Forget Colonialism?

ETHNOGRAPHIC STUDIES IN SUBJECTIVITY
Tanya Luhrmann and Steven Parish, Editors

Forget Colonialism? Sacrifice and the Art of Memory in Madagascar,
by Jennifer Cole

Forget Colonialism?

Sacrifice and the Art of Memory
in Madagascar

Jennifer Cole

UNIVERSITY OF CALIFORNIA PRESS
Berkeley · *Los Angeles* · *London*

University of California Press
Berkeley and Los Angeles, California

University of California Press, Ltd.
London, England

Library of Congress Cataloging-in-Publication Data

Cole, Jennifer, 1966–.
    Forget colonialism? : sacrifice and the art of
memory in Madagascar / Jennifer Cole.
        p.   cm.
    Includes bibliographical references and index.

    ISBN 978-0-520-22846-7 (pbk. : alk. paper)

    1. Betsimisaraka (Malagasy people)—
History.   2. Betsimisaraka (Malagasy people)—
Psychology.   3. Betsimisaraka (Malagasy people)—
Attitudes.   4. Memory—Social aspects—
Madagascar—Ambodiharina.   5. Violence—
Madagascar—Ambodiharina.   6. Madagascar—
History—French Invasion, 1895.   7. France—
Colonies—Africa—Administration.   8.
Ambodiharina (Madagascar)—History.   9.
Ambodiharina (Madagascar)—Social life and
customs.   I. Title.

DT469.M277 B483   2001
969.1—dc21   00-048844

Manufactured in the United States of America
10 09 08
10 9 8 7 6 5 4 3 2

For my parents

Contents

Illustrations and Maps

ILLUSTRATIONS

MAPS

Acknowledgments

The fieldwork on which this book is based was conducted in Madagascar from August 1992 through December 1993, and again in September of 1997 and August of 1999. I did additional archival research in Antananarivo in September 1997 and August 1999; at the Services Historiques de l'Armée de Terre, Vincennes, in August of 1997; and at the Centre des Archives d'Outre-Mer, Aix-en-Provence, in September of 1994 and again in August of 1997. My initial fieldwork in Madagascar was funded by a Fulbright IIE fellowship, a Wenner-Gren Foundation Fellowship, and a Rocca African Studies Fellowship from the African Studies Center at the University of California at Berkeley. My 1997 return trip and additional archival research in France were funded by the American Philosophical Foundation. I should like to acknowledge the Mellon Foundation's support for the Sawyer Seminar Postdoctoral Fellowship on Achieved Identities that I held at the National Humanities Center, Research Triangle, North Carolina, in 1997–98, during which time much of this book was written. A Richard Carley Hunt Memorial Fellowship also helped support the revisions of this manuscript. I thank Kent Mullikin and all the staff at the National Humanities Center for creating a congenial environment in which to work.

I was fortunate to have many teachers who provided me with inspiration and showed me what anthropology could be. Nancy Scheper-Hughes and Gilbert Lewis both influenced my anthropological sensibilities early on. I also warmly thank my dissertation committee at the

..:

University of California at Berkeley—Paul Rabinow, Aihwa Ong, and
Peter Sahlins—for their encouragement and advice. I have learned a great
deal about Madagascar and memory from Maurice Bloch. He supported
this research from start to finish; without his belief in the project I would
probably have quit long ago. Tanya Luhrmann has been an incredibly
generous and inspiring mentor.

This manuscript has benefited from the comments of many readers. I
particularly would like to thank Jonathan Cobb, Michael Cole, Jim Ferguson, Michael Lambek, Tanya Luhrmann, and Rosalind Shaw. Brian
Larkin and Chris Walley each read the introduction in the eleventh hour
and provided helpful comments. William Mazzarella read bits and pieces
of just about everything.

I have had the great fortune to learn from many other anthropologists who work in Madagascar. For discussion, critiques, advice, and answers to my E-mailed queries, I want to thank Gillian Feeley-Harnik,
David Graeber, Pier Larson, Hilde Nielssen, Solofo Randrianja, and
Philip Thomas. I owe special thanks to Karen Middleton, both for friendship and for long ago encouraging me to confront the ambiguities of my
Betsimisaraka material; our discussions about the intricacies of Malagasy "passive agency" and other complexities of ancestral practice have
deepened my understanding.

The members of the Department of Anthropology and Sociology at
Williams College welcomed me during the year 1996–97. I would par-
ticularly like to thank Michael Brown and David Edwards for helping
to make it such an enjoyable year. My colleagues in the Department of
Anthropology at Harvard University have been unstintingly generous in
their support of this project. I would like to thank Begoña Aretxaga, Steve
Caton, Michael Herzfeld, Arthur Kleinman, Mary Steedly, and Woody
Watson. I also owe special thanks to the students in my seminar "Mem-
ory Practices," held in the fall of 1998 and spring of 2000, with whom
I worked through many of my ideas on memory. For her heroic efforts
in copyediting and organizing the manuscript, I thank Wren Fournier.
Amy Young graciously helped with the index and permissions.

This research would not have been completed had it not been for the
help and generosity of many people in Madagascar. I would like to thank
the Ralaizonia family in Antananarivo for taking me in over the years;
it was because of them that I was first drawn to work in Betsimisaraka
country. Tiana Ralaizonia came with me to Ambodiharina to help me
get settled, and I thank him for all of his help and support. Onja Ran-
drianasoloniana took wonderful care of my daughter, Amelia Mazzarella,

when we returned to Ambodiharina in 1997. Louis-Paul Randriamaro-
laza of the University of Antananarivo generously gave me an affiliation
with the university and has generally supported anthropological research
in Madagascar. I thank the family of the person in Mahanoro who is
called Bienaimée in the book: they gave me a home in Mahanoro and introduced me to the world of Ambodiharina, and for this I will always
be grateful.

Words alone are not enough to thank the inhabitants of Ambodiharina and the many villages that surround it. I admire them enormously
for the ways they have learned to see the world. Living among them I
was able to realize what remains one of the best potentials of fieldwork:
to learn to see the world differently through someone else's eyes and
thereby to enlarge one's own vision of the world. Betsimisaraka always
say that you should love all your mothers and fathers equally, so at the
risk of a breach of etiquette I want to especially thank the people whom
I call Ramaresaka, Tsaravintana, Piso, Maman n'i Talata, and my landlady. Pierre deserves special thanks for traveling with me around the area
and for helping with the transcriptions of tapes. Josef died in 1998; without his knowledge and companionship my stay in Ambodiharina would
not have been nearly so enjoyable. The memory of his wisdom and kindness will remain with me always.

I want to thank the acquisitions editor Stan Holwitz at the University
of California Press for his enthusiasm and efficiency regarding this
project. I also thank Laura Pasquale and Cindy Fulton for their help in
shepherding the book through the production process. I thank Bonita
Hurd for her careful and unobtrusive copyediting.

I gratefully acknowledge permission from the American Anthropological Association to reproduce in revised form fragments of my article
"The Work of Memory in Madagascar," originally published in *American Ethnologist* 25, no. 4 (1998): 610–33. A small section of chapter 7
first appeared in my article, "The Uses of Defeat: Memory and Political
Morality in East Madagascar," in *Memory and the Postcolony,* ed.
Richard Werbner, 105–25 (New York: Zed Books, 1998).

I also owe some older and more personal debts. I thank Christina Fink,
Mia Fuller, and Peter Redfield for friendship and support during gradu-
ate school and beyond. I am also grateful to Peter Redfield for sketch-
ing the map of the town that appears in chapter 3. Jimmy Wallenstein
accompanied me during ten months of my first field trip; he also asked
many good questions while we were living in the field. Vero Ralaizonia
and Hanta Rideout first taught me Malagasy. Together with Chris Ride-

out they introduced me to Madagascar and enabled me to stay with their family while in Antananarivo. I thank Karen Barkey, Tony Marx, Jim and Ina Buzard, and Michele Longino for their support during our collective stay at the National Humanities Center; without their friendship it would have been a much harder year.

My husband and best friend, William Mazzarella, read parts of the book and put up with hearing about much more. Without his warmth and humor the world would be a much lonelier place. His kindness and intelligence about all things anthropological—indeed all things—has enriched my life immeasurably.

My parents, Michael and Sheila R. Cole, supported this project in every possible way. They came to visit me in Madagascar and have helped with all the logistical complications of trying to do fieldwork in a place halfway around the world and have a family too. I want to especially thank my father, who read more drafts of this book than he ever wanted to. I dedicate this book to them.

Note on the Text

Betsimisaraka usually write the velar nasal /n/ as *ñ* or alternatively *gn*. I have followed the former throughout this text. Also, in Malagasy there is no difference between the singular and plural noun forms; I have specified where necessary in the text. Throughout the book, translations from French texts are mine unless otherwise noted.

Teknonyms—names that incorporate the name of a person's firstborn child—are common throughout Madagascar: people are frequently referred to as "Mother of so-and-so" or "Father of so-and-so." In Betsimisaraka, this translates to "Reni n'i X" or "Iaba n'i X," respectively. Occasionally, people also use the French terms "Mama n'i X" or "Papa n'i X."

Many of the Malagasy provincial capitals have two names, one in French and one in Malagasy. For the most part, I have used the Malagasy name Antananarivo to refer to the capital city, though in some places in the text, particularly where I cite French colonial sources, the name given is Tananarive. However, I have used the French name for the provincial capital, Tamatave (in Malagasy, Toamasina), and for the northern city Diégo-Suarez (in Malagasy, Antseranana) because my informants used the French names more frequently.

The national currency of Madagascar is the Malagasy franc, or FMG. During 1992–93 the exchange rate was around FMG 1,800 to U.S.$1. By the time I returned in 1997, the exchange rate was around FMG 4,000 to U.S.$1. I have specified approximate amounts in the text where applicable.

Abbreviations

In the case of some organizations, I was able to locate only French or English translations; where possible I have included translations in both languages.

ARDM   Archives de la République Démocratique de Madagascar (Archives of the Democratic Republic of Madagascar)

AREMA   Vangaurd of the Malagasy Revolution (Avant-garde de la Révolution Malagasy)

CAOM   Centre des Archives d'Outre Mer

FMG   Malagasy franc

IMF   International Monetary Fund

MDRM   Mouvement pour la Démocratique Rénovation Malgache (Democratic Movement for Malagasy Renewal)

PADESM   Parti des Déshérités de Madagascar (Party of the Disinherited of Madagascar)

PANAMA   Parti Nationaliste Malgache (National Malagasy Party)

PSD   Parti Sociale Démocrate (Social Democratic Party)

RESEP   Régiments pour la Sécurité Présidentielle (Regiments for Presidential Security)

RPSD   Rassemblement pour la Sociale Democrate

SHAT   Services Historiques de l'Armée de Terre

VVS   Vy Vato Sakelika (Iron, Stone, Branches)

CHAPTER I

Introduction

There are the experiences to which the fixed forms
do not speak at all, which indeed they do not recognize. There are important mixed experiences, where
the available meaning would convert part to all, or all
to part.
                                    — *Raymond Williams*

This book is a study in the processes of social remembering and forgetting through which the Betsimisaraka inhabitants of a small town in east
Madagascar weave together a local world, a world forged in the crucible
of colonial conquest and continually remade and transformed in the context of postcolonial Madagascar. The question I ask is, (How do Betsimisaraka remember the past,) particularly the symbolic and actual violence associated with the French colonial period? In brief, my answer
is that Betsimisaraka have developed certain social practices for shaping
memory, some of which exist throughout much of Africa but have not
previously been analyzed as an art of memory. My goal is to demonstrate
how these practices work and the conditions under which they fail.

My argument will draw upon classical and contemporary social science analyses of the many ways in which the mind extends beyond the
individual. Many of these analyses emphasize that the process of perceiving and knowing the world is fundamentally shaped by the ways in
which people interact with the world by means of artifacts of literacy such
as pens, paper, and a multitude of other aspects of the material environment. I differ from previous writers in this tradition by focusing on the
less tangible but equally efficacious social practices that enable or disable
certain kinds of memories, and on how people use these techniques to
shape how they remember—and thus think about and act upon—the
world.

Revising our conception of memory in this manner has two advan-

tages for theorizing people's memories of the past and the role of these
memories in their contemporary activities. First, because this conception
requires us to focus our analysis on the social and cultural practices
through which individual and social memory are woven together, it affords a way out of the dichotomy that sees memory as *either* locked inside people's heads *or* available only in collective representations and embodied practices of ritual. Second, it requires us to acknowledge that
many traces of the past may be incorporated in the sociocultural environment so that they are not consciously remembered. It is the dialectic
between inner and outer constructions that makes memory such a complex, shifting phenomenon, one that is both unpredictable and central
to social life. And it is precisely because the complexity of memory stems
from the interaction of social and psychological processes that we must
take both sides into account.

In order to study memory as simultaneously constituted by public representations and individual consciousness woven together through social practice, this book develops an anthropological rather than a psychological perspective on memory. There is, I believe, a great deal to be
gained by asking what we can learn about memory by observing how
people engage in the mulifaceted process of remembering in their everyday lives. Throughout this book I pay attention to the role of remembering in the lives of individuals, and I argue that the dual nature of memory makes it a key site at which to examine the interplay of individual
projects and shared cultural forms. My aim is to show how social and
individual memory articulate with one another to shape the ways in which
Betsimisaraka remember the colonial past. The Betsimisaraka memories
that I address here are about ancestors and colonialism, but the problem of how sociocultural practices shape memory, and how people selectively remember and rework the historical past, has many analogues
elsewhere. As many scholars have argued, memory is central to the constitution of subjectivity and identity; contending evocations of the past
presuppose divergent self-understandings and alternative possible futures.
Consequently, understanding how memory works is central to an understanding of social life.

REVERSIBLE ILLUSIONS OF THE PAST

I first went to Betsimisaraka country because I wanted to understand how
historical events were experienced in terms of everyday consciousness.
In 1947, Betsimisaraka had been involved in a violent anticolonial re-

bellion against the French, yet when I first visited Madagascar in 1991 many older people expressed nostalgia for the old colonial regime. The paradox—former rebels talking nostalgically about their departed colonial masters—piqued my interest, and I returned to the part of Madagascar inhabited by the Betsimisaraka to explore how the rebellion was currently remembered by different parts of the population.

Anthropologists today are taught to expect a complex world. Gone forever are the days when we used to perceive cultures as isolates, islands of difference awaiting discovery by the anthropologist-cum-explorer. Our conception of the pristine preexisting localized community as a starting point for anthropological research has given way to a focus on the processes through which community and locality are constructed (Appadurai 1996; Gupta and Ferguson 1997). An important insight gained from this way of conceiving the anthropological object of research is that many of the features that anthropologists once took to be emblematic of an allegedly timeless "culture" have in fact been forged through historical processes of trade, conquest, and colonization in different parts of the world over the last three hundred years (Dirks 1992a; Piot 1999; Shaw 1997; Wilmsen 1989). Cultural difference, we now realize, is not found. Rather, it is historically produced. Just as timeless tradition has disappeared from anthropological analyses, so too has the historyless savage. We now recognize that history exists not only in oral narratives but also in a wide array of rituals and embodied practices (Comaroff and Comaroff 1992; Price 1980; R. Rosaldo 1980; Stoller 1995).

These were the kinds of assumptions that I took with me to the field. During the first few months of fieldwork, however, my contemporary anthropological preconceptions seemed distressingly at odds with the situation I encountered. For example, though I hardly expected people to refer to the past all the time (either in speech or ritual or poetic forms), I nevertheless found myself perplexed by the apparent irrelevance not only of the 1947 uprising but also of the colonial past more generally. What I found when I first arrived in Ambodiharina was a world where people's relationships to one another were constituted through an elaborate moral economy of cattle sacrifice. It was also a world that—in its tone and tenor, its concerns about ancestors, its enthusiasm for cattle sacrifice, and its agricultural mode of subsistence—evoked classic anthropological accounts of African societies from the 1930s and 1940s. It was a world that Meyer Fortes (1945) and E. Evans-Pritchard (1956) might well have invented for an essay exam for Oxbridge undergraduates, a world that contemporary anthropology, with its growing concern with the accelerating interpenetration of local and global processes, claimed had never existed. The local practices that confronted me appeared at first so unquestionably local that it was almost impossible for me to see them as simply an effect of colonial power. Nor could I at first discern any sites or practices through which historical consciousness of the colonial past was produced. In short, at first blush I found myself faced with a world that belied the anthropological wisdom I had been taught.

Of course, there were occasional reminders of the French colonial period. Much to my dismay I found that my unexpected arrival provoked enormous fear associated with colonization. This apprehension was apparent in the rumors that circulated about me ("She's here to claim her grandfather's land! The *vazaha* [Europeans] are coming back!"), sentiments that suggested a keen awareness of past encroachments and the need to protect what people rightfully felt to be theirs. Memories of the colonial past were also evident every time someone who did not know me referred to me politely in French as "Madame-o." Throughout my stay in the village, a slightly mad old woman named Baomaro engaged me in an elaborate charade. "Oh, Madame-o!" she would call out, "the villagers are letting their cows eat my vanilla which we were forced to plant for tax money! And now my harvest is ruined. How will I pay my taxes?" And I would participate in the charade to calm her down: "Yes, Baomaro, I'll look into it right away! We'll get those cows off your land. We'll show those villagers!" Although her ravings were those of a mad woman, the example nevertheless illustrates the fact that memories of the colonial past remained, to be called forth on the appropriate occasion.

Before long, however, the novelty of my presence faded. As it became apparent that I was not the kind of outsider they had previously experienced, I began to be incorporated into daily life. Even so, in this process of integration and normalization, the world that I came to know seemed for the most part to belie the turbulent history of colonization it had undergone. As I listened to the daily conversations about matters of local concern, the way my presence had sparked people's memories of the colonial past seemed relatively trivial—the provocation of a passing anthropologist, and little else. Elders would politely tell me about the colonial period when I asked, but for the most part I had to elicit the information; it did not appear to have any life of its own.

Had I stayed in Ambodiharina for only a few weeks, it would have been all too easy to assume that the colonial period had left little imprint on the villagers. I might have concluded that the importance attributed to the colonial period by Western anthropologists and postcolonial theorists had more to do with their own preoccupations than those of the formerly colonized. I might also have concluded that anthropological insights into the contradictions of living in a world remade through colonialism were unsuited to the rural world in which I was working. But I would have been wrong, for the longer I lived in the village, the more time I spent strolling down the main road with Velonmaro as he explained how the village looked when he was young, the more clearly I could see flickers of the colonial past emerge from among the palm-thatched houses. Gradually, it became apparent that my first impression of a "traditional" Betsimisaraka village untouched by the troubling signs of the colonial past needed revision: there were clearly multiple principles of social organization and multiple histories and experiences of the world interwoven in people's daily experience.

For example, the colonial past was visible in its physical remnants, including the leaning telephone poles, their wires cut and dangling, situated at the northern tip of the town, and the blue-and-white sign, reminiscent of Paris street signs, reading *téléphone publique,* rusted and falling to one side near the ferry port. Traces of the colonial past were also evident in the corrugated-iron-roofed houses, which more often than not were accompanied by what I came to think of as a Creole-style porch, sprinkled in among the one-room palm-thatched huts.

The colonial past was also implicit in the layout of the town, with its wide-cut central road reminiscent of a French village's central *place.* In "traditional" Betsimisaraka villages, people claimed, the great house—the house inhabited by the *tangalamena,* the person in charge of mediating between the living and the dead—was always built slightly higher than the houses of the more junior members of the family grouped around it. But the French had forced people to align themselves with the road. There was also the curious fact that the town contained many different great houses and prayer posts *(jiro),* each indicative of a different extended family. By contrast, early travel accounts described the central east coast peoples as living in scattered hamlets, each containing only one large family. One old man told me, "The reason we have so many prayer posts is that we're all strangers *[vahiny]* from somewhere else." What he did not add, however, was that one of the reasons so many different ancestries had come to settle in one place was that they had been forced to by the French colonial government, which had tried to regroup scattered ancestries into larger villages in order to facilitate corvée recruitment. Fi-

nally, there were the breadfruit trees, the lychees, and the occasional
bonara tree, all of which had been introduced by the French in their efforts to develop the local economy.

The traces of colonialism extended beyond local geography and flora
to a variety of social practices. At least some of the people in Ambodiharina owned coffee plantations and sold what they could of their harvests to a national company in town. Ambodiharina also had an organized council of village elders, one of whom acted as a representative to
the state.[1] People saw it as a mark of status to sleep on a European-style
bed, as opposed to the traditional reed mats, and to sit on a chair instead
of on the floor. Likewise, it was fashionable to wear Western-style clothes
and mass-produced *lambaoany,* the wraps worn by women, rather than
traditional *akanjobe* made from raffia fiber. When they had money,
people bought imported rum rather than drink the local *toaka,* which
many considered dirty and inferior. I once asked Velonmaro why it was
that people switched from *kabala,* the traditional raffia shroud, to the
cheap white or flowered fabric used to wrap corpses today, and why they
now preferred imported rum to *betsa* or *toaka,* alcoholic drinks made
from sugarcane, as the drink of the ancestors. He explained that the
vazaha had brought those customs, that they had forced people to change:
"They said those old ways of doing things were shameful, too dirty, and
so they gave us clean customs." Or as Josef, another elder, explained it,
"When the *vazaha* came we decided that things that were made by *vazaha*
were good. And so we started to use cloth instead of raffia and rum instead of *toaka.*"

What this evidence of the colonial past implies is that Ambodiharina
is clearly double, a hybrid locality forged in the context of colonial rule.
On the one hand, it is a colonial creation, a village built to facilitate corvée
recruitment and designed to fit French notions of what a village should
look like. It is a village in which Betsimisaraka patterns of social organization were reorganized to satisfy the needs of the colonial state, and
where people live with a reified, invented tradition—complete with a
council of village elders and village headmen. On the other hand, it is
also a Betsimisaraka village as people first taught me to see it through
their lens of densely tangled social relations and local concerns. The longer
I remained in the village, however, the more I came to perceive the two
sides of local life as genuinely interwoven in people's experience. Not
only did the French reorganize the Betsimisaraka, but the Betsimisaraka
actively adopted some of these changes, molding them to their own concerns. No one forced them to build the corrugated-tin-roofed houses in

their Creole-plantation style. In part, the apparent irrelevance of the colonial past, and the related elision of a postcolonial present, had to do with the fact that I arrived in the village at a time when the Malagasy state had receded, leaving only the ghosts of old structures behind. But the very fact that it had taken me the length of an extended stay in the village to move beyond people's manifest concerns and perceive the hybrid nature of the place suggested that powerful processes of social memory were also at play that worked selectively to produce an indigenous sense of locality.[2] In fact, it was because these practices of remembering and forgetting so convincingly produced a particular sense of locality that the effects of the colonial past were hard to perceive in the first place.)

Over time, I came to think of Ambodiharina as the Betsimisaraka version of a reversible perceptual illusion. Like Ludwig Wittgenstein's (1953) famous duck-rabbit, which we tend to see *either* as a duck *or* a rabbit, people seemed to emphasize one aspect of their historical experience at the expense of the other; but the alternative aspect would suddenly pop into view, reversing their perceived experience. For the most part the local world of ancestors, rice, and cows dominated, but as I have suggested, the complementary erasure of colonialism was both unstable and incomplete.

Several months into my stay, however, the dominance of local concerns in people's perceptions was abruptly reversed when memories of the colonial past made themselves felt with startling force. Like many other African countries in the early 1990s, Madagascar was in the process of rejecting a state-socialist regime, replacing it instead with a new, self-proclaimedly "democratic" model of government. As part of the process, new elections were held. But adults in Ambodiharina did not see the elections as democratic, or rather they did not see "democratic" as good. Instead they perceived the elections through a prism of terrifying, emotion-laden memories associated with the event that I had initially been interested in learning about, the rebellion of 1947. The intrusion of outsiders on a massive scale, the act of voting, and the atmosphere of political tension that accompanied the elections were interpreted as a prelude to state violence and social chaos. People began to talk about the rebellion incessantly and were visibly upset by the return of what were obviously painful memories. The local concerns that had dominated my stay in Ambodiharina were suddenly eclipsed, while the colonial past and its sequelae were all too visible.

In the pages that follow, I place this memory-story in its cultural and historical context and seek to understand the memory practices that made

it possible. Charles Piot, in his recent book *Remotely Global* (1999), cas-
tigates an earlier generation of anthropologists for failing to realize that
the societies they encountered were both modern and deeply located in
translocal practices. He also rightly takes to task recent theorists of post-
modernity and transnationalism for continuing to contrast the flux of
postmodern and transnational societies with the allegedly static, historically unself-conscious societies of which the "African village" is often
taken as an exemplar.

Piot's insights are symptomatic of a much larger shift in anthropology, for contemporary anthropologists tend to reject the idea that local
experience, conceived of as an isolate, holds the key to understanding.
Instead, social experience is increasingly understood as itself stretched
across local place and translocal spaces of imagination. A central ethnographic problem, then, becomes precisely the way in which "the local"—
as a category of social practice—becomes constituted, contested, and reproduced in everyday life.

Part and parcel of this situation is, paradoxically, the fact that under
certain conditions "the local" actually comes to appear—to local actors
and anthropologists alike—as a unit very much like the self-contained
"field" of earlier ethnographic studies. Indeed, one of my aims in focusing upon the processes of social remembering is to highlight precisely the
conditions in which certain groups or individuals might, through their
social practices, consciously and unconsciously, produce this effect. And
so, my main concern here is not to blame an earlier generation of anthropologists for failing to recognize transnational entanglements. Rather,
I want to illuminate the practices that might make it seem as if a place
like Ambodiharina, which had been integrated into wider networks of
trade and conquest for centuries, was static and remote, even to someone who—in theory—knew better.

On one level, my narrative may appear to be about a rearguard action on the part of tradition against the forward charge of modernity.
And in fact that is precisely how it appeared to some of my informants.
But I prefer to see it as an ethnography of remembering, in which what
is remembered as "tradition" is perhaps the most "modern" construct
of all.

WHY MADAGASCAR

The fourth largest island in the world, Madagascar lies in the Indian
Ocean, just off the coast of southern Africa (see map 1). Although the

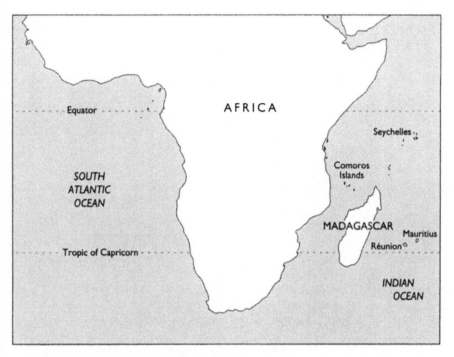

Map 1. Madagascar in relation to Africa

precise ethnic makeup of the island's inhabitants has been subject to lengthy scholarly debate, it is now widely accepted that the people of Madagascar originated in both Indonesia and Africa, settling the island in successive waves somewhere between 400 and 900 C.E. The inhabitants of Madagascar speak Malagasy, an Austronesian language that most closely resembles Majann, spoken in Borneo. Map 2 shows the traditional locations of major ethnic groups in Madagascar.

Madagascar is a particularly compelling place to study social practices of remembering and forgetting because its peoples are famed for their memorializing rituals, which they have often altered in order to retain their historical identity in the face of change. For example, in her book *A Green Estate* (1991), Gillian Feeley-Harnik examines the way Sakalava practices concerning ancestors were central to their efforts to survive the pernicious effects of conquest. Sakalava constructed political legitimacy in terms of ancestors, which were embodied in relics: whoever controlled the relics controlled the crown. Feeley-Harnik suggests that when the Sakalava monarchy had to fight off intrusions from both the Merina and the French, they changed their ways of preserving their

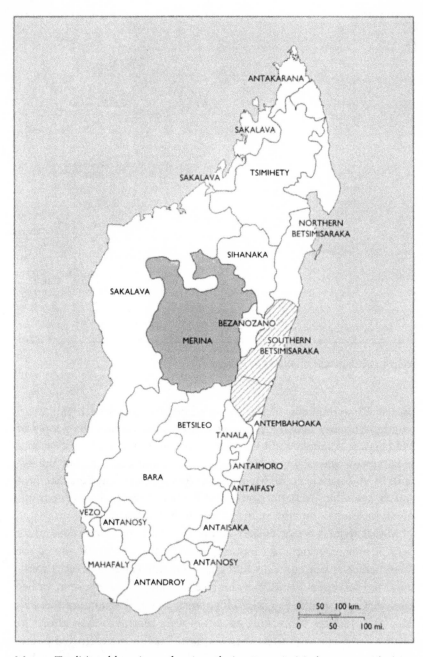

Map 2. Traditional locations of major ethnic groups in Madagascar, with the Merina and southern Betsimisaraka regions highlighted

ancestors. Instead of constructing relics, which could be moved or stolen, they began to build tombs. The transformation, she argues, reflects Sakalava attempts to protect local models of social regeneration in the face of external intrusions. This process continued into the 1970s, when Sakalava efforts to rebuild the royal tomb were fundamentally linked to Malagasy efforts to "reestablish independence—*fahaleovan-tena*—in Malagasy terms in Madagascar as a whole" (17).

Karen Middleton makes a similar argument in her analysis of why the Karembola of southern Madagascar no longer practice circumcision. After the Karembola suffered famine and the destruction of their landscape when the French intentionally released a cactus pest, which destroyed all the cactus stands in southern Madagascar, they gave up the practice of circumcision and simplified their practice of sacrifice, developing elaborate mortuary customs in their place. Middleton shows that, despite the Karembola's overt discourse of impotence and decline, they have "fashioned a world from which foreigners are excluded, an imagined polity to which only Karembola belong" (1997, 366). As with the Sakalava, the elaboration of mortuary practice is fundamentally linked to the people's efforts to preserve historical identity, because the work Karembola devote to building tombs and appeasing ancestors is intimately linked to the reproduction and transformation of their social order.

The same pattern occurs in a different way in an early study by Maurice Bloch (1971b), who claims that there is a close connection between the perils associated with external intrusion, social change, and ancestral rituals. He describes the fact that, in nineteenth-century central Madagascar, the Merina alternated between enthusiastic acceptance of foreign practices and their total rejection. In one dramatic incident, after King Radama II had embraced missionary Christianity, a spirit-possession crisis broke out in which people prepared for the return of a recently deceased traditionalist queen, Ranavalona I. Bloch suggests that rejection of the Western influence is a fundamental aspect of Merina ancestral rituals, which find their contemporary expression in the ways that Merina adapt to new political and economic realities in their daily lives but recreate an image of an unchanging ancestral world in rituals of secondary burial.

Although these studies are informed by somewhat different theoretical sympathies, they all point to the historically constructed nature of ancestral rituals, their role in mediating Malagasy experiences of colonialism, and the creative ways in which Malagasy in different parts of the island reacted to colonial intrusions and transformations alike.

In many respects, the peoples who now go by the name of Betsimis-araka are similar to other Malagasy peoples. They too have highly elab-orated memorializing techniques that make the processes of remember-ing and forgetting particularly available to analysis. Indeed, Betsimisaraka refer to cattle sacrifice, their most developed form of memorialization, by the same word they use for remembering, an analogy that aptly de-scribes the massive amount of memory work this ritual achieves. They also have other ways of memorializing the past, including the observa-tion of taboos and the practice of second burial for which the peoples of Madagascar are so famous. However, owing to their location on the east-ern periphery of the island, positioned between the powerful Merina and the plantation islands of Mauritius and Réunion, they have had a par-ticularly turbulent history that has placed great strain on their resources for controlling their cultural identity, making processes of social re-membering especially prominent.

Prior to colonization by the French, the Merina of highland Mada-gascar forcibly incorporated the Betsimisaraka into their kingdom. The French officially conquered the Betsimisaraka in 1895. Their motivations were threefold. First, an aggressive political lobby from Réunion Island, which depended on Madagascar for supplies of cattle, rice, and labor, advocated formal colonization. Second, rumors of hidden wealth sug-gested there were economic advantages to be gained. Third, French officials gave the British control over the Suez Canal in exchange for con-trol of Madagascar.[3]

As in other French colonies, French colonial policy in Madagascar was at least partially based on the concept of assimilation, the idea that at least certain colonial subjects could one day become "civilized" and French.[4] In practice, French administrators were never sure how French their subjects should or could become, and their desire to assimilate colonized peoples was always tempered by the need to keep them po-litically subordinate (Cooper 1996). Nevertheless, the existence of such a policy implies that the French period left important marks on local identity.

Abstract debates about how to colonize aside, the Betsimisaraka ex-perience of French colonization was deeply disruptive. During colo-nization Betsimisaraka lost their best land to French settlers. They were also heavily taxed and forced to work growing crops such as coffee, cloves, vanilla, and pepper for the cash economy. And they were made to work so much for others, either for settlers or the colonial state, that they had little time to spend cultivating their own rice. As I mentioned, the Betsimisaraka region was also the site of bloody battles in one of the most infamous moments in French colonial history: the brutal repression of a rebellion in which an estimated one hundred thousand Malagasy died. But while decolonization in many parts of the world inaugurated a marked political centralization under the banner of "development," Madagascar—beginning in the late 1970s and continuing through the early 1990s—witnessed a steadily receding state.

When France granted Madagascar independence in 1960, the departing colonial administration handed power to a regime that ensured that French military, economic, and cultural interests would be protected. In 1972, in what is sometimes called a second independence, this neocolonial government was successfully contested by massive student riots. The next few years saw the departure of those French who had remained on the island after independence, as well as a series of different administrations; stability was finally achieved under President Didier Ratsiraka in 1975. Ratsiraka created a military-led government that instituted the policy of Malgachisation, the nationalization of industry and a switch from French to Malagasy as the national language used in the schools (Covell 1989). He also advocated a centralized version of state development, and he focused his efforts in both agriculture and industry on large-scale projects. Investments, financed with foreign loans, went to state-run initiatives like the army's plan to cultivate a hundred thousand hectares of rice and to the creation of new state-dominated agricultural activities, such as a massive soy-bean-growing project (140). While the policy of borrowing and investing money in large-scale development projects continued throughout the seventies, the policy collapsed in the eighties as foreign loans became increasingly difficult to obtain. By the early eighties, the government was heavily in debt and was forced to enter into a series of negotiations with the International Monetary Fund, which continue to this day.

As the government grew ever poorer its infrastructure gradually disintegrated and, throughout Madagascar, the state eventually withdrew from the countryside. When I first went to Mahanoro, the district capital, Betsimisaraka selling manioc and rice, and itinerant traders who had brought their wares from the high plateau, occupied the wide avenues and spacious central square of the town. The once-grand houses with their corrugated iron roofs and spacious gardens were falling apart. Built by French functionaries and Creole planters, these houses, their verandas sagging and roofs rusting, were inhabited by Chinese merchants or Merina and Betsimisaraka functionaries. The state of the houses was indicative of a more general condition of economic decline. In 1989, Madagascar was the twelfth-poorest country in the world, with an average annual income of $230 per person; the national income was half of what it had been in the 1960s (Covell 1989, xiv; Raison-Jourde 1993). Though relatively small-scale production had always been the norm, during the colonial period and through the 1960s, coffee, pepper, vanilla, and cloves had been farmed for export on the world market. By the mid-1990s, however, this trade had dropped to a fraction of its former volume. Because of the poor economy and the fact that the wages paid—even for the socially prestigious job of schoolteacher—could not cover a family's basic needs, most people who lived in Mahanoro made sure they retained access to whatever rice land they had inherited, and they paid people in their ancestral villages to farm it.

The area of Madagascar in which I worked has never been rich, nor has it been a region of large-scale capital investment. As we will see in the next chapter, it is a region of poor settlers and failed economic dreams. But at least during colonial and neocolonial times, Mahanoro had been thoroughly integrated into a wider national and even imperial framework, where one could telephone the capital and order the finest French champagne. By the time I arrived for fieldwork in 1992, however, communication had broken down. The main road from the capital city of Antananarivo to the port and provincial capital of Tamatave (Toamasina) on the Indian Ocean was still paved (see map 3). At the turnoff, which then led to Mahanoro, it became a rutted path that in the rainy season was so muddy as to be impassable. The coast is frequently transected by rivers that empty into the Indian Ocean, so those seeking to make their way either north or south are constantly confronted with river crossings. Since the colonial period, slow ferries designed to transport cars or cargo were found at most river crossings, but at least in the early and mid-1990s, they were usually out of gas or out of order. Instead, most people went by foot or used bush taxis *(taxi-brousse)* or small dugout canoes to get from place to place. During my first fieldwork in 1992, there was one *taxi-brousse* that traveled weekly to Tamatave; it left Mahanoro at dawn and arrived in Tamatave—located only 205 kilometers away—well into the evening. Another *taxi-brousse* traveled weekly to Antananarivo; it took one day and one night to travel the 170 kilometers.[5] In 1992, an Air Madagascar flight delivered mail weekly via Tamatave. When I returned in 1997 the flight had been canceled; mail arrived sporadically by *taxi-brousse.*

The infrastructural breakdown that characterized Madagascar in the

Map 3. Provincial capitals and major towns on the east coast of Madagascar

early 1990s serves as a potent reminder that the apparently ineluctable compression of time and space, which has come to stand as the hallmark of globalization, may in fact be highly uneven and accompanied by new distances and disconnections (see also Ferguson 1999; Hannerz 1996). Particularly for those countries that had aligned with the old Soviet bloc, the end of the cold war meant the temporary cessation of important former aid and the dissolution of state infrastructures. Massive foreign debt and the implementation of structural adjustment programs only exacerbated the situation. As a result, researchers in many parts of the continent found themselves working in communities that were *more* isolated than they had been in the past. For some researchers, the disconnection and the way it has been accompanied by the reemergence of supposedly obsolete social forms have become an overt focus of analysis. James Ferguson (1999), for example, finds in Zambia and the tragic failure of modernization in the copper mines an opportunity to question modernist metanarratives, and argues that we need to develop new tools for analyzing the reversals that have characterized recent history. Much like in the case of Zambia that Ferguson describes, the brief period of disconnection that happened to coincide with my fieldwork also meant an apparent reversal in the direction of social change. This seeming disruption of historical "progress" should also be understood as a matter of the variable density of socially transformative events. Initially, there was a period of relative stasis, during which people's imaginations were at least temporarily focused on very local concerns. But the dramatic disruptions associated with the presidential elections soon intervened. The juxtaposition of these two contrasting moments afforded me a unique opportunity to bring together two areas that I had set out to study—colonialism and social memory—and to ask the following question: What are the social practices that mediate how a particular historical period is remembered?

COLONIALISM AND CULTURE

The term *colonialism* is used in so many different ways—and in recent anthropological discussions refers to so many different kinds of outside domination—that some clarification of the term is required here. This is particularly so in the southern Betsimisaraka region, whose inhabitants have endured many kinds of outside intrusion and control, ranging from, in the nineteenth century, domination by a combination of early Creole settlers and Merina, to French colonialism in the nineteenth and the first half of the twentieth century. Consequently, while the Betsimisaraka sometimes distinguish among these different kinds of foreign intrusions, they often refer to powerful outsiders from different historical periods in similar ways. In the pages that follow, I focus on the period of French colonial rule. However, I also draw upon information about earlier periods and, as far as possible, seek to identify the kind of regime to which I am referring. Nonetheless, it is difficult to avoid some slippage in terminology. As in the situation described by Rosalind Shaw (2001), who found in Sierra Leone that Temne memories of the slave trade are layered with memories of the colonial trade that replaced it, Betsimisaraka memories of colonialism also form a palimpsest. Their memories of slavery—which was practiced in Madagascar prior to 1896—inform their interpretations of French colonialism, which in turn shape how they remember the prior Merina period. Bearing in mind the need to guard against lumping together all types of foreign control in a homogeneous image of power, it remains important to consider some of the ways in which scholars have theorized European colonialism of the sort that I will be concentrating on in the pages that follow.

A number of different anthropological and historical studies have sought to understand the transformations wrought by colonial rule. Their conclusions differ—depending on where and when they examine the effects of colonialism—which highlights the diverse and highly uneven ways in which European colonialism unfolded. Nevertheless, for the sake of clarity, these studies can be sorted roughly into three groups: those that emphasize the power of indigenous agency in mediating outside intrusion, those that focus on the transformative power of colonial rule, and those that struggle to stake out a middle ground. The work of Marshall Sahlins, who attempted to understand how Hawaiians responded to early contact and conquest, exemplifies the first approach.[6] Sahlins (1981, 1985) shows how the fate of the explorer Captain Cook and the making of Hawaiian history were mediated by indigenous symbolic structures. The Hawaiians' response to Captain Cook, Sahlins argues, could be understood only in relation to local practices surrounding the god Lono. Concerned primarily with early moments of contact history, Sahlins characterizes Hawaiians as history makers on their own terms, encompassing and transforming outside intrusions.[7]

By contrast, some scholars who have written about the second wave of late-nineteenth-century and twentieth-century colonialism, the period with which I am primarily concerned here, have tended to emphasize the impact of colonial rule as both negative and pervasive. This perspective is particularly visible in books written by colonized elites who experi-

enced colonial power firsthand. For example, in his study exploring the
psychology of the colonial encounter, the Tunisian Albert Memmi writes,
"The body and face of the colonized are not a pretty sight. It is not without damage that one carries the weight of such historical misfortune"
(1961, 119). Frantz Fanon appears to agree. In *The Wretched of the
Earth,* he writes, "The colonial world is a manichean world . . . As if to
show the totalitarian character of colonial exploitation the settler paints
the native as a sort of quintessence of evil" (1963, 41). The horrible thing,
Fanon goes on to argue, is that eventually, through a process of psychic
splitting and the subsequent internalization of the negative image, the
colonized come to believe the colonizers and to hate themselves for everything they are not in relation to the colonizer's culture.

In thinking about the relative degree to which colonial powers shaped
their colonized subjects, Michel Foucault's conception of power provides
an important tool. In his essay "The Subject and Power," Foucault distinguishes between exploitation, domination, and subjection. Foucault
argues that most analyses of power concentrate on relations of domination and exploitation—the question of who controls whom or, in Marxist terms, how the products of labor are extracted from the producers
and so forth. Foucault emphasizes the third term, subjection. He writes,
"There are two meanings of the word *subject:* subject to someone else
by control and dependence, and tied to his own identity by a conscience
or self-knowledge. Both meanings suggest a form of power which sub-
jugates and makes subject to" (1982, 212). This dimension of power is
likely to be expressed through the manipulation of social forms. For example, the policing enforced by forms of social ordering—the layout of
villages or houses, the control of hygiene—produces new kinds of subjects. Foucault conceives of this kind of power as "capillary," minutely
diffused throughout the social body through specific social practices and
forms of social knowledge. These practices produce new subjectivities,
new ways of thinking and behaving that transform the most basic ways
that people experience themselves.

This Foucaultian conception of power as capillary underlies many
analyses that consider the effects of colonialism as both "sinuous and
hegemonic" (Dirks 1992b, 7). Following Foucault, such studies have emphasized the ways in which colonial categories of knowledge constituted
colonized peoples as an object of study and control in the service of state
power.[8] Through analyses of the tropes and categories used by explor-
ers, missionaries, settlers, doctors, scientists and city planners, scholars
have shown how Africans were discursively constituted as "tribes," the

ways in which administrators and planners sought to bring people into new spheres of social interaction, and how medicine defined disease in racial terms.

For example, in *Colonizing Egypt* (1988) Timothy Mitchell uses a Foucaultian model to examine how colonial officials were able to colonize Egyptians' bodies and minds. He cites the strategy formulated by a French administrator in Algeria as an apt example of what it was the colonizers sought to achieve: "In effect the essential thing is to gather into groups this people which is everywhere and nowhere; the essential thing is to make them something we can seize hold of. When we have them in our hands, we will then be able to do many things which are quite impossible for us today and which will perhaps allow us to capture their minds after we have captured their bodies" (95). This desire to "capture bodies," as Mitchell shows, was a complex process that involved the documentation and regulation of the population from birth to death. It included military control, schooling, the reorganization of social interaction through new forms of architecture, and census taking. Perhaps because Mitchell focuses more on planning than implementation, reading Mitchell one might easily believe that colonial power actually succeeded in capturing Egyptian bodies and minds. Colonial power appears to be terrifyingly effective, diffused throughout the tiny capillaries that traverse the social body, deeply and permanently embedded in people's perceptions of "the real" (xi).

While this notion of power as capillary suggests the penetration of colonial influence down to the most intimate parts of the social body, Frederick Cooper (1994) suggests an alternative metaphor. Pointing to the partial, erratic nature of colonial control, Cooper argues that it is more appropriate to think of colonial power in Africa, at least during the early phases of colonization, as "arterial" rather than capillary. "However much surveillance, control, and the narrowing of the boundaries of political discourse were a part of Europe in its supposedly democratizing era," he states, "power in colonial societies was more arterial than capillary—concentrated spatially and socially, not very nourishing beyond such domains and in need of a pump to push it from place to place" (1533). Cooper's observations are part of a larger trend in imperial history and historical anthropology that acknowledges the profound difference in power relations between colonizer and colonized while emphasizing the contingent and nonmonolithic nature of the colonial enterprise.[9] As Ann Stoler and Frederick Cooper note (1997, 6), "Colonial regimes were neither monolithic nor omnipotent. Closer in-

vestigation reveals competing agendas for using power, competing strategies for maintaining control and doubts about the legitimacy of the venture." In a similar vein, John Comaroff (1997, 165) urges anthropologists to take in the moments of colonial "incoherence and inchoateness,
its internal contortions and complexities."

The implications of viewing colonial power as arterial are exemplified
in Achille Mbembe's 1991 discussion of "the domain of the night," the
realm of dreams that allowed one rebel soldier in Cameroon to fight off
the predations of the French. "In fact," he argues, "the colonial vector
was hardly interested in taking possession and dominating all social sites.
Everything was not perceived to be equally important to the state's reproduction. Which is why there continued to exist, even in the midst of
the space the state did control, a large number of domains that were
non-official and uncaptured. These functioned in an autonomous and
quasi-clandestine fashion." Mbembe further develops the conception of
uneven colonial control when he observes that "the colonized could
choose several possible interpretations of his role, precisely because he
was situated and acted in several social universes at the same time" (95,
my translation).

Though Mbembe is perhaps more focused on the internal contradictions and aporia in state power, both his and Cooper's discussions of arterial power tend to privilege the state, a position at odds with Foucault's
efforts to de-center the state by exploring the ways in which power op-
erates through expert discourse. Nevertheless, the idea of colonial power
as arterial provides a useful corrective to recent Foucaultian analyses of
colonial power, for in moving Foucault from metropole to colony, there
has been a tendency to assume that power works in the same way in both
places (but see Stoller 1995). Supporting the need to revise Foucault's
insights in the colonial context, Megan Vaughan (1991) argues that the
fit between Foucault's conception of modern European power and the
exercise of colonial power is a partial one. Not only did many colonial
states continue to rely on "repressive" modes of power, but other sites,
like the medical power-knowledge complex, were less central to colonial
control than in the metropolitan context. Moreover, she suggests that
colonial power in Africa focused more on groups than on individuals.
As a result, Vaughn concludes that "the extent to which colonialism . . .
treated 'subjects' as well as 'objects', and thus operated through individual subjectivities, is open to question" (11). Like others, Vaughan implies that although colonial power was certainly multiple, it is uncertain
whether it was capillary in Foucault's sense.

Bearing in mind the multiple vectors that constituted colonial power, the metaphors "capillary" and "arterial" provide alternative ways of conceiving of the impact of colonialism in eastern Madagascar. Did colonial power penetrate so deeply into the social body that it had permanent and general psychological effects on how people think of themselves and their world, as people like Albert Memmi and Frantz Fanon implied? Or did it affect some parts of the social world more than others, leaving some areas relatively intact? Is it possible that some domains were so totally transformed that people no longer see or contest their own transformation?

How one answers this question clearly depends on the kinds of practices and institutions that mediate people's experience of state and professional forms of power, and the way they intersect with local practice. As we shall see, focusing on practices of social remembering, which Betsimisaraka conceive of as integrally bound up with access to certain forms of power, suggests that the capillary / arterial metaphor, with its implicit there / not there dichotomy, is inadequate to capturing the ways in which colonial power affected local practices. But it also has the advantage of making visible some of the mechanisms through which colonial rule was implicated in what Terence Ranger (1983) famously called the "invention of tradition," even as it enables an analysis that moves beyond a top-down approach to look at how individuals were implicated in their own transformation (see also Ranger 1993; Vail 1989). Focusing on practices of remembering also allows us to add nuance to the now widely accepted claim that the colonial encounter tended to produce an "acute self-awareness of [a] temporal lag and spatial marginality" (Gupta 1998, 11), for in fact the way peoples on the periphery view the center is at least partially shaped by the presence or absence of certain kinds of memories.

In the following pages, I explore how people remember the French colonial period in one small town in east Madagascar.[10] As will become clear, I play upon *remembering* in a double sense, for I use it to refer to the process of reorganization and transformation (a literal dismemberment and re-membering) imposed by colonial rule and in turn re-membered by Betsimisaraka, and the processes through which people remember or recollect the past. I am interested in the coconstitutive ways in which colonial power re-membered the Betsimisaraka and in turn how Betsimisaraka remember the transformations and experiences of colonialism. Among my concerns in this book is to specify the precise domains and mechanisms through which the transformations wrought by colonization continue to make themselves felt in people's daily lives, as well as

how these interact with people's efforts at social regeneration and transformation in the wake of colonial rule. My efforts to address these issues
have led me to a particular conception of memory.

THEORIZING MEMORY

As with the word *history*, which refers to both the practice of writing
down narratives about the past and the past events themselves, there is
a tremendous amount of ambiguity in the word *memory*. In common
parlance, *memory* has three meanings: the mental ability to store and re-
trieve information; the emotional, semantic, or sensory content of those
memories; and the location where these memories are stored (Young
1995).

Two common assumptions characterize Western cultural models of
memory. First, memory is an individual phenomenon, triggered by outside stimuli, that happens largely inside our heads. Second, memory
works much like a camera, registering photos at the time of the experience that remain unchanged, crystallized images that we can later recall
at will. When we can not easily access a memory, it is not because it is
not there, but because we are looking in the wrong place. These folk notions of memory are simultaneously refuted and substantiated in scholarly writing on the topic. On the one hand, psychological studies of memory refute our commonsense understandings by tending to emphasize the
malleable, reconstructive nature of memory (Bartlett [1932] 1995; Loftus 1993; Neisser 1982; Schacter 1996). On the other hand, the fact that
the study of memory has been primarily the provenance of psychologists,
concerned with the workings of individual minds, reinforces the assumption that memory is an individual cognitive function that is natural and
hence universal.

In focusing on the social practices that articulate individual *and* social memory, this study owes much to three pioneering figures whose the-
orizations of memory represent an early attempt to reunite psychology,
anthropology, and sociology, bringing the individual and the social sides
of memory into a single frame.

HALBWACHS, BARTLETT, FREUD

In his classic study *The Collective Memory*, first published in 1950, Maurice Halbwachs ([1950] 1980) argues that our memories are always constructed in dialogue with our social surroundings. Individual memories

can be interpreted only within a social context, and it is the social context that renders them coherent, allowing them to be narrated. Further, memories are not stored in the brain to be retrieved at will, as the photographic theory of memory would have it. Rather, our memories are constantly reconstructed in keeping with the needs of the present. Since memories constantly change as groups evolve, they need stable anchorage either in space or through acts of commemoration. It is through commemoration that collective memory is localized—given shape, form, and feeling and thus made *memorable.* In turn, commemorations help constitute authoritative versions of a group's past.

   Though Halbwachs was right to emphasize the socially constructed nature of memory and the role of commemoration in enabling narrative memory, his analysis is flawed on two counts. First, his extreme tendency to see all remembering as a product of the social group led him to completely overlook issues of individual or autobiographical memory. And yet the points where one is likely to see tension and change are precisely the junctures between socially constructed memory and individual experience. One need only consider the thoughtful work on popular memory in the context of totalitarian social regimes to realize that practices like commemorative rituals may *shape* individual memory, but they do not entirely *determine it* (see Watson 1994).

   Second, as a student of Emile Durkheim, Halbwachs was heir to many of the same problems that plague Durkheimian sociology. The meaning of the key concept of what "a group" meant tended to be underexplored, and Halbwachs never really addressed the question of divergent memories or countermemories within a group. Generally, his conception emphasized how a homogenous social group tends selectively to represent the past in the interests of the present. Who was doing the remembering—and to what social ends and with what consequences—usually remains unclear.

   Contemporary anthropological and sociological writing on memory tends to share Halbwachs's dismissal of individual memory, focusing instead on public representations of the past. Much of this work emphasizes three intertwined aspects of Halbwachs's work: the political nature of social memory, its localization in commemorative practices, and the way memory supports and sustains a group's identity.

   A key reason that social struggles over memory have become such a popular subject of study surely lies in the connection between memory and sociopolitical identification that Halbwachs was among the first to analyze systematically. Studies that focus on this phenomenon suggest that ongoing social struggles for a variety of resources—including the meaning of events—mediate recollections of the past (Rappaport 1990; Roseman 1996; cf. Schudson 1992, 1995). The close connection between memory and self in turn makes "memory work" politically salient, as continuous memories are often the substance on which claims about identity are based (Bakhurst 1997; Warnock 1987). As John Gillis argues, summing up a view that could be said to characterize the majority of Halbwachs-inspired studies on memory, "Identities and memories are not things we think *about* but things we think *with*. As such they have no existence beyond our politics, our social relationships, and our histories" (1994, 5, emphasis in the original). Many of these studies look to forms of commemoration or rituals like spirit possession as particularly rich sites at which to explore the diverse social struggles through which groups make memories and identities and transmit them to future generations (Connerton 1989; Piehlar 1994; Sharp 1995; Lambek 1998; Koonz 1994; Stoller 1995).

A second key predecessor who explicitly tried to theorize the impact of social structure and practice on individual mental life was the psychologist Frederic Bartlett. Like Halbwachs, Bartlett also argues for the active, constructive nature of remembering (Bartlett [1932] 1995). Whereas Halbwachs based his ideas about collective memory on a historical study of the spatial infrastructure of the New Testament as well as personal reflection, Bartlett drew upon the results of specially designed experimental techniques.

Unlike the great majority of psychologists at the time, Bartlett was actually concerned to make his laboratory experiments resemble real life as closely as possible. Eschewing the term *memory*, which he felt indicated a process locked inside the head, Bartlett chose the term *remembering* to capture a sense of ongoing activity in real-life contexts. His goal was to elucidate the "social determination, direction and modification of processes of remembering" ([1932] 1995, 12).

Basing his conclusions on experiments in which he asked people to either recall a story or particular images after given intervals of time, Bartlett argues that what we remember is shaped by "schemas," a term he borrows, in modified form, from the neurologist Sir Henry Head (1920). Head states that "every recognizable postural change enters into consciousness already charged with its relation to something that has gone before . . . For this combined standard, against which all subsequent changes of posture are measured before they enter consciousness, we propose the word schema" (Head 1920, quoted in Bartlett [1932] 1995, 199).

However, whereas Head goes on to suggest that past impressions are stored in the cortex, Bartlett moves away from a physiological model. He suggests that schemas are best thought of as "organized settings" that refer to "an active organization of past reactions, or of past experiences, which must always be supposed to be operating in any well-adapted organic response" ([1932] 1995, 201). He conceives of these organized settings as a densely layered network of past associations and experiences that constantly rearrange and modify themselves into "momentary settings" as new experiences confront old ones. In turn, memories are a product of this imaginative process of reconstruction.[11]

In recent years, a wave of psychological scholarship has emerged that emphasizes Bartlett's insights into the social nature of remembering (Cole and Cole 1999; Edwards and Middleton 1986; Middleton and Crook 1996; Middleton and Edwards 1990; Rosa 1996; Shotter 1990). These scholars focus on three strands in Bartlett's thought that are of particular relevance to our consideration of the social practices through which Betsimisaraka remember the colonial past. First, these scholars stress his insights into the role of feeling and affect as key features of how people remember. Second, they highlight the importance of Bartlett's concept of conventionalization, a process whereby cultural symbols take on recognized properties through processes of assimilation, simplification, and elaboration as new experiences are assimilated to prior schemas. Finally, several scholars suggest that "conversational discourse" provides an underappreciated side of Bartlett's work that links it more closely with social process (Edwards and Middleton 1986).

David Middleton, Derek Edwards, and John Shotter all argue that, because thoughts must be expressed in language, focusing on discourse provides a natural bridge between mental processes and social practice. Remembering is constituted by the particular discourses of which it is a part, and it is always occasioned by, and subordinated to, the socially constituted needs and struggles of individuals and the social discourses through which they are expressed. In turn, conversational remembering has important social and political consequences. As Shotter points out, "Our ways of talking about our experiences work . . . to represent them in such a way as to constitute and sustain one or another kind of social order" (1990, 123). In highlighting the social and political implications of Bartlett's work, these studies provide a way of linking Bartlett's insights into the role of schemas in remembering to Halbwachs's focus on the politics of commemoration.

I share Halbwachs's and Bartlett's commitment to a social constructionist view of memory and agree that remembering is always entwined with sociopolitical processes. However, I remain uncomfortable with the functionalist assumptions that are part of their legacy, assumptions that are due partly to the short time frame of many of these studies. Is memory infinitely malleable and is it really evoked only because it suits socially constituted needs? Recent Africa-based studies of long-term historical memory suggest that the relationship between past and present can not be reduced to an interest-based model. Carolyn Hamilton (1998), for example, argues that in the case of the history of Shaka Zulu, which dates back to the late nineteenth century, there are powerful limits on the process of historical invention. Her position resonates with Arjun Appadurai's aphorism that the past "is a scarce resource," and his belief that representations of the past are constrained by cultural models of what constitutes a compelling historical narrative as well as the raw materials available for construction (1981). In a different vein of antireductionist critique, several scholars have also argued that we can not emphasize the political at the expense of the moral (see J. Cole 1998; Lambek 1996; Werbner 1995; see also Werbner 1998). Michael Lambek (1996) goes so far as to suggest that we conceive of memory itself as a form of moral practice, a way of instantiating relationships with and commitments to others.

These reservations bring me to Sigmund Freud, the third figure who struggled with the combined individual and social nature of memory, and whose views provide a powerful antidote to presentist arguments about remembering. In his early work, Freud argues that memories of every experience are stored in the unconscious and, although they may not be easily accessible, they remain within. He suggests that in order to save itself from particularly painful or conflictual memories, the ego might ward them off over long periods of time by means of repression. Yet he also maintains that, despite the functionalist demands of the ego, certain habits or practices might indicate a displaced reaction to previously experienced painful events (1965, 1963). In other words, the painful past can easily live on, unwanted, in spite of present needs.

Though Freud privileges ahistorical psychodynamic forces as an explanatory mechanism in theorizing memory, I prefer to read Freud through his Bakhtinian interpreters, who emphasize the complex ways in which practices and speech always carry multiple meanings and are weighted with complex emotions at the same time. The idea of an un- spoken world of memory, a subterranean world that might implicitly structure some aspects of social life, remains useful in trying to theorize the unspoken ways in which Betsimisaraka remember the colonial past in daily life. As Michael Lambek and Paul Antze put it, Freud was interested in "what we commemorate in the patterns we repeat" (1996, xxvii). I return to this question in chapter 8, where I draw on V. N. Vološinov's notion of the "unofficial conscious" as a way of gesturing toward a sociohistorical way of thinking about a subterranean current of memory.

THE MINDFUL WORLD: SOCIAL TECHNOLOGIES OF MEMORY

These early accounts and the subsequent work they inspired go far in the attempt to bring the social and individual nature of memory together. Ultimately, however, each of them tends to emphasize *either* the individual *or* the social nature of memory, and none of them go far enough in theorizing the processes through which the two sides might reciprocally shape each other. In theorizing the social and individual nature of memory, I have found it useful to turn to an alternative tradition of anthropological and psychological writing that sees the process of knowing the world as fundamentally intertwined with the social, cultural, and material world of which it is a part.

In recent years a body of research has emerged that seeks to move beyond subject/object dichotomies by turning to the notion of practice or activity as a mediating device between subjective experience and objective social conditions. For example, Pierre Bourdieu attempts to overcome dualistic notions of cognition and social life. He suggests that the notion of a habitus as "a system of lasting, transposable dispositions which . . . functions at every moment as a *matrix of perceptions, appreciations, and actions*" (1977, 82–83, emphasis in the original) provides a way of dialectically mediating between objective structures and the cognitive and motivational structures they produce. Similarly, Charles Taylor (1979, 48) suggests that social practices form the intersubjective medium of mind. "Meanings and norms," Taylor tells us, "that are implicit in practices are not just in the minds of the actors but are out there in the practices themselves, practices which can not be conceived as a set of individual actions, but which are essentially modes of social relation, of mutual action."

The idea that social practices might shape thought is also apparent in the early work of Clifford Geertz. In his classic article "The Growth of Culture and the Evolution of Mind" ([1962] 1973), Geertz argues that human beings developed in tandem with culture. In other words, there is no such thing as a "pre-cultural" person, no possibility that culture acted only to extend "organically based capacities logically and genetically prior to it" (68). Rather, people and culture (used here in the sense of an extrasomatic set of symbols, meanings, and artifacts) evolved together. As a result, people do not think or feel independently of culture. They think *through* it, for "human intellection in the specific sense of directive reasoning depends upon the manipulation of certain kinds of cultural resources in such a manner as to produce (discover, select) environmental stimuli needed—for whatever purpose—by the organism" (80). Moreover, the context in which thinking occurs is not just "in the head" but "[in] . . . the house yard, the marketplace, and the town square" (45).

Geertz's conclusion—that we rely on extrasomatic symbols and tools to organize the inchoate flow of experience and tell us how and what to think, and that these tools are available in everyday settings—is confirmed and extended in the work of cultural-historical psychology, which sees human mental activity as fundamentally shaped by the sociohistorical setting in which it occurs. According to Michael Cole the central thesis of cultural approaches to psychology is that the structure and development of human psychological processes emerge through culturally mediated, historically developing, practical activity. A key concept in this school of thought is that artifacts—humanly created material objects— are critical in regulating how people think. Moreover, not only did human psychological processes emerge with the practice of making artifacts, as Geertz suggests, but the use of artifacts continually "reacts back" on the people who use them to effect a change in their basic psychic condition (1996, 108).

Perhaps one of the most provocative attempts to argue for the cognitive consequences of a particular social technology is Jack Goody's analysis of some of the ways that writing affects thinking (1977). Framing his discussion in terms of the doggedly persistent dichotomies that plague how Western scholars have thought about observed differences in thinking among "primitive" and "modern" peoples, Goody suggests that one route out of the impasse is to focus on the *technologies* of communication. He goes on to discuss a number of different kinds of graphic representations, including the list, the table, and the matrix, and concludes that graphic representation takes speech and thought out of context, freezing it and enabling it to be analyzed beyond the context of its production. As a result, many of the mental characteristics we associate with literacy—in particular analytical thinking and historical analysis—may be a consequence of literacy, not its cause.[12]

Though Goody has been attacked for giving too much explanatory weight to the technology of writing, independent of the socioideological context in which it occurs, his intuition into the link between social artifacts (like writing or a pencil) and mental processes has been widely confirmed. An important line of recent thinking in cultural psychology argues that thinking is not, as most people tend to assume, an entirely individual, internal process. Rather, "people think in partnership with others and with the help of culturally provided tools and implements" (Salomon 1993a, xiii). Edwin Hutchins, for example, argues that, since people think *through* the artifacts they use, activities and the material artifacts that make them possible—not individuals—should become the unit of cognitive analysis. He calls this unit of analysis—which stretches across individuals to encompass the wider sociocultural environment— distributed cognition (see also M. Cole 1996; Hutchins 1995; Lave 1988; Salomon 1993b).

In this book I draw on these insights and apply them to the domain of memory. However, my approach extends writing on the interaction between culture and mind in two ways. Most studies of how activities shape human mental processes focus on the crucial role of technology in organizing how people think, but few examine the ways that activities themselves are embedded in larger fields of historical struggle. Although I agree that technology is important, I also want to draw attention to what I see as the social behaviors and practices that work like technologies to shape how and what people remember from the past. At the same time, I emphasize the way these behaviors, and the kinds of memories they enable, are part of larger historical processes of transformation: they are part of Betsimisaraka efforts to survive.

Memory does not exist internally, nor does it exist only in collective representations as most anthropological analyses imply. Rather, it exists intersubjectively, stretched across individuals and the wider social and cultural environment that they inhabit. As a result, it is to the social practices that shape memory, and the way these intersect with ongoing historically constituted social projects, that we must turn to understand its workings.

ENTERING THE SCENE: MY POSITION, SOME DETAILS

Contemporary anthropologists have stressed the ways in which ethnographic knowledge is coconstructed, as much a product of the ethnographer's interactions with a particular people at a particular time as the theoretical position taken. Certainly, the account that follows is a result of my interactions, relationships, and intense attachments to particular villagers, who had their own, at times contending, explanations of Betsimisaraka cultural practice and the events that occurred during the sixteen months I was there (August 1992 to December 1993; September 1997; August 1999). Not surprisingly, the same tension between ancestral and colonial modes of social interaction and organization I described earlier also structured how I was received within the village.

If my arrival momentarily made some people remember the colonial period, coloring how I was perceived by some villagers, the particular relationships and attachments that I formed during my stay, which in turn dictated the kind of fieldwork I was able to do, emerged from my interactions with those people in the village who took me in and became my friends. When I decided to work in Ambodiharina as opposed to any other place with a similar history it was because I had met, while crammed together in a *taxi-brousse* traveling to the capital, the granddaughter of a woman who was from there. Jammed together in a physical intimacy I would not usually adopt with strangers, which was then accentuated as we were thrown into each other's laps with every bump in the road, we struck up a conversation. The woman's name was Bienaimée, and when she learned of my desire to live in a village, she immediately offered to introduce me to her family and promised that they would care for me. True to her word, Bienaimée put me in touch with the requisite people and engineered at least the initial, official introduction to the village. But as it turned out, this city slicker of a granddaughter did not know much about local etiquette. When she came to the village ostensibly to introduce me to her poor relations and calm their fears as to my possible motives, her efforts failed miserably and she succeeded only in aggravating existing tensions between the country and town branches of the family. Nevertheless, the connection proved useful, for despite their discomfort with Bienaimée's behavior, her family informally adopted me, providing me with a social network within Ambodiharina. This family's links to Mahanoro were also invaluable in helping me see just what some of the effects of the colonial period were.

Quite early on I learned that villagers had their own ideas about how

I was to do fieldwork: they expected me to interview each *tangalamena* in turn. To do so was not only a sign of respect for the *tangalamena* but also assuaged villagers' anxieties about what I was actually doing in Ambodiharina. Although these somewhat awkward interviews occasionally did turn up an intriguing story or odd tidbit of cultural lore, I conducted them largely out of a sense of loyalty to people's ideas of what counted as important historical and ritual information. I almost always taped formal interviews and transcribed them later, with the help of my friend Pierre, who had the great gift of being able to use examples and associations to help broaden my understanding of various points. However, most of the time I carried a tattered Malagasy notebook with me and wrote stories down verbatim, as people talked. At first it made people nervous ("Oh! She's writing again!" they would titter), but they soon came to accept my strange behavior and even to wait patiently while I jotted down their words. Apart from helping with the endless cycle of rice cultivation, my activities included attending ceremonies—usually cattle sacrifices or second burials—either in Ambodiharina or in neighboring villages in the district.

Whereas the warp of my sojourn was shaped by these formal interactions with a variety of different people, the weft—what made these formal occasions meaningful and imbued them with the drama and passions of people's lives—was provided by the cluster of families that took me in. Whereas colonial memory would define me as other—an "other" with a history of tense, exploitative relations to local people—those who came to know me sought to define me through other possible interpretive frameworks that provided alternative grounds on which we could interact. It was this mutual redefinition that made friendships—however murky and tentative at times—possible. Significantly, those who chose to take me in justified their actions with reference to two contending frameworks, which in turn point to an important form of variation within the village. Though I examine these different groups more closely in chapter 3, let me introduce both here.

I arrived in Ambodiharina with Bienaimée and her uncle, the *delegué* (tax collector), in August of 1992. The *delegué* normally lived in Mahanoro, but he came to Ambodiharina regularly to conduct government business on his rounds through the district. He was initially terribly worried about whom I would live with and who would take care of me. Not actually from Ambodiharina, and wary of leaving a young white woman unattended to live with peasants, he sought to introduce me to many of his friends. Predictably, these tended to be people who had spent time outside the village and who had slightly more education than the norm. They saw their contact with me as part of the new, modern Madagascar. While some members of this group came from other parts of Madagascar, several of them were in fact raised in Ambodiharina and were as well versed in Betsimisaraka practice as the most ancestral of elders. Nevertheless, they were eager to learn about the outside world, about other places and ways of doing things, and they saw their association with me as part of this process. For the time being, key members of this group of self-conscious village "progressives," as they might be called, included Pierre; his wife, Nirina; their neighbor and friend Piso; one of the two merchant couples in the village, Jean and Maman n'i Talata; and the midwife.[13] These people tended to see themselves as different from the other villagers. They also regularly talked about "the locals" as if they were themselves not important constituents of local life. For the progressives, the real locals were people who had never left Ambodiharina for any significant amount of time, particularly to attend school; this parochialism was why, the progressives complained, the locals were so difficult to live with. By contrast, the progressives attributed what they perceived to be their own open-mindedness to the greater number of years that they had spent in formal schooling.

The other group, which grew out of my initial connection to Bienaimée's grandmother, constructed our relationship somewhat differently, in keeping with what might be considered an "ancestral" mode of social integration, one based on kinship. Although this group expanded to include a number of related families, my relationship to Ramaresaka, one of the first villagers to befriend me and take me out to plant rice, is representative. Later, I learned that it was because Ramaresaka was possessed by twelve different spirits, one of whom was a Mauritian trader, that she had dared speak to me; apparently her spirit had been delighted at the sight of another white person. But this was never the public reason she used to justify her association with me when other villagers would tease her about feeding and looking after a *vazaha* (European). Rather than define me as the latest incarnation of a series of dominant outsiders, Ramaresaka and many others chose to define me in more general terms, and they did this quite self-consciously. "She is someone's child," they would say, or "She is young and a student and alone, and Malagasy children too go abroad, and so we must care for her and help her finish her story as we would want for our own children." In so doing they were able to re-create me as a human being, a vulnerable, dependent one at that. This group also included Ramaresaka's husband, the diviner Tsaravintana, as well as one of Tsaravintana's cousins, Solo, and his wife, Liliane, who were closely related to Bienaimée's grandmother. Another person who contributed an enormous amount to my understanding both of Betsimisaraka practice and its relation to the colonial past was Josef, an old man of about seventy who was the *tangalamena* for Bienaimée's grandmother's paternal family. Although in this book I identify which villagers are speaking in which circumstances, when I refer to villagers in the plural I mean primarily this group and the wider networks of kinship and friendship of which they were a part.

I was an outsider, privileged in terms of race and class inscribed willy-nilly in the wider history of colonial contact, and these associations could never be totally forgotten. Yet in the context of daily village life, which assumed intimate knowledge of the local scene, ways of making a living, and particular human relations, I was an incompetent child, as yet unversed in local ways and entirely dependent. I was constantly reminded of the occasion in *Return to Laughter* by Laura Bohannan (Elenore Smith Bowen) when the elders tell her that she is a mere child and they will raise her. The villagers' redefinition of who I was and what it meant for me to live with them in the village enabled them to dispel, as best they could, the ghosts of the colonial past. They redefined me in their own terms, despite my occasionally puzzling behavior and the refractory nature of my otherness that could never be completely mastered. In so doing they created the grounds for our shared interaction. The empathy in the account that follows springs from their efforts to teach me about themselves as much as my efforts to learn. My account springs from the kindness of strangers, who took me in with humor and with grace.

OUTLINE OF THE STUDY

In the next chapter I begin to answer the questions I have raised by presenting a history of the region, taken primarily from French and Malagasy archives. This evidence makes it abundantly clear that the colonial experience was intrusive and violent in ways that justify the expectation that it would continue to play an important role in contemporary life. Chapter 3 introduces the reader to the world of the ancestors as I first learned it, a world that gave the illusion of a seamless coherence and seemed to belie the century and a half of social disruption that, according to the historical sources, preceded it. I also give the reader a sense of some of the different kinds of people living in Ambodiharina, for social heterogeneity—and social struggle—is key to understanding the dynamics through which the colonial past is remembered. The remainder of the book is devoted to examining the different mechanisms through which the seemingly overwhelming dominance of the colonial experience became so muted that it required an extended period of intimate involvement in village life before I could begin to see it. In chapter 4, I examine some of the social mechanisms that Betsimisaraka use to represent and reproduce the past, and I compare their practices to Western conceptions of history and memory. In chapter 5, I explore the intimate link between local power and ancestral memory, focusing on the ways in which these memory practices are intimately entwined with people's social goals, a fundamental part of how they seek to gain power and assert control over their lives. I also show how, in attempting to reproduce themselves in colonial times, many Betsimisaraka drew colonial power into local processes of social reproduction and transformation. Due to the entwining of ancestral and colonial power in the creation of Ambodiharina as a particular hybrid locale, the privileging of the local does not erase the colonial past entirely, although in ordinary circumstances it succeeds in forcing it into the background of people's consciousness. Chapter 6 examines cattle sacrifice, the most prominent social technology of memory, which mediates people's relations to the past as well as their current relations to each other and the sociopolitical context of the present. Like the practices described in chapters 3 and 4, cattle sacrifice privileges the local past. However, as in the previous cases, it is an imperfect mechanism, occasionally allowing colonial memories to intrude. In chapter 7, I examine circumstances in which none of these techniques succeed in muting memory of the colonial past, which comes to dominate local consciousness in a vivid and powerful way. Finally, in chapter 8 I try to characterize and account for the kind of memory processes described in the preceding chapters. This journey—which begins with a view of the past dominated by colonialism, moves to an image of the past as entirely local, and then goes on to consider in varying degrees the complex articulation of the two—repeats my own process of re-membering.

CHAPTER 2

Colonial Interventions into Betsimisaraka Life

Gentleness, fear, apathy, naïveté and credulousness are the characteristics of the race. History shows us that in 1776 the Betsimisaraka chiefs happily offered sovereignty of their country to Benyowski, and the people readily submitted; there was no hostility shown to foreign rule. After Benyowski, Sylvan Roux took his place, followed by Jean-René, who traded with the Hova King Radama I in Tananarive. Soon after Jean-René's return to the coast, Radama I attacked and vanquished him without difficulty. Ever since, the Betsimisaraka, perpetually deceived and oppressed, have never once rebelled against their oppressors.

  —Journal Officiel de Madagascar, *May 1897*

To understand how Betsimisaraka remember the colonial period, we must begin with the historical record. In this chapter, I outline a history of the region using a combination of published works and archival sources.

  As the archival fragment that serves as the epigraph for the chapter makes clear, the Betsimisaraka have long been subject to the dominating intrusion of outsiders. Their historical experience of colonization, first under the Merina, then the French, has provided the crucible in which particular techniques for shaping memory, and with them a certain kind of historical consciousness, have formed. In some ways their experience of colonization was disruptive but manageable; as we will see, many aspects of colonization have been assimilated, others modified, still others erased. But some aspects of colonization were profoundly wrenching, and the marks they have left run deep.

"THE MANY WHO WILL NOT BE SUNDERED"

Soon after France colonized Madagascar in 1895, General Governor Joseph Gallieni imposed a modified form of indirect rule called *la politique des races,* dividing the peoples of Madagascar into different groups according to their customs so as to facilitate the colonial administration. The result of this division and codification, which produced essentialized ethnicities from what were once fluid political groupings, endures today. The census for Madagascar lists twenty different official ethnic groups.[1] The third largest of these so-called ethnic groups, the Betsimisaraka inhabit the east coast of the island, from Vohemar in the north to Mananjary in the south.

Unlike other Malagasy peoples, who are widely known within Anglophone anthropology through the writings of Maurice Bloch (1971b, 1986), Gillian Feeley-Harnik (1991), and Conrad Kottak (1980), among others, the Betsimisaraka never had a centralized kingdom nor any institutionalized form of ranking. Rather, historical sources consistently describe Betsimisaraka as unruly and disorganized, a multiplicity of different ancestries constantly fighting among themselves. The French explorer Alfred Grandidier describes Betsimisaraka country in the late eighteenth century as "the land of many princes. Each village, each cluster of hamlets has its prince, its 'head' *[filohany],* its own independent chief, the head of the family. The inhabitants of the village were simply called the descendants of so-and-so" (1958, 23).

Grandidier cites an account by Parat, written in 1714, that is even more explicit: "The east of Madagascar," he writes, "is governed by chiefs with no power, each controlling only his tiny village, constantly fighting among themselves. They are all traitors" (1958, 23). Hubert Deschamps, drawing on additional historical sources, reiterates the theme of disorganization: "The tribes lived in total independence the one from the other," and "wars between tribes and clans, incited by slave traders, periodically ravaged the country" (1960, 105).

These accounts agree on two themes that remain relevant for understanding Betsimisaraka today. First, local political groupings are small, organized at the level of independent lineages (see chapter 3). Although a French policy enacted at the turn of the century made Betsimisaraka cluster in villages comprising more than one extended family, the ideal of independent households, each controlling its own affairs under the direction of a male elder, remains strong. When I asked one man why the Betsimisaraka had never had a king he replied, "We're too difficult, too feisty. Each man wants to control his own ancestors, his own family. The *tangalamena* sees to all that."[2]

The local ideal of independent lineages, however, has never meant that Betsimisaraka existed in isolation, for they have long been a part of global and regional networks of trade. From the sixteenth century on, Europeans seeking to trade in firearms, slaves, cattle, and rice would stop to exchange goods and stock up at ports along the east coast (Grandidier 1958; Deschamps 1960). In 1596, a Dutch fleet landed in the Bay of Antongil to restock with food and water. In 1598, three more Dutch ships dropped anchor, seeking food supplies and slaves, for which they traded guns. In 1601, the first ships sent by the British East Indian Company arrived. Throughout the seventeenth and eighteenth centuries, traders seeking slaves, cattle, and rice for export to the expanding plantation economies of Bourbon (Mauritius) and Réunion frequently visited the coast.

By the end of the seventeenth century, the east coast had become a sanctuary for pirates, from whence they attacked ships on their way east. English and French pirates intermarried with local women, typically the daughters of elite clans. As one observer wrote, noting a strategy that has long been a means through which strangers are incorporated into Betsimisaraka society, the French "favored marriages of officers, sailors and workers with Malagasy women because it attracted the friendship of the *indigènes*" (Grandidier 1958, 25). These unions produced the *métisse* (mixed blood) pirate princes—locally referred to as the *zana-malata*—who were to have a considerable, albeit temporary, impact on local political organization. Because of their access to superior arms, the pirates, and later their children, began to act as mediators among the different Betsimisaraka clans. As Yvette Sylla writes, "There were two privileged groups on the east coast. On the one hand [were] local clan chiefs whose economic supremacy was reinforced by their access to guns, and on the other hand [were] the pirates who co-existed with the Malagasy but were nevertheless seen as possessing an exterior, superior power" (1985, 21).

During the early eighteenth century the lucrative trade opportunities provided by European traders and pirates, and particularly the introduction of firearms, sparked certain internal transformations, the most important of which was the creation of the Betsimisaraka federation. The story of the formation of the Betsimisaraka federation is one of those events that colonial historians seized on to characterize the different peoples of Madagascar, and it is repeated in truncated form in most missionary and colonial accounts of the region (for example, see Aujas 1907). The version I tell here reproduces the stereotyped feel of many of these accounts, though it is derived from my reading of the French trader Nicholas Mayeur (cf. Mayeur [1809] 1977).

As most chroniclers describe it, the genesis of the federation lies in internecine tensions among different ancestries occupying the east coast. In the first decade of the eighteenth century, the group of ancestries known as the Tsikoa, from the Andevoranto region, grew jealous of the lucrative trade and control of ports enjoyed by the clans farther to the north (Grandidier 1958; Mayeur [1809] 1977). Under the leadership of a warrior named Ramano, the Tsikoa attacked the northern ancestries, looting and pillaging the area to the north of Tamatave. Soon thereafter, the pirate Ratsimilaho, son of an English pirate and a princess from Fénérive, returned from England bearing gold and arms, only to find his people enslaved by the southern clans. At first, Ratsimilaho attempted to persuade Ramano, leader of the Tsikoa, to release his people and return home to the south. When Ramano refused, he called a large political meeting *(kabary)* in which he attempted to convince the other ancestries to unite in order to drive out the invaders.

After a long debate, the other chiefs conferred upon Ratsimilaho the title *filoha be,* or "big chief," and gave him the authority to lead them into battle. They surprised the Tsikoa working in their rice fields and succeeded in forcing them south; from this time on, the Tsikoa were called the Betanimena, or "Covered with Red Mud." But Ramano planned his revenge and later attacked the northerners, only to be driven south again. In order to conquer Ramano, Ratsimilaho allied himself with one of the chiefs of the southern clans. In 1712, the two leaders swore a public oath, marking the allegiance between the groups. It was at this ceremony— which included the sacrifice of a bull—that the group took the name the Betsimisaraka: "the many who will not be sundered." Ratsimilaho also adopted a new name in keeping with his position as leader of the Betsimisaraka: Ramaromanompo, or "he who is served by many."

The Betsimisaraka federation lasted only forty years, scarcely the span of two generations. Deschamps (1960) believes that its demise resulted from the death of Ramaromanompo in 1750 and the failure to find an adequate successor. Manassé Esoavelomandroso (1979) provides a complementary explanation, arguing that the breakdown of the federation was largely the result of internecine squabbles provoked by foreign traders who, in supporting various chiefs in order to obtain slaves, contributed to the endemic factionalism along the east coast. By the turn of the century the federation had dissolved back into myriad little chieftancies, each supported by a different European or *métisse* slave trader, and each fighting for control of a tiny fiefdom.

Two aspects of the history of the Betsimisaraka federation are particularly important to stress. First, the name was initially little more than a political slogan, a wartime rallying cry rather than a name that actually indicated the kind of social organization typical of the region. Second, the federation seems mainly to have initially referred to the northern third of what is now called Betsimisaraka country. In 1803, Chapelier wrote that, unlike the northern Betsimisaraka, who were ruled by the *métisse* descendants of pirates, the southern Betsimisaraka were governed by members of their own "race" and "enjoy tranquility and are not prone to anarchy" (cited in Grandidier 1958, 59). Although the region where I worked is culturally similar to its neighbors, no one ever mentioned having belonged to the Betsimisaraka federation. Historical sources do not reveal exactly when the name Betsimisaraka was extended to refer to the inhabitants of the southern part of the region, but it was clearly in usage by the mid–eighteenth century, following the Merina conquest (M. Esoavelomandroso 1979), and was further reified and codified under the French.

Betsimisaraka, then, are a heterogeneous lot, and what little unity that exists is a product of shared customs and shared historical experience, including being treated as a social entity by powerful outsiders. To give just a small sample of the heterogeneity of the area where I worked, the inhabitants of Ambodiharina cited their ancestral origins as being in highland Imerina, to the south in the region of Farafangana and to the west in the area of Marolambo. They had come to Ambodiharina for diverse reasons as well, which included not only fights among family members that resulted in the founding of new ancestries but also resettlement by the French. What bound the different families to each other as a community was a shared locality that was ritually constituted when the different groups acted as witnesses to the others' sacrifices.[3]

Betsimisaraka themselves distinguish between northern Betsimisaraka and southern Betsimisaraka and, within these divisions, between those who live along the coast and those who live inland "under the bamboo" *(ambanivolo)*. The experience of colonial penetration described here is intended to apply to the Vatomandry-Mahanoro region, and in particular to those areas where people have lived intimately with Merina and French colonizers for a considerable period of time. The experience of colonialism in areas of Betsimisaraka country like Marolambo, where

Merina control was only partial and where Merina or French settler implantation never occurred, may well have been different in important ways.

MERINA DOMINATION

Though eighteenth-century observers described the Betsimisaraka as enjoying "easy tranquility," this situation changed in the nineteenth century, when the diverse peoples of the east coast came under the control of the Merina, the people who inhabit the central high plateau of Madagascar.[4] The Merina conquest of the central east coast was achieved in a series of expeditions between 1817 and 1823. The area around Mahanoro was first conquered in 1823 by Merina armies led by the Tamatavian trader Jean-René, who had sworn fealty to the Merina king Radama I (1810–28); from then on, indigenous inhabitants were subject to a foreign power. Grandidier notes that, "despite their sweet, malleable character," the inhabitants of the regions did revolt, but that the rebellion was easily crushed by Radama's troops, who were able to "totally restore order and maintain it without trouble, despite the fact that the Merina governors exhibited excessive cruelty" (1958, 61, my translation).

Early occupation under Radama seems to have affected Betsimisaraka daily life relatively little (M. Esoavelomandroso 1979). Radama conquered more through oratory than force, and most local princes were granted relative autonomy in exchange for acknowledging Radama as their "father." The political organization of the country was left intact so long as local princes agreed to have a Merina officer at their side. Although Merina settlers did establish themselves locally, they lived mainly as traders and seemed to have bothered the Betsimisaraka relatively little.

As French interest in controlling Madagascar increased over the course of the nineteenth century, however, Merina policy on the east coast changed. Under Radama I, the Merina aimed for unification of Madagascar and the enlargement of Radama's kingdom. Under Queen Ranavalona I (ruled ca. 1828–61), Merina policy shifted to emphasize defense against increasing intrusion from predatory colonial powers and the facilitation of commercial exploitation. It was during this period, which lasted till the French conquest in 1895, that Betsimisaraka suffered the most from Merina presence on the east coast. Betsimisaraka territory was divided into different districts, each town administered by a fort that provided the necessary conditions for political domination and successful commercial exploitation.[5] Mahanoro became one such commercial center, where local produce such as raffia, rice, and cattle were brought for export. But it was the local Merina administrators, not the Merina monarchy in Antananarivo, who had the most to gain. As one contemporary observed, "Everywhere there is some sort of commerce, where local resources can create import and export transactions, the Hova [Merina] have posts, and make a lot of money only a small portion of which sees its way into the state coffers" (Clément Delhorbe, cited in M. Esoavelomandroso 1979, 95).[6] Writing of Merina garrisons on the northwest coast, Feeley-Harnik (1991) notes that the forts were intended both to protect Merina soldiers and, importantly, to incorporate local people into the new regime they represented. Similarly, Esoavelomandroso writes that incorporation was the initial goal of the Merina oligarchy, which incorporated Betsimisaraka into the army and lower levels of the administration.

By the late nineteenth century, however, the "incorporation" seemed to have amounted to little more than taxation and the use of corvée performed by Betsimisaraka for the fulfillment of royal work. From the 1880s on, the corvée for carrying royal packages of imported items, as well as local products like raffia, to Antananarivo increased, and the area around Mahanoro was one of those hardest hit by demands for workers. During certain seasons, those required to fulfill the demands for corvée had barely enough time to return home before they were called to Tamatave yet again to carry more goods. Months were lost carrying packages, maintaining Merina forts, or cutting trees for the queen in Antananarivo that Betsimisaraka were forbidden to cut for their own use. The wealthier Betsimisaraka were accompanied by their slaves, which Betsimisaraka had acquired through internal fighting and raids on Mozambique. The slaves carried food, cooked, and helped their masters with their burdens. Frequently, Betsimisaraka also borrowed provisions to avoid being excessively encumbered along the way. But they borrowed from Merina officers or the local governor, who later used their debts against them and eventually made off with their harvests, slaves, and goods.

The Merina requisition of labor was accompanied by taxation. The declaration that all land belonged to the queen, the basis of the Merina monarchy, meant that each person was required to pay a tax on the land worked. Among the Merina, the tax was neither defined in relation to surface area (like the *hetra* imposed by King Andrianampoinimerina, the king credited with the rise of the Merina state) nor applied to the head of each household, but was applied to "each spade" *(isampangady)*,

meaning each worker. Extended to the provinces, this system led to constant abuse. In the case of the Betsimisaraka, the men were constantly
away fulfilling demands for corvée, leaving agricultural work to women,
children, and slaves. As a result, dishonest officers were able to tax each
worker rather than the head of household: the "each spade" tax, which
should have amounted to thirty kilos of rice per household head, was
often made to amount to considerably more (M. Esoavelomandroso
1979).

The imposition of corvée and taxes must have had a disintegrating,
divisive effect on Betsimisaraka village life, but the intrusions ran deeper
still. The Merina goal of shattering traditional Betsimisaraka organization so that it might be reconceived was implicit in the battle that
Merina officers waged against indigenous Betsimisaraka practices. Betsimisaraka responded by fleeing to the hinterlands to escape administrative control. As a result, the 1881 "Code of 305 Articles," the Merina laws for the administration of the kingdom, contained the following:

> Article 104: They [Betsimisaraka] cannot build houses in the forest without
> the authorization of the government. If people erect, for the purpose of in-
> habitation, houses in the forest, they will be punished with a fine of 10 cattle
> and 10 piasters, and their houses will be destroyed and they must also pay an
> indemnity of one cow and one piaster for each tree cut.

> Article 105: It is forbidden to clear the forest by means of fire with the in-
> tention of planting fields of rice, corn, or other crops. Those areas already
> cleared may be cultivated, but if people clear new land with fire or extend
> those clearings already in existence they will be *mis aux fers* [put in chains,
> i.e., imprisoned] for five years.

> Article 106: Those trees located next to the ocean can not be cut or damaged
> unless it is under the express orders of the government. Whoever damages the
> forest will be punished with a fine of 10 cattle and 10 piasters, and if they can
> not pay will be put in prison until they work off the fine. (Cited in Esoavelo-
> mandroso 1979, 98)

These orders reflected the Merina government's desire to gain political
control over the Betsimisaraka's movement. For many Betsimisaraka—
who inhabited a land crosscut with rivers, lagoons, and streams—the
dugout canoe was (and still is) the most frequently used means of trans-
portation. Faced with the facility of movement enabled by the canoes,
and the excellent hiding places afforded by the dense inland forest, Merina administrators found their agenda difficult to implement. As one Merina bureaucrat wrote to the prime minister, "If the number of our subjects has lessened, as you can probably tell from the attached list, it is

because of the local people's character. They don't want to do their part of the *fanompoana* [corvée] and thus frequently change domicile, moving from port to port" (cited in M. Esoavelomandroso 1979, 100).

The ban on inhabiting *toby*, the provisional houses built near fields in the forest, was decreed for much the same reason. Frustrated by its inability to catch these inveterate nomads, the Merina administration eventually resorted to forced settlement. In 1892, the Merina generals in charge of the region each received a letter from the prime minister asking them to forbid all movement from one port to another without government permission. At the same time, the garrisons and points of administration multiplied; all Betsimisaraka were made to move to large villages and forced to abandon those hamlets judged too small or too isolated. One general wrote, "In order to have them easily at hand for the transport of royal packages we will regroup in five villages all the inhabitants in our circumscription" (cited in M. Esoavelomandroso 1979, 101). This process of relocation was to accelerate under the French.

EARLY CREOLE SETTLERS

When the French disembarked on the rocky point of Mahanoro in 1895, the town was already inhabited by Réunionais, German, and Mauritian merchants; numerous plantations lined the banks of the Mangoro River, where European and Merina *colons* (settlers) grew vanilla, sugarcane, coffee, and cocoa.[7] By 1882, a Réunionais named Fourbon had already built ten buildings "modern for the time" and had two hundred slaves as laborers.[8] That same year, Reverend R. P. Lacomme wrote that there were as many as one hundred indigenous Catholics and around fifty whites living in the area.[9] When Louis Catat passed through the countryside to the west of Mahanoro in 1890, there were twenty or so small plantations, which produced three and a half tons of produce sold for twenty-four francs per kilogram (1895, 121). Although small plantations dominated the local economy, there was also some trade, although less than in other coastal towns to the north because of Mahanoro's inferior port.

The development of the region for small planter-merchants had begun under the Merina in the 1880s. Although the Merina queen Ranavalona I forbade foreigners to own land, settlers nevertheless acquired it through theft and deceit, frequently marrying local women as a way to get around the law (see chapter 5). Esoavelomandroso (1979, 181–82) documents the following example of land theft, as well as some of the

complicities that existed between the European settlers and Merina officials posted to the region:

> Wilson was an English citizen living in Mahanoro in the 1870's who confis-
> cated the land of Illemanga, a Betsimisaraka, after having accused him
> of "stealing a knife and a fork." Terrified that he would be dragged before
> the Hova authorities, Illemanga fled. Wilson then ran Illemanga's wife and
> children off the property and confiscated it. Illemanga's wife and kin com-
> plained to the Merina governor, Rainsolofo, who ignored the complaint. Only
> in 1892, when Wilson's overseer threatened the family with his gun and took
> some of their land bordering on his—which Rainsolofo had himself just
> purchased—did Rainsolofo respond. Moved by self-interest to action, Rain-
> solofo wrote to Wilson to ask him not to enlarge his property and to remind
> him that Betsimisaraka contested his possession of the land. Coincidentally,
> Wilson died a few days later; Madame Wilson sold the vanilla plantation. But
> there were complications. She was supposed to sell the rights to the land that
> she ostensibly purchased from Merina officers. As she did not possess rights
> to the land she could not sell it. Nor would Rainsolofo, scared of European
> intervention, return the land to the dispossessed family of Illemanga.

We do not know the outcome of this story. But it suggests the way that—
following settler implantation, but prior to official French colonization—
land was often acquired through a combination of Merina officers'
complicity and their inability to control the actions of foreigners. Betsimisaraka remained at the mercy of both groups of powerful outsiders.

When France officially colonized Madagascar in 1895, Governor General Gallieni sought to minimize the number of small settlers, favoring
large grants of land to companies.[10] However, land was parceled out in
large concessions mainly in the northwest (Sharp 1993); the east coast
remained the country of the *petits colons* (small settlers), despite French
administrators' efforts to the contrary. Dubbed *marécageux* after the fens
that were a preferred site of habitation, these *petits colons* were poor
Creole settlers from Réunion and Mauritius who had come to make their
fortune.[11] Relatively few actually did. The *marécageux* were small
planter-traders with little capital who took more land than they could
cultivate, married local women, and then proceeded to lead a miserable
existence, living off a combination of subsistence agriculture and money
earned from coffee, cloves, and pepper produced for the world market.
Frequently, they had depots located on their concessions, where they sold
rum and foreign goods and traded with Betsimisaraka for rice, rubber,
and raffia.[12] According to Jean Fremigacci (1976), this arrangement
amounted to "piracy of other means." Writing in 1901, E. Prudhomme
describes the Creole style of house as an "eyesore," while in a report

some fifty years later a French administrator describes them thus: "The *marécageux* live in the bush in a lamentable state. Isolated, lazy, incapable of reacting against any adversity, they prefer to console themselves with alcohol rather than get up enough energy to take care of their antiquated plantations . . . This is colonization in its full degeneracy, of no economic importance, despicable, and condemned to disappear. Yet it is nevertheless European and thus, for political reasons, difficult to abandon totally."[13]

FORMAL FRENCH COLONIZATION

During the early years of colonization, French officials were at some pains to distinguish themselves from their Merina predecessors. The ideology that the French were liberating Madagascar from the rule of despots and leading them toward a more enlightened form of republican government was an important element in justifying colonial rule. As Fremigacci (1993, 28) notes, "The armed expeditions like those led against Dahomey in 1892 or Madagascar in 1895 were no longer seen as manifestations of militarism, but rather the equivalent of the revolution of 1789 in France: They marked the liberation of people from the control of absolute monarchies." Early reports recount how delighted the Betsimisaraka were to be liberated from the Merina, and stress that French authority was firmly established. The reality of Betsimisaraka and French colonial interactions, however, was considerably more complex (see fig. 1).

Despite the concern of Gallieni and subsequent administrators to break what they termed "Hova [Merina] oppression" and to present themselves as liberators of the coastal peoples, French policy tended to reproduce many of the patterns of domination and oppression that existed under the Merina. Moreover, because the French eventually had to rely on Merina middlemen as subaltern functionaries, they became further identified with them from the perspective of local people. To this day, villagers in this area sometimes employ the word *vazaha,* used on the high plateau to refer to Europeans, to refer to Merina, Europeans, and any government bureaucrat or representative of the state. Nevertheless, as I shall argue here, French colonialism differed in important ways from that of the Merina, and Betsimisaraka remain aware of the difference. In particular, French administrators were much more concerned with transforming local societies rather than with simply extracting resources.

With official annexation in 1895, the goal of the French administration was to facilitate pacification, followed by settlement and the subse-

Figure 1. *Danses Betsimisaraka,* 1901. With formal colonization, French
officials occupied the former Merina governor's residence in Mahanoro.
This photo may have been taken during General Joseph Gallieni's tour
along the east coast of Madagascar, during which he visited Mahanoro.
Courtesy of Foiben-Taosarintanin'i Madagasikara.

quent economic development of the region. In order to realize these goals,
Gallieni implemented his policy of *tache d'huile* (literally, oil spot), developed during his campaign in Indochina, a policy that entailed the grad-
ual outreach of services from existing centers to new settlements and the
control of those settlements. At the same time, he implemented a three-
pronged policy of colonial transformation focusing on land, work, and
the restructuring of local societies.

GETTING LAND

One of the primary ways that French colonizers intruded into Betsimisaraka life was by dispossessing them of their land. With the decree of
2 November 1896, anyone could purchase land for five francs per
hectare. With permission from the governor, land was given to those of
French nationality. Between 1897 and 1900, the administration granted
fourteen provisionary titles and thirteen other titles, to land that totaled

187 hectares. By 1900, the district of Mahanoro had around fifty different enterprises run by Europeans.[14]

In theory the acquisition of concessions was supposed to follow a procedure that would protect Betsimisaraka land rights. Each settler was to place a request with the district chief noting the limits of the land chosen, and an inquiry was supposed to be held before the land could be granted. In practice, however, the *colon* would place his request and move onto the land, regardless of who owned it. Other *colons* got land through still less legal means. Fremigacci (1976) cites the story of a *colon* who said it was the era when a trader could become a planter for the price of a barrel of rum. Villagers echoed this story when they told me how they had lost their ancestral land by going into debt buying rum; eventually the land was taken as payment. The story of Ampetika provides some sense of this process. I reproduce it here not only because Ampetika was considered a model concession by Gallieni and other French officials but also because many people in the Mahanoro region see Ampetika as iconic of the displacement people suffered during the colonial period. More than one family living in Ambodiharina had been dispossessed of land at Ampetika, and it was Ampetika that villagers attacked and burned during the insurrection of 1947 (see fig. 2).

HOW AMPETIKA WAS LOST

In 1896, Monsieur Deville de Sardelys requested the concession of Ampetika, three hundred hectares of choice land along the Mangoro near the village of Betsizaraina, a former Merina outpost where royal cattle were kept.[15] The colonial government approved the request. On 12 December 1896 the *proces de bornage,* the public hearing required to title land, was carried out. The government at Mahanoro called a meeting of the villagers and announced to them that following the harvest they would no longer be permitted to work the land. The *chef de village,* Ravimbina, asked that they be allowed to return to land formerly worked by them that one of the governors of Mahanoro had given to slaves from Mozambique following French manumission of slaves in 1896.[16] The governor declined, saying he could not chase the former slaves off land that had been given to them by the government, and then offered the villagers instead the marshland around Betsizaraina. The villagers accepted. At this point Houdoul, the overseer for Sardelys, made the following announcement: "The land of Ampetika belongs to the French domain; you have cultivated and planted here for several years without asking gov-

Figure 2. *La Concession d'Ampetika,* 1901. Many people in the Mahanoro region were forced to fulfill corvée requirements at this concession, which local people burned during the 1947 rebellion. Courtesy of Foiben-Taosarintanin'i Madagasikara.

ernment permission. The government has decided that it is in your interests to give this land to Monsieur le Compte Deville de Sardelys, who will[,] through his management, teach you the art of agriculture. Consequently, if you have planted either rice, manioc, sugarcane, corn or other grains you may harvest them this season, but henceforth you may no longer plant here without M. de Sardelys's authorization." The report on this meeting claims that the peasants then bowed their heads and made a short speech saying that the French were their "mothers and fathers" *(raiamandreny)* and that they would follow their orders. Nevertheless, they begged the government for new land on which to continue farming.

But in 1897 the following petition was sent to Gallieni:

Dear Sir,

We, the inhabitants of Betsizaraina, write you because a *vazaha* from Tananarive arrived here and gathered us together, both big and small, and he spoke thus. "The land of Ampetika to the north of the Mangoro is mine, and I have received it from the *fanjakana* [government], and I am informing you. If you have any complaints speak now." And we responded, "We don't oppose you, sir, because you have received it from the government who is both mother and father, but if you ask of our complaints then here are the words of the inhabitants of Betsizaraina." "This land of Ampetika is where we make our livelihood, it is our means of living and serving the

fanjakana, it is that which allows us to pay the rice tax each year. We
don't go into the forest to burn the woods and plant rice[,] because we
have this land of Ampetika on which to plant rice, sugarcane, manioc,
potatoes, bananas and beans. Also, neither our ancestors nor our fathers
nor our descendants have ever wanted to sell this land. When the Merina
governors came to Mahanoro or when other great persons came from
another province and asked to buy Ampetika[,] they would never get it[,]
because we the owners never wanted to sell it. As they sought land on
which to graze their cattle we gave them other land."

Upon hearing our words the *vazaha* replied, "Go seek other land for
your subsistence, this land of Ampetika is mine and you can not oppose
me." He told us to find other land off which to live, but we can't[,] for
no one wants to give us his land for our subsistence. As we can no longer
work on our heritage, Ampetika, we are complaining to you, the government, for you are our father and our mother. We will certainly die if we
can not use our ancestral land of Ampetika.[17]

Predictably, the petition was refused. It appears that the only reason
the villagers dared petition Gallieni was because a Mauritian faction in
the area also wanted the land and manipulated the villagers in a ploy to
get the land for themselves. The *service des domaines,* the office in charge
of titling land, granted the concession to de Sardelys. Nevertheless, the
story is interesting precisely because Betsimisaraka voices are so rarely
heard in these transactions, and because it shows so clearly where the
balance of power lay. As with most cases, Betsimisaraka peasants were
forced off the most fertile land and made to farm elsewhere. People who
lived in Ambodiharina at this time may not have lost as much land, because the town is located on less-fertile land adjacent to the coast. However, several families who were displaced from Ampetika moved to Ambodiharina. As relative latecomers, they continue to have less-well-placed
rice fields today. At least in some areas—particularly a few kilometers to
the north and west of Ambodiharina, where most of the old *colons'* concessions were located—villages became dispossessed of their best land and
were made to cultivate new land in the interstices between concessions.

GETTING LABOR

French colonizers not only took Betsimisaraka land, but in many cases
they forced Betsimisaraka to work for them cultivating the very land they
had taken from them. Prior to official French colonization, foreign acquisition of labor was officially, if incompletely, controlled by Merina
governors, who sought laborers to augment commerce and agriculture

in the region. Like the French administrators who would succeed him, one Merina governor wrote that he sought to "make the indigenous people in the circumscription, who are naturally lazy and nonchalant, work. Through my administration, I sought to make them work and trade" (cited in Fremigacci 1976, 171). When the *kabary,* the official speeches used throughout Imerina to convey the will of the government to the people, failed, the Merina used threats—such as enrollment in school or the army.[18] Louis Catat (1895, 400) makes it clear that the settlers bought labor from the Merina governors: "The governor in question uses the *fanompoana,* the corvée, to designate such and such a village to provide labor to the concession holders. These men who serve as payment receive nothing but blows, and they all desert. Not daring to return to their villages, they become bandits in the bush. That is how one becomes *fahavalo* [a bandit] in Madagascar." When the French arrived, labor for the *colons'* concessions and labor to enable the new government to build the infrastructure remained necessary for the creation of a successful economy. The tension between these two forces—the government's need for labor on roads and bridges of the colony, and the *colons'* desire to have people work for them—runs through report after report from the colonial period.

The need to obtain labor for both the *colons* and the government, and how this was done, was a major factor in how local people experienced the colonial state. In reviewing the reports from Mahanoro at the turn of the century, two things become clear. First, administrators were caught between what they perceived to be the beneficial, civilizing effects of the colonial enterprise and the need to make a profit. Second, the way in which specific laws and edicts were enacted was partly a result of where the particular sentiment of any given administrator lay. For example, the reports from the administrator Henri Chesse, chief of Mahanoro District at the turn of the century, suggest that he remained concerned about how much work one could fairly demand of the Betsimisaraka, and several meetings were organized with the *colons* to stop labor abuses. Further, he clearly recognized the injustice of requiring the same population to work both on government projects and for the *colons* in addition to producing their own food. In one report from 1899, Chesse ruefully noted that "we can employ only the labor we gain by prestation [e.g., requisition], and produce in this district, once we have stopped sending laborers to the outside [i.e., to the government]."[19] In the case of Chesse's replacement, however, the balance tipped in favor of the *colons,* a fact that

is evident less in his reports to the government than in the clear appro-
bation he received from the various settlers in the district.[20]

Despite constant complaints about how lazy the Betsimisaraka were,
French administrators retained, at least initially, an illusion of easy access to labor. Catat gives a sense of the initial optimism with which the
French viewed the development of the region: "Although the density of
the population is low in this region one can nevertheless procure workers rather easily, mainly agricultural labor. A native worker who is used
for clearing land and other agricultural work should be paid 15 francs
a month plus food, about 750 g. of rice a day and a bit of meat and a
ration of salt each week. The Betsimisaraka, heretofore lazy, carefree
and unproductive, have improved greatly these last few years and now
provide useful labor to the *colons* of the area. The numerous planters
who inhabit the region are never short of labor and they are satisfied
with what they get from the indigenous people"(1895, 16). As colonization progressed, this view changed considerably; by the third or fourth
year of French conquest the illusion of accessible labor had passed and
the acquisition of labor became a major preoccupation of *colons* and administrators alike.[21] Between 1898 and 1900, the government forced Betsimisaraka to work by means of prestation, which was supposed to provide labor both for the government work on the road from Tamatave to
Antananarivo and for the planters. During this time the *colons* applied
for workers directly to the *chef de district,* who would round up the necessary men and women and bring them to the plantation where they were
supposed to work. There were, predictably, desertions, but for the most
part the *colons* obtained the necessary labor.

In 1900–01, this policy changed when the personal tax was increased
and requisition labor was abolished. By forcing Betsimisaraka to earn
money to pay their taxes, the new law was supposed to encourage Betsimisaraka to work for the *colons* and to thereby develop the local economy (see fig. 3). From the start, however, it was clear that few Betsimisaraka would seek wage labor of their own accord, a fact of which
the disgruntled *colons* in the region were keenly aware. For example, de
Sardelys, the owner of the extensive concession of Ampetika, wrote, "I
can not hide from you the painful surprise with which I received the news
that the prestation is to be abolished for both settlers and the state. At
the moment, 2/3 of our workers are provided by the corvée[,] and the
1/3 who remain employed for the whole year agree to work to fulfill the
prestation. If the prestation is abolished all our workers will disappear,

Figure 3. *La Concession de Monsieur Bray, Caféieres,* 1901. During the
colonial era, Betsimisaraka were organized into work brigades to labor
on colonial concessions. Courtesy of Foiben-Taosarintanin'i Madagasikara.

some no longer forced to work, the others having no reason to seek
employment."[22]

From the point of view of the Betsimisaraka, however, forced labor
was constant. In his report, the administrator Martin, who was in charge
of providing workers for the various *colons,* remarked on the devastat-
ing consequences of the end of the prestation from the point of view of
the planter who needed labor. He then noted a "few personal observations": "The Betsimisaraka from Mahanoro have contributed a large part
of the labor for the construction of the east coast road. Out of a population of 8000, 600 were recruited each month for the construction at
Beforona. Upon their return, most were made to work for *colons.* With
all this coming and going only a few months of freedom remained to
him. It is easy to understand that after such a schedule the indigenous
people aspire to tranquility. Moreover certain *colons* have earned themselves the hatred of the local people."[23]

Not surprisingly, few Betsimisaraka volunteered their labor to the *colons*. They failed to pay their taxes and were rounded up by the government and brought to the concessions, where they could work their taxes off instead. As a result, a complex game between the administration, the *colons,* and the Betsimisaraka began as early as 1901. The *colons* were unhappy with the new system because it relied (from their perspective) more on incentive than on force. Meanwhile, the Betsimisaraka grew increasingly resentful of heavy taxation and corvée exacted by the government. The latter was particularly hated by people from around Mahanoro, who were rarely allowed to stay in the district and were instead made to work far to the north, where they had no supporting network of kin.

To avoid paying their taxes and fulfilling the government's requirement for corvée, many Betsimisaraka would hide out on the planters' concessions. As one disgusted administrator described it, the planters' domains were like small fiefdoms ruled by a seigneur who protected his serfs against all interrogation: "This leads me to speak of the *indigènes* [Betsimisaraka] who live habitually on concessions yet who do not comprise the normal personnel of remunerated workers. The planters tolerate the installation of small villages on their land: they allow them to use rice land[,] and in exchange the inhabitants are supposed to work for them one day a week. Every smart *vazaha* thus congratulates himself on having found free labor. How will these miserable people pay their taxes if they earn nothing?"[24]

Legally, what should have happened is that the *colons* paid the taxes of the Betsimisaraka who sought refuge with them, thus acquiring the right to their labor. Instead, most *colons* refused to pay the necessary taxes. Once this happened, a Betsimisaraka who had sought refuge with the planters became an outlaw. Afraid to leave the concession for fear of the authorities, he was left to the mercy of the *colon* on whose land he lived. In 1914, the political report for Vatomandry noted that "to the simple mind of the Betsimisaraka there are two types of employers: those who pay the prestation and demand a reasonable amount of work, and those with whom one can always find shelter but who demand hard labor. The balance does not always lean in favor of the first."[25] Labor abuses multiplied. There is scarcely a political report about the region between 1901 and 1934 in which the administrators do not complain about the Betsimisaraka hidden away on the plantations—tax offenders beyond the reach of the administration yet vulnerable to the predations of the *colons*.

TURNING BETSIMISARAKA INTO SEDENTARY PEASANTS

Intrinsic to Gallieni's strategy for ensuring an adequate labor supply was a comprehensive program for the transformation of Betsimisaraka society that sought to achieve the capillary level of control of which Foucault wrote. His policy included the resettlement of villages, the creation of a cash economy, and the reshaping of local authority structures.

Remaking Villages   Betsimisaraka's propensity to live scattered in their fields, far from any center of state authority, and to flee to the Mananjary provincial border whenever recruiters came by, was a constant source of worry for the administration. In 1904, Gallieni wrote a letter to the *chef de province* explaining the logic behind one of the numerous reorganizations of the short-lived Southern Betsimisaraka District that occurred during the first ten years of colonization: "Once the coastal provinces are thus constituted, it will be easier to react against the excessive individualism of the populations, against this isolation, akin to savagery, with which they seem content, so that in general, agglomerations are reduced to the smallest family unit. This in turn means the absence of social bonds and the slow hatching of needs that must necessarily follow from social groupings. Hence the huge difficulties which continue to confront the administration, who can only have a feeble influence on populations thus disseminated, and the *colons,* whom for lack of any important agglomerations, have great difficulty in procuring the necessary labor."[26]

As part of French administrators' attempts to control the movements of the population, the French passed laws that were intended to reshape Betsimisaraka villages. A village was to be composed of no fewer than twenty people, each paying a personal tax, and was to include no fewer than five groups of houses. Administrators also declared that the house clusters were to be close enough together to foster social solidarity, and located near to a road; they hoped that the clustering and relocation would make the inhabitants more amenable to control by the village chief.[27] They justified this pattern of forced resettlement with reference to humanitarian ideas: "It is under the appearance of a certain constraint, a work of humanity to react against these tendencies of isolation. The development and fixity of agriculture, which thus attaches people to the land and better groups the locals[,] will contribute to good public order and the security of the populace."[28]

Creating Needs and Desires   The worry over movement and habitation was about more than just the need to recruit labor or control the locals easily. Throughout their colonies, the French emphasized the potential connection between forms of habitation and relations among the inhabitants: changes in one were seen as necessarily leading to changes in the other.[29] For example, Timothy Mitchell (1988) notes the fact that, despite the presence of English troops, the colonial government had difficulty in forcing villagers in Egypt to remain on their estates as food producers. As a result, in the 1840s British administrators introduced the "model village." Through the careful construction and ordering of villages, they sought to institute "the new way in which the very nature of order was to be conceived" (44). Likewise, French administrators in Madagascar believed that the creation of "proper" villages would promote social evolution, particularly the creation of new needs and desires. Consider the following administrative report, dating from 1899: "In order to complete our work, we must tighten the ties that bind the different families of the 'Betsimisaraka,' and group together in a few important centers the numerous scattered households. From this, markets will start to be created[,] and once traders come and set up, the *indigène* can not help but covet the 'new' and the 'unknown' and, from this, will begin to seek work: needs will have been created."[30]

The creation of needs and desires was central to the logic of the French colonial system. For the French, this was not only a means to make people want money, and thus to cause them to willingly work for the *colons,* but also a part of the process of making Betsimisaraka French. According to French administrative logic, the products from the concessions would be shipped back to the metropole, while the newly covetous Betsimisaraka would, as Karl Marx argues in his description of capitalist expansion, provide new markets for goods produced in France. In addition, using new kinds of products was expected to help prod the *indigènes* along in their "evolution," an evolution that would end, it was understood, when they became convenient auxiliaries to the French colonial project.

In the early years of colonialism, the French assumed that the irresistible attraction of novelty, combined with the need to provide money for taxes and new patterns of settlement, would "naturally" strengthen social bonds and lead the Betsimisaraka to adopt a money economy. By 1928, thirty years after colonization, French administrators remarked with surprise that Betsimisaraka continued to need remarkably little. As one administrator wrote: "Neither the enticement to dress nor the embryonic worry of material comfort will incite these people to seek profit. It is rather curious to note how few needs have appeared over the last thirty years in the indigenous milieu."[31] Another, writing in 1933, was barely more optimistic: "It is thanks to the many shops that now exist in Betsimisaraka country that the Betsimisaraka has a few new needs. He is forced to seek supplementary revenues in produce sold on the market[,] and today it is rare to find a village not surrounded with several hundred coffee plants[,] of which the benefits serve to augment the standard of living of the owners. But this is only just beginning. His food has scarcely changed. The only transformations that have occurred concern the sales of used clothes and certain cooking utensils."[32]

Total failure, however, was hardly the outcome of French attempts to introduce new habits. French colonial archives represent the successful introduction of coffee as one of the few triumphs among French attempts to make Betsimisaraka more like sedentary French peasants. The French saw growing coffee as intrinsic to this process: while rice allowed (and sometimes even required) villagers to move from place to place, coffee—because it took four to five years to produce and lasted, with upkeep, for around twenty years—made them more sedentary. In turn, increasing sedentarization was supposed to heighten the Betsimisaraka sense of private property. As one administrator gleefully reported, "Today we should represent the Betsimisaraka as sedentary, aspiring to create around his village property that is his alone, that he cultivates with his family and the help of a few workers whom he pays by killing a bull. This new practice appears to be the result of the new practice of growing coffee."[33] The transformation, however, was double-edged. As Jean Fremigacci (1985) points out, planting coffee also had the unexpected effect of liberating Betsimisaraka from their fiscal obligations: the money earned selling coffee allowed people to pay off their taxes and freed them from having to work for the *colons*. Some *colons* even wanted to forbid Betsimisaraka from planting coffee, precisely because it gave them a source of income that enabled them to be more independent.

Changing Local Authority   French administrators realized that the simple relocation of villages was not enough to create a populace amenable to colonial administration. As a result, they sought both to insinuate themselves into local structures of authority and to transform local authority in a direction that would facilitate the villages' administration. Throughout Madagascar, French officials recognized that, for the local populations, legitimate authority resided in ancestors and the living kings and family heads who acted as their intermediaries. They sought to exert authority in both domains.

In an effort to control local people by controlling ancestors among the Sakalava of the northwest coast, French colonial officials tried to steal sacred relics associated with the monarchy (Feeley-Harnik 1991). In highland Madagascar, the French military sought, for similar reasons, to move the sacred remains of kings from Ambohimanga, where they had formerly been buried, to Antananarivo, which was to be the geographical locus of French power (Ellis 1985). Among the Betsimisaraka, where there were no kings to act as conduits for colonial power, the French, like the Merina before them, sought to regulate local, familial ancestral practice directly. Taking their cue from Merina sovereigns who had preceded them, French administrators sought to insert themselves into local hierarchies by imposing taxes on all ancestral rituals. During the colonial period, permission to carry out sacrifices was granted only if all taxes had been paid. In addition, a tax was (and still is) imposed on sacrifices, and it varied in amount according to how complicated the ritual was. For a circumcision celebration *(sambatra),* which lasts at least six days (and used to last an entire month), the tax is more than for a simple vow fulfillment *(tsikafara)* or a funerary sacrifice *(lofo).* A tax also regulates reburial rituals, which for health reasons are supposed to take place during the cold season, between the months of July and October.

Addressing the living, French administrators sought to solidify local groupings and to empower key elders whom they hoped would help them with administration. French policy in Madagascar was characterized by a modified version of indirect rule, in which local "chiefs" were made to work as subaltern functionaries for French administrators (Crowder 1964). At least initially, French administration among the Betsimisaraka followed the *politique des races,* whereby successful government of the populace was seen as dependent on knowing the local social divisions and basing administrative divisions upon them. As one administrator in Mahanoro remarked, echoing Gallieni's orders from on high, "Time and experience have allowed us to study the *indigène* of the region, to the point of penetrating his private life. In order to seize his ways and customs and shape his history, we have divided the population into equal political and administrative districts responding to the preceding order of ideas."[34] The administrative grouping thus formed was to be governed, at the lower level, by people who were members of that ethnic group. As Gallieni wrote in a classic formulation of colonial hierarchy, "European authorities will direct and survey the ensemble, while indigenous authorities will administer the *indigènes,* collecting taxes, overseeing the execution of public work and all other economic and administrative tasks demanded of them" (1908, 334).

Thanks to the encyclopedic writings of Grandidier, whose work—documenting the populations of Madagascar and their respective forms of political and social organization—colonial officials used as a guide for the local administration, French officials knew that the Betsimisaraka had neither kings nor queens. The key to successful government of the populace, they decided, depended on negotiation with a few key elders. Unfortunately, from the French point of view, even these key elders were difficult to locate, so fragmented were local power structures. The early reports are filled with observations about the necessity of grouping the populace under "chiefs" of the same ethnic group, and frustration when they found that "chiefs" thus selected had no real authority. Initial frustration gave way to optimism as colonization progressed, only to be succeeded by disgust as French officials concluded that the locals were in fact incapable of governing themselves. As one disheartened administrator wrote, "As for a Betsimisaraka elite, they are still at the babbling stage *[elle en est encore à ses balbutiementes].*"[35] Moreover, the administrative jobs that these Betsimisaraka intermediaries were supposed to fulfil—including collecting taxes, enforcing state laws concerning the burning of dry rice land, and recruiting labor for the *colons*—made those who executed them highly unpopular. As one official noted, it was only those indigenous officials who brought "constant and at times brutal" pressure to bear on local people who got things done: "Local attitudes toward the indigenous functionary vary according to how much pressure the functionary places on the population when he attempts to extract taxes or get workers for the prestation. There is a close link between the attitude of the population and the methods of the functionaries: those who are able to obtain what we ask of them exert constant, sometimes brutal pressure. The people do not like them."[36] Most people, it seems, dreaded the job and tried to avoid it. As one old man put it, "They'd call us together and make us choose a *chef de village,* and we'd all run away. You never knew *what* they might ask of you. But the *vazaha* would not give in, and they would call us all together and make us choose someone. He was supposed to be our 'post to lean on' *[andry iankinana].*" By 1903, a scant seven years after the implementation of the *politique des races,* local administrators decided that Betsimisaraka were unfit to rule. Although a few indigenous functionaries remained, people from the high plateau replaced the majority of them.[37] This only further reinforced local perceptions of *vazaha* and Merina as more or less the same thing. In addition to choosing key individuals for participation in the colonial system, the French sought to rearrange the village administration. The French were impressed by the Merina institution of the *fokon'olona,* which King Andrianampoinimerina transformed by restating from on high the functions that it had had previously. In his analysis of the *fokon'olona,* Maurice Bloch (1971a) suggests that the effect of this move was to allow the *fokon'olona* to appear to function as it had previously while changing the source of authority. The French extended this process, following the Merina example by making the *fokon'olona* into an arm of the state.

Among the Betsimisaraka *fokon'olona* means simply "all the people who live in a particular place" and was originally less an institution, like a village council, than a principle for collective decision making.[38] Be that as it may, French administrators sent to Betsimisaraka country perceived the *fokon'olona* to be an institution that *did* exist in Imerina and that *should* exist on the east coast. As one early administrator remarked wistfully, "The *fokon'olona,* which would facilitate administration, does not exist here, and the villagers move about with ease."[39] In 1902 the French decided to solve the problem, and a decree was made that allegedly "brought" the *fokon'olona* to the east coast as part of their plan to spatially reorganize the Betsimisaraka and create the villages that they thought ought to exist. Thirty years passed, however, and, as with so many other elements of the colonial project, administrators ruefully observed their failure: "The *fokon'olona* . . . should be of great service to the administration. At least on the high plateau, the *fokon'olona* are perfectly organized, and fulfill their obligations spontaneously and without requiring administrative pressure. Because of the complete difference in mentality between Betsimisaraka and Merina, or perhaps because the influence of the conquering Merina is negligible in the region, the *fokon'olona* in the district are not interested in the question. Being of minimal sociability, they do not feel the sentiment of solidarity that is the basis of this institution."[40] Despite this administrator's complaints, the *fokon'olona* was in fact adopted by the Betsimisaraka and remains the mechanism through which villagers interact with the state to this day.

THE MISSIONARY PRESENCE IN AMBODIHARINA

Along with the French administration and *colons,* French Catholic and Anglican missionaries also attempted to transform Betsimisaraka practice and to bend it to their own conceptions of spirituality. Some fifteen years prior to colonization, a visiting Catholic priest noted that there were already a hundred Betsimisaraka converts, though generally Mahanoro and the surrounding area were known as an Anglican area.[41] In Ambodiharina, two churches were founded: one Anglican in 1911, and one Catholic founded somewhat later. The anticlerical secular humanism of early French administrators meant that there was little collaboration between the government and the churches in the first years of colonization. In fact, Gallieni sought explicitly to diminish clerical power by closing missionary schools and creating government schools in their stead, though the school he established in Mahanoro was closed within a few years because of lack of funds (Thompson and Adloff 1965). With succeeding governors this policy changed, and from 1940 until the creation of the *loi-cadre* in 1956, which marked a loosening of French control over Madagascar, administrators attempted to eradicate local practices by going so far as to tear out the prayer posts *(jiro)* where ancestral sacrifices took place.

For the most part, however, missionaries in the Mahanoro area appear to have focused their efforts on the eradication of spirit possession rituals, in which the spirits of dead ancestors or nature spirits possess people. The missionaries' success has been mixed. Although inhabitants of upcountry villages continue to perform these rituals, contemporary practice in Ambodiharina has been reduced to the spontaneous emergence of ancestral spirits during the all-night celebrations that follow sacrifices (see chapter 5). At various points in time some individuals have chosen to abandon the practices through which they constructed their relations with ancestors and to attend church instead. But at least a handful of these more radical churchgoers have realized that they also need contact with their ancestors, and have chosen to reestablish their connections to ancestors after a time. Comparatively speaking, however, churchgoers represent only a handful of the population. For those who are active in church, funerals include hymn singing and a mass before departing for the tombs, but these practices have been incorporated—albeit at times unevenly—into local practices related to ancestors.

THINGS FALL APART: THE REBELLION OF 1947

Although many different aspects of the French colonial regime penetrated deep into Betsimisaraka daily life, the single event that marked the high point of colonial intrusion was the violence that took place during the rebellion of 1947. The rebellion was a response to the contradictions and material hardships that Malagasy experienced immediately preceding and during World War II. During the war, the colonial administration loosened its control of indigenous politics. This context of comparative freedom enabled the growth of the Mouvement pour la Démocratique Rénovation Malgache (Democratic Movement for Malagasy Renewal, MDRM), a political party whose leaders—two Merina who previously had been involved in anticolonial politics, Joseph Ravoahangy and Joseph Raseta, and the Betsimisaraka Jacques Rabemananjara—advocated independence within the context of a French Union.[42] At the same time, the colonial administration increased its demands on the resources and people of Madagascar to unbearable proportions in the name of the war effort. The growth of an organized independence movement, paired with increased suffering at the hands of the colonial administration, created the ambience favorable to revolt.

The rebellion began at midnight on 29 March 1947. Malagasies armed with spears and the occasional gun attacked French administrative centers, military garrisons, police stations, French concessions, and Malagasies who sympathized with the colonial regime, burning buildings and killing a number of French administrators and *colons*. The revolt erupted at a number of different points on the east coast, including military garrisons located at Moramanga in the center of the island and Manankara in the southeast. Over the course of the next two months, fighting spread to cover most of the east coast of the island as bands of rebels moved from village to village, forcibly inducting men into the rebel army as they went. In each of the places in which the rebels gained control, they created an autonomous Malagasy government under the direction of one of the rebel leaders.

Officials declared the rebellion over in December of 1948, when they had defeated the last of the rebels. A full twenty months of fighting had passed. Jacques Tronchon (1986), author of one of the first books to examine the rebellion seriously, estimates that during the long campaign of 1947–48, 550 French died, while 100,000 Malagasy were executed, tortured, starved, or driven into the forest. Even according to official accounts, 89,000 Malagasy died, about 2 percent of the entire population of 4 million; over 11,000 were killed as a result of military action (Allen 1995, 47; Tronchon 1986, 70–74).[43]

Caught between the brutality of the French and that of the rebel army, rural Betsimisaraka suffered throughout the events. Civilians witnessed horrible atrocities as the rebels killed people who had collaborated with the French regime. In many places rebels systematically mutilated their victims, and bodies were found riddled through with spear wounds, cut into pieces, their genitals torn off. Others were carved into pieces and fed to dogs, or the dogs too were killed, tied to the body and thrown in the water.[44] The rebels left notes out on the road warning people what would happen if they disobeyed. One directed at the French read as follows: "Look you French: do you see what our little knives can do? Here is the Gendarme. His genitals are stuffed in his mouth." Many rebel documents reveal a concern to fight a just war, and explicitly order rebel soldiers not to kill Malagasy, Chinese, or *métisse* Malagasy.[45] Nevertheless, the testimony gathered by gendarmes from Nosy Varika, the region to which most of the people from Ambodiharina fled, gives some sense of how the rebels operated. One rebel prisoner described being sent to requisition food from the local population. When a fifteen-year-old girl refused his demands, on the grounds that he was a rebel, he took his knife and hit her across her lower back "wounding her gravely."[46] Another described how the local *chef de canton* was stabbed to death, then hacked into pieces and thrown in the river.[47] Still another man described being sent to murder a local *colon,* then asked to go back and chop off the man's right hand to prove to his general that he had completed the job.

The French way of killing was equally brutal but more efficient. Senegalese and Moroccan soldiers attacked and burned villages suspected of harboring rebels, or tracked the rebels through the forest, at times firing on anyone wearing a raffia shirt.[48] French planes flew low over villages spraying them with machine gun fire or dropping bombs and grenades that Betsimisaraka peasants often mistook for tobacco holders. Once people had fled into the forest, hunger, a less spectacular killer that eventually took more lives, exacerbated the initial violence. The rebel reports reveal a veritable obsession with food: my impression is that more people worked for them gathering food supplies than actually fought in battles, an observation that corresponds to the high rate of death by starvation documented by Tronchon (1986).[49]

The effects of the rebellion did not end with the last submissions in 1948. As Maureen Covell (1989) observes, the repression of the revolt was draconian, and in some areas the siege was not lifted until 1956. At the national level, the French reacted to the rebellion by blaming the leaders of the MDRM. Two of the deputies—Raseta and Ravoahangy—were sentenced to death; the third, Rabemananjara, was condemned to forced labor for life. Thousands of low-level officials were tried in order to prove their affiliation with the MDRM; frequently, torture was used to extract confessions. Often their titles were revoked or they were exiled to re-mote corners of Madagascar as punishment.

More locally, colonial administrators used the rebellion to justify a series of new and repressive policies. In effect, a recolonization took place throughout the island. As Françoise Raison-Jourde (1997) writes, an ob-session with "administrative contact" characterized the years following the rebellion as French officials sought to monitor ever more closely the allegedly docile and apathetic Betsimisaraka who had, to their surprise, risen in revolt. This increased surveillance was accompanied by the bla-tant abuse of power in the countryside, as French administrators sought constantly to exert their power by humiliating Betsimisaraka peasants whenever they made their administrative rounds. In a memoir written in the early 1990s, Jacques Dez, a French administrator to the Nosy Varika region, provides one example that gives a sense of what the post-1947 French-Betsimisaraka relations were like: "At Sahasinaka in 1951 an ad-ministrator created a new personnel procedure . . . When he wasn't satisfied with the welcome he received in a village, he made all the men stand in a line, and, perched on his jeep, made them walk towards him. The village men were made to walk towards him while he, his arm held out, knocked off their hats" (cited in Raison-Jourde 1997).

Given the nature and extent of the atrocities, followed by the even more violent repression of the rebellion by the French, it is not surpris-ing that villagers in areas affected by the rebellion were left traumatized in its wake. Administrative reports for 1948 describe people in a state of shock, noting that the Betsimisaraka, once known for their laziness and unwillingness to work for settlers, now worked quietly, without joy or resistance.[50] In 1949, one local official observed that the *indigènes* were characterized by lassitude and despair, their faces still "haunted by their sufferings."[51]

Another official observed that, when the government tried to institute new elections in an attempt to hand power over to a local regime sym-pathetic to the French, people refused at first to vote. "They fear this form of politics," he wrote, "that goes beyond the local level, because it spreads hate, violence and death."[52] When a second round of elections was held, some people did finally vote, he noted, but they did so out of fear of the state rather than out of political conviction.[53] The fear of state politics appeared to be spread throughout much of the east coast. As one administrator remarked, "The people voted in the last legislative elec-tions because they thought they were obligatory, but they were hardly interested." In Ambodimanga du Sud, located to the south of Ambodiharina, "everyone left after having voted and no one awaited the results. Everyone voted for the candidate who had been approved by the administration" (cited in Raison-Jourde 1997, my translation). The trauma remained.

ASSESSING THE COLONIAL EXPERIENCE

The peoples who inhabit the central east coast have good reason to call themselves "the many who will not be sundered" (Betsimisaraka). The invention of the name in the eighteenth century may have been intended for different purposes preceding the intrusions described here, but it turns out to have been remarkably prescient in light of the Betsimisaraka predicament during the next 150 years. The Betsimisaraka have, perhaps from the beginning, been a decentralized group always on the edge of devolution, a tendency that their colonizers constantly played upon. While Merina domination focused primarily on exploitation of local people through forced labor and taxation, French colonization involved a concerted effort to transform the Betsimisaraka's way of life. In particular, French authorities sought to rearrange local structures of authority and people's spatial relationships, and thereby to create a stable peasantry that would produce, consume, and labor in the manner desired by the French colonial state. Although the intrusions were somewhat less invasive under the Merina, both sets of outsiders disrupted local societies by pulling Betsimisaraka out of their own communities and rerooting them in larger collectivities, and by changing the very grounds on which Betsimisaraka could interact with one another.

Yet if French colonization transformed some aspects of Betsimisaraka society, it never achieved in practice the level of control that French administrators hoped for. What is most striking about French administrative reports for the region is how discouraged administrators sound. Again and again, administrators wrote that the Betsimisaraka were happy to obey but refused to change. It seems ironic in retrospect, but administrators prior to 1947 even claimed that there was no danger of an anticolonial political movement forming locally because the natives were too lazy and disorganized. While some administrators blamed the supposed failure of colonial policies on the climate or the Betsimisaraka's inherent laziness, others observed that the acquiescence worked as a kind of passive resistance. Indeed, it seems that colonial administrators at the turn of the century were well aware of a point that would be emphasized by studies of resistance some ninety years later: that apparent acquiescence and passivity in the face of force are one way to deal with unwanted authority (Adas 1992; Scott 1990). One administrator explicated this view quite clearly when he wrote: "The higher notions of patriotism or social responsibility are nonexistent, and replaced by obedience to the *Chef de District,* who is the indispensable regulator of collective life. The other side of the coin, however, is constituted by this natural apathy[,] which we must always emphasize. The *indigène* will never object to a task but rather seek to avoid it. If he has not understood, then he will not be controlled. The thing will be easy for him."[54] By 1948, the year following the rebellion, the despair—the sense that colonization failed to transform Betsimisaraka hearts and souls as it had initially set out to do—permeated the reports of the French colonial administration. One report remarked, "What is terrible is that the Betsimisaraka respects the force that we represent, not the beneficial concepts and practices that this force should permit us to realize."[55]

The preceding narrative suggests two points, both of which are relevant to understanding the hybrid nature of Ambodiharina and the larger questions of postcolonial consciousness that have preoccupied anthropologists. First, Betsimisaraka were profoundly influenced by the French colonial experience, which was constituted in interaction with transformations wrought by prior waves of outsiders like the Merina and the early Creole settlers, and there is good reason to expect the colonial past to play an important role in contemporary Betsimisaraka life. After all, Betsimisaraka now live in multiancestry villages, and they have created a special council for handling their relations with the state. They use new kinds of materials for building their houses and they try and gain extra income by selling coffee, pepper, and vanilla to a local export company. They are also deeply marked by the experience of state violence. Second, Betsimisaraka successfully resisted many changes, making colonial transformations unevenly distributed. Though they now live in multiancestry villages, this new form of spatial organization has never made them entirely dependent on a money economy. They enjoy extra income from selling coffee, but they continue as subsistence farmers who grow rice. The administrative structures to speed state administration remain in place, but it is difficult to mobilize Betsimisaraka in collective projects: people still try to control their own affairs. The question remains, however, as to how these transformations left by the French colonial period have been interwoven with local ways of life, and how Betsimisaraka remember this period now that they live in the postcolonial era.

CHAPTER 3

Local Worlds

Daily Village Life

They all tampered with the laws that lay down who
should be loved and how. And how much. The laws
that made grandmothers grandmothers, uncles uncles,
mothers mothers, cousins cousins.

—Arundhati Roy

If one continues south from Mahanoro about ten kilometers, the remnants of the motor road encounter the Mangoro River, a broad expanse of water that empties into the Indian Ocean. It requires forty-five minutes to cross the Mangoro in a dugout canoe—except when the rains have made it totally impassable. On the other side of the river is Ambodiharina, the village where I decided to settle (see map 4).

Ambodiharina is the largest village in the subdistrict of the same name.[1] If one has just arrived from Mahanoro and stands at the landing spot of the ferry or dugout canoe, one realizes that the town is flanked on three sides by water. Facing north, one looks out at the huge sweep of the Mangoro, where people use nets and traps to fish from small canoes. To the west one looks across the canal called the Sahave, an offshoot of the Pangalenes, the web of canals that the French created and that run along the east coast of Madagascar, enabling the transport of produce on slow barges. On the other side of the canal are the rice fields, organized into neat, named areas and divided one from the other by small earthen walls. The banks of the canal are where people do their washing and, until three wells were built during the time I was there, where most people got their water for cooking. People also cross the canals daily to go to their rice fields. Looking out from the banks of the canal, one occasionally sees a party of women knee deep in the mud transplanting rice, or perhaps a

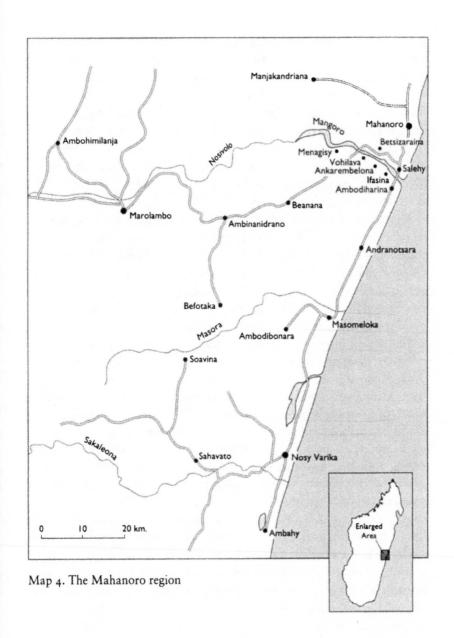

Map 4. The Mahanoro region

group of boys driving two or three cattle around to soften the mud in a field prior to transplanting. More frequently, one sees pairs of men and women working together: a woman transplanting rice while a man removes grass from the paddy close by. Or if it is harvest season (December and May-June) one might see a party of people standing chest-high in golden fronds of rice, gathering bouquets of rice by hand with a small knife and placing them into a basket. Turning toward the east, one sees still more rice paddies and then the lagoon. Finally, one might catch a glimpse of the sandbar that separates the lagoon from the impossibly fierce waves of the Indian Ocean.

Palm trees bend gracefully over the road that transects Ambodiharina from north to south. Throughout the day, when people are in their fields, the town is largely deserted, except for children playing and old people shooing chickens away from rice set out to dry. In the evenings, however, it comes alive, and on moonlit evenings adults sit outside their houses and chat while clusters of small girls gather to sing in the moonlight, beating out the rhythms on bamboo tubes filled with seeds. As one walks south past the last house cluster one comes upon fields of manioc, sweet potatoes, pineapple, and then, farther on, the forest. Within this larger division more paths transect the town from north to south and east to west. Most households occupy neat squares in a grid, the boundaries between one family cluster and the next marked by fences of ever-growing plants called *hasina* (a word that means both "power" and "efficacy") for its ability to grow almost anywhere. Each family cluster includes a house, a kitchen, and sometimes a granary. Oriented along the north-south axis of the town, the rectangular thatched huts, made of traveler's palm, are set on small posts to elevate them slightly off the ground. Near some houses one sees *jiro,* the prayer posts cut in the shape of a bull's horns, at which cattle sacrifices take place. Occasionally, instead of a *jiro* one finds just a tangled mass of *hasina* plants with the bleached craniums of sacrificed bulls perched haphazardly on top. Fruit trees, such as breadfruit, oranges, mangoes, papayas, and coconut, grow around the edge of the town, which is where trash and refuse is swept each morning and, occasionally, burned when too much has accumulated. This was how the village looked in 1992 and 1997 (see fig. 4 and map 5.) Except for the growth in population, which now numbers around 1,500, and the addition of the cement schoolhouse, it appears to have looked much the same at the turn of the century, when Joseph Gallieni, the French general who conquered Madagascar, passed through. Describing the village at this time the general wrote, "After five hours we reached Am-

Figure 4. Rice drying in a village courtyard, 1993. Along the coast, Betsimisaraka harvest rice with a small knife and gather it into bouquets, which are
then laid out to dry. Photo by Jennifer Cole.

bodiharina, a Betsimisaraka village of 350 inhabitants, built at the edge
of the lagoon in the midst of fruit trees and small gardens separated by
fences" (1901, 96).

At one time the layout of the houses in Ambodiharina corresponded
to the order of arrival among the different families and the power struggles between them. Betsimisaraka society comprises many different ex-
ogamous clans or "kinds" *(karazana),* which I also refer to as ancestries.
People often, though not always, identify the first ancestors as a brother-
sister pair. While the clans were originally associated with a particular
territory, today they are nonlocalized groupings of people who share a
common family origin and taboos and who have built their tombs in the
same clearing. Although certain clans extend over several different villages, so that one finds people in many villages claiming that they are,
say, Zanavohitra, it is rare that the clan finds expression in actual practice. For example, on one occasion the entire Zanavohitra group came
together to do some work on the tomb of their founding ancestor. The
assembly of the entire ancestry was so unusual that the people I was with
kept commenting that they had no idea who all their relatives were, and
that without this kind of event one might accidentally marry one's kin.

Within this large, only rarely actualized grouping exist multiple
smaller lineages, each associated with a particular *tangalamena* and his

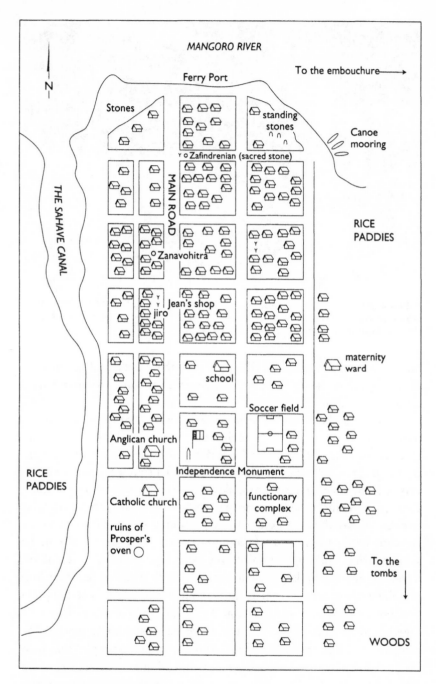

Map 5. Ambodiharina, 1992

descendants. Ideally, each *tangalamena* inhabits a particular great house *(trano be)*, while the other members of his family live either in the houses surrounding the central courtyard, where sacrifices take place, or in homesteads of their own. This group usually shares the same tomb and participates in the expenses associated with sponsoring rituals. Betsimisaraka trace descent through both their mother's and father's lines, and like other groups in Madagascar they say that people have "eight parts" *(valo-ila)* or "eight ancestors" *(valo-razana)*, four from each parent. But people always say that fathers' claims on children have priority, a sentiment captured in the oft quoted expression "The father's foot is stronger" *(tongo-dray mahery)*. Though most people tend to live nearer their father's great house, they almost always participate in the rituals associated with their mother's great house as well, and some people may even choose to live with their maternal kin.

While there are twelve different officially recognized ancestries in Ambodiharina, great houses are constantly proliferating: when families quarrel, the most common response is for a man to split off, setting up a new great house for his own descendants. As one woman put it, "Each likes to rule in his father's house." Although the splitting of houses does not necessarily entail the splitting of tombs, eventually the descendants of the new great house will want control of their own ancestors as well, and a new tomb will be built.

Like many other peoples in Madagascar, Betsimisaraka perceive the north as "the root of the people," the preeminent direction, symbolic of political and spiritual dominance. In Ambodiharina the family that inhabits the northernmost tip of the town is the Zafimalaone. According to official town history, the Zafimalaone came when three brothers fled from a place called Ampahana, located somewhat to the north near Vatomandry. They swam the Mangoro River and miraculously made it to the other side alive. The point at which they crawled out of the water is called Ankarembelona (literally, "where they came up alive"; from the words *to bring up [akarina]* and *alive [velona]*).[2] The youngest brother settled in Ankarembelona, the middle brother settled in Ifasina, and the eldest brother settled in Ambodiharina. The eldest brother, called Ingahimalaza, was celebrated for his magical powers that enabled him to live in the Mangoro for a month without getting wet. As a result of his phenomenal powers over the water, the other ancestries residing in Ambodiharina recognized Ingahimalaza, his father, Fohirandrana, and their descendants as the true masters of the Mangoro River.

Or so goes the official story, for throughout Madagascar the idiom of ritual preeminence often naturalizes and masks the actual use of force. Not surprisingly, what little can be gleaned from the archives about the area prior to Merina conquest tells a story very different from the one glorified in local legend. Leguéval de Lacombe (1840), the French trader who accompanied the Merina king's emissary, Jean-René, on his conquest of the east coast describes Fohirandrana as a fearsome warrior. When Jean-René showed up to try and make Fohirandrana submit to Radama, Fohirandrana would not so much as stand up to welcome Jean-René, organizing instead a clever surprise attack against the unsuspecting Merina. Grandidier also refers to Fohirandrana as a local chief who had conquered the other families in the area.

Fragments of history I heard from various people in Ambodiharina supported this version of events. For example, Ravale, the *tangalamena* for the Zafindrenian, the ancestry who in many ways competed with the Zafimalaone for preeminence, said that the Zafimalaone had fled to Ambodiharina when they had been tricked into giving their muskets, obtained in slave trading with the English, to women in another ancestry. The men took the purloined muskets and turned on the Zafimalaone, who fled but were able, in turn, to conquer the groups bordering the Mangoro. Outside the context of recounting official stories and always on the sly, people from other families would mention that Ingahimalaza, perhaps the most famous Zafimalaone ancestor, had been a fearsome warrior and despot. Laughing, another *tangalamena* recounted that Ingahimalaza used to stop people passing through the town and, with his spear point resting lightly on their foot, ask them where they were going. Or as Pierre's father, a man who was a Zafimalaone descendant, but who had a rather irreverent attitude toward his ancestors, put it, Ingahimalaza had gained control of Ambodiharina the way Saddam Hussein had taken Kuwait: through force.[3] But such comments were rare, always accompanied by nervous laughter. According to official history, it was power inherent to the Zafimalaone that enabled them to control the water. Although—as we shall see in subsequent chapters—the question of *which* member of the Zafimalaone had power over the water was subject to debate, the power of this ancestry over the water was recognized, and never seriously contested, by the other ancestries.

In addition to the Zafimalaone, a number of different ancestries formed the core of the northernmost portion of the town, including the Zafindrenian, the Zafindrembola, and the Zanavohitra. Another family whose history figured prominently in local legend was called the Andrebakara, and their courtyard was located to the south of the old town. From what

I could piece together, this group came at the time of the French conquest in 1896, when the Vorimo clans from the west, who had fought periodically with the groups living along the coast, came to drive out the Merina (see M. Esoavelomandroso 1985). Ravale, the *tangalamena* for the Zafindrenian told the story this way:

> There were men who came from the west, very black, and the people here asked them, "What is your purpose?" And the men replied, "We've come to kill the Merina, to drive out the Merina, but not Betsimisaraka." They wanted to steal the Merina's cattle, their riches, of course. So we asked them, "How will you know [who is Merina and who is Betsimisaraka]?" And they forced people to speak. And if you said *lananana* [i.e., if you used the Merina style of pronunciation to speak the word for the bamboo tube in which people on the east coast carry water] they killed you, and if you said *lañañana* [the same word, but with the Betsimisaraka pronunciation] you were spared. At that time the Andrebakara were making their way to the north, seeking work up in the vanilla plantations in Antalaha. There were three brothers who were good at spear fighting. And we asked them to be our friends and to stay and fight the marauders. So they stayed as our army, and we gave them rice land over at Befotaka [literally, much mud, the name of a rice field] to farm. They are our protectors, and so that is why they live to the south, at what was the edge of the town.

This group marks the outermost limits of the "old town," with its hierarchy of different great houses.

As throughout Madagascar, people in Ambodiharina had kept slaves, but I never found out if the fact that the Andrebakara were the Zafimalaone and Zafindrenian's "soldiers" also meant they were their slaves.[4] Prior to manumission in 1896, some families had owned slaves, primarily people captured in raids; but older people kept silent about this topic, only occasionally referring to it in oblique, guarded ways, and younger people tended not to know much about it. It was only after I began to understand the political organization of the town more clearly that I realized that three of the families that people claimed to be Zafindrenian were in fact the descendants of the Zafindrenian's former slaves. By the time of my second visit in 1997 I was able to identify who the Zafimalaone's slaves had been. But slavery was not the live, profoundly divisive issue that it remains in areas of the high plateau, a phenomenon that I attribute partially to a process of directed forgetting.[5] Intriguingly, people explained that following manumission they had often performed the ceremony that creates blood siblings (see below), or else they had performed a ritual cleansing and then intermarried with their slaves. But people were, for the most part, unwilling to raise these old inequalities;

in some cases I knew of, older people had intentionally avoided passing this information on to their children, stressing that since the French had come everyone was free.

Though this old hierarchy (masters of the land and their former slaves) is symbolically inscribed on the order of houses in the northern portion of town, as one moves south the careful spatial mapping of precedence fades. Today, because the population has expanded, many people whose ancestors had belonged to some of the founding families live far to the south, where they have more room to spread out and build comfortable courtyards. As several people explained, new families "begged for blessing" from their elders, which permitted them to move to the south and create new courtyards. What this means is that, once one moves past the Andrebakara courtyard, there are no real neighborhoods in which a particular family occupies a particular part of town; rather, the different kinds of people seem jumbled up indiscriminately. Descendants of the founding families are able to claim precedence because their great house—the house of their ancestors—is located in the northern tip of the town.

The ritual hierarchy of different families that embodied old struggles between ancestors was rarely visible in the interactions I saw every day. Instead, villagers exhibited what I came to regard as a kind of radical autonomy. Why did Pierre go fishing while Tsaravintana went to clear land? "Each to his own work." Why does Ravale live to the south when his great house is to the north? "Each to the place he likes to live." As Ramaresaka summarized this viewpoint, "Each to his own work. Some plant rice, others coffee, some clear land. [Living] people must search for food, search for that which will make them living, and they must always find it. There are no neighborhoods, but each goes to the place she chooses; but if there is work to do [raha misy asa atao] then you must go to the great house. Each to his own story. The story of Tsaravintana [Ramaresaka's husband] will be different from mine."

The notion of "each to her own . . . ," of individual fate or fortune, was echoed on other levels as well: each to his own taboos, each to her own ancestors, his own illness, her own cause and day of her death.

"Each to his own work, his own place," said Ramaresaka, "but when there is work to do everyone goes to the great house." This sentence contains a key ambiguity, for the word she used for work—asa—has two meanings. The first use of asa indicates private, domestic work related to making a living—planting rice, clearing land, gathering kindling, and so forth. The second use of the word is also tied to the notion of making a living but in a different sense, for it concerns the ritual activity that enables communication with ancestors, the source of power on which the social order is based. One could, then, rephrase the sentence as "Each to his own *livelihood,* his own place, but when there is *ancestral work* to be done, all go to the great house."

Ramaresaka's simple statement contains within it a critical observation about what life is like in Ambodiharina, for it underscores the fact that people's attempts to make a living are always carried out on two planes. First, on the most obvious level, one can not help noticing how deeply absorbed people are in farming rice, which is the literal source of their subsistence. But as Ramaresaka's statement implies, "making a living" also involves negotiating a densely layered network of social relationships, which for Betsimisaraka includes both the living and the dead.

In the rest of this chapter I explore the different domains of subsistence activity and social relations that make up the texture of daily life in Ambodiharina. In particular, I try to give the reader a sense of the different kinds of people who live in a place like Ambodiharina, and the ways their gender, age, and life experience enable them to pursue some goals and projects and deter them from others. As will become clear in subsequent chapters, the variation internal to Ambodiharina— the fact that everyone does *not* have the same goals, dreams, or life experiences—is a critical factor in the larger processes of social remembering and the articulation of individual and social memory, with which we are concerned.

The texture of daily life presented in this chapter creates a radical disconnect from the image of Ambodiharina one gains from the historical sources, for as the reader will see, a history of invasive colonialism is noticeable primarily by its absence. Traces of colonialism *are* here, evident in the material signs of the colonial past—such as a road, tin roofs, and the standing stone monument to independence—as well as in who benefits from certain social divisions in the town, in who has good land, and in who continues to enjoy certain kinds of privileges rooted in the past. But people did not talk about the events of the colonial period, nor did they commemorate it; nor did they *seem* affected by the violence that occurred. The French empire had come and gone, and centers of power had shifted dramatically. But at least some—though, significantly, not all—of these people appeared to still talk and act as if Ambodiharina were the center of the world.

MAKING A LIVING

Heat blazing down. The women—babies tied snugly to their
backs, children trailing behind them—head for the fields to scare
away the fody (a species of weaver finch) that threaten to eat the
newly sprouted rice. The men are still planting cassava, but more
and more are starting to clear land for dry rice. There is little to
eat, and, for able-bodied men and boys, days not spent in the fields
are used to go to Ampetika—an old colon's concession, now a
national export company—where they buy sugarcane for fifty
Malagasy francs and bring it back to the village and sell it for one
hundred Malagasy francs. Women weave mats or smoke fish and
give it to their husbands or brothers, who carry it into the country
to trade it for sweet potatoes, bananas, and manioc. Everyone is
short-tempered and selfish from hunger. (Field notes, October
1993)

When I first arrived in Ambodiharina, what struck me most about
people's lives was their intense locality and the huge, endless, and often
repetitive effort that people put into making a living. The inhabitants of
Ambodiharina are subsistence rice farmers who plant their rice primarily in paddies made in the marshes that flank the village. There are two
seasons for growing rice, one in which rice is planted in August and September and harvested in November and December *(vary oraka)*, and a
second in which rice is planted in January and February and harvested
in June *(vary vato)*. December and January are considered times of plenty,
but by April or May, when the first crop has been eaten and the second
is not yet ripe, many people are hungry. In addition to growing rice, almost everyone raises manioc, sweet potatoes, pineapples, bananas, and
lychees. Sometimes people also keep small gardens for growing *ro*, the
leaves that, together with rice and, ideally, fish, make up a complete meal.
When I brought seeds from California as small gifts for people, several
people started to build gardens with fences and make small *potagères*.
Depending on the season, people eat manioc, breadfruit, or sweet potatoes for breakfast. A stew made of manioc or breadfruit is often eaten
as an accompaniment to rice at lunch, particularly when people are trying to fill their stomachs with heavy foods before spending an afternoon
working in the fields. In times of scarcity, people are forced to fall back
on crushed manioc leaves or the cooked and dried fruits of the *via*, a local marsh plant that people consider both tasteless and hard to digest.

The effort to feed oneself and one's family, to keep people clothed, and to supply enough baskets to store one's belongings in takes an enormous amount of energy. As Ramaresaka put it, "Living people must seek for food, and they'll always find it"; their days are largely dedicated to this task. Typically, men's days start with a trip to the fields to the south of the village, where they dig cassava, or possibly sweet potatoes, for the morning meal. If the man is a good fisherman, it may also start well before daybreak with the laying of fish traps on the Mangoro, or possibly even a fishing expedition at sea. For women, the day begins with their going to the nearest source of freshwater, where they bathe, wash the dishes from the night before, and fetch water for coffee using long bamboo tubes *(lañañana)*. Women then make coffee and start to peel and cook the manioc that the men have brought back. Once people have eaten breakfast, they take to the fields, and the banks of the canal are busy with people being rowed across to the rice paddies. On rainy days, women often stay in and weave baskets, while men take the opportunity to repair fishing nets or weave new ones.

Although the outline of people's days remains roughly the same throughout the year, the seasons dictate which activities people spend time on. For example, when I arrived in August the men had already cleared the rice paddies, and people were in the middle of planting their second crop. Women spent all day gathering shoots of rice that had been planted in small nurseries and tying them into bundles to transplant to the fields. Often, a married couple and their children do all the work themselves. For certain jobs, however, like softening the fields for planting or doing the actual transplanting, people need extra help. In these cases, nuclear families rely on their extended kin, or they hire young women or men in search of cash. For example, Tovolahy and Babette, a young couple with whom I often ate (and whom I'll talk more about later), had children too young to work, so they often hired Babette's unmarried brother to help with transplanting in exchange for food and rice. Babette's mother-in-law, Liliane, however, always hired a group of girls to get the transplanting done quickly. She paid five hundred Malagasy francs a day plus coffee and the main meal as compensation.

At certain points in the agricultural cycle, especially if their fields are far enough away, people may actually move to live by them. This is particularly true in October and again in March, when the rice has begun to sprout and people spend entire days in their fields watching for flocks of *fody*, which can descend en mass and ruin an entire crop. Days spent living in the fields can be fairly quiet as the family works alone, the younger children often cooking while their parents work. Many people, however, idealize life in the fields, saying that that was how people used to live before the French had made them live in towns.[6] When I came to visit Ramaresaka and help her harvest rice on newly cleared land to the south, for example, she apologized for leaving me on my own in the town, saying that when she was small her father would take them all to the fields to live and work on the rice. They would take other children with them, she said, the children of their friends, and they would all play, tumbling around like puppies in the straw. Now, she said, she just could not get rid of the habit *(tsy mety afaka)*. People often described living in the fields as peaceful, cool, and spacious, a reference not only to the expanse of rice land they could see around them but to how living in one's fields contrasted with the heat and crowding of the town. The heat they referred to was more than just the literal heat of the burning, sun-soaked sand on which the town was built, for it also included the metaphorical heat of social relations and the awareness that daily intimacy inevitably led to fights. People also worried that the old ancestral rice paddies were yielding less and would no longer support them. As Ramaresaka explained, "You want lots and lots of land to eat from, so you can give some to each child and they can have their families and you can feed people when guests come. And it's good to be far away from everyone so you don't fight with your neighbors!"

No matter how many fields they plant in a given season, people's rice crops always remain vulnerable to the weather. People are constantly trying to hedge their bets, but most live all too close to the margin. For example, in March of 1992, when people's second harvests had already started to grow, heavy rains came, swelling the river. The paddies that lined the canal were flooded, and most of the rice ruined. Observing the damage that had been wreaked on people's rice along the canal, Celine, a woman in her twenties, commented that she and her husband tried to avoid that problem by planting rice either in fields along the canal or in some paddies located farther back, depending on the weather. That same year, three paddies from which Babette and Tovolahy had hoped to get a good harvest were completely ruined when the river overflowed its banks, smothering the rice in debris carried by the water. Rather than waste his money by hiring people in an attempt to finish planting rice, Tovolahy decided to stop planting for that season altogether and to fish instead, sell the fish upcountry, and then use that money to buy rice while it was still cheap during the May harvest. Tovolahy and Babette were lucky: they were young and strong. Tovolahy was a gifted fisherman and

Babette was good at weaving. People without other options continued to plant rice, but they seemed tired and depressed, dragging themselves out to the fields that they knew were going to provide only a paltry harvest.

There is a cement market hall or bazaar that was built during the French colonial period, but there is no weekly market in Ambodiharina. When I was there in 1993, the market stood empty, except when children occasionally sold a few fish from the morning catch to get money (usually under a dollar) to buy the coffee, sugar, and chewing tobacco that most people feel they can not go without. Requests that villagers actually use the bazaar were a regular part of every government meeting in the schoolhouse. By the time I returned in 1997, the government's constant admonishments to use the bazaar rather than traipse about the village selling fish appeared to have taken effect, and people were actually using it to sell extra fish or the small quantities of produce they had grown in their *potagères*.

Young men often obtain discretionary income by catching fish, which their wives then smoke and carry in baskets to sell in Mahanoro or take upcountry for a better price. But fishing is always considered an activity morally inferior to farming rice. Solo, whose nine sons were all excellent fishermen and whose catch often meant that the family ate better than most, said that fishing was really "a game." Similarly, Ramaresaka complained that some grown men "don't work [e.g., don't grow rice] but just fish all day." Nevertheless, cash obtained by selling fish remains an important supplement to local income. After the seasonal arrival of *vily* (in French, *bicek*), a kind of smelt that people consider a great delicacy, young women catch as many as they can and then have either their husbands or brothers carry the catch the ten kilometers to the market in Mahanoro, or they salt and dry it. Much petty trade is turned inland toward towns that can be reached on foot or by canoe, where people have kin with whom to stay. People also move back and forth between Mahanoro and home to buy commodities like cloth that are not sold in the town.

Although all families in the village own land, some families have more productive and better-positioned rice fields than others. But no one ever talked to me about colonial land policies being the root of their troubles. During 1993, tensions arose when several households—including those of Ramaresaka and Tsaravintana; Tsaravintana's cousin Solo and his wife, Liliane; and the six married children of the latter—decided to increase their landholdings by breaking new land to the south of the vil-

lage. No one contested Ramaresaka's new land because it was well beyond the last rice fields. However, when over time it became clear that
Solo and his children were going to get a good harvest off the land in
what, for most people, was a bad year, another family started to complain that their ancestors had farmed that land long ago. The man who
picked the fight was called Anselme; he was one of the better-educated
people in the village and had actually been a member of the French navy.
Like many others in Ambodiharina, Solo's family thought Anselme was
snobbish because he "knew paper" and would use his competence in negotiating the state bureaucracy to bring a trial in Mahanoro. In response,
they were quick to try and find people whose "eyes had seen" whether
Anselme's ancestors had actually farmed that land or not.

Under normal circumstances the fight should have come before the
town council *(fokon'olona)*, who would have likely decided either in favor of the person whose ancestors had farmed the land or the person
least likely to sell the land. If the town council had been unable to decide the dispute, it would have been sent to the court in Mahanoro, which
was precisely what Solo and Liliane wanted to avoid because of the expense and the time lost working their fields. In this case, however, the
government intervened before anything could happen (though not before they had invested the labor in clearing the land). The forest ranger
announced that no one was allowed to work that land, and that all of
it—including Ramaresaka and Tsaravintana's new land, which had not
been locally contested—was a protected area because of the presence of
raffia palms. Luckily, Solo and his family, as well as Ramaresaka and
Tsaravintana, had enough old land to farm, and they could revert back
to cultivating those fields. Ultimately, internal struggles and incipient inequalities among villagers were subordinated to the will of the state,
though the lingering bad feelings between the families remained.

It is important to stress that the tensions I have just described indicated a jostling and competition among relative equals rather than sharp
disparities in wealth or status. To be sure, the inequalities that did exist
mattered enormously to people in Ambodiharina, and they sometimes
meant the difference between enough money to buy medicine or see a
doctor, and death. But in terms of actual amounts of money or daily living conditions, the disparities seemed fairly small. Generally, everybody
ate the same sort of food and wore the same sort of tattered clothing.
Except for the local merchant, the carpenter, and teachers, they all had
the same level of elementary school education. The most significant social and economic division occurred between those who lived only off

the land and those who had some other source of income—usually former members of the military, who had a right to a government pension.
This is a rough distinction, however, as the general impoverishment of
the government meant that every functionary also farmed rice. At the
time I was in Ambodiharina, Anselme was the only surviving man who
had been a member of the Malagasy branch of the French colonial army.
His pension amounted to more than most people's, and as a result his
cash income was considerably higher than those of the other villagers,
though he too needed to farm rice. Anselme had legally married a woman
who, according to state law, would receive his pension upon his death.
However, Anselme had subsequently left this woman and lived with another, with whom he had had ten children. At the time of my second
visit, Anselme was quite ill, and people spoke with more than a hint of
malice of the struggle over the pension that would surely ensue when he
died. As the story of his struggle with Liliane and Solo over land implies,
his education, and his intimations that he would use it to secure himself
a better place in the village, made him both envied and disliked by many.
These relationships and the reasons for the conflicts had historical roots
in the colonial past, but on this occasion they were not particularly visible, nor did the people involved in them seem to care.

The daily round of rice work, which occupies so much of people's
energy, is punctuated by various events—deaths, fights, the arrival of
someone from the outside, or simply a ball or large ritual. For example, Monique's death, which occurred when she was out cutting breadfruit and slipped, fell, and broke her neck, caused considerable uproar.
Monique was a middle-aged woman whose father, Foire, was the younger
brother of Bototsara, one of the key *tangalamena* among the Zafindrenian, the ancestry that had competed with the Zafimalaone family
for precedence and lost.[7] Foire had become a teacher and had settled in
the south for his work. When he died, his brother Bototsara claimed
that he had not contributed to the construction of the family tomb, and
refused to allow him to be buried there. As a result, he was buried on
his concessions in the south. The death of an adult was always cause
for discussion, but Monique's death scandalized people because it was
premature. Everyone believed that the ghost of her dead father had killed
her because Bototsara had refused to allow him to be buried in the family tomb. Though Bototsara countered by saying that Foire had not contributed to building the tomb, people continued to hold Bototsara responsible, claiming that, as the older brother, he had the responsibility
of caring for his younger brother as a parent would a child. Many even

whispered that Bototsara had bad magic, called "not-two-courtyards" *(tsy roa kianja),* which allowed him to flourish at his family's expense.

Another notable scandal occurred when one of the *tangalamena* went out early one morning to check on his cattle and saw a young man, dressed only in red shorts, disporting himself with a cow. The *tangalamena* immediately returned home and told his wife, at which point word spread throughout the village. But despite prodding, the *tangalamena* refused to divulge the name of the presumed culprit. The incident was repeated everywhere, and people snickered as they told it. Who, they asked, could possibly be so indecent as to "marry" a cow? Many also observed that the cow had been irreversibly spoiled—it had experienced that which "was not done by people" *(tsy fanin'olona).* Because it had been polluted, it could no longer be used for a sacrifice. Moreover, no one would knowingly buy a despoiled cow.[8] Rumors continued to fly. Finally, one night, among a band of drunk young men relaxing after the day's work, the joking went too far. One of the men, a certain LeJean, was accused of having "married" the cow. He stormed to the doorstep of the *tangalamena* who had seen the event and swore that if he was not innocent of the deed then his ancestors were dogs. For southern Betsimisaraka, cursing one's ancestors by calling them dogs is the worst possible thing to say, and it usually requires, at minimum, cleansing with rum or, ideally, a bull. LeJean was made to pay a fine and cleanse his ancestors with rum. Meanwhile, the *tangalamena* who had witnessed the event refused to say who had done it, his silence thereby exacerbating the uproar. He eventually fled to his wife's rice fields in a village to the south in order to avoid the social tension he had created around him.[9]

Although these two examples illustrate how tensions in internal relations might interrupt the flow of everyday life, disruptions to daily routine—both good and bad—often came from the outside. In 1992–93 the major event that caused considerable disturbance in Ambodiharina was the presidential election, which I treat at length in chapter 7. But more mundane events, like a homecoming or a stranger passing through, might also stir things up, becoming the subject of gossip for a time. One kind of recurrent event that always threw up some kind of scandal was the ball, which was usually accompanied by a video. Balls were organized by a Merina man named Raymond, who lived in Mahanoro but made extra money by bringing his electric generator to the outlying villages, where he would show videos, followed by all-night music and dancing. The balls were held on average every two months—more frequently in the harvest season, when people had a bit of pocket money. They would attract everyone between the ages of ten and about thirty-five, and the music would start at sundown and last until sunrise. Outside the schoolhouse, women would set up small stalls with tiny kerosene lanterns and sell shredded papaya salad, small fried fish, and cassava bread.

Young people loved the balls—they were a welcome relief from the monotony of working rice. But as I mentioned, they were also always the source of scandal, as inevitably both men and women would get incredibly drunk and then go off and have one-night stands, often followed by their getting caught by their spouses. After the ball that took place on June 26, Malagasy Independence Day, Ramaresaka and Babette told me with evident glee that six couples had broken up. They proceeded to regale me with the details of who had cheated on whom, who had caught whom in *flagrante delicto*, and what kinds of gifts the men had had to give to get their women back. The "electric balls" (as opposed to the "traditional" accordion balls that accompany sacrifices) were so frequently a cause of dissension among young couples that many actually discussed them during marriage negotiations. Typically the marriage negotiator might say something like: "We know that balls are a big source of tension for couples. Are you going to attend them or not? Will you only attend them together?" Of the three formal weddings that I attended during the time I was in Ambodiharina, no couple said they were not going to attend balls.

Homecomings might also interrupt the flow of everyday life. Sometimes these homecomings were sad, as people came back to Ambodiharina having tried to make it in town (usually Tamatave) and failed. When Jacqueline, her three scrawny children in tow, returned to live with her parents, people hardly seemed to notice. Her husband had died, and she had been too poor to stay on her own in Tamatave; her arrival seemed to be perceived as yet another burden on the already overburdened household. I would see her standing listlessly in her courtyard, watching other people go about their work, not quite fitting in and not quite sure of her place. At other times she would tell people about her experiences of town life, comparing the prices of basic foodstuffs and muttering about how expensive things were.

The story of Babette's uncle Mamy, which captured people's imaginations for a time, provides a sense of how a more dramatic homecoming might affect everyday life. Mamy was a member of the Régiments pour la Sécurité Présidentielle (Regiments for Presidential Security,

RESEP), Ratsiraka's special army corps. He was granted permission to go on leave, and hitched a ride from Antananarivo to Mahanoro, planning to head straight for Ambodiharina. However, by the time he arrived in Mahanoro it was after dark, and Mamy knew that he could no longer safely cross the dark expanse of the Mangoro. Instead, he decided to spend the night in town, and went to the house of his kinspeople. The evening started to go wrong when he was turned away from the door: they said they had room for his bags but not for him! (To refuse to help kin is immoral and adds to the sinister tone of the story.) So Mamy asked if he might leave his bags and go in search of a place to sleep. He had not gone but a few yards when he heard the unmistakable music and singing of a spirit possession ceremony. Thinking these were "good" people, healers, and that here was a place to pass the night, Mamy knocked. He was ushered in and told to take off his shoes, as is customary. He was given a sarong *(lambaoany)* to wrap over his uniform, which is also customary for spirit possession ceremonies. He was given a glass of lemonade. And then, or so the story went, Mamy went crazy and lost control of himself. He was found a few hours later—with no shoes and every cent in his pocket gone (supposedly FMG 180,000, worth $100 at the time), wandering dazedly near the church—by the priest, who picked him up and brought him to the hospital. By the next day Mamy's kin had heard what happened and gathered in Ambodiharina. He remained in the hospital for another day, by which time his kin decided to bring him home to Ambodiharina. Mamy returned home and appeared to be better. The next day we gathered in his father's house as the villagers filed in to greet him; the story of his encounter with the scheming spirit-possession leaders was recounted again and again, and he was congratulated on his safe return to his ancestral homeland.

The gossip around Mamy's return—which I heard while planting rice and again that evening at the shop—centered on the "bad people" in Mahanoro; but it turned out that, like the scandal around Monique's death, it too involved demanding ancestors. As Babette explained—when I asked her why, if Mamy was sick, they had insisted on bringing him home to the ancestral great house—the "real" reason Mamy had fallen ill was a vow he had made to his dead mother that he had failed to fulfill. The example, in turn, brings us back to Ramaresaka's comment that "when there is work to do everyone goes to the great house." In order to illuminate what is at stake in these kinds of events, and the role they play in shaping people's concerns, requires a consideration of ancestors.

JOSEF: ANCESTORS AND *TANGALAMENA*

In the slow afternoons of summer, before the new rice shoots of the winter crop were long enough to transplant, I would spend hours on end with Josef, slouched in the shade by his house, shooing away chickens that came too near the rice laid out to dry (see fig. 5). Quiet and retiring but with a wry sense of humor, Josef had spent his entire life in the village, except for the times when he had been sent by the French to Tamatave for corvée. Josef came from one of the better-educated families in Ambodiharina: his father had been an early convert to Anglicanism and had been among the villagers who joined the MDRM and later died in prison; his sisters and brothers had all been mission educated. Anselme had gone off to join the navy, Jesoa had become a *chef de village,* and two of his sisters had been trained as *maitresses de couture* (seamstresses). Josef remembered the days of the French; he greeted me with a "Bonjouro" the first time he met me, and from time to time would come out with clichéd statements like: "Tous les hommes doivent les impots" (All men must pay taxes). And he always answered my questions about the colonial past. But it was hardly this aspect of his experience that he emphasized, for Josef was most preoccupied with the difficult work of being a *tangalamena.*

Betsimisaraka order the world in terms of a hierarchy that runs from Zanahary (God) to ancestors to the *tangalamena;* people say that the ancestors are powerful because they are in direct communication with Zanahary, who "hears all things."[10] In addition to mediating between the living and the dead, Josef was responsible for resolving conflicts among descendants. He perceived both of these tasks as difficult, dangerous work. The *tangalamena's* words and deeds, emotions and thoughts, Josef explained, are endowed with the power to both harm and heal by virtue of his contact with the dead. "*Tangalamena,*" Josef told me, "are masters of the good and masters of the bad."[11] Moreover, he continued, they do not just talk but use one of several different substances thought to enhance contact with the ancestors—particularly honey, but also rum, *betsa,* and white clay *(tany ravo)* — when they want something to be done. In short, they are privy to greater communication with the dead and can use this to their own ends. Josef was quick to stress, however, that the power intrinsic to the work of *tangalamena* is always matched by its danger, for mishandling the affairs of "children," as all other members of the group are called, can result in sudden death *(maty tampoka).* Positioned between the living and the dead, Josef could be killed by either

Figure 5. Spending time with Josef, 1993. Josef served as the *tanga-lamena* for his mother's ancestral great house *(trano be)*. Photo by Jennifer Cole.

the "sadness of the children" or the "anger of ancestors." He was vul-nerable to illness-inducing, murderous blame *(tsiny)* from both directions. Moreover, to lead people into immoral behavior or harming others, or to harm his own descendants, would be suicidal for him. One way to do this was through speech, as speech is considered a particularly potent form of action (see chapter 5). As Josef observed, he heard a lot about the foibles and misdeeds of his children, but he talked little because speech held the possibility of harming his descendants. Reflecting generally on what his work was like, Josef commented, "Ancestral law is terribly difficult! You must know how to bend and compromise. The *tangalamena* must be neither too hard nor too soft. He must resolve all conflicts in the great house and not let them go to court. If he fails to fulfill his duty as *tangalamena,* then the ancestors may kill him. Struck dead! 'You did not take care of the sadness of the children,' [the ancestors] say to you. When anything happens in the family, the ancestors show themselves to you."

The *tangalamena's* privileged relation to ancestors and their dual role as holders of ancestral memory and dispensers of blessing means that *tangalamena* must be selected carefully. Ideally, the person chosen as *tangalamena* is the oldest in the male line. In reality this ideal is frequently compromised. According to purely structural considerations, it was Anselme, Josef's older brother, not Josef, who should have been chosen as *tangalamena.* When I asked Josef why he had been chosen, he explained that while Anselme had gone off to join the navy he had remained at home in Ambodiharina. As a result, he was more versed in ancestral ways. But it was not only a matter of who knew ancestral practice better, for Josef was quick to add that living in the context of European institutions was likely to change people, making them easily angered. Those who live away for too long are thus not considered fit to become *tangalamena.* Even those who stay home might be prevented from acceding to the position if their families judge their character to be inappropriate for the task: that was what had happened to Geoffrey, a badly behaved man who, in a drunken rage, had told his father to lick his foot. Afterward, no matter how much he demanded the position of *tangalamena* as his own, Josef said, his family would not allow him to lay claim to that power.

Because of his work as *tangalamena,* Josef remained keenly aware of the influence ancestors have over people's lives and of the difficulties people encounter as they set about the business of negotiating ancestral power. Josef told me that ancestors move among the living, watching them and guiding them in their decisions: a thin fog covers them, and so they are invisible but present nonetheless. "They're here in this house right now," he said. He also explained that the dead continue to enjoy the same food, drink, and music and continue to behave much the same as when they were alive. Ideally, the relationship between ancestors and descendants is one of mutual respect and reciprocity. "Ancestors," he explained, "[are] supposed to bless their descendants and make them prosper, and descendants [are] supposed to reply by recognizing their ancestors, remembering them with gifts and sacrifice." As Josef put it, "You look for wealth, your rice prospers, you find cattle or money: all of that is blessing bestowed by ancestors." The problem was that this relationship, which is ideally conceived as positive, always contains the potential to "turn" *(mamadika),* meaning that either party might betray the other. For example, descendants might blithely make off with ancestrally rooted power and willfully forget all about the true, moral source of their success. Occasionally, they might even promise the ancestors a bull of their own accord and then not come through with it, absorbed as they are with the business of daily life. People always assume that it is characteristic of the wily ways of living humans to take without acknowledgment—meaning steal—and forget, intentionally or otherwise, the ultimate source of power.

"You see Telolahy?" he asked me. "Well, he promised to throw a circumcision but doesn't have enough money to sponsor the ceremony. And so he's taken honey and begged the ancestors to postpone the sacrifice. The ancestors had been looking for their promised bull, and so he fell sick, and only when he brought the bull from Vohilava [a neighboring village] did he get better again." Telolahy's story ended happily because he was eventually able to get the bull, but Josef emphasized that the ancestors give credit *(manome bon)* only once. If one promises to sacrifice to the ancestors but then takes too long to fulfill that promise, the ancestors will accuse one of lying: "You promise, 'I'll give a bull this year,'" explained Josef. "But you don't have a bull, not enough rice, not enough sugarcane. Slow! And the ancestors come and say, 'Where was that thing you promised? You! You're lying!' Sickness! Death! You're forced to give. *Vazaha* don't have that—you finish a house, and that is it. But here, we fall sick before we realize."

As Josef's words imply, "living people" are always trying to fool ancestors, to get their power without giving in return. It soon became clear, however, that ancestors, for their part, tend to be overly demanding of their descendants. For example, one day I brought news that Josef's older brother's wife, Marie, was to do a flourishing sacrifice—the sacrifice people do when they have had many children—in her father's town. That was all I knew at the time, but without even hearing the explanation from the parties involved (who were obviously closely related to Josef and would almost certainly come around in the next few days to talk things over), Josef already knew what had happened. He immediately exclaimed,

"Ahhh, when you prosper then you really suffer. Of course Marie's [paternal] grandfather wants a bull. After all, when Anselme did his flourishing celebration here for our mother [he nodded toward the old tree where his family performed sacrifices], I called our ancestors, and then had Marie's father come up and name hers, while I presented the bull. So of course Marie's ancestors know a bull was given to her husband's ancestors, and now they're competing [miadilahy] for their own. Really, it spreads illness around. Things [e.g., ancestors] you should not call, you call, and then you are forced to give." Josef was not alone in his sentiments.

The demanding nature of ancestors—the fact that people who are so poor in life can exert so much power in death—is one of the imponderables of life in Ambodiharina. As my landlady, Reni n'i Marriette, put it, "So many things oppress the Betsimisaraka! Here, we do not have anything, but ancestors are always demanding. When they are living they do not have a thing, but once dead they become a big prince and beg!"

Not only are ancestors greedy, but other people in the community often provoke the demands that ancestors make of the living. People often blame their fellow villagers for spitefully causing the ancestors to pay more attention to their descendants than their descendants might want. "The loose mouths of people" is the phrase that villagers use to explain how people come to sacrifice to the ancestors despite themselves. As Josef explained, "The dead watch the living. And they see that their children and grandchildren have done really well, their daily life is good. Or other people will speak: 'Those people over there are really flourishing and doing well.' The ancestors hear and will come and ask for a bull in sacrifice: 'Give to us, for you have a good life.' So Zanahary hears and makes them ill; Zanahary quickly hears all things."[12] Josef's words convey the unspoken competition that exists among all the villagers, which is mediated by their diverse relations with different ancestors. The inhabitants of the village bear witness to each other, to their neighbors' successes and failures. Their observations and subsequent comments are a kind of moral policing of the community, ensuring that no one can "profit" without recognizing the true source of their good fortune. Or another way to put it is to say that everyone is a potential, even probable, witch until they are forced to "remember" their ancestors and make their success socially appropriate (cf. Fisiy and Geschiere 1991). Precisely because ancestors are greedy, making demands of their descendants that those descendants can barely fulfill, their demands and the way in which they

force the living to mobilize their resources in sacrifice are integral to local political struggles, which often revolve around the process of building up or erasing people's memories (see chapters 5 and 6). Those who
seek power through ancestors always do so at their own risk—and this
in effect sums up the dilemma of what it is to be a *tangalamena*.

RAMARESAKA: PARENTS AND CHILDREN

If Josef taught me about ancestral politics from the perspective of an active participant, emphasizing the way the shadow world of ancestors plays
a part in local struggles over power and authority, Ramaresaka taught
me that many of the same concerns pervade parent-child relations among
the living (see fig. 6). In many ways Josef and Ramaresaka shared similar life experiences: both had lived through the colonial period, and both
had spent most of their time in Ambodiharina, although Ramaresaka had
also lived for many years in her husband's village upcountry. Ramaresaka, however, was less educated than Josef, a fact she blamed on the
disruption caused by the rebellion and its aftermath, when her parents
had hidden her away upcountry lest she be raped by the Moroccan and
Senegalese soldiers charged with pacifying the country. Like Josef, Ramaresaka knew the history and the secrets of the village. It was Ramaresaka who first told me that, whenever the Mangoro threatens to
flood, Ingahimalaza and Fohirandrana, the ancestors for the Zafimalaone,
appear in a tiny canoe so quick the eye can barely see it. And when I told
her I had heard about a man who had married his mother's brother's
wife, a relationship that is normally prohibited, it was Ramaresaka who
made me realize that the relationship had been more than a mere breach
of taboo. She made the forbidden relationship come alive, describing how
madly in love the couple had been, and how they had often sneaked off
to stay together in the family's house in their coffee forest.

Like Josef, Ramaresaka also identified herself through her ancestors.
One of the first things she did when I met her was to allude to her powerful lineage by telling me that her ancestors, the Zafindrenian, were
among the first to settle the town. They had given land to Mozambi-
cans, she said, a delicate way of signaling to me that her ancestors had
been powerful enough to own slaves. Many people told me that "women
do not know much about ancestors," and in fact women are not allowed
to invoke the ancestors or sacrifice cattle, which effectively bars them
from participating in the formal domain of ritual politics. Many people
also claimed that women do not know how to "talk" properly and

Figure 6. Ramaresaka preparing *kadaka,* a dish made of cooked cassava, 1993. Cassava is considered poor people's food—something to fill the belly while villagers wait for their rice harvest. Photo by Jennifer Cole.

would be incapable of making the speeches required for ancestral events (see also Keenan 1974). Such formal statements aside, however, many older women know every bit as much about ancestral history as men do; they simply are not empowered to use it in the contexts where it most matters.

Nevertheless, for Ramaresaka, "knowing ancestors" remained a matter of pride. She used to comment scornfully that women who were too lazy to find out the reasons behind a sacrifice lost their *zo*—a word that means "rights" and that people used to refer to the honor that comes from participating in social life. But because Ramaresaka was somewhat younger than Josef—perhaps in her fifties—and because she was a woman and thus intimately involved in raising children, it was to parent-child relations, love, and marriage that our conversations returned again and again. Looking at Ramaresaka's preoccupations gives some insight into family relationships from the particular perspective of a middle-aged woman.

Ramaresaka farmed rice with her husband, Tsaravintana, and their children on land she had inherited from her father, but she lived with, and spent most of her time with, Tsaravintana's family in an area they had settled far to the south of the village. She had been married three times—once when she was very young to a man from the village just across the river, again in the prime of her life to a man who lived up-country, and then, after he had died, to Tsaravintana. She had borne nine children, one with her first husband and then eight with her second husband. Only five had lived.

Ramaresaka explained how Tsaravintana had courted her:

> He came and greeted me, and asked to marry me. I wasn't ready yet, and so he just gave me some money and went away. I thought to myself, "I'm going to use this money to carry [i.e., support] my children." And so I used the money to pay people to clear a rice field. Then one day he came back in a canoe with food, sugarcane, rice, pineapples, and bananas. A little boy brought up the food. And then he just sent the boy who had rowed him here home. And he stayed, and we hadn't even slept together, nothing! As it turned out, he had read his divination beads and knew I wouldn't throw him out. I asked him if he could care for all my children and he said he could. And he started to gather the money for pots and pans, and finally we got the money for our marriage. We made our marriage with the blessing of the elders.

Ramaresaka and Tsaravintana had never had children of their own, and I sometimes felt that changed how Ramaresaka felt about their relationship, for she would often refer nostalgically to her previous loves and always emphasized that marriage was made by Zanahary, so that one could not really choose who one got. Together with Tsaravintana, however, she raised her uncle's last-born son, LeKetra, whose mother had died in childbirth; her granddaughter Vevette; and Nirina, a girl they had adopted from the south.[13] Their house was located in a courtyard shared with other members of Tsaravintana's family, including the old matriarch, Ravola; her grandson Antoine, who supported her; and Tsaravintana's two nephews, Legisy and Tovolahy, and their wives and children.

As a result, there was always at least one neighbor or family member hanging out at their house, usually gossiping about someone else's be-havior. In addition, because Tsaravintana was skilled at divination *(sikidy)* and healing, people who wanted to understand what ailed them—which often turned out to be improper social relations—were con-stantly dropping by. Ramaresaka taught me what it means to be a mother, to care for and raise children, and how one is supposed to behave in daily interactions. Almost every conversation I had with her came back to the themes of who loved whom and how much; she was quick to see these themes not only in her own life but also in the constant flow of gossip about other people that circulated through the village.

As I mentioned earlier, Betsimisaraka reckon descent through both their mother's and their father's lines, inclusive of the eight great-grand-parents. People also make new connections through marriage, which is ideally conceived as the exchange of children and hence the acquisition of new sets of parents. Some people also make relationships through blood siblingship *(fatidrà)*, a bond created by means of a ritual in which people subject each other to a mutual curse should one person betray the bond, but which, if honored properly, creates a whole new network of kin on which people may rely.[14] The fact that there are different ways of creating relationships, combined with a belief in personal lot or des-tiny *(anjara)*, means that people seem to be able to choose where to live and how to spend their time. They are also attached to numerous dif-ferent places. For example, Velonmaro, Ramaresaka's uncle, had coffee concessions down south near Masomeloka, where he had married, but the rice fields inherited from his father were in Ambodiharina, and he owned still other rice fields inherited from his mother in another village upcountry. Ramaresaka was also connected to several different places, for she had coffee land that she had owned with her second husband to the west, as well as rice fields in Ambodiharina, and though she was ul-timately forbidden to farm it, she had cleared new land to the south with Tsaravintana.

According to Ramaresaka the relationship between parents and chil-dren, like the ancestral descendant relationship that it mirrors, is ideally supposed to be one of reciprocal love and honor. Parents are supposed to love their children, to nurture them physically, and to protect them from possible harm. In return, children are supposed to love and honor their parents. In both cases, the emotions of love and honor are perceived as visible in either party's willingness to contribute goods and labor to the other's well-being. This idealized parent-child relationship is em-bodied both in proverbs and in ritual practice. For example, one proverb holds that "children are like your horns," comparing children to the strength of a bull. When I asked Ramaresaka what this meant, she explained the proverb in the following terms: "Whatever you want to do, you lean on your children. Your children are your protectors, so you say you have horns. When they're still small you carry them on your back, and later they become your horns." The idealized image of the relationship is also acted out in rituals carried out every December and again on Malagasy Independence Day, June 26, when children return home and ritually honor their parents by bringing food (typically chickens and rice) and a bit of money. Though the rituals take place on Christmas Day and Independence Day, the ritual structure is clearly modeled on the rituals that used to take place during the Merina ritual of the royal bath. During that ceremony, which was elaborated upon at the end of the nineteenth century, Merina kings and queens transferred blessing to the kingdom. The ritual was practiced by the Merina, and then in the areas conquered by the Merina, prior to colonization by the French. Whereas under Merina conquest the ritual was used as a means of symbolic and actual incorporation into the Merina state, today people interpret the ritual as constitutive of ideal parent-child relations.[15] Parents receive the proffered "honor," which is still called by the Merina term *jaka pandroana,* utter a few conventional words of blessing, and then produce their own rice and chicken to add to the pot: each feeds the other.

While general cultural practices constantly invoke the importance of parent-child relations, Ramaresaka drove home how profoundly the parent-child relationship shaped every aspect of people's lives. For example, when Ramaresaka's daughter and son-in-law showed up with the ritual gift of food and money associated with Independence Day two months later, Ramaresaka radiated happiness, telling me that her children were "remembering their mother" by bringing the "food that is never used up." When her daughter and granddaughter went upcountry for a few days to help their friend harvest coffee, Ramaresaka was despondent, even though she had urged the girls to go help their family friend. "Children remove your lice and fleas," she told me. "To be without children is total poverty, they are your wealth and your comfort, and those you raise will always remember you—most especially daughters always remember their mother." Or as she put it on another day, "Children are like your mirror, you love to see them glitter." Tsaravintana was every bit as involved. In 1999, I arrived to find Vevette, Ramaresaka's granddaughter, off visiting her father's kin to the south. But two days had not passed before Tsaravintana was off to get her. "I just miss her too much," he said, and headed south, his small sleeping bundled tied to his knife and slung over his shoulder.

Ramaresaka seemed to enjoy remarkably affectionate relations with her children, but for most people the ideal of a reciprocally nurturing relationship is generally fleetingly and imperfectly achieved. Precisely because of the wide variety of choices that people have in terms of where to invest their loyalties, the question of who loves whom, and how much, is a constant topic of conversation. Parents could be grasping and cruel, trying to live parasitically off their children's wealth or, more commonly, favor one child over another. For example, one day Jacqueline, the young widow with three children who had returned home from Tamatave, came to visit Ramaresaka, clearly dejected. When I asked, Ramaresaka explained that Jacqueline's mother saddened Jacqueline because she favored her sister's children over her own. "You see," she said, "she always carries Josie's child on her back, although Jacqueline's is smaller! Poor Jacqueline, she'll have to leave and go back to Tamatave." Another time, a woman who lived to the south came by to finish a cure that she had arranged with Tsaravintana. Tsaravintana was not home, but Ramaresaka explained that the woman's child had almost died, sickened by his father's ill feeling toward him. Ramaresaka commented with disgust that some people like only the children who live in their house, while others also like the children of their sisters and brothers.

The stories that Ramaresaka told me about how parents favored one child over another were matched by equally frequent stories about the tensions that marriage created in the relations between parents and children. The Betsimisaraka marriage ceremony explicitly states that each family gains a child: ideally one was supposed to treat one's in-laws as one's parents. In reality, however, marriage creates conflicting interests, first because people tend to marry several times, creating relations of half-siblings, and second because it represents the point at which a man or woman begins to focus on building up power and wealth of his or her own. Though in practice most women leave their natal households and go to live with their husbands' kin, no one ever seemed particularly concerned about the fact that a woman's loyalties are divided between her family of birth and that of marriage. By contrast, men are supposed to be primarily concerned with reproducing ancestral connections, and people often perceive a man's loyalty to his spouse as conflicting with his loyalty to his parents and sometimes even to his children. It is a tension that runs throughout people's lives. "The biggest problem," Ramaresaka explained, "comes from people's children whom you take [in

marriage]. When you take 'other people' [*olon-kafa*, non-kin], some take
a liking to you and are kind, while others don't. You see Yvonne [Ra-
maresaka's daughter by her second marriage]? She is very lucky to be so
well treated by Iaba n'i Sambimanana [her father's younger brother]. After all, she is the daughter of his dead brother. If there were another wife
[married to Iaba n'i Sambimanana], there would almost certainly be trouble. It's sure that a wife wouldn't want her wealth to be lost to someone's else's child. But Iaba n'i Sambimanana is good-hearted, and he honors his responsibility. That is why Yvonne is so lucky."

When Saboena came to consult Tsaravintana about what was ailing
her, a similar story emerged. Saboena was a middle-aged woman living
alone with her son and daughter-in-law. Together they raised a pig to
sell, which Saboena fed daily.[16] When the time came to sell the pig, however, the son and daughter-in-law kept the profits. "Poor Saboena," Ramaresaka commented. "Do you see how her children treat her?" Another
time when I showed up, Ramaresaka told me about the problems
Ravola, the old matriarch who lived in the courtyard and who was too
old to do more than sit and shoo chickens away, was having. "You see
how Ravola raised Antoine," she asked? "Well, now Antoine has run off
with his mistress. Together they are taking all the rice that they farmed
on Ravola's land. Ravola came crying to me today and said, 'Oh how I
regret that I've raised him.'" For Ramaresaka, daily existence was shaped
by these minute struggles over love and loyalty, played out in a context
where people had relatively little to share.

TOVOLAHY AND BABETTE: YOUTH

*When Tovolahy would get home from a morning of fishing in the
ocean, we would all crowd around as he poured the contents of
his fishing bag, sewn from a plastic flour sack, onto an old mat.
The rest of us would watch Babette separate the different fish into
the small piles in which they would be sold. She would give one of
the smaller, less edible fish to the little girls, Zana and Vevette to
play with. They would dance around with them, tugging at their
whiskers and poking the green-speckled eyes until the fish would
begin to stink, and they would grow tired of their game and move
onto something else. As we moved aside, Ramaresaka's eyes
sparkled mischievously at me. "The general has divided it all,"
she said, nodding toward Babette; "there is nothing left for the
kin." (Field notes, March 1993)*

Throughout this chapter I have referred to Tovolahy and Babette in passing, but it is worth pausing to consider what life was like from their perspective and what they can tell us about young adults in Ambodiharina.
At the time I first met them, Tovolahy was twenty-seven and Babette was
in her early twenties, maybe twenty-two. Tovolahy had done a year of
military service in Sainte Marie, and after he had finished he had stayed
for a while on the island before returning home. He had fathered a son
by a young woman, something that I learned from his mother, who said
that some day maybe they would go get the child. When I asked her why,
she said, "What, not take something that belongs to you?" reflecting the
widespread assumption that people belonged to their father's kin. But
for the time being Babette ruled the roost, and she wanted that child to
stay far away with its maternal kin in Sainte Marie.

Both Tovolahy and Babette had gone to the local primary school, and
both could read and write, slowly, saying the words as they read. Babette was pretty, sure of herself, and fierce, but she masked her fierce-
ness with laughter most of the time. My favorite image of her is the memory of her cutting across the soccer field that lay in the middle of
Ambodiharina, her three-year-old daughter, Zana, and her six-year-old
son, Legros, in tow, skipping along (see fig. 7).

In many ways Ramaresaka's criticism of Babette for pushing Tovolahy's kinspeople away was correct: Babette worried about her family
and her wealth alone, and she really was not much interested in sharing
it. Though young men are known for occasionally making trouble and
fighting at balls, when it comes to marital relations it is young women
that people complain about most: they are perceived as highly desirable
because they enable the founding of new families, and deeply trouble-
some because they pull a man away from his kin. Like many young
women, Babette was in the process of building up her personal and material resources, so that later her children would give to her. Her parents
were not around. Her mother had had the misfortune to die on the 26th
of June, Independence Day, and no one had attended the funeral.[17] Both
her uncle and her father were in Ratsiraka's army, the RESEP, and both
were stationed away, in Tulear and Antananarivo, respectively.

In this context, Babette seemed interested in, above all, creating
wealth and a home she could control. Despite her youth and the fact that
her father and uncle had experience of other parts of Madagascar and
Tovolahy had lived away in the army, Babette and Tovolahy had a shared
vision of how to create wealth and a home that was centered primarily
on local means of subsistence. They would often denigrate life in Ma-

Figure 7. Babette holding a rare bird that Tovolahy had trapped,
1993. The couple lived comparatively well because of Tovolahy's
skill at trapping and fishing. Photo by Jennifer Cole.

hanoro and the way one had to buy everything there. They both worked
remarkably hard in the fields, supplementing their rice work by catching and selling *vily* when these came available. Babette was also adept
at weaving and selling baskets. Tovolahy seemed more cautious and he
had a happy relationship with his parents. Babette, however, who had

only her uncle to answer to, made it clear that she did not hesitate to stand up to elders. Whenever we talked with Ramaresaka about how in the "old days" people had chosen spouses for youth, Babette expressed her outrage declaring, "I could never finish that [i.e., obey that]." And when she disliked the way her uncle followed *his* wife's opinions, slighting the family, she was not afraid to express her displeasure by refusing to give the symbolic offering of money and rice that re-creates the family hierarchy each Independence Day. Tovolahy seemed to acquiesce to her desires, to the dismay of his kin. By the time I returned in 1997, Babette and Tovolahy had split up and Babette had gone off with her father's sister to live in the large market town of Ambatondrazaka. Zana and Legros had been absorbed into Tovolahy's parents' household, and Tovolahy lived a few houses away with a new partner. He had not yet claimed the child in Sainte Marie.

VILLAGERS "NOT OF THE VILLAGE"

Thus far I have considered aspects of local experience and categories of people whose visions of the world focus on local social relations and local ways of prospering. Josef, Ramaresaka and Tsaravintana, Tovolahy and Babette—despite their different ages and genders, all these people shared a desire to make their lives in Ambodiharina free of outside control. Yet there was another group of people important to mention, for despite the fact that they did not see themselves as "of the village," they were part of a category of people who exist in every Malagasy village. They also are crucial to my larger question of how people remember the colonial past. I am describing the group of people I earlier referred to as "local progressives," such as the carpenter Pierre, who also worked as my research assistant, Piso, Jean, Maman n'i Talata, and the midwife, whom people referred to as Rasage. All of these people shared the fact that though they lived in Ambodiharina, they did not particularly want to. They felt stuck and out of place, and they constantly referred to the others, people like Babette and Josef, as the "real" villagers. Piso seemed to have it particularly hard. She was from the northwest of Madagascar but had gone to live in Antananarivo as a maid. It was while she was working as a maid in a bar in Antananarivo that she had met Hervé, who was from Ambodiharina and whose sister owned the bar. They had come back to try and raise their children in Ambodiharina; but Hervé had been detained in Antananarivo during most of my first visit, and so when I got to know Piso she lived alone with their three daughters. They lived in the house of Hervé's uncle Bototsara, and since Bototsara hated Piso he was always making her miserable.

Piso felt trapped: she was stuck taking care of her ailing mother-in-law, who had had a stroke, felt disliked by many of the villagers, and mourned the lack of opportunities in the village. Local customs that other people so valued she simply saw as obstacles to much-needed change. For example, she saw the custom of blood siblingship as a barrier to progress. "You know," she would say, "the reason why this place never progresses? Well, take blood siblingship. Someone does something, but they are related to so-and-so who is related to so-and-so through blood siblingship. So you can't prosecute, you can't do anything. And so you just sit there." More than anything, Piso hoped local circumstances might change.

But though she felt trapped, she worked incredibly hard so that her children would not be. She soon realized that the children acquired only rudimentary learning at the local school, from which the teacher was absent most of the time. She saved up and spent all of her extra money so that her eldest daughter could go to the Catholic school in Mahanoro. And Piso's horizon was never limited to Ambodiharina. Instead, she was one of the few people who had enough money to pay for batteries for her radio so she could listen daily to Radio Madagascar. Indeed, she once told me she would feel like she was suffocating if she could not listen to her radio; she even brought it out to the rice fields with her. She also had regular contact with the capital, as well as her home near Mahajunga. After I left Ambodiharina, she was the one person who made a consistent effort to write me.

Like Piso, Jean had come to Ambodiharina because of marriage. He had first worked as a taxi driver on the route from Antananarivo to Mahanoro, where he had met his wife, the daughter of a large Indian family who owned most of the shops in the small villages between Mahanoro and Nosy Varika.[18] Jean and his wife, Maman n'i Talata, ran the local shop, making sure that their eldest daughter, too, went to school in Mahanoro. Maman n'i Talata was gentle and much liked by most local people. Jean, however, would sit behind the counter of his shop, his Petro-Max gas lamp burning, his cheeks bulging with tobacco, and hold forth on the savagery of the locals.

Piso and Jean were people who had come because of marriage and had never quite fit in, holding themselves apart from the locals and seeing them as "less developed" and "other," as the "real villagers," while they were not. Pierre was somewhat different. He had been born in Am-

bodiharina, and all his family lived there and in the surrounding countryside. He had, however, spent time at school in Tamatave, coming close
to passing his baccalaureate. Eventually he had returned home, but he
knew carpentry and repeatedly made extra money by building things for
people, though he and his wife also farmed rice. If Piso and Jean scorned
the locals, Pierre compassionately understood them and their points of
view, even if he felt himself to be apart. When I once asked him which
history mattered more to him, the history of Madagascar that he had
learned at school in Tamatave or the local history of his ancestors, he
said school history did not mean much, but that if he had not learned
the history of his ancestors, he would feel ashamed.

THE ILLUSION OF THE LOCAL

The people of Ambodiharina have lived through a good deal of disruption, even an extended cultural assault, but the world of Betsimisaraka
daily life is nevertheless a world that many anthropologists might recognize from the earliest African ethnography. The pervasive power of
ancestors, the cultural elaboration of the parent-child relationship as a
model of authority and mutual dependence, the importance of elders,
and the emphasis on reciprocity and equality—these are aspects of many
lineage-based societies that Africanists have documented. We now know
that the appearance of such locally embedded practices as tradition is a
paradoxical effect of the local dialectic of modernity, and the history
sketched out in chapter 2 suggests that Ambodiharina is, in many important ways, a hybrid locale. But people do not experience it that way
in their daily lives. The colonial past is the ground upon which most
people unself-consciously tread. And here the Betsimisaraka are hardly
unique, for none of us, as Nietzsche ([1874] 1980) famously pointed out,
can live historically all of the time. Historical consciousness—memory
itself—is always produced by particular social practices and it is always
socially occasioned.

CHAPTER 4

Between Memory
and History

Betsimisaraka Imagine the Past

One night their country was invaded by the tanks of
a gigantic neighboring country. That had brought such
a shock and brought such terror that for a long time no
one could think of anything else. It was August, and
the pears in their garden were ripe . . . Mama had invited the pharmacist to come and pick them. But the
pharmacist neither came nor even apologized. Mama
was unable to forgive him, which infuriated Karel and
Marketa. They reproached her: Everyone else is thinking about tanks, and you're thinking about pears. Then
they moved out, taking the memory of her pettiness
with them.

But are tanks really more important than pears?

—*Milan Kundera*

How are we to understand the apparent erasure of the colonial past
among a people for whom life was severely, often brutally, disrupted?
How is it possible that Betsimisaraka live among the visible remnants of
the colonial past, yet that past appears to be absent in every significant
way from the intimate round of their daily lives? We always see life from
a particular perspective, and that perspective is partially created through
representations of the past that highlight some aspects of experience and
neglect others. Selective representations of the past explain how a par-

ticular constellation of relationships in the present came to be. Might the particular practices through which Betsimisaraka represent the past and shape memory occlude the visibility and cultural salience of the colonial period and the ways in which it disrupted their lives? I begin my answers to these questions by considering the Betsimisaraka in light of a long-standing debate in the social sciences about people who do, and do not, "have history."

OF HISTORY AND PEOPLE WHO SUPPOSEDLY LIVE WITHOUT IT

The question of how to understand differences in historical conscious-ness has a long historical past, having emerged alongside the discipline of anthropology in the age of exploration and the heyday of European colonialism. Confronted with the different ways societies imagined their relationship to the past, missionaries and colonial administrators initially sought to understand different forms of historical practice according to an evolutionist paradigm, which held that all societies moved from a state of savagery to civilization. One criterion used to distinguish "civilized" from "primitive" peoples was the presence of written records: "civilized" peoples were said to have historical records and could therefore write histories. "Primitives" were said to rely primarily on oral accounts of the past embodied in myths. According to this view, history—defined as a written chronicle of past events—presupposed writing because the pres-ence of written documents enabled people to take events out of context and compare and analyze competing accounts, thereby allowing a criti-cal distance from the past (Goody and Watt 1963; Goody 1977). Because oral narratives about the past were often recognized as only partly re-ferring to actual events, elaborate techniques were developed to elimi-nate the distortions inherent in oral testimony, to get as close as possi-ble to "what really happened" (Vansina 1985).

Social organization, in addition to literacy, provided another impor-tant predictor of who would or would not "have history." In their in-troduction to *African Political Systems* ([1940] 1987), Meyer Fortes and E. Evans-Pritchard eschewed evolutionary models even as they adopted evolutionary categories in synchronic form. They argued that one is more likely to find an elaborated mnemonics of past events among those people characterized by centralized forms of power, particularly monarchies, as opposed to lineage-based societies.[1] Judged from either of these per-spectives, Betsimisaraka—an oral society until literacy was introduced during the nineteenth century, and characterized by decentralized social organization—appear to be a paradigmatic example of "people without history."

With the fading of the high colonial period and the increased interconnection between European metropoles and their former colonies in the 1980s, an alternate view emerged. Anthropologists now seek to avoid the ethnocentrism in thinking that all history has to look like our history and recognize that ideological structuring inheres equally in Western historical representations of the past (White 1973, 1987). In place of assuming the old binary oppositions (oral/literate, primitive/civilized), we seek instead to understand the diverse cultural practices through which the past is imagined. To borrow a felicitous phrase, we now recognize not only that culture is historical, but that history is cultural (Lambek 1998). Most studies now take as their starting point the assumption that all societies "have history," and from there seek to determine the particular modalities through which, say, an oral society constructs its relationship to the past.[2] Many studies emphasize three sites as being critical to the construction of historical consciousness: landscape and the way it encodes narratives about the past (R. Rosaldo 1980; Feld and Basso 1996; P. Thomas 1996); oral history (Vansina 1985; Delivré 1974; Feeley-Harnik 1978; Cohn 1987), and ritual (Connerton 1989; Lambek 1998; Sharp 1995; Stoller 1995).

Despite agreement that the dichotomous thinking of the past oversimplifies reality, I have found it useful to use a European version of the "great divide" theory as a tool for analyzing the particular social mechanisms through which Betsimisaraka represent the past. In particular, I draw upon the distinction between the embodied nature of memory and the reflective, self-conscious, and distancing qualities associated with history (Halbwachs [1950] 1980; Nora 1989; Davis and Starn 1989). Maurice Halbwachs offers one influential formulation of this dichotomy, arguing that collective memory is a "current of continuous thought, . . . not at all artificial, for it retains from the past only what still lives or is capable of living in the consciousness of the groups keeping the memory alive" ([1950] 1980, 80). In contrast, he suggests that history, because it is written by professional historians, who are presumably external to the groups they write about, is largely concerned with introducing demarcations into the stream of lived experience. Where history is a record of events, Halbwachs claims, memory is a repository of tradition. And where history emphasizes difference and separation, memory highlights resemblance and continuity.

In his study of French national memory, Pierre Nora (1989) elaborates on Halbwachs's distinction, explicitly linking it to parallel debates on differences in modern and traditional (one could substitute *civilized* and *primitive*) ways of relating to the past. Nora proposes that "memory is exemplified by primitive or archaic societies," whereas "history is . . . characteristic of how modern societies, propelled by change, organize the past." Echoing Halbwachs, Nora further suggests that memory is "integrated, dictatorial . . . unselfconscious . . . ceaselessly reinvent[ing] tradition." "'History' is voluntary and deliberate." Memory implies retaining an emotional bond with the past. In contrast, history, which requires "analysis and criticism" (8–9), suggests distance from the past. For both Halbwachs and Nora, memory appears as organic nature in contrast to history's culture (Davis and Starn 1989).[3]

Summing up these discussions we might say that they imply two distinct dispositions toward the past that are partly enabled or shaped by certain kinds of technology. The first disposition characteristic of history attempts to document change, and it is made possible partly by the sheer mass of information that a technology like writing enables one to accumulate. The second disposition typical of an ideal type of memory tries to create emotional connections to the past. Though neither Halbwachs nor Nora acknowledges the presence of individual psychological processes in memory, their discussions of the term in relation to history, which include phrases like "ceaselessly reinvent[ing] tradition" (Nora 1989, 8) and "a current of continuous thought" (Halbwachs [1950] 1980, 80) are modeled on the continual updating we think of as characteristic of individual memory.

These debates about the difference between memory and history are highly problematic. First, the use of binary oppositions reinvigorates the dichotomous thinking that has long plagued European attempts to understand other forms of historical practice. Second, the discussions assume that some imagined entity ("the West") is a place where there is a way of relating to the past that everyone shares. Yet we know such generalizations do not hold. If some professionals in, say, England devote their lives to writing histories based on archival records, the great majority of Englishmen and -women may never read those histories and may constantly reinvent their relationship to the past. Third, it assumes that *memory*—what people remember from the past—does not influence the writing of history, and that *history,* in terms of what historians write about the past, does not always seep into people's memories.[4]

To be sure, the generalizations characteristic of these discussions are unable to account for the particular nature of Betsimisaraka historical consciousness. Nevertheless, as ideal types they provide useful points of comparison through which to understand the precise ways in which Betsimisaraka construct their relationship to the past. As I demonstrate in the following pages, the mechanisms and practices through which Betsimisaraka represent the past lie somewhere between memory and history and combine elements of both.

BETSIMISARAKA VOCABULARY CONCERNING THE PAST

Turning to the Betsimisaraka and their constructions of the past, we find that they too have words for *history* and *memory*, but that Betsimisaraka ways of conceptualizing these words do not map comfortably onto the memory/history dichotomy. The term most likely to be translated as "memory" is *mahatsiaro*, which literally means to "make not set apart." The translation is important, for it shows that, like Frederic Bartlett ([1932] 1995), Betsimisaraka conceive of memory as a process (remembering) not an object (memory). Although the word is sometimes used in the simple sense of "I didn't remember to buy fish at the bazaar," the most culturally significant understanding of *mahatsiaro* is the remembering that is supposed to take place between descendants and ancestors. The connection between remembering and ancestors became particularly apparent when I asked a series of different people—men and women, young and old—what the word *remembering (mahatsiaro)* meant, and every single one said that it meant remembering ancestors. As Tsaravintana put it, "*Mahatsiaro?* It works in many ways, like you remember to beg for blessing from your parents whether you live here or follow your spouse to go wherever. First, you have to beg for blessing from your elders." The equation that people make between remembering and the ritual act of begging blessing, the core of Betsimisaraka religion, suggests that Betsimisaraka imagine remembering as a morally charged act of identity assertion, which they accomplish by renewing particular ancestral connections. It also implies a relation to the past that depends far more on individual agency, on the necessity of making those connections, than Halbwachs's or Nora's conception of memory as unself-conscious reinvention implies.

We encounter a similar kind of difficulty in mapping when we look at how Betsimisaraka conceptualize the word *tantara,* which throughout Madagascar is typically translated as "history."[5] However, the work of several scholars of Madagascar indicates that the relation to the past typical of *tantara* and the Western notion of history are not strictly synonymous. For example, writing of the Merina, Alain Delivré (1974, 164) defines *tantara* as "the ensemble of customs, privileges and situations which are the actual product of history." Similarly, Maurice Bloch (1998, 108) writes, "*Tantara* does not abolish time but in it the passage of time is not cumulative . . . Rather in *tantara* the past is seen as precedent" (see also Beaujard [1991] and Feeley-Harnik [1978] for discussion of this term).

In these descriptions of *tantara,* the vision of the past implied by the word contains elements of memory as well as history, for it moves in two directions at once, transmitting information about the past without necessarily leaving that past behind. If anything, the explicit goal of *tantara* is to bring the past into the present, a point that further connects it to memory. This interconnection of history and memory in local practice is most apparent in the fact that people interpreted both terms as being about making ancestral connections. So close is the association between *tantara* and ancestors that the same words are used to describe seeking historical knowledge and begging for ancestral blessing (*mangataka tso-drano*).

The lack of correspondence between Western and Betsimisaraka vocabularies for referring to the past makes it imperative to examine how the indigenous terms are used in daily life. They are different from one another, as are memory and history, but in ways that are specific to the Betsimisaraka. Understanding this specificity is crucial to understanding how the colonial past is remembered in contemporary life.

MAHATSIARO AS MEMORY

Starting with the local concept of *mahatsiaro* (remembering), we find that the practices associated with it are situated between memory and history as ideal types. The complexities of the concept are particularly evident in the saying "We are the ancestors' stones." Betsimisaraka sometimes use this expression when people behave in ways that willfully erase the traces of ancestors' work. For example, by selling ancestral land, they are leaving the ancestors with "no standing stone." Literally, a standing stone (*tsangambato*) is a megalith that is sometimes erected to commemorate an event, but it usually substitutes for a body that has been lost and can not be brought back to the ancestral tomb.[6] Standing stones are thus memorial objects, made to last forever.

That Betsimisaraka villagers compare themselves to the ancestors' standing stones must be understood in the context of the striking lack of enduring material culture characteristic of this region of Madagascar. Unlike in the central part of the island, there are no huge stone tombs scattered over the countryside, nor are there elaborately carved funeral memorials depicting the life and times of the deceased, as there are in the southeast. Nor, as among the Sakalava of the northwest, is there a royal center or cemetery, concrete reminders of a precolonial past. In fact, very little endures in a Betsimisaraka village. The houses made of traveler's palm rarely last more than ten years and require constant renewal. Untended, they succumb quickly to the heavy rains and occasional cyclones, the traces of their brief existence soon erased and forgotten. The tombs are made primarily of wood and rot all too quickly in the damp earth. In likening themselves to standing stones, then, Betsimisaraka suggest that their very bodies are the most important memorials to ancestors.[7] The memory of ancestors is not permanently fixed onto tombs or stones, the proverb implies, but remains internal. What this means is that the practices aimed at memorializing ancestors are far more pervasive than a simple invocation of them in ritual. Rather, they are embodied in people's continued willingness to keep the memories of ancestors alive, which they achieve by living, as closely as possible, the way they perceive the ancestors lived.

In particular, memories of ancestors are created and sustained in what, following Nora, I call "sites of memory." For Nora (1989, 12) "lieux de memoire originate with the sense that there is no spontaneous memory, that we must deliberately create archives, maintain anniversaries, organize celebrations . . . because such activities no longer occur naturally, that without commemorative vigilance, history would soon sweep them away." Though Nora suggests that lieux de memoire characterized modern societies like France and might have predicted that people like the Betsimisaraka would have a "milieu of memory"—a kind of society so infused with tradition that it did not need to self-consciously create links to the past—this is not in fact the case. Betsimisaraka emphasize the fragility of their links to the past, and they work to maintain these links by investing their efforts in particular "sites." I concentrate on three key sites of memory that are the major mechanisms through which Betsimisaraka represent the past: the practice of taboo, houses, and the ritual practices surrounding tombs.

These sites are important because taboos, houses, and tombs are all key structures through which individual projects are realized and brought to fruition. Though each of the memory practices differs in the particular forms through which ancestors' memories are created, what links them together is an underlying belief that human effort imbues sites—whether words, places, or practices—with an individual's personal desires and ambitions. This belief is similar to Marx's notion that human intention is externalized through labor: objects created with one's hands—or in the case of the Betsimisaraka, even one's voice—are the product of one's goals and intentions that come to inhere in the material world (see also M. Cole 1996). For instance, if a woman weaves mats for her nuptial house and then later divorces, she must leave the mats behind for her husband's use. If, however, the husband remarries he is expected to remove the mats and return them to the woman. The mats are part of the first woman's ambitions to marry and create a successful household and, hopefully, descendants. To have a rival sleep on mats made with her hands, in essence mocking the first woman's aspirations, would be a huge insult. The family's *tangalamena,* or even the village council, would discipline any man who disrespected his former wife in such a manner. Although this example clearly shows the connection between human labor and the externalization of individual ambition, it does not include one critical fact: ancestors' memories—which are made through a complex mix of now-dead people's historically specific ambitions and contingent predicaments—are kept alive through their descendants' actions.

TABOO

One of the key practices through which Betsimisaraka simultaneously represent the past and shape memory in the present is respect for ancestral taboos.[8] Each person has a set of ancestral taboos that he or she must obey or risk the consequences.[9] Since Betsimisaraka typically marry several times, and people inherit their taboos from both their mothers and their fathers, taboos—things one's ancestors have said are forbidden to do or eat—are highly individualized. It is common to see certain family members cooking some kind of food, forbidden to another member of the household, outside in a special pot so as not to contaminate the inside of the house or the normal cooking utensils. Reflecting on what he perceived to be the uniqueness of Betsimisaraka practice, Solo remarked, "Antaimoro [a neighboring group to the south] don't have many taboos, but we Betsimisaraka have a lot. What makes that happen is that from my father's ancestral custom we don't eat crocodile, while from my mother we don't eat *varika* [a kind of lemur]; and from my mother's father, whose ancestral house I guard, we don't eat black or striped eel. My wife, she doesn't eat bulls without horns or goat. So our children, they have to respect all those taboos, and if they don't their mouths will be filled with sores." Here it is important to note that there is nothing anomalous about any of these animals: the notion that they are "matter out of place" does not apply (see Douglas 1966). Rather, "tabooed things" came to be taboo by ancestral fiat. Because a particular ancestor decided not to eat striped eel or wood pigeon, a certain kind of lemur or crocodile, the animal was defined as something "not eaten by the ancestors." But this did not mean that the ancestry who shared the courtyard next door could not eat it, or even that people living within the same house could not have different taboos, as they inevitably did. As everybody said, each to his own ancestors and each to his own taboos.

Paul Connerton offers a useful way to conceptualize taboo as a memorializing practice when he argues that "the past is sedimented in the body" (1989, 5), and that rituals of incorporation—body postures, movements, table manners—are one of the ways the past gets reproduced. The focus on ritual and the embodiment of memory fits well with taboo as a memorializing practice, because taboos are about incorporating the past into the present by refraining from certain kinds of actions.

Taboos held by individuals or communities are generally acquired in two ways, reflecting two slightly different mechanisms through which the past impinges on the present. First, ancestors create the most powerful taboos when they externalize their preferences and intentions in words, and descendants subsequently internalize these ancestral proclamations through refraining from particular forms of action. For instance, taboos might take the form of "last words" (farabolana), words that are particularly powerful because they are uttered just prior to death. Some people's last words are powerful because they are a "good request" (e.g., advice) left by the ancestors. As Josef put it, "Here is the path to take, here are our kin. You must not forget it! Because he [the dying person] has seen that which came before and guarded it and wants to leave it for his children. That is what makes last words powerfully efficacious!" Others interpreted "last words" as the expression of displeasure or anger, anger that was difficult to erase because the speaker was dead. Botoroa explained, "Last words? Like, 'If I die, don't give me the wealth [cow] of so-and-so,' or 'Bury me here and not there.' Anger makes that happen. And he who said it is dead, so who can remove that? No matter what, it remains his speech—words cut off. Even if you kill a bull it won't come off—but if they're still alive you can coax and cajole them and cleanse it with a sacrifice. 'I said something too harsh and now I remove it.' But it has to be he who spoke the words who removes them."

Parents may also project their memories into the future by intentionally uttering a curse, which has the power to bind future descendants (see also Graeber 1995). Tathen's grandmother, for example, explained that her family was forbidden from eating *sokoza,* a tiny bird. The bird had rescued her ancestors from bandits by screeching: it prevented the bandits from finding her ancestors hiding in the bush. Saved by the *sokoza,* one ancestor had been so moved that he (or she—Tathen did not specify, and the ancestor might have been either male or female) declared that all his descendants were tabooed from eating *sokoza.* Equally frequent were tales of how an ancestor had almost died eating a particular substance and then had declared that substance taboo for his descendants. One of the Zafimalaone ancestors, for example, had almost died while eating *lango,* a savory dish prepared by grilling still-green rice. Furious, he cursed his descendants, saying that they would die if they were foolish enough to eat *lango.* Another family told me that they were forbidden from building a house with a veranda, an architectural addition that became popular during the colonial period as Betsimisaraka adopted some of the building styles of the Creole settlers. One of their ancestors had been injured while sitting on a veranda, and had cursed his descendants, saying that no happiness would ever come to them were they foolish enough to build such a European-style house. Thus, as people respect the taboos imposed by ancestors—by avoiding specific activities or refraining from eating particular kinds of foods—memories of those ancestors come to dwell in the very bodies of their descendants.

The second way that people create taboos is through their attempts to protect the power of medicines. Compared to when an ancestor projects his or her will into the future by uttering a curse, this practice involves a less direct shaping of the present. However, ultimately the logic is the same, because taboos created through people's efforts to protect the efficacy of magic are also indicative of the way that the sediment of people's past projects structure present actions. Most people I knew maintained that all medicines were potentially efficacious and that the trick was to find the particular kind that worked well for oneself. In order to remain efficacious, however, the power inherent in medicines had to be maintained.

Although some taboos are attached to particular medicines intended for people, often they are meant to protect and nurture the power of a particular place (I am here translating the word *hasina* as "power." For a detailed discussion of *hasina,* see chapter 5). When my friend Babette started suffering countless toothaches, she became persuaded that she had accidentally consumed a forbidden food.[10] Her illness sparked a discussion about taboos and how people got them. As she explained, "Sometimes you burn a field clear and there are no animals that burn. But if there are, you have to go to the diviner to take care of the land. When Tovolahy's dad cleared the new land he found two kinds of snake had burned, and [he] went to see Tsaravintana, who read the divination beads and told him not to work on Thursdays so as not to suffer and die. Or sometimes your baby is sick and you take [the child] to the diviner, who sees there is a day like this or like this you must respect to guard the power of medicine." In theory, taboos acquired in association with treatment given by a diviner might subsequently be removed. In practice, what tends to happen is that people forget about the original medicine, which was never physically preserved. They continue, however, to honor the original restrictions, voluntarily refraining from engaging in the prohibited actions, whatever those might be. Ultimately the origins of these taboos are forgotten or "carried to the grave," thereby becoming taboos associated with the land that anyone who farms that piece of land is forced to obey.

The taboos that affect an entire town illustrate particularly clearly how taboos that were originally meant to preserve the power of medicines become enduring structures of memory carried out in daily practice. Ratsara, the *tangalamena* from the neighboring village of Benavony, described the taboos that its inhabitants were supposed to honor: "It is prohibited for us to raise pigs [and] *dokitra* [a large domestic bird similar to a duck, found in Madagascar], and red clothes can not be washed in the stream. But for pigs, you can bring them on the path near the town, and *dokitra* may be raised forty meters outside of town. Those caught breaking the taboo must sacrifice a bull. We cleansed this town two years ago on the 26th of June." To my question "Where did these taboos come from?" he responded, "The sun crossed this town, and so we decided to fix it through divination. That is why we no longer raise pigs. *Dokitra* are taboo because they don't talk. They are tabooed to protect children going to school. They are tabooed so that all schoolchildren may speak out clearly."

Ratsara's explanation reveals densely layered assumptions about how taboos bring the past into the present and structure everyday life. Every town has a set of shared taboos that must be obeyed by all the inhabitants. Often, these derive from the peculiar vulnerabilities of the village in relation to the natural surroundings. In this case, the village was built from west to east, instead of along the north-south axis typical for most towns in Madagascar. As a result, when the sun moved along its trajectory from east to west it "crossed the village," a condition that people believed contravened the natural order of things and required magical intervention. In Ambodiharina, the vulnerability of the town stems from its occupation of a tiny tongue of land surrounded on three sides by water. People believe the major taboo of the town protects the town from flooding: it is forbidden to drag a canoe across the town from west to east or vice versa. Instead, one must take the longer and more tedious route of rowing around the northernmost tip of the town and back down the selected side.

Taken together, these examples reveal the diverse ways in which ancestors' memories are created through taboo, for they demonstrate how taboos crystallize around the personal predicaments and challenges faced by prior generations of people. Whether one creates a taboo as a direct expression of individual will ("No descendant of mine shall build a house with a veranda"), or attempts to fulfill one's personal ambitions by respecting taboos meant to enhance the productivity of one's fields, the creation and subsequent following of taboos is intimately entwined with people's individual projects of self-realization. Taboos embody the experience and desires—even the accidents and bad moods—of those born before, and those who come after inherit them, for better or worse. Respecting taboos is ultimately about remembering the ancestors who imposed them by extending their projects into the present. People might not recall the exact reason a taboo came about, yet they are nevertheless forced on a daily basis to refrain from actions that they would otherwise take. After all, it is considered a lucrative business to raise and sell pigs, and most people would much rather take the shorter route by dragging a canoe across a narrow strip of land rather than row laboriously the long way around. By obeying ancestral prohibitions—shaping actions to confirm to ancestral demands—people honor the past as their ancestors experienced it. In so doing they create a form of "lived memory" that collapses the distance between themselves and the past, creating a *milieu de memoire*—a world suffused with the past—in Nora's terms.

HOUSES

Like taboos, more concrete sites of memory such as houses and tombs also work to simultaneously represent the past and create memory. With houses and tombs, however, the practices through which people sustain ancestors' memories shift the emphasis from embodiment to a dialectical movement between actual practice and the material structures in which prior ancestral intentions are said to inhere. In a general sense, people remember "ancestors' ways" when they occupy particular seating positions within the house. For example, as with many other peoples of Madagascar, Betsimisaraka associate the northeastern corner of the house with ancestors; because men are believed to be closer to ancestors, they are supposed to occupy that corner. In turn, women, typically associated with the hearth, tend to sit in the southwestern corner of the house, near to where the hearth is located. By sitting in these stereotypical positions, which in turn reflect local ideas about gender and which kinds of people are "closer" to ancestors, people bring the past into the present by reenacting what is perceived as an ancestrally sanctioned hierarchy between men and women. In this sense, "remembering ancestors" stands metonymically for tradition.

Yet many of the practices associated with houses are less about respecting tradition in a general sense than actually about keeping alive the memories of specific ancestors, most especially one's father. Like taboos that express the will of one's ancestors and their process of "self expansion," houses are also seen as a key site through which individual ambition is realized. In turn, children—sometimes a woman but more frequently a man—are supposed to continue to enact their father's projects. Specifically, they are supposed to occupy their father's house. Typically a family designates someone to live in their father's house, because if left unattended the house has the potential to make the family members sicken and die. People explain this by saying that the ghosts of the former inhabitants check back at the house every so often to make sure that it is inhabited. While it is acceptable for people to leave their houses to "seek wealth," people assume that one consumes wealth at ancestral locales, which implicitly honors—and strengthens—ancestors. As Jacqueline put it, "You search for booty in the forest but you eat it in the town."[11] If a visiting ancestor failed to find any ashes in the hearth, he or she would come after one, forcing one through illness to reinhabit the house. Perhaps because they can envision a time when it will be their turn to impose their memories on their descendants, older men who have made their fortunes often accept these constraints with good-humored resignation. Josef, for example, claimed that he never left home anymore to travel around, not even for ceremonies, because whenever he traveled, he inevitably dreamed the ancestors were looking for him. So, though

Figure 8. An ancestral great house *(trano be)*, 1993. Ideally,
the *tangalamena* lives in his ancestral great house. Photo by
Jennifer Cole.

he had built a fancy house with a corrugated tin roof, he did not dare
inhabit it. When he first tried to move in, he had fallen sick. He interpreted this illness to mean that the ancestors wanted him to occupy the
original great house located a few feet away. And so, he said, he never
went anywhere at all but just sat and guarded his ancestral great house.

In this way, Josef implied that he inhabited and produced a *milieu de memoire* by continuing to enact the projects of his ancestors. Josef's example, moreover, was hardly the only one; over the course of my time in Ambodiharina, I knew four different people, three men and one woman, who took up occupancy in their fathers' houses because they had fallen ill. It was the act of living in their fathers' houses that was perceived as keeping alive his memory—which in some cases was folded into a generalized "ancestral memory"[12] (see fig. 8).

TOMBS

Though houses and taboos are the major sites through which people self-consciously remember the past on a daily basis, Betsimisaraka identify the tomb as the most important ancestral site of memory.[13] Like houses and taboos, remembering ancestors by taking care of their tombs is also partly about extending ancestral projects into the present. Overseeing the building of a tomb and its maintenance, and then mediating between the ancestors who are buried there and their descendants, is among the primary ways that men gain and exert their power. In turn, having descendants honor one's memory at one's tomb is the key sign that a person has indeed achieved the status of a powerful ancestor.

Ideally, then, people represent tombs as places where they draw on, and nourish, their ancestors' memories.[14] Considering tombs to be the "real root," the center and "heart" of the ancestry, people I knew invested a huge amount of resources and energy in sustaining the generative power of ancestors buried in them.[15] Older villagers maintained that in earlier days the power of tombs had been protected by hiding them deep in the forest, away from marauding bandits, and by hedging them with numerous prohibitions. For example, people were forbidden from even approaching the Zafimalaone tomb without one bull leading the funeral procession and another following it. They had also dared approach only with muskets in hand! Today, these prohibitions have been largely removed, a concession, people maintained, to the growth of the town, which has forced people to build and cultivate in the area near the tombs. As Rafaly, a *tangalamena*, explained, ancestral power (*hasina*; see chapter 5) exists in the ancestral courtyard and the great house, but most especially at the tomb: "The most generative place is at the tomb, there where ancestors reside. You can't just do anything, can't go near to where tombs are. Even myself, the elders never took to see burials.

But now it has become a game. Children of sixteen or eighteen years old can go alone to where the ancestors are buried to gather kindling." What endures, however, is the profound belief that, as with houses, it is above all the act of taking care of tombs—investing one's effort and money in them and, implicitly, in the ancestors who lie buried there—that continues to keep ancestors' memories alive.

The necessity of actively maintaining ancestral-memories-in-tombs becomes apparent when we consider the flimsy materials from which most tombs are built.[16] Although today, more and more ancestries in Ambodiharina have copied the Merina custom of building huge cement tombs—and these are certainly a mark of prestige—the majority of villagers continue to struggle with the wooden tombs that they say are traditional.[17] Typically, the cemeteries look like small clearings in the forest, with stakes, occasionally made in the shape of crosses, sticking out at the eastern ends of what appear to be mounds of dirt (see fig. 9). At the bases of the stakes lie piled rusting tin plates and spoons, half empty bottles of rum, and various personal effects, including rotting straw hats, an occasional patent leather purse, even perhaps a toy doll. The site is entirely unprepossessing. Each of the mounds contains a tomb, made from eight pieces of wood cut from the same kind of tree cobbled together, roughly resembling a canoe, but with rounded ends.[18] Corpses (which are called by the same word as for "ancestor"—*razana*), wrapped first in a blanket and tied securely seven times, are piled one on top of the other within the tomb.[19] Men and women have separate tombs. It is hard to judge how many bodies actually fit in a tomb, but one often gets the impression that they are rather crowded. A piece of wood larger than the others is placed as a lid on the tomb, which is then covered over with sand and dirt.[20] The overall effect this creates is that the ancestors are protected from the elements, but just barely. There is no caulking on the tombs, which are so shallowly buried that the uppermost portion of the tomb, the huge piece that acts as a lid, inevitably pokes out of the ground.

But in the fragility of tombs lies their genius, for they require periodic attention, which is, at the same time, a way of making descendants remember their ancestors. Just as ancestors punish their descendants who "forget" and so neglect their houses, ancestors also inflict illness on descendants who forget to honor ancestral memories articulated through their tombs. As a result, remembering ancestors is much more than simply thinking about one's dead grandmother as one walks quickly and fearfully past the tomb to collect kindling on the outskirts of town. It is

Figure 9. A Betsimisaraka cemetery, 1993. This cemetery includes the tombs
of several different families, all of whom are members of one descent group;
separate wooden tombs contain the bodies of men and women, and each tomb
is marked by a wooden stake. Photo by Jennifer Cole.

an active process, one that requires descendants' work and money: descendants' bodies, their blood and sweat, are quite literally the ancestors' memorial stones. Sometimes this effort is put into replacing tombs,
sometimes into building new, cement tombs, and sometimes into just assuring ancestors—often specific individuals—that the living continue to
fulfill the desires of the dead.

For example, one mortuary sacrifice I witnessed was held for a
woman who, according to local custom, should have been buried with
her father, but who instead was buried in the same cemetery as her husband at her request.[21] The entire ceremonial speech given to the assembled village centered on how the woman had had certain desires that her
husband and children then struggled to fulfill. Likewise, at a ceremony
that marked the completion of a cement tomb and the successful transfer of the ancestors' bones to their new house *(tranon-drazana)*, as tombs
are sometimes called, the speech centered on how a piece of work started
by the ancestors was faithfully finished by their descendants: "Even if it
took a very long time, yet we managed to finish this tomb. The elders
stood, family of Maniry, Radaka, Vanonabelona, Tabola, stood up and
worked on this huge project. Yet as we don't choose the day of departure, they went home to sleep [*mody mandry*] with Zanahary. Later, we

children were made standing, and we did what was necessary to finish [their] work."

When the speech was finished the respondent answered, embellishing the host speech-maker's words: "In the days before the elders worked on this tomb, yet if it was started by the elders, some did not sleep together, nor wake together and did not see each other. If the elders sought to build it, the work was never completed. So too not all projects may be completed and sometimes they are stopped. If it became like a sleeping bird, your children who came later still desired to complete it. Our elders had a project they spoke about. We too must plan to do something good for our ancestors. At that time they did not break vows to Zanahary: if the elders planned to build a tomb you did not forget but continued their work. It was completed, truly assembled by you." In emphasizing the continuation of the ancestors' past into the descendants' present, the speech emphasizes the collapsing of distance between the different epochs. At least according to the sentiments publicly expressed at the tomb, it makes no difference that ancestors and their descendants only partially overlap in life, for even in death, ancestors continue to direct and shape their descendants' lives.

HISTORY IN MAHATSIARO

The emphasis on descendants' continuation of ancestors' projects, practices like taboo, and people's relations to houses and tombs—all gesture toward a way of relating to the past that seems very close to memory in ideal terms. It is a vision of the past where the past invades the present, and where the present gets its power (a theme I take up in more detail in chapter 5) from a carefully maintained relationship to the past. Viewed from this angle, the primary meaning of remembering *(mahatsiaro)* closely approximates memory, and Betsimisaraka do indeed appear to inhabit Nora's definition of *milieu de memoire*. Yet further examination reveals that the same practices that ideally create memory also encompass tendencies associated with history, though writing per se is only minimally involved. First, people in fact express a critical relationship to the past typical of history; it may not involve critically comparing written accounts, but it does involve a certain sense of skepticism about, and distance from, the past. Second, the practices through which people remember ancestors often bear, albeit unintentionally, the traces of particular historical epochs. Let us consider in turn each of the ways elements of history infiltrate *mahatsiaro.*

"TIMES HAVE CHANGED": CULTIVATING CRITICAL DISTANCE

Precisely because people are afraid to talk about the dead by name for fear such talk might conjure them up, they talk instead about the much safer topic of where the dead reside. Thus, one of the ways that ancestors' memories are kept alive is indirectly, through people's talk about the different "sites of memory" in which ancestors' memories are said to inhere. However, where the emphasis on connection to ancestors would lead one to expect an unself-conscious relationship to the past, Betsimisaraka discourse on ancestors' memories is more ambivalent, and people are sometimes even highly critical of ancestors' demands. Repeating ancestral actions is, as we saw, the stated ideal. In reality, however, people find themselves faced by new demands and opportunities in the present, and they often feel torn between the moral obligation to repeat the choices of their ancestors and the need to move forward and forge their own lives—and the potential for future memories. As a result, the need to memorialize ancestors is a constant source of discussion and reflection actively experienced in terms of personal dilemmas and conflicts. The fact that people are constantly debating the relative merits of maintaining ancestral memory, and critically judging how far they have come from an idealized ancestral past, implies a distance from the past that Nora associates with "history's call for analysis and criticism" (1989, 9). Remembering ancestors *(mahatsiaro)* is hardly an unself-conscious reflex but shares at least some of the distancing and subsequent analysis associated with a "historical" relationship to the past.

For example, ideally, remembering ancestors by respecting their taboos becomes a form of bodily memory so ingrained in people's daily routines that it is almost automatic, part of the world that goes without saying. In reality, however, the restrictions imposed by ancestral taboos are a constant source of tension, as people break them both by accident and on purpose. Because respecting taboos is ultimately supposed to augment and protect the ancestral power inherent in the land, forgetting to respect taboos is believed to have material consequences that people live with and think about on a daily basis. Repeatedly, people told me how tremendously productive the land used to be, but that it had lost fertility because nobody respected taboos anymore. This failure was explained as either a result of people's incessant self-interest or their inability to meet ancestral demands in the face of changing circumstances and increasing hardship. Rasoa, a former wife of the *chef de canton,* explained the dynamics of the process: "Nowadays there are no fish in the river, no smelt *[vily]* in the embouchure. No one observes the taboos! The last-born children, they just think about money now, don't share anything. The ancestors are angry, and so they don't give to us. Before, when you did something wrong you had to cleanse it, had to sacrifice a bull to the embouchure. But these days no one forces people to bring out a bull." To my question "People really used to make people cleanse broken taboos?" Rasoa responded, "Eeeeee! Once when a man came from Nia-rovana, he tried to drag his canoe across town rather than rowing around. Taboo! We made him get a bull and cleanse the transgression, but now no one does that anymore. You see now, Monique and that woman fought on the embouchure and no one made them cleanse it, and so the power of the land has decreased. The community is still angry, but no one does anything."

Rasoa may not cast it quite this way, but her words speak to the central tension in Betsimisaraka practice between memory and forgetting. Too much memory, like too much forgetting, leads to death. The one requires an impossibly perfect replication of ancestral life, the other the cutting of ties through which meaningful identity is made. The trick is to negotiate a balance between the two, to "brush death for life" (Feeley-Harnik 1991, 46; see also K. Middleton n.d.). Yet as life got progressively more difficult, people explained, the precarious balance of retaining a past while creating a future grew increasingly difficult to achieve. Time and again I was told that in the "old days" ancestral taboos had been so numerous as to make many actions well nigh impossible. People had been unable to cross the Mangoro with gold, they had been unable to farm on many days of the week, they had been forbidden from marrying Merina, and sometimes they had even been forbidden from going north. With changes brought by colonization, people had been forced to remove taboos. Nevertheless, the consensus remained that the removal of taboos, which people equated with the obliteration of ancestral memory, necessarily affected the efficacy of the land. Either unable or unwilling to respect the desires of the ancestors all of the time, people were forced to live with their lessening power in the world.[22] Official discourse emphasized the desirability of memory *(mahatsiaro)* and the way in which people honor ancestors' memories by reenacting the past, but people's experience, their attempts to live in a new world with rules imposed from the old, made them keenly aware of the difference between the two. The awareness of a gap between an idealized ancestral past and the weakened present was always there.

More concrete structures of memory, such as houses, also reveal the tension between replicating ancestors and the reality of difference and change.[23] For example, the ideal of a son maintaining his father's memory by inhabiting his father's house is not always achieved in practice. Sometimes, the sentimental links that tie generations together grow too distant, or the burdens of memory too much. Pierre's father, for example, found himself confronted with two houses, one belonging to his father, the other to his uncle, and discovered that the ancestors expected him to live in both.[24] Unable to satisfy the competing ghosts, and terrified of the retribution that he knew would ensue, he opted to burn his uncle's house, destroying the power of the house and with it the ability of the house to haunt him. Likewise, people's great-great-great-grandchildren were sometimes referred to as the "offspring who burn houses" *(zafimanorotrano)*. After five generations it was assumed that the links that bound ancestors and descendants together had faded; therefore, no sentimental reason would prevent the descendant from getting rid of the house so as to avoid the responsibility of caring for it.

But burning a house is only the most drastic measure, an infrequent action that people dare attempt solely with more distant relatives. Often, the dead father wins out, at great inconvenience and cost to the living, as the child is forced to drop whatever he or she is doing and move back home. Moving against one's will is felt to be a tremendous burden, since people portray the experience of living in a particular place as one of growing used to the land's customs, a part of realizing one's individual fortune or destiny *(anjara)*. Sarafina, Liliane's sister from upcountry who had come to help with the transplanting, expressed this kind of sentiment when she said she was used to planting rice on dry land, and just could not get used to transplanting seedlings into mud. In general, people felt that habits gained from living in a particular place were not easily lost, a belief expressed in the proverb "The color of the land is taken by the potato."[25] Complaints like Sarafina's were grounds for moving or inhabiting one village rather than another, except when ancestral demands changed the parameters altogether, forcing the living to submit to the will of the dead.

Koto's story strikingly illustrates the entanglements created by the expectation that the living will fulfill and extend the desires and ambitions of the dead, and the way this is further complicated by struggles among living siblings as they try to divvy up the responsibilities of common ancestral care. Koto's father was a Betsileo schoolteacher who had moved to Ambodiharina from the town of Fandriana with his wife when Koto was small. Soon after arriving in Ambodiharina he divorced his first wife, who returned home, and married Josephine, Bienaimée's grandmother. They had several more children, and Koto lived with, and was raised by, Josephine until his father divorced Josephine and married another local woman. Following the rebellion of 1947, Koto's father returned to Fandriana, taking his third wife and all of the children with him. He died soon after, bewitched, his widow claimed, by jealous kin. His children languished uncared for until their kin from Ambodiharina went to fetch them. By the time I arrived, the children were already well into middle age, settled with families of their own in Ambodiharina and Mahanoro. Eventually the family learned that their father's house in Fandriana stood empty, and that someone would need to go back to live there. Nobody wanted to go, and so nobody volunteered. Finally, Koto's better educated, successful younger brother pointed out that Koto was the eldest son, and he managed to half persuade, half force Koto to go. Forced to leave the life he had grown accustomed to over some forty years and return to Fandriana, Koto was sacrificed to ancestral memory, while his brother remained comfortably attached to his new life in Mahanoro. For Koto—and even for the other family members who remained in Mahanoro but were somewhat uneasy about how things had turned out—the maintenance of ancestral memory was anything but unthinking.[26]

ENCODING EPOCHS

Finally, when we look closely at the different practices that constitute ancestors' memories, we see that the semiotic means through which Betsimisaraka commemorate ancestors sometimes indicate specific historical periods. Betsimisaraka may claim that they "are the ancestors' stones," implying that memory of ancestors is entirely internal and unthinking, but as the previous pages make clear, in reality ancestors' memories are constructed dialectically, through the interaction of people with particular cultural practices and material sites that exist in the world. Moreover, because Betsimisaraka ancestors were people who lived during a specific period, the historical forces operating at that time shaped their choices, preferences, and options, as well as the mundane materials through which they created ancestral memory. This circumstance implies that the sites, practices, and materials through which Betsimisaraka produce ancestral memories carry the traces of prior epochs.

Turning to the examples of taboo discussed earlier, we find that several of the taboos refer directly to events, experiences, or problems associated with particular historical periods. Although the divisions are hardly formalized, Betsimisaraka tend to refer to time in three major periods. The time of the fighting *(tamin'ny tonta)*, refers to the period during the eighteenth and nineteenth centuries when the slave trade produced continuous raids and fighting between ancestries along much of the east coast. The time of the *vazaha (fahavazaha)* refers roughly to colonization by the French, although I sometimes heard it used to refer to events that took place under Merina rule. Finally, people talk about "since we came up from the flight" *(avy niakatra tamin'ny filofana)* to mark the time from the end of the 1947 rebellion to the present.

In the case of Tathen's taboo against eating *sokoza,* the tiny bird who rescued her family as they hid from bandits, which I discussed earlier, the taboo refers directly to "the time of fighting" *(tamin'ny tonta)*. In contrast, the taboo against building a house with a veranda refers specifically to a style of building introduced by Creole settlers during the nineteenth century that later become popular with Betsimisaraka. The story behind the taboo, which relates how the veranda had fallen on an ancestor who then forbade his descendants from building houses with verandas, is ambiguous. On the one hand, it can be read as mocking the ancestor who rejected colonial architecture, otherwise considered a sign of wealth and status. On the other hand, it might also signify resistance to colonial domination, symbolized in the architecture of the Creole house, since Creoles were, after all, the people through whom colonial domination was most directly felt. Either way, the existence of the taboo and the injunction to obey it potentially invite reflection on the colonial past.

The taboo against raising *dokitra,* which applied to the entire village of Benavony, provides another example of taboos' potential to encode different epochs. People said the taboo was enacted so as to enable their children to speak out clearly in school. The taboo is particularly interesting in light of a self-protective strategy used by the people of Benavony for their advancement in colonial times. Though located farther away from Mahanoro than Ambodiharina, and somewhat off the main road, Benavony is a village in which many people cooperated with the French; one of the most powerful local subaltern functionaries came from Benavony. As Ratsara proudly told me, his descendants now live in France. In turn, this man was pivotal in helping people to protect their ancestral land from theft by *colons*. Rather than completely rejecting new practices brought by the French, the people in Benavony actively embraced them, hoping to thereby improve their position. Schooling, which became particularly important under the French, was a critical part of this process, reflected in the taboo meant to enhance children's performance that exists to this day.

For Betsimisaraka, people as moral entities are historically produced through cumulative relationships. These relationships, which are constructed in historically specific circumstances such as an attack by bandits or a falling colonial-style roof, are performatively constituted and kept alive through the bodily practice of taboo. In turn, the practice of taboo—keeping those historically produced relationships alive in the present—creates a certain form of historical consciousness, characterized by the accumulation and juxtaposition of taboos that derive from different historical epochs but coexist in daily practice. As Michael Lambek (1998) notes regarding Sakalava conceptions of history, there is not so much an effective displacement of one time by another as their accumulation and mutual resonance.

The traces of past epochs, particularly the colonial period, are similarly visible in the location of certain houses, which reflects not only enduring ancestral-descendant relationships but also relationships that crystallized in a particular way because of specific historical events occurring at a given time. Houses in general may represent an idealized, unchanging ancestral-descendant link, but houses in particular are built in specific places because of events occurring at a precise point in time. The fact that the remembrance of ancestors is embedded in houses creates the potential for reflecting on why the houses were built in one place and not another—for historicizing one's links to ancestors as well as memorializing them. For example, as I mentioned in chapter 2, *colons* appropriated much of the best land for growing coffee around Ambodiharina. When the French left, some in 1960 and others in 1972, much of this land was freed up, though some of it continued to be legally owned by the departed French. Soon after, the town accordion player, Razafy, left his home and moved west to where he could grow coffee. But it was not long before his father's ghost started to afflict him and forced him back to the ancestral house in Ambodiharina. In short, as people explained to me, Razafy was prevented from taking advantage of the new land because his father had been prevented from doing so during colonial times. Ironically, the injustices inflicted on Razafy's father because of colonial rule continued to affect Razafy in postcolonial times, albeit for very different reasons. The house in Ambodiharina, and Razafy's occupation of it, came to stand for the particular predicaments created by colonization.

The memorializing practices that create tombs as sites of ancestral memory also work in many of the same ways as houses do to encode the historical past. First, as with houses, the location of tombs reflects the particular predicaments and choices faced by the ancestors who built them. For example, as I mentioned earlier, villagers say that they used to build their tombs deep in the forest (An'ala mizina—literally, the dark forest; the name of the forest where several ancestries' tombs are located), safe from potential desecration by marauding bandits. Today, some people's tombs remain in the forest where they were originally built. Attending to those tombs—the inconvenience of hiking in to them and the spooky quietness created by the trees—always reminds people of why they were built there. With colonization, however, the constraints around where to build tombs and how to maintain them changed. For one, the seizure of land by *colons* meant that some families chose to move their tombs to avoid trespassing on European-controlled land. Several people I spoke with also said they had moved their tombs in response to demands by the French.

The adoption of new memorializing practices, in addition to new materials used to care for ancestors, provides another example of how making and maintaining memories of ancestors also potentially encodes the historical past. For example, many people I spoke with, both young and old, distinguished between materials used in caring for ancestors that they considered traditional and those that had been introduced by the French. New materials include cement used in the building of some tombs, purchased cloth, and imported rum, which all signify the colonial past in a positive way, for they suggest that the colonial encounter provided Betsimisaraka with new, and what they perceive as superior, ways of constituting ancestors' memories.

Finally, the practice of remembering ancestors that takes place during the Betsimisaraka observance of the Fête des Morts, the Catholic day of the dead, explicitly encodes the colonial past. The work of memorializing ancestors during the *fête* refers to the colonial past in two ways. Most obviously, the *fête* evokes the colonial period because it was introduced by the French. But the foreign origins of the practice are underscored—and hence consciously remembered by some participants—because accomplishing the *fête* requires people to contravene ancestral custom in ways that initially scared them. As Rafaly mentioned earlier, it used to be prohibited to go anywhere near the tombs unless there was a death, and even then it was impossible to bury people without the sacrifice of a bull. Sometime during the colonial period, however, perhaps in conjunction with their attempts to create a national day of commemoration, French administrators encouraged people to go out and clean the area around the tombs. Reflecting back to the start of the practice, several people I knew recalled that an "order" had come from above telling them to clean the area around the tombs on November 1.[27] Terrified at the idea of breaking ancestral custom and incurring the wrath of the dead, several ancestries whose tombs were located close together pooled their resources in order to cleanse their transgression with the sacrifice of a bull. When they inaugurated the custom, they did so by announcing to the ancestors that this was a new form of caring for ancestors introduced by the French; they also begged the ancestors not to punish them for departing from ancestral custom. But people remain aware of the day's colonial origins: I heard one family argue that they should not continue to observe the day on the first of November, the day chosen by the French, but should move it to Malagasy Independence Day.

Remembering ancestors during the Fête des Morts also encodes historical referents by incorporating commodities and practices into the ritual that have come to stand synecdochically for the colonial period. During the celebration, for instance, people weed and clean the area around the tombs, sometimes even planting flowers, a French custom that in other contexts they mock. They also light candles and may sing Christian hymns or kneel to pray. Perhaps most important, villagers offer their ancestors a variety of luxury items, including coffee, European-made rum, and candies (Cole and Middleton 2001). Though all of these items are available locally—usually imported from China and having little to do with France—they are still perceived as having originated in the colonial period and are considered emblematic of French ways. Thus, where a bone-turning ritual creates memory by assuring ancestors that descendants continue to fulfill their commands and emphasizes the continuity of ancestors' ambitions with those of their descendants, the day of the dead encodes specific references to the historically shaped nature of those links. In giving their ancestors coffee and imported rum, villagers not only remember their relation to ancestors but remember them as particular people whose lives, desires, and preferences were shaped during the colonial era.

TANTARA AS MEMORY

If Betsimisaraka practices associated with the concept of *mahatsiaro* (memory) combine elements of memory and history, the concept of *tan-*

tara (history) similarly implies a conception of the past located between memory and history from the opposite side.

NAMES AS *TANTARA*

The most striking way in which *tantara* represents a construction predicated on the continual updating, rather than fixing, of the past is in the equation that people make between *tantara* and names. For example, late one afternoon not long after my arrival in Ambodiharina I was talking with Ramaresaka and her uncle Velonmaro, who had agreed to tell me their *tantara*. We began our discussion casually enough, chatting of this and that, but the moment I asked whether they could remember their ancestors' names—my feeble attempt to construct a genealogy—the atmosphere changed. Silence fell, followed by nervous, tittering laughter; I had stumbled onto a highly sensitive topic. After the initial wave of embarrassment passed, Ramaresaka, always the tireless teacher, took it upon herself to explain why one could not just name ancestors:

> We can recollect [their names], but unless there is rum we cannot cite them. They are kings, who reside with Zanahary and the [other] ancestors. They're already with Zanahary and you can't speak about them mindlessly, mention them without reason. Yes, you need a reason. That's why they hate when you speak about them, why there are so few words about them. It is difficult to speak before Zanahary. First you beg a little, you beg for blessing from them because when you speak of them they come, little by little, and gather around you. Your eyes don't see them, but they enter your mind and their names come, so-and-so and so-and-so. You remember them all.

This equation of names with *tantara* was evident on other occasions as well, when I would offer rum prior to asking for *tantara* and people would start to call out their ancestors' names, though it was really the stories associated with them that I wanted.

As these examples imply, ancestors' names are the quintessence of *tantara,* to be evoked only in the context of ritual, which partly explains the significance of the aphorism "Names never die" *(Ny anarana tsy mba maty),* frequently quoted in the village. As the proverb has it, "Living people don't shed" *(Olombelona tsy miofo*—meaning they only live once), but their names live on through ritual supplication, when they are called on to witness and sanctify their descendants' lives. The key cultural moment when Betsimisaraka call ancestors' names is during the invocation that takes place during a sacrifice, a topic I discuss at length in chapter 6. For our purposes here, I want to highlight the fact that conceiving of ancestors' names as history implies an orientation toward the past that privileges the automatic updating and integration of the past into the present and appears very close to being memory. After all, the lists of names called at sacrifices are fairly truncated, and the *tangalamena* who call out the names always rely on the support of their kinspeople in order to remember the full list. But to say that the lists are totally fluid or that they have no anchoring in particular historical periods is to overstate the case. Like taboos that can evoke particular time periods, names of some ancestors stand synecdochically for particular epochs because of the stories associated with them.[28] For example, Fohirandrana, the apical ancestor of the Zafimalaone, is celebrated for having fought a magical battle with Ranavalona I when her armies came to conquer the area around Mahanoro. His name remains a symbol of local power. By contrast, when the Zafindrabe family call their ancestor Sampson, the only person in the village to join the Parti des Déshérités de Madagascar (Party of the Disinherited of Madagascar; PADESM), the puppet party created by the French colonial administration, they evoke him as an ancestor. But for many older villagers who come to witness the event, he is the only person who betrayed the MDRM during the 1947 rebellion.

Further, though the use of writing to record ancestral names is not systematic, some ancestries do record ancestors' names in an ancestral book *(bokin-drazana)*, a practice that appears at first glance to be leaning toward the practices of inscription associated with history. When I first arrived in Ambodiharina and expressed my interest in *tantara,* most people urged me to speak with *tangalamena: they* would know everything I needed to learn as *they* held the ancestral books containing precious ancestral secrets. These books only confirmed what Ramaresaka and Velonmaro's reaction to my request for ancestral *tantara* made clear: one of the most important kinds of *tantara* is the particular genealogical linkage that binds ancestors and descendants. But where writing down ancestors' names might be taken to imply a certain critical distance from the past typical of history, people are always quick to downplay it, emphasizing instead the kind of embodied connection created through memory. Most *tangalamena* boast that they are so familiar with their ancestors' names that they never need the external support implied by the use of a book; using books as an external aid to memory was seen as a crutch signifying an undesirable distance from ancestors. Like Velonmaro and Ramaresaka, who suggested that, given the appropriate context, the ancestors "just come" when one calls them, Josef also stressed the mystical, lived nature of the ancestral-descendant connection. "When you hold the stick," he commented, referring to the ritual stick used in sacrifice (also called *tangalamena*), "there isn't anything you don't know. The stick holds it all—it comes out in dreams and tells you how to complete the ceremony the following day."

TANTARA AS INTIMATE KNOWLEDGE

Still other aspects that link *tantara* and memory are evident in Ramaresaka's use of the word *tantara* in the following passage:

> Some people can explain *tantara,* other people can't. Some people are ashamed to speak and can't find words. Some people grow old, too tired, and can't advise their children. Maybe they even die without having taught their children! Talk like: "This is the way you live, this is the way you make your living, these are the ways of the government, these are the ways to work, these are our roots." Some people don't talk much but do their work. If you live in a place, then you will know. Maybe you hear, maybe you don't—maybe you are still carried away by youth and games. But you don't forget—later, even when your parents are dead, then it all comes back to you. Of all my children, it's Vevette here who will really know ancestral ways.

When I asked her why, she replied, "Because the others left and went away, but she never leaves my sight." By emphasizing the unself-conscious relationship that people have to the past, Ramaresaka uses *tantara* in a way that strongly resembles Halbwachs's and Nora's conception of memory. *Tantara* is here imagined not as grand, heroic, and far away but intimate and mundane. It is not a narrative of the reigns of kings but stories about the generative relationships of one's own parents that seeps into and colors the details of life, such as what one eats or how and where one farms. According to this vision, *tantara* encompasses the implicit, often unarticulated knowledge that comes from watching people die, learning how to behave, and observing things such as how to handle certain violations and which trees to place in particular parts of the house so as not to offend certain tree spirits. It is acquired just by living in a place and paying attention to how things are done, something that is unavoidable if one participates in the daily flow of village life.

The distribution of who knows *tantara* also reveals the connection between memory and *tantara*. Halbwachs claims that the close association of historical narratives with particular families distinguishes memory from history. He observes, "Collective memory differs from history[:] . . . it is a current of continuous thought whose continuity is not at all artificial, for it retains from the past only what still lives or is capable of living in the consciousness of the groups keeping the memory alive. By definition, it does not exceed the boundaries of the group" ([1950] 1980, 80). Likewise, for Betsimisaraka, *tantara* (historical knowledge) and access to power embodied in ancestors are available only to descendants of a given ancestry. Although all the villagers in the town may have heard the story of the Zafimalaone, for example, no one but the *tangalamena* (and other elders) of the Zafimalaone ancestry can legitimately bestow that knowledge on someone else.[29] The stories of the different ancestries in Ambodiharina invariably overlapped and intersected. Often when I discussed one group's history with a *tangalamena,* we would find ourselves on the topic of another's. When this happened the *tangalamena* I was speaking with would invariably tell me to contact the *tangalamena* of the given ancestry and speak directly with him, as he was the only person who could rightfully dispense the knowledge.

TANTARA AS HISTORY

Faced with the social distribution of *tantara,* or Ramaresaka's vision of the past and its integration into the present, it is tempting to conclude that *tantara* is the same thing as memory and that Betsimisaraka do indeed inhabit a *milieu de memoire* as Nora might have predicted. Yet just as certain facets of history—critical distance, the signs of previous historical periods—slip into the ways in which Betsimisaraka build their connections to ancestors *(mahatsiaro),* so they are also visible in local conceptions of *tantara.*

Indeed, as the use of the word *history* to translate *tantara* implies, the word also refers to narratives of past events set within a chronological framework. In particular, one important kind of *tantara* is a chronicle of how specific ancestries came to live in particular places and the order in which these ancestries arrived (see chapter 3). As I mentioned earlier, Betsimisaraka tend to divide the past into the "time of the fighting," the "time of the *vazaha,*" and the "time since the rebellion." Many of the arrival stories I was told were anchored firmly in one of these epochs. Ratsara, for example, described how one of the ancestries in the village he lived in had come there because they had fled bandits farther to the south, a description that probably refers to the "time of fighting." The group had most likely been forced by the social unrest created by slave trading along the east coast to break their ancestral connections and move to a new place (see Larson 2000). Likewise, several ancestries explained the history of their settlement as a direct result of colonial interventions into local life. Take, for example, the story of Vohilava, a town to the west of Ambodiharina and adjacent to the Mangoro River, whose history was told to me by the *tangalamena* Iaba n'i Zakatiana:

> In Vohilava there are two kinds of people, and each used to have their own town. One part was called Vohilava and the other part was called Tanambe. A *chef de canton* came from Ambodiharina and combined the two towns—only a bit of forest separated the two. The *chef de canton,* Petard was his name, came and asked, 'Why is this town divided in two?' And the elders said, 'Those people are from over there in Ambohitsara, and the *vazaha* took their land so they moved here.' So the *chef de canton* said, 'You can't do that, but must make one town of the two parts. You live so close together but act separated. You must join together.' When the towns joined together it became the one long town you see now, and that's why we call it Vohilava [Long Town].

Still other ancestral *tantara* recounted how families had been forced to leave their ancestral fields and join the settlement at Ambodiharina as part of the "thirty-roof law" imposed during the colonial period (see chapter 2). The Zafindrabe family, for example, had previously inhabited a small camp *(toby)* in the marshes to the south, until they were forced to come live in Ambodiharina, in keeping with colonial regulations. Similarly, Botoroa said that his ancestor had begged permission to move their place of residence from Ambodiharina to an area to the west, and had even promised the official that he and his family would be able to fulfill the corvée requirement. In both of these examples the forms of *tantara* clearly have more in common with history than the almost mystical connection to the past that Halbwachs, Nora, and, as should be clear, Betsimisaraka identify as characteristic of memory.

INCIDENTAL HISTORY, DELIBERATE MEMORY

Having reviewed a range of cultural practices through which Betsimisaraka construct their relationship to the past, we are now in a position to characterize Betsimisaraka historical consciousness and how it relates to the events of the colonial period. Juxtaposing a sense of connection to the past with self-conscious inscription and a sense of distance from the past, Betsimisaraka confound the memory/history dichotomy by combining elements of both in novel ways. If the focus on embodied knowledge characteristic of memory pervades some aspects of Betsimisaraka discourse on *tantara* (history), certain facets of remembering *(mahatsiaro)* clearly incorporate the ability to encode specific periods and the critical attitude we have come to think of as characteristic of history.

The Betsimisaraka's practice in regard to the past is aimed less at the commemoration of events or periods than of relationships. The focus on relationships tends to privilege local concerns, but because ancestors were once historical actors whose lives were shaped by particular historical predicaments, the act of commemorating them partially records the periods in which Betsimisaraka have lived. For example, construction of sites of memory—the ways Betsimisaraka have created relationships between ascendants and descendants, the places they are able to build their houses, the kinds of things that make them angry or grateful and cause them to impose taboos—are themselves indicative of a changing world. Moreover, remembering ancestors requires that descendants use diverse media that tend to indicate the predicaments, preferences, and material choices experienced by Betsimisaraka at particular epochs. The colonial past is woven into local practice, but as the context in which the text of ancestral commemoration is played out.

In characterizing the nature of Betsimisaraka historical consciousness, the distinction made by psychologists between deliberate and incidental memory proves useful. To deliberately remember how to get to your friend's house means to make remembering the directions to the house the deliberate goal of the action. If on the way you pass the house you lived in as a child and remember your childhood, then that memory of your childhood is called incidental memory: it is incidental to the deliberate goal of getting to your friend's house. The memory of your childhood tags along, so to speak, with the memory of how to get to your friend's house. In keeping with the memory/history distinction I have used here, we might think of Betsimisaraka constructions of the past as intentional memory and incidental history: what is aimed at is connection to ancestors, but those connections are themselves historically mediated. I should stress the fact that to say that Betsimisaraka's historical consciousness is incidental to the work of connecting with ancestors is not to say that it does not matter. Rather, my intent is to suggest that historical consciousness emerges from people's efforts to connect with ancestors, for as they work (even ambivalently) to create an unchanging connection to the past, people are constantly faced with the reality of change. This gap appears to entail a particular bittersweet structure of feeling that, if not quite captured in the term *nostalgia,* is certainly a poignant awareness of the passing of time that many scholars have identified as characteristically modern (Osborne 1995). The essence of Betsimisaraka historical consciousness is that, although they desire and fear connection to ancestors, they live with the knowledge that perfect connection can never be achieved.

CHAPTER 5

The Power in the Past and the Colonial in the Ancestral

Public concerns with memory . . . can be considered
screens on which a culture projects its anxieties about
repetition, change, representation, authenticity and
identity.
                                        —*Michael S. Roth*

The last chapter examined the practices through which Betsimisaraka historical consciousness takes shape; this chapter addresses the complementary questions of how these practices articulate with the social hierarchy and how Betsimisaraka try to manipulate their links to the past in their daily lives. The following discussion of how Betsimisaraka use the past complements the insights provided by the previous chapter in several ways. First, analysis of local forms of historical representation reveals that Betsimisaraka value connections with ancestors, but this analysis does not tell us why this should be the case. Second, my discussion in the preceding chapter shows that Betsimisaraka have several practices for shaping memory and for deliberately trying to make people reproduce the past, but these practices alone do not tell us much about change. However, more than the process of reproducing the past is at stake; after all, if Betsimisaraka really did endlessly accumulate their parents' taboos and farm only their land, eventually they would be so circumscribed they could not move. Finally, although I have shown that ancestral sites of memory encode the colonial past, I have not explored *how* this process actually happened. The key to understanding these interrelated processes is the local negotiation of two different kinds of power: the power people perceive to be rooted in ancestors, and the power of colonial settlers and the state.

Looking at how people try to use and manipulate the power of the past also helps illuminate how the ancestral and colonial pasts became entangled with one another in the production of Ambodiharina as a particular kind of locality. In Ambodiharina, the practices through which people construct locality are bound up in the ways in which both individuals and communities seek to realize particular projects, a process that requires people to harness the power of the past. Over time, colonial power has become deeply implicated in this process. I should emphasize, however, that there is nothing historical about these processes in the sense that history is over and done with. Rather, the processes critical to how colonial power was woven into ancestral memories are ongoing ones, as a current generation of Betsimisaraka take advantage of new sources of power made available in the postcolonial era.[1]

ANCESTRAL *HASINA* AND THE SOCIAL ORDER

To understand how ancestral and colonial pasts have become entangled in the creation of Ambodiharina and their subsequent evocation, we must begin by considering the practices associated with people's assumptions about how to obtain a happy life and the forces that constrain their ability to do so. Betsimisaraka conceive of power in terms of a shapeless essence or force, called *hasina*. In daily discourse, Betsimisaraka repeatedly emphasize ancestors when they talk about *hasina*. As I was told again and again, "The ancestors have *hasina* above all other things. They have honor and respect, as they are one with God, the place from whence we spring." More generally, Betsimisaraka say that *hasina* is first produced through ancestors' mundane actions while they are alive, then simply by virtue of their death. In other words, through daily activities like farming rice, building houses, producing and raising children, and dying, ancestors imbue the land and village around them with their *hasina*.

The problem from the descendants' point of view is that the ancestral *hasina* inherent in the world they are born into is never stable or fixed. Rather, it is likely to diminish, even disappear, if it is not maintained. The need to "remember" ancestors in order to maintain their power is an important mechanism that forces people to partially reproduce the past. Though the association between power and memory pervades Betsimisaraka practice in relation to all of the sites of memory examined in

the last chapter, the practice of spirit possession and other kinds of healing helps illuminate the workings of one facet of the underlying logic.

THE DYNAMICS OF RECIPROCAL MEMORY: SPIRIT POSSESSION AND HEALING

In much of the literature on Madagascar as well as other parts of Africa,
spirit possession is a key practice through which people construct historical consciousness of the past—including the colonial past.[2] In Ambodiharina, however, this is not the case. Rather, spirits are usually
identified as either wood or water sprites or people's ancestors, though
these ancestors are never identified in any specific historical way. Talk
about spirit possession is more a way of imagining the nature of ancestral power than it is about remembering or reconfiguring the colonial
past, a process that takes place through cattle sacrifice, as we shall see.[3]

People refer to spirits who possess people as *biby, tromba,* or *raharaha.*
Since there happens to be no *tromba* leader in Ambodiharina, there is
no organized context for possession, and people only rarely and spontaneously become possessed during ancestral ceremonies. For the most
part, possession remains latent, a potential that people talk about a lot
when referring to why some people are sick or have good luck. Many
people believe that descendants are especially vulnerable to inheriting
spirits from people with whom they had been particularly intimate. Nirina, for example, acquired her grandmother's spirit when she was caring for her grandmother while she was terminally ill: the spirit "moved"
(mifindra) from her grandmother to Nirina. Rahely, another young
woman, occasionally became possessed by her grandmother's spirit.
People said that the grandmother had loved to dance and so would show
herself on happy occasions. Ramaresaka similarly expressed the idea that
possession and memory of ancestors are linked, when she insisted that
possession was one way for ancestors to "remember" their descendants.

The basic premise underlying the practice of spirit possession in Ambodiharina is that people gain power by allowing their bodies to become
vessels through which the ancestral past inhabits the living present.
Ngelina, for example, once told me about a woman who lived in a neighboring town who had had a "spirit standing on her," and that, because
she had obeyed its taboos, the spirit had given her a bull that appeared
mysteriously from the sea. A stipulation was that she had to lend the bull
to whomever wanted to take it to trample rice fields, for example, so

long as they brought it back to her at night. No one, Ngelina insisted, had seen the bull arrive. The woman had received an order from her *tromba* to build a corral, and all of a sudden the bull appeared. Ngelina finished the story by nodding at me conspiratorially: "You know," he said, "if you get a *tromba* and obey its taboos, they bring you great wealth."

Ramaresaka made the connection among spirit possession, remembering ancestors, and power even more explicit: "Some people remove *tromba*, get rid of ancestral trouble. There are people who want to eat pork [the most common food taboo imposed by *tromba*] and they come and try to get rid of it. It's a spirit they say, all lies! Yet it's an ancestor standing, remembering themselves in your body. Some ancestors give blessing, others make you sick, but both of them you get rid of because you can't stand not eating pork. Yet sometimes they bless you, maybe you give birth to many, many children and not one dies." Ramaresaka returned to the topic some months later. "Ancestors," she explained, "had family, children, and grandchildren who lived here, and at times they 'remember' their children and show themselves to their children in dreams." She went on to say:

> If it is a good dream, then you know it signals ancestral blessing. You think of them, "Ah, mama showed herself to me, there wasn't anything wrong, I just saw her." The first time I gave birth alone, my grandmother showed herself to me—my father's mother, and she was a famous midwife and knew how to birth people, like a *sage femme*. And when I bore Njira, my daughter, she appeared to me; that very night I gave birth. We came up to town [from the hut in the fields]. "Who to get as a midwife, who to get?" everybody was asking. "Don't bother, I said, I'll bear her myself." My three brothers-in-law were there in the great house and I was in the kitchen—there were many people gathered. I bore the child and went to get the placenta: I pushed and pushed below my navel and it slipped out and I turned it over and looked at it to make sure nothing remained inside, but it had all come off. And I cut the umbilical cord, cut it myself, master of the child [*tompon ny zaza*]. I washed the baby and tied her umbilical cord with thread and put her down and I slept. My brother-in-law asked me where I would lie-in, at the center or at the hearth, and since I'm not tabooed from being at the head of the hearth I stayed there. My ancestor's arrival gave me the force to cut my own child's umbilical cord. She remembered me: "I choose to place my force in your hands," she said. So now I've helped to bring forth many children while on this earth, and never hesitated but helped deliver many children.

The empowering nature of reciprocal memory holds equally true for other kinds of non-*tromba*-inspired healing as well. For example, for the Zafindralemy, a Betsimisaraka clan famed as bonesetters and masseurs, it is the explicit recognition of the power of ancestors that gives certain members of the lineage the power to heal. All a family member had to do was go to an elder and place a coin in the palm of that person's hand and request a blessing, at which point the elder was supposed to transmit ancestral power by saying, "I place the power of my hands in you." Similarly, Tsaravintana claimed that although one could learn the techniques of divination by studying, the real ability to heal simply came from ancestors. It was the submission to ancestral dictates, the recognition of their power, that gave healers the ability to cure others and earn a bit of money for themselves.

In light of this equation between commemorating ancestors and getting their power, the emphasis on memory *(mahatsiaro)*, addressed in the last chapter, becomes clear. Betsimisaraka have a vested interest in attempting to reproduce what Pierre Nora (1989) characterizes as a *milieu de memoir*, for it is in sustaining ancestors' memories that the power required to maintain a happy life is achieved. Yet as I have suggested, striking the delicate balance between remembering ancestors and becoming consumed by their memories is always tricky. Again, people's talk about spirit possession gives some idea of the dilemmas involved. The case of Nirina, who had inherited her grandmother's spirit, is an apt example. The spirit symbolized her closeness to ancestors because it had been inherited from her grandmother. In reality, however, the spirit was more a curse than a blessing, because it was apparently a spirit that hated the excrement and urine associated with children and made Nirina unable to carry a pregnancy to term.

Even Ramaresaka, who tended to sentimentalize the potential benefits of ancestral memory and castigate the laziness of the living who failed to protect it, described the negative side of *tromba* when I asked her why she did not take part in the spirit possession parties that were so popular in villages upcountry:

> Some people with *tromba* hold parties *[mirombo]* in the new moon, but I don't do that. Each to their own spirit, and each to their own way. *Tromba* upcountry like lots of noise, but the ones here don't like it so much. You have to be careful—you get sick and then they "sit" on your children. That's how it went with me. My grandmother on my mother's side, when she had just died her *tromba* "sat" on me. I couldn't see it, it just came. But for it to sit on your children while you are still living? I was sick for three months, shat blood. It wasn't in a celebration but in illness that it first appeared, and that's why I don't *mirombo*. A woman cared for me; she said to stop eating pork and I did. That is when they first came out—some of them I don't even know what language they speak; maybe it's my great ancestors from across the water.

Ancestral memory is double-edged. If one side is about descendants remembering ancestors and getting their power, the other side is about ancestors remembering that they have descendants whom they can control. In this respect, Betsimisaraka practice is similar to what David Graeber (1995) argues for Imerina, where memories of ancestors are always contiguous with the violence they might inflict. It is as if human attention alone makes power benevolent; some people I knew claimed that pieces of land or even old standing stones that were not cared for anymore became cruel *(masiaka)* because they lacked a master or someone who tended them.

LOCALIZING POWER: HOUSES

Though local conceptions of spirit possession illuminate the way remembering stands as a local gloss on what power means and how it works, ideas about spirit possession fail to convey the intensely localizing nature of ancestral power. As occurs in many other parts of Madagascar, Betsimisaraka ancestors express their power by pulling people back to a center, rather than by policing boundaries (see also Lambek and Walsh 1997; Graeber 1995). The practices surrounding houses and tombs best illustrate this aspect of ancestral power. As I suggested in the previous chapter, the need to maintain ancestral *hasina* in houses and tombs causes ancestral sites of memory to pull descendants to them like magnets, rather than letting them scatter and create new sites of memory of their own. The intensely localizing power of one's father's past projects sedimented in particular sites is particularly evident in the case of Girard, a man who lived in a village to the south, whom I first learned about from Tsaravintana. I had come home from the fields with Ramaresaka to find Girard slumped in one corner looking depressed and Tsaravintana, the divination beads spread out before him, explaining to Girard the precise cause of his sickness. Later Tsaravintana explained to me what had happened:

> Girard is the son of my sister. When he was still tiny, his father, who had been a teacher, died, while in the midst of trying to complete a house with a corrugated tin roof. Since Girard and his siblings were too young to live on their own, their father's brother raised them. As an adult, Girard was aware that he should complete the house, but didn't have control of the money to do so. Eventually, when he was old enough, he obtained his father's pension. Soon after, however, he fell sick because his father's ghost wanted him to complete the house. Though he is working on the house now and has almost finished it, he fell sick yet again because his father's ghost is angry that he hasn't finished

it quickly enough. He thus came to me seeking medicine against blame *[ody tsiny]* to try and stave off his father's demands until he can gather the material resources necessary to complete the house and hold the house-opening ceremony.

Girard's case clearly shows how the power embedded in Girard's father's memory forced Girard to spend the inherited pension on completing his dead father's project. But even completion of the house was not enough, for his father's ghost expected him to live in the house as well. Since Girard would have preferred to live in Ambodiharina, where he had kin on his mother's side, he assuaged his sense of displacement by visiting Ambodiharina frequently. I would inevitably find him ensconced in the local *betsa* shop, talking and drinking *betsa* at the end of the day; but only a few days would pass before he would be forced back to his father's home in the south yet again.

Drawing on the ideas of Michel Foucault (1988), we might characterize this close connection between power and the practices associated with remembering ancestors as a particular kind of technology of the self. As I mentioned earlier, Foucault sees the production of subjectivity as fundamentally tied to processes of knowledge production through which people become conscious of themselves as subjects. Technologies of the self are one particular kind of technique "which permit individuals to effect by their own means or with the help of others a certain number of operations on their own bodies and souls, thoughts, conduct and way of being, so as to transform themselves in order to attain a certain state of happiness, purity, wisdom, perfection or immortality." Foucault further suggests that each technology "implies certain modes of training and modification of individuals, not only in the obvious sense of acquiring certain skills but also in the sense of acquiring certain attitudes" (18). In Ambodiharina, the power of ancestors is closely tied into the practices through which they are remembered. In turn, remembering ancestors works as a powerful technique of the self because people produce themselves as particular kinds of subjects through the work of remembering their ancestors, which, as I have described, pervades people's lives in multiple ways.

HASINA IN THE WORLD AT LARGE

The ancestral power–memory *(hasina)* that is so highly constraining, which draws descendants in to support the projects of their dead ancestors, exists in tension with other kinds of *hasina* that people perceive to exist out in the world. Betsimisaraka say *hasina* exists naturally in the rocks, trees, streams, and rivers, all of which are potentially powerful. One study of the inhabitants of the far northeast of Madagascar mentions a man who, while looking out over the landscape beyond his house, remarked, "It's all *fanafody* [medicine]" (Hurvitz 1980, 65). Though the man referred particularly to the natural potential for making charms, his statement indicates more generally that anything—rocks, trees, water, spots of land—may potentially prove a source of power and potency. The Betsimisaraka I knew would agree. Moreover, because of their long history of interaction with powerful outsiders, villagers remain keenly aware that other people and their practices hold power as well.

Though Betsimisaraka distinguish in rhetoric between *hasina* in ancestors and *hasina* derived from other sources, actual practice blurs the distinction on several counts. First, the *hasina* that inheres in ancestors, the *hasina* that derives from trees and rocks, and even the *hasina* said to inhere in certain practices are not qualitatively different. They are dangerous, yet generative, forms of power and potential that may lead to the realization of one's desires and yet always need to be appeased. More important for my argument here, "nonancestral" *hasina* can become appropriated and "ancestralized" through people's attempts to lead fulfilled lives—that is, through their attempts to find new sources of power and harness them to their particular projects for personal fulfillment, which eventually include the act of constructing themselves as powerful ancestors.

For example, people say that one reason the Mangoro River is powerful is because of the ancestors who dwell there. As we saw in chapter 3, the Zafimalaone gained control of the Mangoro through military conquest, but in official discourse villagers naturalized the Zafimalaone's power by saying it was simply a result of ancestral *hasina*. As Rafaly, the wayward *tangalamena* of the Zafimalaone ancestry, proudly explained, "The Mangoro gets its *hasina* from the strength of ancestors. All ancestors are powerful, but the ancestors of the Zafimalaone were powerful in the water. In the days before, there were many bandits who came to attack. The Zafimalaone ancestors would order their cattle to travel by water rather than on land to avoid the attackers. No matter who else claims they derive power from the water, if they aren't the descendants of the Zafimalaone then their words don't have *hasina*." What Rafaly did not say is that the power of *hasina* can move two ways. If people sometimes appropriate *hasina* "out there" and make it ancestral, then so too over the course of generations, as the power of a family waxes and wanes, what was once the *hasina* of specific ancestors becomes naturalized, a part of the landscape in which people live. For example, Liliane once told me that when she had lived in their house located to the south, she kept dreaming of a little girl whom she assumed used to live there; it was as if the spirit of the dead girl had become a part of the land. Likewise, it is not inconceivable that, some time in the future, people living in Ambodiharina will say that there is *hasina* in the Mangoro but will not connect that *hasina* to the Zafimalaone.

The intersection of ancestral and nonancestral *hasina,* and the struggles that occur as people seek to draw nonancestral *hasina* under their control in order to make it part of their social world, lies at the heart of Betsimisaraka political process. At the same time, this interplay between ancestral and nonancestral *hasina* accounts for the fact that translocal processes like colonialism have helped constitute Ambodiharina. The basic tension that runs throughout local practice is between sources of power that derive from the accumulated actions of one's ancestors and those that exist outside ancestors but have the potential to enable people to create new and different futures. In order to understand the interplay between the two, we must pause for a moment to consider two other factors, what Betsimisaraka refer to as *rangitra* and what Stanley Tambiah (1985) once aptly dubbed the "magical power of words."

RANGITRA

The first factor that significantly shapes people's ability to access and profit from power embodied in places is their *rangitra*. Simply put, *rangitra* is the spirit that accompanies each living being, tree, and rock and that makes specific people and sites powerful. One *tangalamena* described the concept of *rangitra* as follows: "*Rangitra* is the spirit that lives with people from the time they are small until they die. It is the *rangitra* that makes small children play and speak to themselves. You know, when you see children playing, talking to themselves, that's their *rangitra* they speak to. God [Zanahary] only looks and sees where you go, but the *rangitra* goes with you everywhere and protects you. You seek money and you find it, seek rice and have a good harvest, seek health and never fall sick. Your *rangitra* makes that happen." Many Betsimisaraka believe that the true productive potential in each person is unlocked when an individual is able to pair his or her *rangitra* with a person, place, even a house that has the same, or complementary, *rangitra*. If a person moves out to clear new land and brings in particularly good harvests, it is believed that the land is of "one *rangitra*" with the person. Or if someone lives in a house for a long time and bears many children, people will say the *rangitra* of the house and the person go well together. Conversely, if later someone else moves in and does not prosper, people will say that the house's *rangitra* does not go well with that of the new person. These same conceptions operate in assessing marriage. For example, if a couple is married and always has good harvests, then people will say they are of one *rangitra*. The idea suggests matching and fulfillment. Conversely, if the man leaves and marries a new woman but then brings in a bad harvest, people will say their individual *rangitra* do not combine well. For married couples whose *rangitra* are poorly matched for whatever reasons, ritual intervention through a diviner or a *tromba* expert is required.

The following story reveals some of the ways that people use *rangitra* to explain either compatibility or misfortune. One day as I returned from a trip to town, Nirina, Ramaresaka and Tsaravintana's daughter, greeted me with the news that their puppy, the black one with the white stripe on its head, had died. Its *rangitra* had killed it, she said. Puzzled, I asked Tsaravintana what she meant.

> That puppy has a *jiny* [a word occasionally used in place of *rangitra*], he's "strong headed"; there is a powerful spirit in him. But that dog, its markings, the white stripe on the black face, are those of a cow—for a dog to have that kind of a marking is to steal another's fate [*mangalatra anjara*]. So his *jiny* killed him, as they decide your fate. If your *jiny* is strong and good, then you will flourish with lots of rice and all your children will thrive. The *jiny* leads you to good fortune—rice, coffee, money, children. All living people have them. You see how Tovolahy and Babette are getting on so well now? It's because they purged themselves of illness. For a while there, when they lost the canoe and the fishing net, they were constantly fighting. Tovolahy would take [FMG .50] for cigarettes and Babette would get mad at him; so I made them apologize to the ancestors and Zanahary for their fights, to spray water [*mamafy rano*] on one another. And now they no longer fight but confer and get along on everything. "That is what we must do to make ourselves living," they say, and so they have the same *rangitra*. They are of the same mind and life becomes easy.

Babette's and Tovolahy's petty marital disagreements, attributed to incompatible *rangitra*, proved relatively easy to cure. Other couples, however, suffered more severely from the problem of ill-matched *rangitra*. In one case, a girl I knew married and became repeatedly pregnant, but all of her children were either miscarried or stillborn. The couple's failure to produce a healthy child was attributed to incompatible *rangitra*, and the couple was ultimately persuaded by their parents to divorce and marry other people, with whom they each managed to successfully reproduce.

The concept of *rangitra* is used to explain both good and bad fortune, or why it is that one person is able to do something and another is not. The infinite variety of *rangitra,* some weak and others strong, some good and others bad, explains why the same people may farm the same piece of land but one brings in an excellent harvest while the other brings in a mediocre one. The emphasis on difference, individual fate, and fortune exists within families as well as between them. Parents, for example, are said to have *rangitra* different from that of their children. As Ramaresaka explained, "Some parents have cattle and rice fields that they leave to their children. And the children squander it all. The cattle die, they sell off the rice fields—they don't have the same *rangitra* as the parents for making things flourish." Even children of "one stomach"—the colloquial term for children born of the same mother, an important expression of shared identity—have different *rangitra*. As Liliane put it, "Many people of one stomach all go out to search for fish in the water, and some get fish while others don't, but it's the same water and they all go together—that is *rangitra*." Alternatively, when people begin to explain unfortunate outcomes—such as why they went fishing in the same stream as everyone else but did not get any fish—they might say their *rangitra* had fought, and that another's had won. Similarly, people often put duck eggs in with chicken eggs for a hen to brood. Either the ducklings or the chicks would survive but never both, because their *rangitra* would fight.

Rangitra are critical to the process of self-fulfillment because they enable people to take advantage of *hasina* inherent in the natural or social world. The fruitful coupling of *rangitra,* often achieved through speech, is perceived as finding one's true lot or portion in life *(anjara),* the unlocking of the productive potential of *hasina* through pairing with another (see also Feeley-Harnik 1991).

UNLOCKING *HASINA*: THE MAGICAL POWER OF WORDS

A final principle that underlies people's attempts to access *hasina* is the potential for speech to call forth the power of *hasina* in the world. Concern with speaking and hearing is widespread in Betsimisaraka practice and evident in many facets of daily life, the most pervasive and mundane

being the elaborate greeting etiquette used throughout southern Betsimisaraka country. Louis Catat, writing in the nineteenth century, described the practice:

> The Merina walks silently by you but the Betanimena gives you a *finaritra*
> [literally, pleasing].[4] Sometimes two natives walking in opposite directions
> will stop and put down their burdens and chat. To see them absorbed in in-
> terminable conversation one would think they are the oldest friends but it
> is not so; indeed frequently they have never met before. According to the
> customs of the country one tells the other from whence he comes, where he
> goes, the purpose of his trip, [and] interesting news along the way. In order
> to remember it the second repeats to the first everything he has said and the
> first speaker corrects him at each point. Once this has been accomplished
> the second begins his personal account and the other repeats it. This is how
> they spread news. This method is inconveniently long[,] but it must be ob-
> served that time has no great value among the Betanimena. (1895, 123)

Although *finaritra* has fallen out of fashion and is only occasionally
used by old men at ceremonies when they self-consciously play up and
exaggerate their proximity to ancestors, a similar style of greeting, including an elaborate call and response, continues to be used today. The
point I wish to emphasize here is that repetition is important in validat-
ing a speaker's words because it shows that the listener has in fact heard.[5]
Speech requires an answer in order to validate it, to render it meaningful. Drink formally presented to guests has to be "announced" and "responded" to; merely to drink without speech means that the relationship implied by presenting rum does not exist. Similarly, in any kind of
group meeting, etiquette demands that one person speaks and then someone, often the eldest present, answers, beginning his response with
"Words not answered are terribly difficult." Answering the words means
the speech was really made; only crazy people speak alone. It is the formal speech and the response that together make relationships socially
recognized, in essence giving them *hasina*.

Words are used to "awaken" and activate powers inherent in objects
as well as ancestors. For example, the diviner chants, "Wake up, wake
up, wake up!" to the divination beads as he stirs them before sorting
them out. Likewise, speech is used to communicate with ancestors. For
example, people use speech to invoke ancestors in order to inform them
about small household matters. More dramatic is the piercing yell that
the *tangalamena* lets out *(mikoka)* when, and only when, he wants to
get the ancestors' attention. Finally, the power of speech is most dramatically revealed in the long speech given by the *tangalamena* to the

ancestors just prior to the sacrifice of a bull, in which the "sadness of a family" is communicated directly to Zanahary and the ancestors.

Once uttered, spoken words take on a force of their own that extends beyond the context of their utterance. The ability of words to have a material effect on the world means that people feel ambivalent about conditions that cause them to lose control over words. For example, when women or men first approach a dead relative they often break out into a keening song, telling the deceased about their memories and beseeching them to carry messages to other dead relatives. People explain that the bereaved person's emotions "grew too much" and forced them to speak. In general, however, women are perceived socially as more emotional and thus more liable to create trouble through their inability to control their tongues (see also Keenan 1974). By contrast, men are perceived as having greater control of words, and their ability to control their words and temper is one of the ways people construct men as subjects fit to hold the power associated with ancestral knowledge.

Whether words escape unbidden in grief or anger or are uttered intentionally as a vow to a rock or tree, their power to awaken and call forth *hasina* that may otherwise lie dormant in ancestors and things can never be taken lightly. In daily intercourse people are tremendously careful of what they say to and about one another because they know that idle words might actually make something happen; one definition of a child is someone who speaks without thinking. Thus, to talk about someone's hypothetical death comes close to murder. One way to prove one's innocence when wrongly accused is by swearing on water, thunder, or ancestors *(mifanta)*; people assume that if the person is guilty, the power that the words awaken will kill him or her. Likewise, as I mentioned in chapter 3, to talk about someone's success is one way to draw the attention of ancestors to him or her, a theme I will return to in more detail in chapter 6. For instance, I once asked Josef about rumors in town that a certain *tangalamena*, who was quite a theatrical and gifted speech maker, was going to sponsor a circumcision celebration. He did not dare ask him, Josef said, as to do so would be to "awaken illness." Another time Josef told me that one of his more distant nephews, a *tangalamena* from another ancestry, came to him to ask about the original site of their prayer post *(jiro)*. Josef knew that the original site of the post was now a trash heap where children defecated and adults urinated. He chose to keep quiet, however, because he knew that his speech would provoke the ancestors to demand a bull to remove the filth and dishonor brought about by forgetting.

In sum, voice is one of the ways in which the power of *hasina* is awakened and brought into the social world. People try to control *hasina* through vows or by invocation; but outcomes are never certain, because, to be effective, speech must be heard not only by living witnesses but by the ancestors. The effect of speaking to ancestors (or rocks and trees) is always ambiguous, because you find out only later if "they" were listening or not. There is always the possibility that, despite your best efforts, the ancestors will turn a deaf ear. Likewise, there is always the possibility that the rock or tree you invoke will not be powerful *(masina)* after all, at least for you.

APPROPRIATING POWER: REPRODUCTION AND TRANSFORMATION

Having shown how local ideas about prosperity and social reproduction are rooted in ancestors, we are now in a position to consider the fact that, when people reproduce local contexts, the contingencies of history mean that they also inevitably produce new contexts (Appadurai 1996; Sahlins 1985). The distinction between ancestral and nonancestral forms of *hasina,* mentioned earlier, is central to the process of creating local history, because Betsimisaraka may choose to move away from ancestral locations when they are able to appropriate sources of power outside the ancestral domain. The central dynamic is one of periods of stasis combined with movements across the land. The discovery of new forms of *hasina* is always a potential threat to the reproduction of ancestral memories. While sometimes these new sources of power are incorporated into preexisting local structures, thus building up old ancestral sites of memory, at other times they enable people to create new sites of memory of their own, which always entails the potential erasure of the sites of memory left behind.

VOWS

Perhaps the most common way people try to gain access to *hasina* is through vows, a practice in which people use speech to awaken the powers that inhere in particular places. When the vow is successful, and the person actually obtains what was wished for, people typically say it was because of complementary *rangitra* that a particular object or place proved efficacious for a particular person. For our purposes here, two kinds of vows must be distinguished. On the one hand, some vows are made to sites of ancestral memory, like houses or tombs. These vows exemplify how people draw on ancestral power in negotiating daily life. On the other hand, there are vows made to new sources of *hasina*—such as a rock or tree or piece of land—and these vows always have the potential for subverting the ancestral order.

Vows to Ancestral Sites of Memory   Vows are made for every sort of endeavor undertaken by people, but some of the most common are requests for children or some kind of administrative post or honor. Another frequent theme is the tensions and trials created by villagers' inevitable and necessary, yet uneasy and vulnerable, connections to the wider world of which they are a part. There are two steps to any vow: making it and, later, fulfilling it. While smaller vows may be fulfilled using honey or fabric, more important vows require the sacrifice of a bull. Typically a person who wants to make a vow seeks out his or her *tangalamena,* either the one associated with the mother's or the one associated with the father's house, depending on which ancestors the person wants to invoke; the *tangalamena* then calls various people to act as witnesses. If the person making the vow arrives at the home of the *tangalamena* unexpectedly, this could merely mean that he calls over his wife and children sitting in the yard or cooking in the kitchen next door. Though the haphazard calling in of any available person appears to be no more than the casual throwing together of a group, it is critical to the efficacy of a vow that others *watch* it occur. Honey and rum are placed on an eating mat in front of the eastern door, the ancestors are called, and the request made. Witnesses then drink rum to seal the vow.

The story of Reni Rasoa gives some of the flavor of a common vow. Reni Rasoa was the widow of the former *chef de canton,* a government functionary, and thus entitled to his pension after his death. However, she found that dealings with the Malagasy bureaucracy were slow and difficult at best, an impossibly complicated waste of time and money at worst. For years Reni Rasoa tried without success to get her husband's pension. Eventually she vowed to her husband's great house that if she succeeded in receiving the pension she would give the ancestors three bottles of *toaka* rum and three bottles of *betsa,* to be drunk in the house built by her husband. Shortly thereafter, Reni Rasoa borrowed enough money to go up to Antananarivo to see the government officials responsible for the pension. She returned two months later, the voyage having taken considerably longer than she had planned, with the money in hand. The next week, we were all called to the great house to witness as she "paid" the vow *(manefa voady)*.

Frequently those forced by livelihood or circumstance to live outside their ancestral homeland *(tanin-drazana)* make vows while away from home, which they then fulfill upon safe arrival in their natal village. The story of Babette's father, Zafisoa, provides one example. Zafisoa had joined Ratsiraka's special army (the RESEP), as had several of the villagers. To be a member of this special group and to serve Ratsiraka was considered a great honor, given the association between serving Ratsiraka, who claimed Betsimisaraka ethnic identity, and serving one's ancestral homeland. At the time of the fulfillment of the vow in 1993, Zafisoa had been away from the village for several years. During his posting in Tulear, Ratsiraka's troops fought with opposition party groups (Forces Vives). Upon his return to the village in 1993, Zafisoa gathered many people together in his father's house, which in this case was not the official great house.[6] His cousin Telolahy, who controlled the ancestral house, spoke, announcing to the assembled group the reason they had been called.[7] He explained how Zafisoa had lived far away in the province of Tulear, and how scared he had become during his work in the army, causing him to make the vow. He concluded by saying he was now fulfilling the vow.

In these examples, the vows were made to ancestral sites of memory. For Reni Rasoa and Zafisoa, the aim was to draw on ancestral *hasina* in the fulfillment of private ambitions, and both of them "returned to the root" to pay their debts. Neither of these vows was particularly radical, because both implicitly upheld the established ancestral order by reinforcing the power embedded in sites of ancestral memory.

Vows That Awaken Power "Out There"   The stakes are different, however, when people discover new sources of *hasina* that exist out in the world. Take the following example. I had come to the small village of Niarovana, to watch the sacrifice of a bull that was to take place not in town, as was customary for celebrations, but at the sponsor's house in the fields. The man who was holding the sacrifice, who also happened to act as his own speech maker, explained the motivation behind the sacrifice: "We have cultivated here and have borne children—eleven children all born here—and they all lived, and whatever we attempted to do prospered. We built a house in town. It was finished, and the spirit in the land spoke to us: 'If you've fulfilled your heart's will, your children number eleven, your grandchildren five, your fields are prospering, then it is because of us, and we beg you—give to us, for you have flourished.'"

This man's speech reveals a striking example of getting lucky and find-ing *hasina* "out there." The real power generating prosperity was that of the spirits that lived in the land. In this case the spirits were of "one *rangitra*" with the man, and this helped him realize his personal ambi-tions for prosperity. Tavo Robert, one of the local elders, explained why the man had to thank the spirit through sacrifice:

> Living people, according to what makes them living people, must search, search for that which they can do to benefit themselves and their descendants. There is the land—forest, a forest of palm, and the man comes seeking and cuts it down, clears it and cultivates that which he desires to plant there. At first he plants all kinds of things on the land, but what he really seeks is that crop which will bring him money—coffee or cloves or pepper—those crops that will benefit him he must plant. But the meaning of the coffee sacrifice is this: It is not the coffee that begs and needs a cow but the land on which it is planted, where it was slashed and dug and worked, the forest that is cut down on which to plant—land is powerfully efficacious *[masina]* and you turn it topsy-turvy! There are Malagasy customs [e.g., divination, or *sikidy*]; and you do that and the spirit on the land appears. The spirit says, "There was forest here and you came and cut and burned and planted, and we helped you and bless you in this place. The thanks you must give is to sacrifice a bull to me." That's what the spirit in the land says through the *sikidy*—it's the *sikidy* that tells you, makes it happen that way. And some people don't learn through divination but it comes to them in their dreams. The ancestors become dreams in your head and they tell you, "You've benefited a lot from that land: there is something there that has blessed you and given you a good harvest from this forest, from us, so now you give to us too."

Josef echoed Tavo Robert's words when I returned to Ambodiharina af-ter the sacrifice and went immediately, as I always did, to tell him what I had seen. His comments only further emphasized the power of nonances-tral spirits in the creation of prosperity, which was always read as evi-dence of *hasina:* "It's not your own will that makes you prosper, but the creature *[biby]* that lives in the land that pushes good things on you. It's like someone who raises you and cares for you—the luck that comes from the land. Here you are, searching for something, and that which you seek is given. If you don't give back, then the creature may push illness on you too. They would say, 'You promised and now you've lied to us and we've been waiting here,' and all of a sudden you can't seem to get well but are constantly sick." As Josef's words imply, the spirits who inhabit the land—who complement personal *rangitra,* thus enabling people to realize their ambitions and achieve prosperity—are not unstinting in their generosity. Their gifts of fortune, like the gifts that one receives from an-cestors, are always exacted at a price: they call for a sacrifice in return.

Since one must always invoke not only the spirit in the land but Zanahary and the ancestors as well, sacrifices break new ground, marking dominion over the land, the movement from space to place, in Michel de
Certeau's terms (1984). In turn, the sacrifice creates the necessary pre-
conditions for the creation of future households and new ancestries. As
a result, new forms of *hasina* and the sacrifices they generate hold potentially larger, historical consequences.

Briefly put, a successful scenario might look like this: a man goes out
to farm, finds a place in which he prospers, and settles down. Eventually, the spirit in the land demands that a sacrifice be made in payment
for the good fortune and prosperity it has fostered. Because *hasina* must
be honored at the place where it is found, the sacrifice must necessarily
take place at the actual site from which one has profited. To do otherwise is implicitly to give the honor and respect to another place, a huge
insult to the spirit from whom one actually derived some benefit and likely
to provoke retribution. When I asked Tavo Robert why the man in
Niarovana had sacrificed his bull out in their camp in the fields, rather
than in town, his response made clear the importance of honoring the
particular place: "Why did they sacrifice the bull here and not in town?
Terribly difficult!" (He whistled slowly under his breath.) "The land begs
for a bull yet you sacrifice the bull in town? Not permissible. Like a vow—
if you make a vow to a tree, then you sacrifice the bull at that tree, if the
vow is made at a stone, then at the stone you fulfill your vow. If you
make a vow at the great house, then you fulfill it there; but you can't
change the place of payment. It is the spirit in this land, not the ancestors, who beg for the bull."

Though no one would dare voice such a thought, sacrifice marks the
moment of ancestral conquest and appropriation, because henceforth the
prosperity will be seen as stemming from ancestors and not the spirits
of the land, a point that resonates with Maurice Bloch's observation
(1986) that, in Merina ritual, violence done to substances representing
nature symbolically appropriates natural power into the social world of
descent. After the sacrifice, as with any sacrifice, the bull's tail and horns
are hung at the top of the house as proof to God and any passersby that
the sacrifice was indeed carried out. The effect of this practice is to mark
the house as a great house, which in turn suggests that the eldest male
who inhabits it is a *tangalamena*. Though no division may occur at the
time, the scene is already set, for the moment there is an internal conflict
the man who has the house can always decide that the conditions are
right to seize control of his own ancestors and move away.

The link between fulfilling vows in sacrifice and drawing the lines of future division is evident in the following story. Botomena, the *tangala-mena* from a neighboring town, once told me that he had explicitly forbade his brother to throw a circumcision celebration in Ambodiharina. When he realized that the celebration was to be in part the fulfillment of a vow, he acquiesced because he knew that to prevent his brother was to place him at risk for ancestral retribution. But he warned his brother of the danger involved: "Remember what I say now in the morning, for if those who've seen with their eyes have gone [i.e., if all witnesses are dead], then the children will say, "We'll make standing [a great house] of our own."

Since either seizing one's ancestors for one's own projects or moving away from home and fulfilling one's fate inevitably implies division, either act potentially leads to conflict with the ancestors and elders one leaves behind. I came back to the case of the Niarovana sacrifice in a later discussion with Tavo Robert, when I asked him whether next time the man from Niarovana who had sacrificed in his fields could set up a prayer post and start a town. Tavo explained that "each person founds a town in the place that pleases him, the place that blesses him—he can start a town there if he begs the way from his parents. [He'll say,] 'This is the place in which I've prospered, and so I will sponsor a circumcision sacrifice here and erect a prayer post.' If no one objects, then he can do that, as it was the place that made him prosper, and he can form a new town. But only when he has permission [*fafy rano*] from his family in Niarovana can he go to live there. If the family doesn't agree, then he can not do it. He must beg the way from his family, and only then can he move there.

When I pushed him farther, asking what might happen if the family did not agree he continued, "He would be disciplined [*voakabaro*]! His family would prohibit him; they might say that this is the land where you search for booty, for plunder, all that benefits you and makes you living, but the *jiro* [the word is used here to stand synecdochically for ancestral connections] remains here in town; the town is here. If he ignores the wishes of his family he will be lost to them. They will say goodbye to him and his family, and stay here in town.

Tavo Robert was not alone in emphasizing the risk involved in attempting to break off from one's ancestry of origin and form one's own great house. Josef, who had earlier claimed he "never went anywhere" because the ancestors always came looking for him, also focused on how difficult the process was, particularly the political significance of giving blessing: "For a *tangalamena* to give blessing is to give the supplicant power. If someone asks to separate from you and set up their own great house *[trano be]*, then it means that they know what to do. They already have control of their ancestors. In this case you give blessing in your mouth [implicitly here the mouth is contrasted to the heart, as deception is opposed to sincerity], and then you go listen at his sacrifice, but you never speak or tell him what to do. The root can no longer speak when children leave. It is strictly forbidden."

Indeed, as if to discourage people from creating potential divisions by trying their luck at finding new sources of *hasina* and breaking away, frequently people told morality stories about attempts to do so that had failed. In addition to countless stories about people who had departed from ancestral ways and suffered the consequences, there were numerous stories about people who had gone to break new land and fallen sick. This kind of land was usually referred to as *tany masiaka* "cruel land," a reference not so much to the land as to the spirit that inhabited it. As Babette explained it, "There is land on which long-dead people have been buried, and if you don't have the same *rangitra* as the people who are buried there, the land becomes cruel. That land doesn't have the same *rangitra* as you." Terrible things are believed to happen to people who have the misfortune to try to live in such a spot. I heard of one case at an old woman's wake, as people sat around waiting for the moment when we would carry the corpse (to which no one seemed to be paying much attention) to be buried, which I recorded in my journal:

Talk turned to the story of Mazava, a woman, and her husband, Simon. Mazava was sick while she was pregnant, hemorrhaging irregularly. They had worked new rice land to the south, and the rice crop was good, too, but as it happened the land was cruel (masiaka ny tany). The woman became ill, and in the ninth month of her pregnancy she started to cramp and the baby was born dead. The couple went to the diviner who immediately declared that the land was cruel—there was a creature (biby). This was further confirmed as someone had seen bull innards lying around when in fact there are no cattle on this land. Someone said that other people had worked the land before, and two of their children had died before they realized the cause and moved. People had told the couple not to work the land but they wouldn't listen, and now the child is dead and the woman still sick. The women

attending the corpse shook their heads when they heard the story.
The people had known it was dangerous land, and still they had
tried to work it, in the vague hope that somehow their rangitra
might produce a different effect when paired with that of the land.
(Field notes, February 1993)

Of those people who find sources of power that enable them to pull away
from ancestral places, many seek to further the process of implantation,
to create progressively deepening, thickening roots that will tie them to
a place and make them masters of the land. This process always entails
implicit ancestral legitimization: the person proves the "truth" of his
choices through his success, which is read retroactively as a sign of ancestral approval. Conversely, serial deaths always proved that ancestors
had not acquiesced to the move. In one of the more extreme examples I
heard about, an ancestry had split off to start their own house, only to
have two successive *tangalamena* and their speech makers die gruesome
deaths. The children of the people involved attempted to "return to the
root," but the original *tangalamena* would no longer accept them, and
so they remained cut off and adrift, unable to negotiate their relationship to their ancestors yet vulnerable to their wrath.

   If people are successful, however, then much later, long after everyone
has forgotten the initial colonizing process, their children will liken themselves to plants and say they have roots in a particular place. They might
even say their ancestors "have *hasina*" in the water—or this or that hill
or rice paddy—thereby naturalizing and dehistoricizing a situation that
is in fact a product of history. They will also probably employ the word
for the stake used to tether a bull to graze *(antòka)* to convey the idea
they are firmly tied to the locale. Most certainly, they will recite histories
recounting their ancestors' movement away from the place of origin. In
the telling, the ancestors will be remembered and the creatures of the land
forgotten. But this will be only the end result of what is in fact a tortu-
ous process of implantation, fraught with peril, one that inevitably involves a continuous struggle between the people who set out to find their
fate and the ancestors, great house, and *tangalamena* they left behind.

HOLDING ON WHILE LETTING GO: NEGOTIATING
ANCESTRAL POWER-MEMORY WITH *TANTARA*

This picture of a progressive separation from ancestors, as offshoots of
ancestries move out to colonize new space, is mitigated by the fact that,

in order to be truly successful at creating new "sites of memory," Betsimisaraka must achieve the paradox of leaving their ancestors while also
taking them along. Recasting Annette Weiner's insight (1992) into contradictory processes of exchange in terms of space, we might think of
this phenomenon as "holding on while letting go." The necessity of moving without losing one's ancestors becomes clear when we consider that,
for Betsimisaraka, ancestors are the root of social identity. Betsimisaraka
believe that "having ancestors" is synonymous with having powerful ancestors, and powerful ancestors are the mark of a powerful person (see
also Feeley-Harnik 1978). Conversely, not having ancestors is tantamount
to being a slave, the ultimate condition of nonbeing (see Feeley-Harnik
1997). To be without ancestors means one is reduced to invoking and
worshiping other people's ancestors: the honor and respect that should
contribute to the growth of one's own ancestry are siphoned off, and they
contribute to the growth of another. Though slavery was abolished soon
after the arrival of the French in 1896, and though Betsimisaraka have
worked hard to suppress that aspect of their past, they continue to use
the different positions of master and slave—their associated meanings—
as an idiom for expressing dominance and subordination within the
village.

For Betsimisaraka, "knowing history," is the key to resolving the contradictory need to move to new places while still retaining one's ties to
the past.[8] Since, unlike some other Malagasy groups, Betsimisaraka do
not take relics or water or earth imbued with ancestral power with them,
history *(tantara)*—the knowledge of ancestors' names needed to invoke
ancestors and sustain their power—is the means through which people
separate from, and reconnect with, their ancestors in new configurations.
It is one's ability to maintain connection to ancestors despite separation
that signals the *intentional* nature of the division, distinguishing it from
slavery, in which one becomes forcibly separated from one's ancestors
and dependent on the ancestors of another. Conversely, not knowing ancestral names, particularly in the case of an adult male, places one at a
serious disadvantage, because it means one does not have the knowledge
necessary to negotiate the power embodied in the past. As Josef commented, not knowing one's ancestors is to be like "someone for sale that
couldn't speak."

Having *tantara* is part of being a meaningful person: both men and
women gain honor from knowing about the past. For men, however,
knowing *tantara* is absolutely crucial to being an independent person,
for it means that a man can independently negotiate his relationships with

ancestors. As a result, knowing *tantara*—the ancestors' names, as well as why taboos originated or how a family came to inhabit a particular place—signifies that one is a political player in local terms. Though a man might not know any personal details about the particular ancestors involved, if he knows their names and where they lived and were buried, that information alone will enable him to act independently in the context of ritual. Ideally of course, *tangalamena* are given the power to negotiate with their ancestors by their family, "introduced" to the ancestors, and blessed with the injunction "Don't lose your fate! May you carry the weight of the ancestors." Many people even claim that if a person who had not been introduced were to stand up and start calling ancestors, the ancestors would say, "Who is that? This isn't our child," and strike him dead. But like the morality tales mentioned earlier, the warnings exist precisely because any man can be a *tangalamena* if he dares.

THE SOCIAL DISTRIBUTION OF HISTORICAL KNOWLEDGE

The close association between *tantara*, ancestors, power, and ritual action places knowing ancestral *tantara* at the heart of what it means to be a political subject, to be able to know one's world and control it. The association of age and historical knowledge is pervasive. As the proverb says, "I am a child born of the evening, and when my eyes opened, it was the day's night."[9] This proverb is frequently cited by *tangalamena* at sacrifices before they begin the invocation over the body of the bull, or before they launch into any display of knowledge about ancestors. It implies that the speaker, though presuming to speak, is a mere child, someone who arrived too late to know the secrets of the past.[10] It also embodies local notions of who "has" *tantara* and who does not, and who has the right to speak about it, emphasizing the connection between age and *tantara* and the inevitable loss of knowledge that people assume will occur with the passing generations.

In contrast to older men who are assumed to have de facto knowledge of *tantara*—sometimes even when they do not—women and young people are assumed not to possess extensive knowledge of *tantara*, which in turn replicates their more fragile connection to ancestors. Though as I mentioned earlier, many older women do, in practice, know quite a bit about *tantara*, young people generally do not. This point was made repeatedly throughout my stay when I would ask young people about their genealogical connections to other groups and would receive only vague answers in response. Typically, shared kinship was inferred from shared

activities, like making collective contributions to funerals within the town
or hearing a common ancestor called at a sacrifice. I once asked a youth
of about twenty how he was related to the people who lived in the neighboring courtyard. Although he could not specify the exact links, he did
insist they were "one people" because they attended all ancestral events
together. This is not to say, however, that younger villagers and women
never seek out *tantara*. For example, one young woman I encountered
was interested in her ancestral history so that she might learn about her
claim to a particular rice field.[11] I also met several young people who
tried to learn about *tantara* in order to avoid committing incest. In response to my questions about *tantara*, Loira, a young woman, commented
that she did not know much about how people were related to each other,
but that she really ought to, as that way if she moved far away she would
not accidentally marry a kinsman.

    Although both men and women know *tantara,* only men can use it in
the context of ritual action. I was even told that, because women could
not act for themselves in ritual, they were like "things you had to carry"
(raha indô). As a result, the act of "making history," of pushing beyond
the maintenance of ancestral sites of memory in order to make new ones,
is highly gendered. Both men and women are subject to ancestral demands. Women, however, are associated with memory, or the processes
of reproduction—for instance, they teach their children taboos so that
ancestral power will be maintained. By contrast, men are imagined to be
full historical actors who may try to transcend the bounds of ancestral
constraint and make history on their own terms. These dichotomies mask
the complexities of practice, of course, for women give men the children
that make them generative and enable them to create new ancestral sites.
As the groom's family says when they supplicate the bride, "Give us a
hill, give us a town," an explicit reference to the fact that women create
the possibility for men's self-expansion.[12] But the contrast between the
two, and the explicit association of the act of making history with men,
endures.

TRANSMITTING *TANTARA*

If knowing *tantara* is central to what it means to be a political subject,
the related process of transmitting *tantara* is key to how people as local
subjects are produced. One of the primary ways Betsimisaraka try to ensure this process is by making people participate in the work of caring
for ancestors, which is intimately tied to their ideas of growth and self-

expansion. Take, for example, what Ramaresaka told me when we returned one afternoon from a bone-turning ceremony *(famokarana)*, the
ceremony in which bones are exhumed from an old tomb, sorted, and
placed in a new one. She had been describing how she had helped prepare her parents' bodies after their deaths, and was thus used to seeing
"difficult things" *(raha sarotra*—the euphemism for death). The act of
thinking about her own sentimental education raised more general issues about the transmission of knowledge:

> What ever happens now, from the time my parents died, or when my child
> died, I've seen it all, difficult things. If there is some work to be done, I never
> flee, am never disgusted, but I look. That is what makes me a woman and
> gives me the character of a grown person *[maha toetra olona maventy]*. I look
> very carefully [at] what people do, for living people don't live forever but must
> pass through the road of death. If you have children who are already grown,
> male or female, then you must show them the truth as you know it. Power-
> ful things [e.g., death] or joyous ones [you show them all]. Some people are
> spoiled: "I'm still young," they say; "my parents are still living." And though
> they may watch, they never take up their hands and work. They only look
> from over there, but don't dirty themselves—just watch. Like a Madame! But
> even Madame too must do that which is done by people.

What is most striking in Ramaresaka's account is her emphasis on participation as a route to learning about ancestors and "how things are
done." Ancestral events like death, bone turnings, and sacrifices often
provide the context in which ancestral histories are passed on, so that
acquiring *tantara* is intimately bound up with the process of maintaining ancestral power.

For more discursive forms of knowledge, like ancestors' names, people
may take advantage of a break in the ritual proceedings to ask for a formal lesson. For instance, during a sacrifice I once watched a man of about
forty ask his *tangalamena* to teach him his genealogy so that he would
not commit incest. After the requisite rum had been presented, enabling
the *tangalamena* to name the ancestors without fear of retribution, the
tangalamena asked the man to recite his genealogy as he knew it, gently
correcting him as he went. Particularly in the case of new *tangalamena*,
the knowledge that connects "knowing ancestors" with the maintenance
of their power is transmitted contextually, as the need occurs. What this
means is that quite often a man who knows very little about ancestors
can work as a *tangalamena*. The requisite knowledge needed to perform
his ritual function is then imparted verbally the night before the sacrifice,
and reinforced in the context of performance as the elder members of

the ancestry whisper the ancestors' names to the new *tangalamena,* who then actually calls them out.

As the equation of transmitting history with "giving blessing" (hence power) implies, teaching people their ancestral history theoretically helps ensure the reproduction of the local order by enabling people to connect with ancestors. But teaching people *tantara* also creates the potential for subversion, because once people know about their ancestors they can use this knowledge to their own ends. Perhaps because the elders who hold ancestral *tantara* know the potential risks involved in empowering others, the act of imparting historical knowledge often entails the symbolic augmentation of the ancestral power–memory and the people who control it.

Again, we encounter the importance of localization. For example, in order to "get history" the person who seeks historical knowledge must position himself or herself as a ritual supplicant and beg for history *(mangataka tantara)* in exactly the same manner in which he or she would beg for ancestral blessing. And whereas those who hold ancestral history sit quietly and wait, those who need to know about ancestral history must work to find it. For example, Josef once explicitly refused to attend a sacrifice in a neighboring town—one where he could have easily returned home for the night—because he claimed the organizers only wanted him to come so they could ask him about shared ancestors that he knew about. But it was inconceivable, Josef said, that he should go to them to discuss ancestors. Rather, it was the person seeking knowledge who should come to Josef and "beg for history." It is always the junior person, the child, who must recognize and seek out the power that comes from knowing about the past.

Moreover, younger people must demonstrate their respect for the power embedded in the past—their willingness to submit to its weight and use it wisely—before elders will hand it over. One *tangalamena,* for example, explained that he would give any child who came and begged for history the information, but the child had to be eager to learn.[13] Botomena also highlighted the pairing of volition and the acquisition of historical knowledge when he described how he had actively sought to submit to the power of the past, seeking stories from his mother's brother prior to his death. Upon being named *tangalamena* for his mother's ancestry, Botomena also had gone to another, older *tangalamena* and asked him how he was supposed to go about things. "I'm someone just learning to work,"[14] he said, and the old man taught him how to control his anger, to keep honey on hand for ancestral contact, and the other secrets of successfully maintaining an ancestral great house. All these examples illustrate that the desire to learn and the willingness to assume a subordinate position are critical to "getting history": the person must recognize the power of the past and submit to it willingly and eagerly in order to obtain it.

THE ANCESTRAL IN THE COLONIAL
AND THE COLONIAL IN THE ANCESTRAL

When the French colonial government began to create new structures for colonial rule, they further multiplied the structures of power with which Betsimisaraka were forced to contend. Betsimisaraka continued to work on their projects of building up sites of memory, but colonial power shaped the ways they could do so. As a result, the colonial past was drawn into the process of making ancestral sites of memory.

Like ancestral power, colonial power also had a localizing effect, and it impinged on Betsimisaraka's projects primarily by forcing them to live in some places and not others, in keeping with the needs of the settlers and the colonial state. Since the key colonial project with regard to this area was the creation of a cash economy, localization took primarily two forms. First, in order to free up the land for settlers to use, the French had to prevent Betsimisaraka from inhabiting ancestral locations. Second, they had to keep Betsimisaraka close enough to serve as a labor force. To this end, the French not only imposed settlement patterns but enacted *laissez-passer* laws that were intended to keep Betsimisaraka within easy reach of the corvée recruiters. The localizing projects of the colonial state thus had an important effect on the precise patterning of ancestral locations that characterizes the area today and that is reflected in the various "arrival histories" that are central to local history *(tantara)*.

Although colonial power constrained some projects, it enabled others. In many cases Betsimisaraka actively incorporated into their plans the opportunities provided by colonial structures, using them to create new sites of memory. One of the key ways Betsimisaraka incorporated structures brought by colonialism was through their interactions with the settlers, some of whom were French, but the majority of whom were Creoles whose fathers had married local Betsimisaraka women and settled down, a process that began during Merina times and accelerated under the French.[15] In the relationships created with settlers we find a secret history of women, for marrying their daughters off to Creole settlers was one way that people created new sites of memory for themselves, thus making history in local terms.

Betsimisaraka feelings toward these *voanjo* (literally, seeds), as they were called, are extremely ambivalent, for they were seen simultaneously as the "worst part of colonization" and as an important source of power. Bena, an old man who lived in a neighboring village, emphasized the negative side:

> Colonization? Enslavement. There was the corvée of the "thirty days" [the length of corvée]. The *vazaha* who lived in Mahanoro, they took the sisters of our *raiamandreny* [literally, mothers and fathers, or elders] and married them and bore children. We call them *voanjo*. Those *voanjo* really brought slavery—they really brought the worst with them. They brought the "thirty days," the palanquin, always obeying them. Everything they did. No truth. Toward the end they made us harvest rubber, and if you finished your task or not they would beat you, slap you—here is the proof [showing his scarred forearms] . . . That's the cruelty we suffered during the colonial period, inflicted by the *voanjo*, the children of *vazaha*, who married and bore children with Betsimisaraka.

For those Betsimisaraka who were related to the *voanjo*, however, the picture was not so clear-cut. Some people used their pretty daughters to create new connections with *vazaha*, or the daughters themselves sought out the privileges that came with marrying—or, more often, being the mistress to—a *vazaha*. As Neivo explained, "If the girl was really pretty, then the *vazaha* would give her parents money in exchange for land. Then later, when there was a [land] fight, the wife would act as a witness to the deal. The parents were happy their daughter had married a *vazaha*, yet those [family members] who didn't get land were mad." Rafaly, whose father's brother-in-law was a French settler nicknamed "Napoleon III," talked about how useful having a *vazaha* in the family was. His father's brother-in-law had made Rafaly's father his right-hand man, trusting him with the job of carrying the money made at his concessions all the way to Mahanoro. In return, the settler had protected him, cutting deals with the district officers to prevent them from taking Rafaly's father or any of his family members away for corvée. Likewise, Napoleon III had actually given Rafaly's father's family a concession on which to work in an area where he could easily protect them, displacing other people in the process. When I asked Rafaly if other people had not hated his family for taking their land, he simply laughed and said they would not have dared. His laughter rang hollow, however, when he finished by saying that the new concession was destroyed by rebel troops in 1947, at which point Rafaly's family had returned home to Ambodiharina.

For some families, however, the kinship ties forged with settlers enabled them to create new places of permanent connection. Take, for example, what Velonmaro told me about Prosper, a man whose mother was Betsimisaraka and whose father was a Creole settler. I had asked about Prosper's children. Velonmaro responded by telling me about Seneka, Prosper's illegitimate son with a Betsimisaraka woman: "Prosper didn't recognize Seneka formally, because he was afraid of his wife, but he pretended Seneka was a worker. But you could see how much he loved Seneka—he treated him as his right arm, which marked Seneka as special. And Prosper's mother loved Seneka too—she knew he was her grandson because she'd heard people talk. But they hid it all from Madame Prosper." Seneka eventually negotiated with his uncle to be able to stay at his father's concession, and his descendants continue to farm there, and to sacrifice there, to this day.

Though Seneka's story highlights the crucial role of women in mediating access to the colonial settlers, at other times men tried to gain access directly to the economic opportunities brought by the colonial state. Take, for example, the story of Bienaimée's maternal great-grandfather, Sampy. As Bienaimée's aunt Marcelline explained, Sampy had owned a little shop at the southern end of Ambodiharina, down by the church. He had earned a lot of money trading and had begged permission (nangataka tso-drano) from his family in Ambodiharina to move to the west, where he could cultivate more fertile land. Marcelline continued: "He had lots of coffee, lots of cloves and vanilla and pepper, and because he was so rich he became friends with a vazaha and the vazaha helped him get his land measured. You see, among Malagasy, wherever there is a prince, people gather. Well, Sampy paid more taxes and so he got people to work for him—you know, he could ask the chef de canton for laborers to work off their taxes. He had what makes you rich here: money, coffee, cattle."

Like Rafaly's father, Sampy was punished for his connection to the vazaha in the settling of accounts that took place during 1947. Nevertheless, the systematic attempt made during 1947 to erase the inequities that began during the colonial period—by both destroying concessions and killing cattle—never quite worked. Sampy managed to survive 1947 with much of his wealth intact, and the jealousy directed at his family lingered on. "In 1959," Marcelline continued, "there was a huge cyclone and the town flooded. And so the older brother's family said it was disgusting there [referring to their hatred of their wealthier younger brother] and they couldn't live there. So they moved a few feet away and created Taviranambo II." In the case of Sampy, too, the opportunities brought by colonial rule enabled him to constitute a new "site of memory," one that his descendants continue to inhabit to this day.

Finally, a third way that ancestral sites of memory became entangled with colonial power was through Betsimisaraka's attempts to use the settlers in order to avoid the colonial government's demand for labor. As Ramaresaka explained, "People suffered so much. They would try and make things just a tiny bit easier and go and live with the *vazaha*. You would get a job working in the *vazaha's* house, and Madame, she would test you, leaving bits of money, small change, here and there. And you would go and find the money and say, 'Here is your money, Madame!' And only after a very long time would she begin to trust you. Your family too would come begging for jobs, looking for ways they too could squeeze up against the *vazaha* and make things a little bit easier." Boto's story provides an apt example of someone who actually "went to live with the *vazaha:*"

> The times of the *vazaha* were terrible. At that time you needed thirty roofs to make a town. I worked for the *vazaha*; we lived on the *vazaha's* concession in order to escape. I didn't grow up in my ancestral homeland but with the *vazaha*. The government *[fanjakana]* would send you hither and thither and you would work for a week or ten days, or sometimes you'd serve thirty days. *Forcè! Lavangady* made Betsimisaraka suffer.[16] You'd do it despite yourself, for life is sweet. But your own work would go unfinished, as the government was the stronger. You'd carry your own work in your hands, the government's on your head. I suffered for a long time, and only now have times relaxed. So we'd work for the days and be gone for months. You'd know the months—you'd start the first and follow the *vazaha* month and get off on the thirtieth or thirty-first. Two months you'd sit in town, and then they'd pick you again for the thirty days' work—that's what happened to me. So we'd hide with the *colons*, live in camps in the fields. "Child grown up in the Bonara forest, never seen the corvée but flees." That is what people would say about us.

Boto's family gained protection from the *vazaha* at a high price. I figured out the cost of their strategy for survival only during my second trip to Ambodiharina, in 1997, when I asked Josef why Boto's family had so little land in comparison to the other families. Somewhat shocked by my tendency to uncover inequalities that people tried their best to forget or ignore, Josef looked at me askance, then revealed what could happen to a person who tried to take advantage of new opportunities: "They were almost lost. They went to work for the *vazaha,* and when they came back, his cousin had taken their land and said, 'Well, too bad, you left.' The children, they seem like strangers, and that family struggles. They're like people who've just arrived. They left their home and so they struggle. They've come back to their ancestral land, but it is like it isn't their ancestral land anymore."

When I queried older villagers about their personal experience of the colonial past, forced labor and taxation were inevitably the recurrent themes of conversation, the sources of their greatest suffering and the points on which their imaginations now fix. Yet one might also argue that the most vivid image around which ideas about colonization crystallize is that of the palanquin, the covered chair in which villagers carried colonial officials throughout Africa. Countless people—both those who had lived through colonial times and those who were born well after it was over—told me about the palanquin. They never failed to mention the fact that people riding in them urinated and defecated on those below. Josef once commented, with his usual gentle, rueful smile, "They must have deemed us Betsimisaraka less than human to act that way." Surely there is no more appropriate symbol of one people's exploitation by another than the image of the colonial official carried on the very backs of the Betsimisaraka? Few indeed were the older men who had not suffered the indignity of working as porters carrying the palanquin.

Although Betsimisaraka reflections might lead us to think that the occupants of the palanquin were always French, Betsimisaraka and Merina also inhabited the palanquin, for they were incorporated into the local ranks of the administration (see chapter 2). The palanquin thus symbolizes not only French abuse of the Betsimisaraka but also the ways in which French power gave Betsimisaraka new ways to abuse each other. And it suggests the other colonial structure on which the Betsimisaraka drew: the administration. Like the people whose interaction with settlers potentially enabled them to create new sites of memory, local functionaries could take advantage of their new power to rearrange ancestral locations to their own advantage.

The story of how the "master of the Mangoro," the person who ritually controls all matters associated with the Mangoro River, came to live upriver at Ankarembelona, and not down at Ambodiharina to the east, at the edge of the embouchure, provides a good example. As I discussed earlier, the Zafimalaone were an ancestry that inhabited three villages, founded by three brothers, along the Mangoro. Ankarembelona lay to the west, Ifasina in the middle, and Ambodiharina at the edge of the embouchure. With their conquest of the area, the Zafimalaone seized control of the water, which along the east coast of Madagascar marked one as master of the land, as it still does today.

According to local logic, it is indisputably the village located to the east on the embouchure that is the most sacred locale, and it follows that the master of the Mangoro would also live at the embouchure. In fact, however, it is a descendant of the youngest brother, located some distance away in Ankarembelona, who bears the title master of the Mangoro and dons the bright red, princely robe whenever ritual action is required. The roots of this inversion lie in the colonial period. The man who was chosen to be *chef de canton* lived in Ambodiharina in order to fulfill his administrative duties, but he happened to be descended from the youngest brother of the Zafimalaone, who had settled in Ankarembelona. Using his power as a functionary in the French administration, the youngest brother decreed that his kinsman in Ankarembelona should be named master of the Mangoro. Not everybody in the ancestry agreed, particularly the descendants of the eldest brother, located in Ambodiharina, who later split off and formed their own ritual group. But the transfer of power that occurred during the colonial period stuck: today people perceive the descendants from Ankarembelona as the legitimate masters of the Mangoro. The descendants of the brother in Ambodiharina continue to protest their seniority, but no one chooses to listen, and whenever the water requires ritual action they turn to Ankarembelona, seat of the last-born son, who was made great through a colonial twist of fate.

COLLECTIVE NEGOTIATIONS

So far I have focused on the ways that individual people drew colonial power into their sites of memory; however, this process also took place on a collective level that bears mentioning here. In particular, the ancestries that inhabited Ambodiharina at the time of the colonial conquest responded to forced resettlement by absorbing the colonial intervention into prior notions of community, incorporating the town-as-colonial-creation into older ways of constructing community through ritual. Recall that, historically, Betsimisaraka symbolically constituted themselves as a group by using the ritual of sacrifice. When the French colonized, they widened the Merina path that runs down the east coast, building a motor road that divides the town in two. People absorbed the road into their local ways of coordinating the relations between different ancestries. As we will see in the following chapter, when one ancestry undertakes a sacrifice, it needs another ancestry to act as a respondent or witness to the event. What the inhabitants of Ambodiharina have done is appropriate the division created by the French to organize who acts as a witness to whom. If someone on the right side of the road undertakes a sacrifice, then someone from the left acts as a witness, and vice versa. Moreover, the categories that villagers use today to coordinate this process are the names of ancestries that were formalized during the French colonial period. When I first arrived in Ambodiharina, people were quick to tell me that there were "ten official ancestries" in the town. But as time wore on, it became clear that the actual social relations were much more fluid and complex; the list was a bureaucratic convention that had emerged during colonial times as a tool to decide who would be called on for corvée.[17] People continue to use the list for convenience in their dealings with outsiders, whether the government or the recently arrived anthropologist. In much the same way, the *fokon'olona,* or village council, is also a colonially created institution that people continue to use as a tool to deal with the state.

AMBODIHARINA AS A HYBRID LOCALE

In the introduction, I suggested that Ambodiharina sometimes appeared to be *either* ancestral *or* colonial, but as this chapter has made clear, such an either-or view is untenable: Ambodiharina is a hybrid product, simultaneously ancestral *and* colonial. Unlike some Malagasy towns that remain administrative constructions to which people go when they have to interact with the government, and then go home, Ambodiharina is inhabited in the fullest sense of the term, animated by local people, local structures, local stories, and local ghosts. This is no model colonial village. But it would be foolish to underestimate the power of what the French did, or to claim that Ambodiharina is entirely a creation of the Betsimisaraka. Rather, Ambodiharina is a Betsimisaraka village that in its present form has been constituted in complex ways through people's interactions with colonial power; it is a compromise formed in the interaction between translocal and local projects.

Perhaps one of the most profound ways in which colonial intrusions have been incorporated into contemporary Ambodiharina is through the men and women who sought to find their fortunes and locate new sources of power by taking advantage of opportunities that were created during the colonial period. These opportunities included economic changes that occurred as some Betsimisaraka started to combine subsistence agriculture with at least small-scale production of coffee and a tiny bit of pep-

per for the world market. They also included the advantages of participating in the colonial hierarchy—like joining the colonial army or
becoming a functionary. And for women, these opportunities included
marrying—or at least having informal liaisons with—local *colons*. In
the process, people created the potential for new inequalities, as well as
the new sites of ancestral memory that are so critical to the construction
of local history.

This process of colonizing new places, whether occupying new land or
moving one's house to Mahanoro, would have surely happened anyway—
the process of making space into place (de Certeau, 1984])—and asserting
ancestral dominion over new sites is a fundamental dynamic of Betsimisaraka social life, as I have shown. But the colonial apparatus changed
the particular ways in which it could happen. As a result, colonial power
became partially productive of new Betsimisaraka subjects, particularly
the men who actively "made history" by creating new ancestral sites of
memory in new kinds of locales. Women were active in this process as
well, as the story of Prosper and his illegitimate son with a Betsimisaraka
woman suggests. But perhaps because brides usually go to live with their
husbands, and because patrilineal ancestors are thought to have a
stronger claim on their descendants' movements, I did not hear of any
contemporary stories about problems with sites of ancestral memory that
had been created because of the movements of women. This bias reflects
the general bias in Betsimisaraka practice that tends to privilege the ancestral sites of men as well as their historical actions.

The disparities produced through people's unequal access to colonial
power continue to structure some aspects of people's relationships to this
day. They continue to affect people because some of them have ended
up with more access to the structures of the state—schools, health care,
the bureaucracy—than others. In much the same way in which the Merina, who were more thoroughly integrated into the colonial system, have
maintained their power in postcolonial Madagascar, so those Betsimisaraka who profited from colonial structures enjoy more comfortable lives
today. The redistribution of power among Betsimisaraka that took place
under colonial rule has thus far proved remarkably stable. I suspect this
may be true for Madagascar more generally.

And so, in trying to realize themselves and fulfill their ambitions, or
even in just trying to survive, people like Rafaly's father, Sampy, Boto,
and the proud Zafimalaone functionary all contributed to weaving colonial structures into the very substance of local worlds. The outcome of
the interaction depended on the contingencies of history and could take

many forms. Sometimes colonial power allowed people to create new sites of memory. At other times it allowed them to rearrange prior ancestral locations to their own ends. And sometimes, the strategies backfired, as in the case of Boto, whose loss of land to his brothers at home suggests that he may not end up with any "site of memory" at all. But what all of these efforts at dealing with colonial power worked to produce was the uneven terrain over which Betsimisaraka today must travel.

CHAPTER 6

Memory

Official and Unofficial

Consider the herd grazing before you. These animals
do not know what yesterday and today are but leap
about, eat, rest and digest and leap again; and so from
morning to night and from day to day, only briefly
concerned with their pleasure and displeasure, en-
thralled by the moment and for that reason neither
melancholy nor bored. It is hard for man to see this,
for he is proud of being human and not an animal and
yet regards its happiness with envy because he wants
nothing other than to live like the animal, neither
bored nor in pain, yet wants it in vain because he
does not want it like the animal. Man may well ask the
animal: why do you not speak to me of your happiness
but only look at me? The animal does want to answer
and say: because I always immediately forget what I
wanted to say—but then it already forgot the answer
and remained silent: so that man could only wonder.
                                    —*Friedrich Nietzsche*

Nietzsche might have perceived cattle as an emblem of forgetting, but, for
the Betsimisaraka, cattle sacrifice is the most highly elaborated practice
through which social and individual memory are simultaneously articulated, transformed, and sustained. People spend much of their meager sav-
ings by sacrificing cattle, and they do so partly because they believe cattle
sacrifice can heal them of illness and even save their lives. As a result they
get passionately excited about cattle sacrifice, talk about it, judge how a
given ritual is performed, and worry about how to afford one. Aside from

rice farming, cattle sacrifice was the major practice that people were most eager to teach me about, and they took the most care and time doing this.

By focusing on cattle sacrifice, as the Betsimisaraka do, we can begin to piece together answers to some of the questions raised in previous chapters. First, as we have seen, the local aspect of the "reversible illusion" tends to dominate life in Ambodiharina, shaping people's concerns and preoccupations most of the time. Second, the "ancestral" aspect of this perceptual illusion, though perceived as local, is not local in the sense of being "outside" the processes introduced by colonialism. Rather, since at least the eighteenth century it has been historically constituted and reconstituted *through* people's interactions with both Merina and French colonial power. The practices through which Betsimisaraka imagine the past, and the fact that the past is a source of power, shift perceptions of the past toward the local, but these practices never entirely erase the competing narratives of translocal experience. This seepage is evident in the ways that Betsimisaraka have woven the signs and practices associated with colonialism into their ancestral sites of memory, and in the way these signs and practices continue to mediate people's interactions in the present.

Sacrifice helps illuminate this process of seepage because it is the major mechanism through which nonlocal practices have been woven into daily life in Ambodiharina. The practice of sacrifice works as an interpretive filter through which the meanings associated with a host of different practices, including structures introduced by colonialism, are locally reconfigured. More specifically, sacrifice is an art of memory—a way of selectively shaping people's memories and perceptions—and it is key to understanding how the nonlocal becomes local, how what is perceived as local is constantly transformed, and how the local comes to dominate people's perceptions in everyday life. The practice of sacrifice reworks people's relationships according to a double hierarchy: diachronically, in their relationships to their ancestors and the colonial past; and synchronically, in their relationships to one another and the postcolonial state of Madagascar. Yet even in cattle sacrifice the colonial past—and postcolonial present—seeps through. Despite people's best efforts, the consensus about the past and present that is precariously achieved in ritual is constantly contested.

THE SYMBOLIC POTENCY OF CATTLE

For anyone familiar with E. Evans-Pritchard's 1940 and 1956 studies of the Nuer, or Godfrey Lienhardt's 1961 study of the Dinka, the fact that some African peoples constitute their social relations through cattle seems like part of the accepted anthropological lore. For those less familiar with this literature, the importance of cattle as a mechanism for both imagining and constituting society needs some introduction. Betsimisaraka enthusiasm for cattle sacrifice has both historical depth and emotional salience. As the key ritual through which descendants create and affirm their links with ancestors, cattle sacrifice is central to the articulation of hierarchy, figuring in every political regime through which Betsimisaraka have lived. For example, the French colonial ethnographer Alfred Grandidier described the connection between political independence and having control over one's *jiro*, or prayer post—the tree carved in the shape of a bull's horns at which sacrifices to ancestors are made: "There was only one *jiro* for each family, before which they prayed, performed circumcisions and so forth. When the tribe from the north was defeated [in war], they no longer had the right to a *jiro*, and all their prayers were made to the *jiro* of the southerners, the victors. The *jiro* is like the altar of the tribe[,] and a new one was created when the chiefs moved from one village to the next because the *jiro* could never be removed" (1958, 69).[1]

Likewise, an eyewitness account of Ratsimilaho's accession to the role of leader of the Betsimisaraka in 1720 describes how the event was solemnized with the sacrifice of twenty cattle.[2] With the encroachment of European powers, Betsimisaraka used cattle sacrifice in their dealings with Europeans as well. When the princess Betia, descendant of the Betsimisaraka leader Ratsimilaho, ceded the island of Sainte Marie to the French, a bull was sacrificed. Witnesses observed that "this promise [to cede the island] was solemnly made by all the chiefs of the country, following their custom and making a vow on a bull which then served as a feast of rejoicing[,] and this ceremony was made in the presence of *l'Etat Major* of the *Vaisseau La Paix*" (Mantaux and Adolph 1972).

Even before official colonization, the French realized that controlling people's ancestors was one way to control people, and they tried whenever possible to use sacrifice to manipulate the political identifications of the populace.[3] Throughout the colonial period, French administrators staged rituals of cattle sacrifice as a way to demonstrate their munificence and to reward and mollify the Betsimisaraka. They sacrificed a bull in Mahanoro each Bastille Day, which peasants from the surrounding villages were supposed to attend.[4] After the rebellion of 1947, French officials drew on their knowledge of local custom to construct rituals of pacification (and humiliation) in which cattle sacrifice was used (Valensky 1999). Throughout the colonial period they also imposed a tax on any cattle to be killed, thus linking ancestral rituals with state consent (see also Bloch 1986). These practices did not begin with, nor end with, French colonization. Much of the time, French officials were borrowing from practices begun by the Merina, and politicians in postcolonial Madagascar continue to use them now that the French have gone. In 1993, President Didier Ratsiraka also used sacrifice as a way to construct his relationship with local communities, offering a bull to each district in thanks for electoral support.

But to read the significance of cattle only in terms of present and past state projects would be a huge mistake. Rather, the reason successive regimes have tried to appropriate the ritual of sacrifice is precisely because its experiential and emotional significance endures to the present day. The importance of cattle as culturally constructed objects of desire is best illustrated through popular culture and lore. During my fieldwork in 1992–93, one of the most popular songs throughout Madagascar was by Michel Patrick, a singer from the provincial capital of Tamatave; in it, the singer touted the virtues of using cattle to get things done the "Betsimisaraka way."

BIBY AOMBY

Ny Ranomasin'i Tamatave zalahy
Manitsy manaranara
Miheritreritra ny tanindrazana
Raha mampitehitomany
    Faritra faraparani'Tamatave
    Zalahy faran'i Loterie
    tsimanimanina tsy akory
    Ahatsiarovanana fomban-drazana.

Aomby eee ia.
Aomby eee ia.
Loharan-karenentsika Madagascar ny aomby
Antsika samy manana ny fomban-drazana
Fanaovana raha n'i Tamatave ny aombe e!
    Aomby eee ia.
    Aomby eee ia.
    Loharan-karenentsika Madagascar ny aomby!
    Manolo tsoro, Manolo tsoro
    Manolo hasina, Manolo hasina.

Aomby maaaa.
Aomby maaaa.
Tsy azo anaovana sangisangy, biby ny aomby.
Hany aomby!

Soro aomby eee!
Biby masiaka.
Fanoro lahy ee.
Alamino o, ia misy aminay ary ny aomby!
Eny e! Anaovana fombandrazana, ny aomby e!

Lazan'i Betsimisaraka raha tona
Ilaina anaovana joro ny aomby.
Manadia lazan'i Betsimisaraka raha tena ilaina
alana voady ny aomby,
Mandidia lazan'i Betsimisaraka ra tena ilaina
hitokonan trano ny aomby.
                                                                —Michel Patrick

POWERFUL CATTLE

The Sea of Tamatave
Glittering cold
I think of my ancestral homeland
And I want to weep.
        The province of Tamatave
        The last of the lottery
        It's not that I long for it
But I recall my ancestral tradition.
Cows, mooooo!
Cows, mooooo!

The treasure of we Malagasy,
We each have our ancestral customs,
To do things in Tamatave you need cows!
        Cows yes!
        Cows yes!
        The treasure of we Malagasy,
        Cows!
        Present prayer, offer prayer
        Offer sacredness, offer sacredness.

Cows mooooo!
Cows mooooo!
You can't joke around, a cow is a beast!
Food, cow!
Prayer, cow!
A cruel and savage animal.
Savage creature!
Be cool, we have cows over here!
Yes, for completing ancestral customs, cows.

The voice of the Betsimisaraka speaks,
We need cows for sacrifice
Cows are necessary for completing vows,
Spread the word, for opening a house you need cows!

This song was on everyone's lips the entire time I lived in Ambodiharina. Small boys whistled it while they guarded cattle on what was supposed to be the soccer field in the middle of the village. Young women
sang it as they transplanted rice. Old people sang it for me when they
tried to convey the importance of cattle among the Betsimisaraka. "You
know," they would say, "just like in that song . . . "; and they would start
to hum. The fact that Betsimisaraka find cattle so evocative of their ancestral homeland that remembering them makes the singer "want to
weep" is ample reason for the Betsimisaraka to use cattle sacrifice to evoke
their ancestral homeland. On both a symbolic and material level, cattle
sacrifice is crucial to how people imagine community and constitute a
"local" world.[5] To understand how this works, one must first gain a sense
of the ritual, to which I now turn.

THE VARIETIES OF INTERACTIONS WITH ANCESTORS

As the reader will probably realize by now, Betsimisaraka invoke their
ancestors for a variety of different reasons using a variety of different
media. They frequently use rum and honey for small jobs, for instance,
because these provide quick and relatively cheap ways of asking ancestors for help or thanking them for fulfilling a vow or restoring their purity when people have engaged in activities likely to diminish ancestral
power. For example, after a young couple, Lili and Josee, fought, Lili
cursed Josee, saying her ancestors were dogs. Lili's enraged father-in-law
made sure that he "washed the ancestors" with rum before he would allow Josee to return home with Lili. Coconut oil *(ilo)* is also frequently
used as a purifying substance (it is often used to cleanse women post-
partum). Some people argue that, in order to cleanse ancestors after they
have been cursed or insulted, coconut oil has to be present with the rum
to guarantee the efficacy of the transaction.

But of all the different ways of communicating with one's ancestors,
cattle sacrifice is the most important, the most beloved, the "really real"
event on which people lavish the most wealth and effort. When a foreign friend suggested that other animals might do as well as cattle—
after all, why not pigs, goats, sheep?—people said, no, it was only cattle
that could (echoing the Nuer) "substitute for the lives of men" *(Aomby
misolo ny aina olombelona)*. In fact, people were fond of pointing out
that Merina ancestors accepted other animals in blood sacrifice (or so
they said), something *they* would never dare try, an implicit slur on the
lax nature of Merina ancestors as opposed to their own. The origin story

that people told to explain why cattle had been chosen to substitute for the lives of men went as follows: "Cattle and men had made a pact. The cow complained that she couldn't 'make herself living,' so the man said, 'OK, I'll feed you, but in return, I'm occasionally going to sacrifice you to pay for my sins.' And the cow agreed."

Local folklore aside, part of the reason that cattle sacrifices are viewed as appropriate thanks for ancestral bestowal of health, prosperity, and fertility surely lies in the sheer quantity of wealth and effort that people invest in sponsoring them. Perhaps the hardest part is finding enough money to purchase the bull or cow. Betsimisaraka are not a pastoral people and most of the people in the village do not own cattle. Of those who do, few, if any, own more than two or three at a time.

Every year in the summer, when people have money from the rice harvest but before the ritual season begins in September and October, Betsileo, or southerners, come through town bringing cattle for sale. I was told that a bull purchased for FMG 100,000 in Betsileo country would go for FMG 150,000 once it reached the coast, indicating that the owners were able to increase their profits by half.[6] In 1993, a calf purchased in its mother's stomach cost about FMG 80,000, while adult cattle cost around FMG 250,000. By 1997, when I returned to do a sacrifice of my own, the price of a large bull was FMG 750,000. At this price, a bull costs three-quarters of the average yearly income of $250. Depending on how much time the family has to gather up their wealth, they may try to earn money for the bull by selling rice and other produce or, in an emergency, may trade land for a bull.

People estimated that the base cost of a simple sacrifice was around four sacks of rice and sixty liters of local rum and *betsa*, which cost around FMG 150,000, in addition to the cost of the bull. Plenty of coffee for the guests must also be found, as well as a side dish, usually ground manioc leaves or perhaps sweet potato leaves or beans. Since coffee and sugarcane for making rum do not grow well in Ambodiharina, most people try to obtain these products upcountry, where they are cheaper. A few days before the sacrifice, young men are sent into the forest to chop kindling, while young women are sent to gather the traveler's palm leaves upon which the sacrificial meal will be served (see fig. 10).

Though any event can be dealt with through sacrifice, there are several institutionalized reasons for sponsoring a cattle sacrifice. For example, there is a sacrifice that takes place for the fulfillment of a vow *(voady)*. There is also a sacrifice that celebrates having borne many children *(fahavanonana)*. When the children are mainly male this becomes

Figure 10. Pounding rice for a circumcision celebration *(sambatra)*, 1993. The ceremony begins when women pound a special kind of rice associated with power and wealth. Photo by Jennifer Cole.

a circumcision celebration *(sambatra)*, though nowadays the actual circumcision is usually performed separately, either by a man who specializes in the operation or, occasionally, by a state-certified doctor. Finally, there are two other institutionalized kinds of sacrifice: the "house washing" or "house entering" *(fafy trano* or *idiran trano)* ritual, which inaugurates a tin-roofed house; and the coffee-cleansing ritual *(fafy kafe)*, which marks a particularly abundant coffee harvest. Often, these reasons for sacrifice are combined, so that a single bull can be used to complete an astonishing amount of ritual work.

What follows is a description from my field notes of the very first sacrifice that I witnessed, only a month into my stay in Ambodiharina, to which I have subsequently added a few points of clarification. I use the description to convey what sacrifice is like and then to tease out both the official and unofficial memory-narratives woven into the performance. I want to preface this description with a plea to the reader to have patience. Reading about other people's obscure rituals is always difficult, and it is all too easy to dismiss what follows as "weird native customs." In fact, to dismiss cattle sacrifice as exotic trivia would be a mistake, because rituals of cattle sacrifice are highly political events through which Betsimisaraka continually renew and constitute the memories that are central to their identity as a people. As we shall see, however, like all efforts to produce a particular reality, cattle sacrifice is only partly successful.

ZAKATIANA'S SACRIFICE, SEPTEMBER 1992

Early morning. We set out for a village to the west of Ambodiha-rina, where a sambatra sacrifice was to be held. My friend Dere explained that, though many people may have known—because of the constant flow of gossip and rumor—that a sacrifice was to be held, none would count themselves invited until they had "received the call." I was happy to have received an invitation, and I had the best possible guides, for we were traveling with Zafilahy, Dere's brother-in-law and one of the most respected tangalamena in the area, and his grandson Alain. We found some-one to row us across the canal and headed off along the path lined with coffee plants, which borders the Mangoro River. A few feet from the edge of the town, a crowd of young men reeking of local rum rushed past us, on their way to cut the prayer post (jiro) that would be erected for the sacrifice. We lingered momentarily at the edge of town, until eventually we heard people shouting that the jiro had arrived.

The mothers of the children to be celebrated (renin-jaza), each holding a white flag representing a child to be circumcised, joined the party of youths and began dancing at the edge of the village.[7] Jostling with the young men, they wrestled the jiro back and forth while singing, "Zakatiana [the master of the sambatra] isn't stingy with his rum." Only when the speech maker for Zakatiana's great house appeared with rum for the dancers did they enter the town. They danced through the town, the men straining to carry the jiro, the women dancing around the men in a dance called a mandahy lahy—"to make men." On reaching Zakatiana's great house the party faltered, and the speech maker shouted directions at the youth, telling them to dance the jiro six times clockwise around the house. The speech maker accompanied the youths, grasping a wand of hasina, the ever-growing plant that Betsimisaraka use to signify growth and efficacy. As the youths danced around each new great house or jiro, the speech maker demanded rum or

*locally brewed beer for the dancers, and the speech maker
from another house would bless the proceedings by bringing
out more rum.*

*Meanwhile, young boys took turns climbing up the prongs
of the jiro; by associating with the jiro, cut to resemble the horns
of a bull, it was hoped they too would obtain the sharpness and
strength of a bull. A young man watching the proceedings explained that the reason the youths danced around each great
house and prayer post was to "make their hasina the same."
Eventually all the houses in the town had been danced around,
and the party made its way back to Zakatiana's great house.
At this point, the tug of war between the youths and the young
women carrying the prayer post intensified, the women bouncing
and pulling the post back, the men tugging to bring it forward,
in a motion that was clearly intended to mimic sexual intercourse.
The jiro was pulled in and then out of the house again, until
finally the boys won out and the jiro was brought into the great
house, where it was propped up against the southern wall, to be
guarded by the elders.*

*At this point, everyone retired to various houses to eat, and—
finally—we went off to find Zakatiana to present him with our
contribution to the celebrations. We went into the house, and an
elaborate exchange began as Zakatiana greeted us, announcing
that he rejoiced, an allusion to the official reason for the ceremony.
Zafilahy responded, saying that we had "heard the call" and come
to rejoice with the hosts. At the same time, he pulled out and
presented a bit of money that we had gathered together.[8] (Dere
explained that later we would be given meat from the sacrificial
bull in exchange.) Zakatiana responded again, thanking us for our
attendance and the self-abnegation this implied: "You to the east
have come to join us, you have heard the call and you have come,
given of yourself (nahafoy tena), put down your work and your
livelihood, come to join us and rejoice and dance [with us], and
we are happy that you will attend and share [of yourself]. Here
is a small meal to mark this event."*

*Zakatiana then reached around the palm-stalk barrier and
brought out a bottle of local rum, which we proceeded to drink.
Meanwhile, Zakatiana's brother wrote down our names and the
amount of our contribution. Before we could leave the house,*

however, a man who seemed almost blindingly drunk interrupted us. He was pale, with striking blue eyes, and he kept coming up to me and insisting on speaking French. "Bonjour, Madame," he would say, then trail off into a slur of words I could not understand. "Bonjour," he would say, swaggering toward us. His name was Guy, but that was all I learned about him then, and in any event I was somewhat scared of him and happy to have Dere distract him so we could make our escape.

That night an accordion ball was held in the great house to guard the newly cut prayer post against possible desecration. At dawn a new group of young men whose fathers and mothers were still living (velon-dray, velon-dreny) set out to get the "haughty tree" (ramiavona), a special kind of tree that helps add generative power to the celebration[9] (see fig. 11). Once again the youth ran pell-mell into the forest, where they cut down the tree that they had identified earlier and carried it back to the town. As when they carried the prayer post, the youths stopped at the edge of the town waiting for libations of rum before they would proceed. The mothers-of-the-children joined them, and a tug of war began over the tree, pulling it back and forth in a sawing motion. The tree was danced around each great house, and once again the dancers stopped periodically to demand more rum, which was always produced. Shortly thereafter, stalks of bamboo and sugar-cane were brought out and danced around the house in a similar fashion.

By then most of the community had gathered; nevertheless, a town crier was sent round shouting, "Man or woman, young or old, Zakatiana will beg for blessing now, on the courtyard. Put down your work and your livelihood—the call is made. Come one, come all."[10]

Next, the jiro was brought out of the eastern door of the house and planted alongside other jiro from previous years. The mothers-of-the-children danced around the newly erected jiro. At this point, everyone retired for lunch. Following lunch, Zakatiana called the assembled crowd to announce the reason for the sambatra. Throughout his speech, members of the crowd—particularly the mothers-of-the-children, their eyes heavy from rum and their faces smeared with sweat and lipstick—were screaming encouragement and stuffing small coins into his pocket.

Figure 11. Climbing the "haughty tree" *(ramiavona)*, 1993. Several of the ritual sequences at a circumcision ceremony *(sambatra)* are meant to ensure that the sponsor's descendants receive ancestral blessing, as when the boys celebrated by the ceremony climb this tree and are handed coins as symbols of ancestral blessing. Photo by Jennifer Cole.

SPEECH MAKER: *We greet all who have come! Zakatiana is here to sambatra [celebrate], and we call those on the edge of the water [the villagers]. Greetings.*

RESPONDENT: *We are well! Zakatiana is here to sambatra and has called the assembled people. We the assembled have come.*

SPEECH MAKER (WHO HAPPENED TO BE ZAKATIANA
   HIMSELF): *Father of Zakatiana had only the prayer post inherited
   from his mother, and thus Father of Zakatiana conferred with his
   mother's brother [zama] and was given permission to make standing
   a prayer post to his father. And he saw that Iaba n'i Solo [Zakatiana's
   brother] bore a son: "Oh Father," said Iaba n'i Solo, "you are making
   a prayer post for men; we too have fathered sons, let us sambatra
   together." "Ah," replied his father, "let us do it! Screw her really hard
   so that she may have another [son]." Wheee!!!! [The crowd goes crazy
   cheering.] By this time I was already a grown man, had fathered four
   brothers, and Iaba n'i Zakatiana had four boys who still needed to be
   "celebrated." Together we sambatra, together we have fathered sons.*

    *And along with that I promised secretly to throw a circumcision
   [celebration], but I didn't, and so I fell ill. A strong man had to carry
   me all the way to Marotsiriri [the Catholic dispensary], and I was not
   cured; and they carried me to Mahanoro, and I was not cured; and they
   sent me all the way to Vatomandry, but for six months I didn't stand.
   My family carried me. "Aha," I said to my wife, "I am ill." And as my
   wife said, "I will not leave my husband until he is dead." [He recounts
   the conversation:] "You won't leave me?" "No, unless you are dead, I
   shall never leave you."*

THE CROWD, SHOUTING: *Yes, that is true, that is true!*

ZAKATIANA: *During that time, my wife gave all she had and nursed
   me; my sister too returned to nurse me, but then returned home, and
   only my wife remained to nurse me.*

THE CROWD, SHOUTING: *Your words are clear! They are clear!*

ZAKATIANA: *And one day my wife and youngest daughter went to
   market, and when they returned my wife told me, "Your daughter
   said that if daddy can walk again, let us go and buy meat." That is
   what my daughter said. I am alive still, I am cured, and it is not meat
   at the bazaar we shall eat but the Luminous Head [a nickname for the
   bull, referring to the white stripe down his forehead], here at home.*

THE CROWD GOES WILD, SHOUTING: *Oweeeeeeee.*

ZAKATIANA: *It is the blessing of God and the ancestors that has fulfilled my wish. It is true I am cured! Zakatiana has stood and returned
   from Vatomandry to Ankarembelona, with a cane to Vohilava. "If I am
   living," I said to Razafy, "then fatten Lemaryse well [another nickname
   for the bull], for when he is fattened we eat together!"*

THE CROWD: *You speak well, you speak well!*

ZAKATIANA: *I have fathered sons! I was sick and now I live. Together we
   eat the bull. WHEEEEEEE . . . And Razafy said to me, "Don't worry,
   I will kill the bull raised alone." And he fattened the bull. And when
   it was fattened we spoke and decided to sambatra! The bull is fat, the
   newborn is a boy, [and] even a small child can make a wish: "If my*

father is cured we will buy meat at the market." Ah, but this is not meat at the market but the hump of the bull [the fattiest and hence most desirable part of the bull] that we eat. I was moved that my child knew these things, this little girl here!

THE CROWD, CHANTING: *Speak! Speak! Speak!*

ZAKATIANA: *And I too asked myself what to do to thank my wife, my sisters, my family [for caring for him while sick]. Some thank with coconut oil [ilo, symbolic of purity], but I thank you and I wash your hands with a bull. I begged the ancestors and I am truly cured.*

THE CROWD: *We greet you, cured!*

ZAKATIANA: *I wash my wife's hands, my children-in-law's, my sister's, my younger brother's, my children's with the blood of the bull. And together with that, Razafy was sad: "My older brother may die." If my older brother lives, we will eat the bull! And before the ancestors he promised. And together with that [my daughter], Denyze spoke, "I may never see my father, for he is sick and may die, and so too I am sick. If my father lives, I will greet him with money, one thousand Malagasy francs" [fifty cents at the time]. [Denyze walks up and hands her money to her father, thereby fulfilling her vow.]*

THE CROWD: *He speaks well!*

ZAKATIANA: *That is why we kill the bull. Along with that [is] the wish I just recounted. To raise children is difficult; many are the children that we cared for. These children that we raised were still crawling or just learning to stand; for those just crawling the ground was covered with dirt, yet the small children ate it. And this too will be cleansed when we eat the Luminous Head!*

THE CROWD: *He speaks well, he speaks well, he speaks well!*

ZAKATIANA: *And with that, Razafy, my younger brother, was harmed through the will of God. Living people don't sin in heaven but here on earth. Razafy went to prison. The government imprisoned him and he has returned. We cleanse him! Along with that, Radany too went to prison, and his family suffered and mourned for him: sad was his father, sad was his mother, ahhh . . . But we don't choose what God does. It was not willed. We cleanse Razafy and we cleanse Radany with the blood of the bull.*

THE WOMEN WHO HAVE MARRIED MEN IN ZAKATIANA'S FAMILY START CHANTING: *Many offspring, many offspring, many offspring!*

ZAKATIANA: *And another reason: if there is that which is fat, it is tsaky [the salty, fatty food that accompanies alcohol consumption]; and I warned Jean-Paul, but he was carried away in his drunken state and he ate eel, yet that is something his ancestors don't eat; yet it is fat and desirable. We cleanse that. That is to say, we purify him so that he won't eat it again, or [turning to Jean-Paul, teasingly] will we have to perpetually purify you?*

THE CROWD (JOKING): *Don't eat it anymore old man, don't eat it any more!*

ZAKATIANA: *Along with that, Zafindrahoarine is very difficult: he doesn't let anyone stay in the house when he goes to plant [a reference to a family taboo]. Yet the descendants grow, the grandchildren are numerous. As Zakatiana's father said, "The bull is fat; we have chosen this day to sambatra. Remove that which is taboo and let it become that which is good. That which is not taboo shall also be good." That is what Zakatiana's father said, and that is why we kill the bull!*

And Rasamy did his military service, did his military service to serve his country.

THE CROWD: *A good thing, that!*

ZAKATIANA: *But his parents here thought of how, while away, he would eat what the ancestors didn't eat, under the orders of a vazaha. We cleanse all that! We wash his mouth. That is why the Luminous Head is brought out.*

THE CROWD: *He speaks well! He speaks well! If you are up for it, we'll kill another [bull] in the morning.*

ZAKATIANA: *And along with that, the family is numerous. There are those wishes that we dare say, and those wishes that we dare not present; small desires and small wishes are like confession [likened to Catholic confession]. Even if you tell no one, God will hear it; those who have made private promises not revealed before the world, those we wash.*

THE CROWD: *He speaks well!*

ZAKATIANA: *I live in the town of Vohilava, truly. There is a house I bought to the south, over there . . . and that house, it was not I who built it. The man who sold that house suffered until I bought it, and this land here, this house here, these haven't yet had any customs. And according to our customs as Betsimisaraka, when you have a tin-roofed house you must mark it with a bull. We enter and bless that house! And we present it to you. That too is a reason for killing the bull.*

THE CROWD: *He speaks well! He speaks well!*

ZAKATIANA: *There is a house to the west of that one. This house is already dilapidated. And this house too hasn't yet had any customs, the reason being that when the house was new the bull wasn't yet fat. There is a kitchen to the east of this house; this kitchen was built by a carpenter who took pains to finish the roof. This kitchen, the floorboards were smoothed and finished, but at that time the bull was not yet fat; but now the bull is fat and we mark the house!*

THE CROWD: *He speaks well! He speaks well!*

ZAKATIANA: *And along with that I call you, the people, I call you to celebrate, to dance and rejoice with us, for we are joyous, for we call not with rum but with a bull. And with that, we call you not to fight. You see, there are those youths who, having drunk rum at home, will create problems here; for this we have no pity. There are many young men here, some who have just come from the army, and they will tie up those who create any problems! And this big house here, it has already been "entered with a bull," but some repairs were made, and we make this known to you. And along with that, according to the proverbs, it used to be that the earth was pierced by trees, but today [it is pierced] with iron. The fence of the nation is the state. Thus if we kill a bull, we have knives and pots, and the knife is not dull; yet we begged permission from the state. We obtained permission.*

THE CROWD: *He speaks well! That is the request for permission!*

ZAKATIANA: *Here is the ticket [waiving the receipt in the air)]. When you leave here to go home, some of you go to Ifasina, others go to Antanambaorampitso, some go to Menagisy [villages in the area]: don't say it was a wounded bull that was slaughtered, but a bull that was sacrificed by Zakatiana, for he had permission! I have finished. Those are the reasons we kill the bull.*

The crowd was by now almost delirious with excitement. When Zakatiana had finished, the respondent, a small man who strutted up and down to the delight of the crowd, answered him, carefully repeating what Zakatiana had said but embellishing the story with local context as well as proverbs. At this point, a woman I had never seen before, also drunk, attached herself to me. Her name was Giselle, and I was told she had been married to a vazaha, the man who had been the foreman for government works in Mahanoro. Unlike all the other women who were dressed in their holiday best, most of them in dresses made of cheap flowered cotton, with the local wrap (lambaoany) tied around their waists, Giselle was dressed in what must have been her conception of la mode: tight, golden bell-bottom pants and a black shirt, a kerchief around her head. She kept following me around calling to me, "Ahh Chérrrrieeee, viens ici, Chérie," demanding money for cigarettes, then for more rum. Other people seemed amused by her antics, and eventually someone intervened, just before the most important part of the sacrifice was to begin.[11]

At this point the bull was brought out and the young man who had been responsible for caring for it, along with some other

young men, ran it through the town. I could not help thinking
that the bull seemed tame, even nonchalant, in comparison to
the people who shrieked, "A bull, a bull!" in delight and fear and
careened into doorways. A few young men who were more daring
(and ritually protected by magic charms) tried to wrestle the bull,
but soon gave up. The boy who had cared for the bull then proudly
led him in a circle around the great house, another occasion for
display and "giving honor" (manome voninahitra) to the house
and, implicitly, to the ancestors associated with the house.

   Eventually, the bull was tethered to the prayer post, and young
men came forward to wrestle him to the ground on his left side,
tying first his back legs, then front legs together, with his head
facing east. A small eating mat was placed to the east of the bull's
head, at the foot of the prayer post, and rum, betsa, white clay, and
honey were placed upon the mat. A boy whose father and mother
were still living smeared white clay on the bull's head, and the bull
was cleansed with water. At this point the invocation was ready
to begin. Zakatiana's father, the tangalamena, walked carefully
to each jiro and poured a bit of rum on each one. He returned to
his position behind the bull, grabbed hold of the staff used to
strike the bull, and began to address the bull:

> *Before I speak to Zanahary and the ancestors I must address you,*
> *the bull. We know that you agreed with Zanahary to pay for the*
> *sins of the children of living people and your flesh is eaten by us.*
> *Having presented you to Zanahary and the ancestors, your flesh*
> *must be eaten by us. You cry out? You should cry out for it hurts*
> *to have your throat slit. You shit? You should shit for it hurts to*
> *be bound in ropes. You look at me? Then bless me, for I hit you*
> *not to trample the fields but to present you to God and the*
> *ancestors. So agree—for you carry a heavy weight in order to*
> *benefit the children of humans. So agree, and may all that you*
> *do today bring us great blessing.*

In reply to my query, Zafilahy explained that cattle and humans
are of equivalent hasina. To kill cattle needlessly, without meaning,
he emphasized, is to create a restless and vengeful ghost.[12] He
stressed that for the bull to resist his own death is perceived as
a sign that fate or the luck of the day might not be in favor of the
sacrifice. The removal of guilt is a precaution, so that no matter
what the bull does, blessing will result. It is also an apology, as the
bull is made to die instead of the human beings for which he stands.

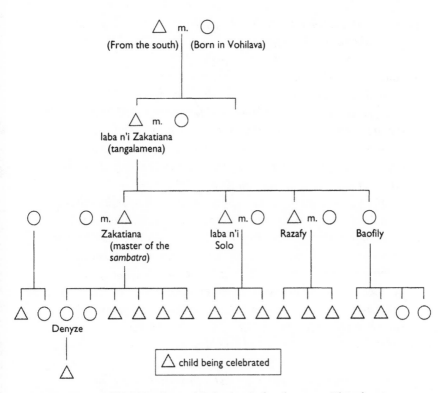

Figure 12. Partial kinship chart of Zakatiana's family, 1992. This chart sketches out the relationships among the key participants at Zakatiana's *sambatra*.

Once the apology was over, the tangalamena let out a piercing cry in order to get God's attention. Then, just as the speech maker explained the meaning of the sacrifice to the assembled community, so the tangalamena announced it to God and the ancestors. At this point the invocation began in earnest, and the tangalamena began to list ancestors' names (see fig. 12). This was the invocation (tsitsika), the part of the sacrifice that people always specified as "really it" (tena izy). The ancestors were called one by one, first the men and then the women. The tangalamena did not know all the names of the different ancestors variously connected to his grandchildren, and so a group of elders gathered around him and whispered names to him so that none might be forgotten. The old men jostled together, calling questions to each other like, "Who was so-and-so's mother" or "Any other women who've married into our group?" reminding each other of the myriad different connections

so that all the ancestors might be called to eat.[13] As each name
was called out, the tangalamena struck the bull with his stick
saying, "Here is the bull, come and eat" (see fig. 13). This process
continued with proper names until the connections began to grow
more distant, at which point only the names of particular tombs
and towns were called. While the older men worked at remembering in order to bring blessing to themselves and their descendants,
the women and children were busy gossiping, joking, and tending
babies among themselves, and seemed happily oblivious to the
more serious negotiations going on.

At this point young men stepped forward to actually kill the
bull. To do so, several men held the beast's head down with a
pestle normally used for shelling rice while another man hacked
at the animal's throat with a knife. The young men then started
to cut apart the animal, reserving particular parts for specified
people. The tangalamena received the right side of the animal's
chest and hump, considered the most honorable portion. His
speech maker received the left side, and the person who had
cared for the animal received one of its feet in addition to some
meat. The division continued, so that eventually every member
of the community received at least a tiny piece of the bull.

At this ceremony, as at many others, an accordion ball (lava
tsynatohy) immediately followed the sacrifice on the ancestral
courtyard, and then a second invocation to God and the ancestors
was made over small pieces of grilled meat. Then, because this
ritual was a sambatra—a ritual aimed at, among other things,
turning boys into men—the taboo (fady), which is intended to
ritually protect the children about to be circumcised, went into
effect. The faces of the mothers-of-the-children were marked with
white clay, as were those of the mothers' brothers (zama). Each
of the mothers' brothers was also given a piece of one of the
bull's right ribs, strung onto a piece of raffia, to wear. For the boys
who were supposed to be celebrated, small packets of seeds were
wrapped in leaves and tied to their waists. The points of the prayer
post were smeared with fat from the bull and sprinkled once again
with rum.

By now it was afternoon, and the "tabooed men" (mpifady)
ran, carrying the bamboo sticks, down to the Mangoro River,
where they scooped up water and then ran back to the town.
Once again, they danced their way through the town, sprinkling

Figure 13. *Tangalamena* invoking the ancestors at Zakatiana's sacrifice, 1993. In order to make sure that the *tangalamena* does not forget to call any of the ancestors during the invocation, many elder men, and occasionally women, gather round him to present names *(manatoro anarana)*, which he then calls out as he strikes the sacrificial bull. Photo by Jennifer Cole.

the crowd with water. That night, the mothers-of-the-children and the tabooed men spent the night guarding the children in the great house. I asked what the tabooed people were tabooed from, and was told that they could not engage in sex or any unclean behavior, as it would harm the children.[14] Toward dawn, boys whose fathers and mothers were still living ran to get "water not crossed by birds," not "touched by women," and brought it back to the great house, where it was placed in a mortar at the eastern door of the great house.

At this point, the key participants ran down to the river—the boys carried on their uncles' backs—and washed their feet and faces in the water. The bamboo was filled once again with water, and the key participants came rushing back to town, spraying the crowd with either water or rice they had carried with them to the river.[15] The tabooed men and women and the boys now reentered the great house, and the boys were passed, screaming, to the tangalamena where he sat, shrouded in a curtain, over the mortar full of sacred water. All of the boys had been circumcised already by a local specialist; the tangalamena simply pulled down the boys' pants, exposing their genitals, and mimicked a cutting motion, then passed the boys out the eastern door to their waiting uncles. The taboo was now over; the rib bones and the seed packets were removed and placed in the roof over the eastern door of the house.

The last moments of the ceremony arrived. The tangalamena and male elders gathered in the great house to complete the ceremony with the asoasony, the presentation of the fattiest cooked meat to Zanahary and the ancestors, and to make one of the final requests for blessing. The head of the bull was placed in the eastern door of the house, its horns tied with six reeds and its right nostril stuffed with a leaf. Rice was scooped from an enormous pot and piled high on a mat; six specially cut leaves were stuck into the pile. The tangalamena took a bite of meat; someone rushed him to start serving meat from the back, and he snapped irritably that he had not finished eating. The tangalamena then called God and the ancestors, though he did not bother to list each one. He informed them that yesterday they had been called to eat the raw meat and today they would eat the cooked meat, and he requested their blessing. Later, Dere explained that this was also supposed to be the moment when the ancestors would be sent home; otherwise, they would surely stay and wreak havoc upon the living. The invocation over, the fatty stew was divvied up and served to people more or less in order of their precedence, with portions being passed outside to where the mothers-of-the-children and other women were waiting. Once the meal was finished, the special leaves were placed in the roof of the house, next to the seed packets and the rib bones.

Zakatiana, the sponsor of the ceremony and son of the tangalamena, now stood up to say a final word of thanks and parting. Before he could finish, however, the man who had responded to the sacrificial speech (kabary) the day before announced angrily that no rum had been served in parting, following the sacrifice, and demanded that it be served now. Wearily, Zakatiana produced the rum; words of parting and thanks to the participants were formally announced once again. We went to thank Zakatiana, who gave us our share of the bull to take back with us. As we walked out of the house Zafilahy explained that our earlier cash contribution did not mean that we had "bought" the meat. Among the Antembahoaka to the south, he continued indignantly, each

*family paid perhaps a thousand Malagasy francs when they
attended a sacrifice, and they could be sure to walk away with
a thousand Malagasy francs' worth of meat; but here the master
of the event bought the bull so that all might receive blessing.
The Antembahoaka treated the bull like dead meat bought at
the bazaar. Here among Betsimisaraka, he continued, it signified
ancestral blessing. We headed toward home. (Field notes, September 1992)*

OFFICIAL MEMORIES

Since sacrifice always reflects the particular struggles of a specific family, no two sacrifices are identical. Nevertheless, whereas the particular ways families try to create official memories are specific, the vision of what official memory should look like is widely shared. In order to honor this tension between the specific and the general, my analysis of Zakatiana's sacrifice relies heavily on the speech transcribed above, but I also draw examples from other sacrifices that I witnessed to fill in the picture of how sacrifice, as memory practice, works.

DIACHRONIC NEGOTIATIONS

Sacrifice mediates and shapes Betsimisaraka perceptions of the past along two intertwined axes. First, people use it to simultaneously constitute and negotiate ancestral power. Second, they use it to rework their relationship to the signs and practices that form the legacy of French colonialism.

Building Ancestors and Negotiating Their Power   The primary meaning that emerged from Zakatiana's sacrifice was the mutually beneficial relationship between ancestors and descendants, in which ancestors bless their descendants with good health, children, and prosperity and descendants respond by offering their ancestors gifts of sacrifice. Zakatiana remarked on his good fortune at various points in the speech, using a variety of expressions: "I have fathered sons! I was sick and now I live. Together we eat the bull." In this respect, his sacrifice resembled the analysis given by Maurice Bloch (1989), who argues that, among the Merina, ancestral rituals are fundamentally about the exchange of ancestral blessings for descendants' acts of honoring the ancestors. Sacrifice thus contributes to the construction of official memories by creating a highly public and emotionally charged spectacle in which the ideal relationship between ancestors and descendants is acted out.

At the same time, Zakatiana used the sacrifice as an occasion to negotiate his and his family members' relationships with various "sites" of ancestral power–memory, particularly ancestral taboos. There were three ways in which people in Zakatiana's family sought to reinstate an ideal relationship with ancestors that had been compromised by violations of taboo. First, Zakatiana referred to children who had "eaten filth," a reference to the fact that children crawling around are likely to eat excrement off the ground. This particular form of "washing" was common, and it took place at almost every cattle sacrifice I witnessed, as people tried to raise their children in ways that were "pure" and "clean," thus maintaining their relationship with ancestors.

Second, Zakatiana used the sacrifice to restore family member Jean-Paul's links with their shared ancestors after Jean-Paul had broken a taboo. In this case, Jean-Paul apparently had broken his taboo because he had been unable to resist his desire to eat a fatty food: "If there is that which is fat it is *tsaky*. I warned Jean-Paul, but he was carried away in his drunken state and ate eel, yet that is something his ancestors don't eat; yet it is fat and desirable." One can almost hear the sympathetic craving in Zakatiana's voice. This example is particularly interesting because it illustrates the ongoing tension Betsimisaraka experience between honoring ancestral memory and fulfilling personal desires, and the way this tension plays a particularly important role in structuring the lives of men. Adolescents and young people know their taboos; everybody, except very small children, does. But adolescent boys are more likely than others to challenge ancestral authority embodied in prohibitions; it is part of their sentimental education as men who, as political agents, may one day challenge ancestors. Moreover, because men tend to travel more, including beyond the confines of the ancestral land, they are more likely than women to be exposed to things "not eaten, not done" by the ancestors. Whatever the cause of the violation, it is symbolically erased when the *tangalamena* purifies the person by feeding him or her a piece of the sacrificial bull dipped in blood. As Zakatiana's father explained about the practice more generally, "You remove the filth and replace it with something good."

The third kind of negotiation that took place at Zakatiana's *sambatra* was an explicit attempt to rearrange the family's connections with their ancestors by actually trying to remove a taboo. As I have suggested, people claimed taboos were good because they protected the power of the land, but they also found them constraining and wanted to avoid them, particularly when the taboos had harmful consequences for descendants or prevented people from engaging in activities that might benefit them. This negotiation is evident in the part of the speech where Zakatiana announced that "Zafindrahoarine is very difficult: he doesn't let anyone stay in the house when he goes to plant." Though I never discovered the origin of this rather bizarre taboo, people I reported it to later interpreted it to mean that the particular family was forced to all go out to plant rice at the same time. The taboo was removed because they found it inconvenient and difficult to obey. Other taboos were not only inconvenient but also dangerous. For example, one prominent ancestry in the village, the Zafindrenian, was prohibited from circumcising male children before they performed the celebratory circumcision sacrifice. This taboo was considered especially cruel and arbitrary because, as cattle grew more expensive, *sambatra* were performed later and later. Eventually, a child, one who was ten years old by the time his parents managed to have the operation and the *sambatra* performed at the same time, died. As a result, the members of the ancestry decided that the prohibition was particularly unbearable, and each family contributed a bull in order to remove the taboo.

The tendency to use sacrifice as a means to erase the constraining power of ancestors embodied in taboos seemed fairly widespread.[16] Again and again I was told how numerous the taboos used to be and how the "children of the evening," the latest descendants of the ancestors, "begged and begged and so were freed" from various restrictions. Several taboos I heard about at other sacrifices clearly had their origins in the topography of power created under Merina and French rule, some aspects of which people found outdated in the postcolonial period. For example, at one ceremony a youth sought to make his living as a butcher, carrying cattle from the south up to Tamatave in the north, where he could sell them for a profit. He had been foiled in his plans several times, and finally had learned through divination that he was subject to a taboo that had been imposed when his ancestor had declared that "no descendant of mine shall go to the north." When I told Josef about the taboo, he speculated that it was perhaps due to the fact that in the past Merina and French had forced Betsimisaraka to "go north," either for corvée or to join the army. In turn, this interpretation suggests that in the past the taboo might have operated as a mechanism of reterritorialization, against the pull of the colonial state. More recently, however, circumstances had changed, and the taboo made the young man unable to take advantage of trading opportunities because he could not pursue business options in the north. At the next family sacrifice, the taboo was removed.

Recasting the Colonial Past   At the same time that sacrifice reworks people's relationships with sites of ancestral memory, it also reworks people's relationships with the signs and symbols of the colonial past. I encountered several different ways in which the colonial past entered into people's concerns during sacrifice; I will take up the specific way colonial practices manifested themselves in Zakatiana's sacrifice, before turning to other examples. Two of the negotiations that Zakatiana included in his speech were about "washing" houses that had tin roofs—one house he had purchased from someone else, and one he had built himself. In the speech Zakatiana said, "According to our customs as Betsimisaraka, when you have a tin-roofed house you must mark it with a bull." What I subsequently discovered was that this kind of sacrifice was in fact created during the colonial period, when settlers and agents of the colonial administration inhabited tin-roofed houses. Whether Zakatiana perceived the ritual as an attempt to transform meanings associated with the colonial period is debatable, and is a question I will return to in chapter 8. But what I want to stress is that initially the ritual was explicitly aimed at transforming tin-roofed houses, once signs of colonial power, into signs of ancestral power.

Though Zakatiana incorporated the process into his *sambatra,* thereby foreshortening the invocation, the full invocation for a "house washing" sacrifice explicitly notes that the house is made differently than a typical "Malagasy" house. For example, the boards that serve as floorboards in a traditional house are used to form the wall, and wood for the frame is often bought in other parts of the country. Finally, the corrugated-tin roof and the nails are imported, or at least used to be, from abroad. Given the symbolic significance of the house as a site of ancestral memory, and the ideas about social relations and hierarchy symbolically encoded in Malagasy houses, it is understandable that new ways of building might require ritual action.[17] People told me that the necessity of sacrifice stemmed from the way tin-roofed houses combined styles of house building and materials that came from antagonistic social orders, which posed a potential threat to the inhabitants. As the *tangalamena* Ratsara explained, "Let's say I covet the house with the corrugated iron roof over there, I covet the functionary's house over there. I decide to make one too. So I take the corrugated tin from overseas, I take the nails that come from overseas, I take palm thatch, and floorboards. But those things—they're not the same. You take the *vazaha* and you take the Malagasy and you mix them. You make the *vazaha* and the Malagasy like kin so that they won't harm the people that live in the house."

Despite Ratsara's portrayal of the Malagasy and the *vazaha* as reified, mutually opposed social orders, actual practice defies such easy dualisms. First, possession of a *vazaha*-style house is seen as something positive because it indicates power and wealth. But it also suggests the thorny problem of unequal access to wealth. Since local cultural logic associates custom with place, to live in a *vazaha* house is in some ways to "become *vazaha*." The house sacrifice reverses this process, for sacrifice forces people who live in a *vazaha* house to give up their wealth in order to affirm their loyalty to ancestors. On one level then, the ritual implies that, despite the fact that people with wealth live in tin-roofed houses like *vazaha*, they are not *vazaha*. But the ritual also reconfigures the meanings associated with tin-roofed houses by taking something that signifies colonial power and making it stand for ancestral power. Once the ritual is completed, what was once the functionary's—perhaps the *chef de canton's*—house is no longer perceived as the symbol of an alien and dominating order but is recast as an "ancestral" site of memory. In this way, the ritual appropriates the power that people accumulate through their associations with *vazaha* and reconfigures it in order to constitute the power of their ancestors.[18]

The coffee-cleansing ritual, or *fafy kafe*, is another important form of sacrifice that mediates people's perceptions of the colonial past, though it was not in fact incorporated into Zakatiana's *sambatra* speech. Where the house ritual seems clearly linked to people's historical experience of the power of settlers and administrators, embodied in the grand house of the planter or the *chef de canton*, the *fafy kafe* seems more closely tied to people's experience of French efforts to create a market economy. Earlier I mentioned that coffee was the crop from which the *colons* made their money. It was also the *colons'* coffee that Betsimisaraka were made to care for and harvest, and it was coffee that Betsimisaraka were themselves supposed to plant as a cash crop in order to pay taxes. Josef explained to me that an order had come "from above" telling everybody to plant a certain number of coffee trees, among other things: "You'd hear, the chief is coming, the chief is coming! And you'd run and clean around your plants. Coffee! Sweet potatoes! Manioc! And they'd come looking for it, and if you didn't have the required number—fifteen days in prison in Mahanoro."

Although Betsimisaraka took to growing coffee and even made enough money from it that they could buy out their obligations to the *colons*, coffee nevertheless came to symbolize a system of exchange and a system of social relations antithetical to their own. In particular, because it was a cash crop, coffee was associated with the acquisition of unseemly quantities of money. Ramaresaka explained to me the origins of the coffee sacrifice:

> It used to be that few people drank coffee—people who had money drank coffee, princes drank coffee. Coffee used to kill those who planted it *[manofa]*. You'd plant coffee and get huge sacks, and all of a sudden you'd go from not having to having. It was too much for their heads! Their heads would turn with the money! They would go to the Chinese merchant to sell their coffee and get cash, and some would be too embarrassed to take the money. Stop, stop they would say! It is too much money. And the merchant would write your name down and give the remaining money to your wife. And some would throw off their ugly raffia clothes and buy fabric. Too much money and their heads would turn! So they started to do the *fafy kafe*—like something transgressed.

As I mentioned earlier, *fafy kafe* is the name for the sacrifice performed specifically when someone's coffee has been particularly fruitful and has brought the owner great wealth. Like the "house entering" sacrifice, it extends the basic sacrificial sequence to encompass a new practice, this time by publicly announcing in the speech the amount of coffee that has been produced and by pouring the blood of the sacrificed bull directly onto the most productive coffee tree. And as with the house sacrifice, people's intent is to assign new meanings to the practice even while they symbolically appropriate the power associated with colonial practices and use it to build up the power of ancestors. What is striking about both of these cases is the fact that the rituals attempt to enact a symbolic reversal: French officials no longer draw Betsimisaraka labor and wealth into the colonial system, and instead Betsimisaraka draw the signs of colonial power into *their* system.

Practices like the *fafy kafe* and house cleansing thus help constitute the power of ancestors, potentially increasing the inequalities among families. Paradoxically, however, people also use these rituals to erase inequalities between ancestries that result from people's differential access to colonial power. Botoroa, the *tangalamena* from a neighboring town, told me about the origins of the ritual: "Coffee came recently but didn't rule in the days before. It was only when Europeans got the land that coffee came, but there wasn't any before. *Fafy kafe* is mimicry. Someone's coffee prospered and so they killed a bull, and someone copied him and the disease was catching. You show off that you have something good, and the disease was catching!" What Botoroa did not need to explain was that, because people believe that neighbor's gossip is what makes ancestors demand a sacrifice in the first place, Betsimisaraka use sacrifice to "even" relations with each other, a point I will return to and discuss in more detail when I examine synchronic negotiations.

Today as in the colonial past, rituals like the *fafy kafe* and the house cleansing and even the washing ceremonies for new soldiers are also partly about forcing wealthy, lucky people to spend their wealth in pursuit of blessing, which is supposed to be shared by all. The fact that people try to use sacrifice to control the emergence of inequalities was evident when Ramaresaka observed that people used to say that coffee would kill its owner if that person did not perform a sacrifice. Social tensions are also implicit in the name of the ritual, for the word *fafy* can also mean "cleansing" and is used to refer to the practice of removing the harm caused by the breaking of a taboo or the violation of proper behavior.[19] As Ramaresaka observed while talking about Betsimisaraka success at coffee production, "It was like something transgressed." Although her statement is ambiguous—in Malagasy it is difficult to tell if "it" refers to coffee or the land—my interpretation is that the "transgression" lies in the way that even the small inequities created by coffee production reshaped social relations among the Betsimisaraka in ways that sacrifice sought to reverse.

Several stories about sacrifice, two of which I will cite here, suggest that people deliberately use sacrifice to erase the effects of colonial rule on their relationships to their ancestors and to one another on an ad hoc basis. Significantly, both of these examples were about conversions to Christianity.[20] While many people in Ambodiharina had entered the local church at one time or another, only a handful of families were actually "enthusiastic Christians," though as far as I could tell, the attendance of the latter at church appeared to complement, not compete with, their ancestral connections. For some of their better-placed relatives, however, increased involvement in church-related networks made some people question, even abandon, their ancestral identifications. One case that Ramaresaka told me about involved her father's older brother, Ramahazosoa, who had been a "big Christian" and who had moved west of Am-

bodiharina to break new land and farm. He built a cement house, Ramaresaka said, knew French, and was wealthy. At home, she said, they
used to pray—all the children prayed and even worked in the church.
When he died, however, one child fell sick and one child went crazy. The
reason, it was later determined, was that when they had done a circumcision ceremony they had failed to call the ancestors. Shaking her head
with amazement, Ramaresaka noted that they had just killed the bull,
like someone killing a chicken. Finally, they had come to the conclusion
that the reason they were sick was because they had given up the ancestors' ways. Since their uncle had never abandoned their ancestors, they
called him to perform a sacrifice in order to apologize for what were, in
effect, transgressions provoked by missionization, and they promised that
they would return to ancestral ways. So now, Ramaresaka said, they pray
and do ancestral customs.

Pierre told me about the second case, which involved his uncle who
"threw down" the tail of the bull—symbolic of the role of *tangalamena*
and one's connection to ancestors—when he converted to Christianity.
His younger brother, however, preferred to keep his relationship with
ancestors, and he picked the bull's tail out of the dirt. He held a sacrifice
to cleanse the bull's tail in order to restore its power and generally for-
malize his renewed commitment to maintaining the power of ancestors.
The example reveals both the variety of reactions to missionization and
the way sacrifice contributed to this variation by enabling people to commemorate or erase their relationship to ancestors' memories according
to their particular personal commitments.

SYNCHRONIC NEGOTIATION

If sacrifice is an attempt to mold the ways in which the power of memory reorders the relationship of the present to the past, it is also profoundly concerned with people's relations in the present, which people
attempt to mold while keeping an eye toward the future. This emphasis
on synchronic relationships is evident in the "equalization" sacrifices I
just described, which were aimed at shaping how the colonial past mediated people's relationships to each other. There were also four other
kinds of synchronic negotiations that recurred in the sacrifices that I attended, though only two were relevant to Zakatiana's particular performance. First, people used sacrifice to negotiate their relationships with
other family members. Second, they used it to negotiate their relationships with members of the wider community. Third, they used it to for-

malize or dissolve existing social relationships. Fourth, they used it to mediate their relationship to the postcolonial state.

Negotiating Family Relationships   In Zakatiana's sacrifice, the primary negotiation that took place was his "cleansing" and honoring of those family members who had cared for him while he was sick.[21] As he said in the speech, he did not cleanse them with mere coconut oil but with the much more awesome, grandiose blood of a bull. But Zakatiana's use of sacrifice to transform his relations with his contemporaries, limited as it was to cleansing people who had been polluted by caring for a sick man, was minimal compared to many of the other sacrifices I saw. It was also touching, since he was actually behaving according to local ideals by honoring people who had fulfilled their kinship obligation to him. Much of the time, however, people use sacrifice to repair tears in the social fabric, making social relations that were less than ideal conform to what people wished they were. For this reason sacrifice is often referred to as the "big knife that removes knots," because it repairs flaws in social relationships, smoothing over imperfections as a knife removes imperfections from a tree.

Since many times the consequences of fights linger on because people awaken *hasina* when they get angry and curse each other, people often take sacrifice as an opportunity to revoke words that might potentially hurt themselves or others. In one sacrifice that I attended at a village up-country, the sponsor's speech revealed that he and his sister had started to clear adjacent plots of land. They had fought over the land when the sister declared, "My wealth doesn't make you living and your wealth doesn't make me living," which meant that the man would be unable to prosper from farming that land. Later, they made up, and the brother ended up buying the sister's land. Eventually, he used the sacrifice to mark an official end to the fight and to remove his sister's curse so that it would not affect his ability to prosper from the land.

Other kinds of negotiations involved curses that people had foolishly imposed on themselves in a momentary reaction to anger or grief that they later regretted. One speech maker at a sacrifice narrated the story of a young woman who bore two children in another town and then, upon moving home to Ambodiharina, bore a third. When this last child died the woman spoke out in grief saying, "It is better not to have given birth at all than to give birth only to have the child die," which was tantamount to saying she would never bear children again. Later, the woman changed her mind, but found that her words had already taken effect and she was unable to conceive. At the next family sacrifice, she arranged for the speech maker to "return the words" in front of the bull and replace them with the following: "But she thought again—perhaps it is better to give birth once after all. To give birth, to flourish, that is why we sacrifice the bull." This same speech also described the suffering of a widower: "Velonjara took a wife from Antanimay, and his wife died while the children were still small. He spoke thus, "Ahh, if my children are not yet grown I'll never marry again." Again, the curse was ritually removed, enabling the widower to remarry.

Remaking Community   A reworking of the sponsoring family's relationships with the wider community is another important kind of negotiation that figures centrally in how people imagine what sacrifice is about, though it was not a part of Zakatiana's speech. I first learned about this aspect of sacrifice when Reni n'i Jacqueline told me about her husband's relative from upcountry, Lemontana. Lemontana was structurally an important elder for Reni n'i Jacqueline's husband, and so it was with some dismay that she recounted the problems that Lemontana had run into with his family. Reni n'i Jacqueline explained that Lemontana's family and the wider community had been angry with him and had forced him to "bring out a bull" or risk being tied to the foot of the prayer post and having the ancestors invoked over his very body. I eventually met Lemontana, and asked him what had happened. He replied:

> I asked permission from the government to make *betsa* and got the patent. But instead of being happy, my family was upset and jealous because it meant an end to their own dealing on the black market. I didn't tell them not to make beer. Instead, I said go ahead and make *betsa* and use it for ancestral purposes but not to sell, so they wouldn't get caught. I went to Mahanoro to take care of business, and in my absence they sold *betsa* and were caught. The gendarme had already passed by and warned them once before. Upon my return from Mahanoro they accused me of having turned them in. The villagers insisted I sacrifice a bull or they would expel me from the village [*Ho ariana raha tsy manome aomby*]—so the villagers forced me to pay a bull. If I had been expelled I couldn't have lived. I am not self-sufficient; I depend on my family. I also wanted to continue to make *betsa,* for which I had just received the patent.

Though Lemontana's story was the only example of someone during my stay who "brought out a bull" to stand in for his sins, once I started asking people about the practice, numerous people discussed times in the recent past when this had happened. For example, several people re-

counted examples in which villagers less privileged by colonial opportunities had used sacrifice as a way to settle accounts with their more
privileged family members and neighbors. Pierre, for example, told me
about Rafaly's father, who, as I discussed in chapter 5, was related to a
colon. He had bragged about his power relative to his fellow villagers
by citing the proverb "Ahh, but the children of the blackbird are pitifully
beaten by the children of the falcon!" As soon as French power lessened
in the 1950s, the villagers were able to take their revenge, forcing him
to throw a sacrifice in order to "wash" *(mamafy)* his haughty words or
be expelled from the village. A similar case recounted by Tovolahy and
Babette had clearly entered local folklore, because it had occurred well
before their births. They told me of a man who had made so much money
growing coffee that he proudly bought shoes and stomped on everyone's
feet at the next village dance. When people complained, the man laughed,
saying, "Oh, that's not me stepping on your feet. It's robusta!" the species
of coffee from which he had earned his money. For his arrogance, he too
was made to apologize through sacrifice. The most dramatic reparational
sacrifices took place in 1947, when the rebel army forced everyone who
had been friendly with Europeans to "bring forth a bull" in order to establish their loyalty to the ancestral order. Looking back at sacrifices like
the *fafy kafe* or the house washing, one can easily imagine that the rituals emerged through people's efforts to smooth just these kinds of social
tensions.

Creating and Dissolving Relationships   Lemontana's story of almost
being disowned raises another aspect of how relationships can be either
created or dissolved through public vows made in sacrifice. Although informal fostering among kin is the norm, it is not uncommon for a childless couple to choose one or two of their sibling's children to adopt formally in sacrifice. Though Zakatiana's sacrifice did not include such a
transaction, a later sacrifice that I attended in the same village did. A
couple had raised two children, lavishing both care and wealth on them.
The speech given at the sacrifice declared they would now formally adopt
the children. Generally, children who have been "made standing" *(nitsangana)* are considered the legitimate heirs to the adopting person, and
any subsequent disputes over land or moveable wealth brought before
the village council will generally be decided in their favor. As Ramaresaka observed, performing the ritual of "making standing with a bull"
was just as if one had recorded an adoption in the registry at Mahanoro.
    But if relationships could be formalized through sacrifice, they could

also be terminated, as Lemontana's story implies, and it is possible, albeit rare, to "throw away" a kinsperson. One story Pierre told me was about Bototsara and his son Jonasy. Jonasy had lived with his mother as a boy and later came to live with his father, as older children often did. He stole things—first a bit of coffee to sell for money to go to a ball, later a little rice—and was caught. His father warned him not to steal. When he was caught stealing yet again, his father dissolved the relationship by calling the community; giving his son a knife, hoe, and pot; and swearing over the body of a bull that the boy was no longer his son. In this case, the bull was sacrificed and the community ate it, thereby giving their consent to the expulsion. Not surprisingly, perhaps, hardly anybody would talk about this incident. Except for Pierre, who dared resist the collective flow of forgetting, the fact that Bototsara had once had a son named Jonasy had apparently been successfully erased from collective memory.

Negotiating with the Postcolonial State   One aspect of contemporary social relations that figured prominently in Zakatiana's sacrifice and entered into almost all of the sacrifices that I attended concerned people's relations with the postcolonial state. The presence of the state is evident in the ending words of Zakatiana's speech ("It used to be that the earth was pierced by trees, but today [it is pierced] with iron. The fence of the nation is the state."), a reference to the way the current regime imposes a tax on sacrifice, as had the French and Merina regimes before. But what is most fascinating about how contemporary state-local relations enter into sacrifice is the way in which people repeatedly use sacrifice to assert symbolic control over those who have been pulled away from local control, into the embrace of the state. In much the same way that certain aspects of people's colonial experience became institutionalized, whereas other aspects are dealt with on an ad hoc basis, certain aspects of postcolonial experience are both symbolically important and recurrent enough to be institutionalized in sacrificial practice. In particular, Betsimisaraka have developed ways for dealing with their experience of the army and prison, two social institutions that people identify as being quintessentially of the state. In Zakatiana's speech, the most prominent negotiation of this type concerned Razafy, a family member who had been to prison, and Rasamy, who had done his military service.

In both cases, the assumption behind the negotiation was that these men had been forcibly made to neglect their ancestral taboos. The notion that recruits to the army or prisoners are forced to participate in a system that is antithetical to ancestral power brings us back to the cultural logic noted earlier that associates custom with place. Betsimisaraka believe that ancestral power embodied in taboos is only efficacious within the context of the ancestral land. As proof, they cite the fact that ancestors only punish their descendants' violations at home; some people even told me that ancestors would not dare punish their descendants by making them sick while they were away, because they are afraid of *vazaha*. Whether my interlocutors meant that Betsimisaraka became *vazaha* while away, or whether they meant that the ancestors were so scared of *vazaha* that they would let them take away their descendants, remains unclear. But given that taboos are one way that ancestors control their descendants, it seems likely that the forcible neglect of taboos imposed on soldiers and prisoners is a powerful way to symbolize their appropriation by the state. In turn, the washing of people in sacrifice simultaneously cleanses returned soldiers of the violations suffered at the hands of the colonial state and reappropriates them as children of ancestors, hence subject to ancestral control.

But it is crucial to emphasize that, although Rasamy and Razafy's reappropriation was largely symbolic, this is not always the case. Particularly when the army recruit or returnee is responsible for sponsoring the sacrifice, sacrifice plays an important role in drawing wealth earned while away back into local control. The case of Mamy that I mentioned in chapter 3 provides a good example. Recall that Mamy was a member of the RESEP, Ratsiraka's special corps, and that he had fallen sick immediately upon his return from the army. Though people initially thought that he was made sick by the medicine given him by the bad *tromba* people in Mahanoro, they subsequently decided that the illness was caused by his mother's demands for a sacrifice in thanks for his success. Consequently, much of Mamy's visit was spent arranging for the sacrifice to take place the following year; when I returned three years later it had already been completed.

Mamy's story illustrates how sacrifice can have a powerful reterritorializing effect, as ancestors assert their control over both people and wealth in relation to translocal processes of state power (see Cole and Middleton 2001). Once on ancestral soil, even the soldier is beholden to the same moral obligations as those who continue to inhabit their ancestral village. Moreover, the returnee is particularly vulnerable to ancestral demands for cattle. After all, he or she has been away, and other family members have probably already paid their dues. When this person returns home, people assume that he or she must have prospered while away. In turn, their gossip is likely to make the returnee the object of his or her ancestors' attentions all the more quickly. For the returnee, sacrifice is inevitable; in Mamy's case his ancestors' recognition of his return and their subsequent demand for a sacrifice were unusually swift.

Witnesses   Finally, before I turn to alternative memories embedded in sacrifice, one last practice must be examined. This practice, "witnessing," is structurally built into the ceremony as a whole. Recall the fact that my visiting party had to go to Zakatiana and present our small contribution, and that he responded by thanking us for having "put down our work." This little ritual marked us as witnesses. We were important for the ritual in two ways. First, our presence marked the sacrifice (or any ancestral supplication) as a "good," legitimate social activity, one meant to bring blessing rather than harm. As one *tangalamena* explained to me, "Good things need friends, but for bad things no witnesses are needed, so that no one may see your heart's intentions. If something is good then you alone can not complete it. There must be a friend to make it true— for good things, friends *(namana)* are needed."[22] Second, as part of the series of endless guests on the morning of a sacrifice, each of us bearing a bit of money and leaving after having drunk a glass of rum, each contributed to making the sacrifice powerful. My repeated questions as to why the other villagers were necessary at all (given how jealously the meat is guarded) only provoked exasperation from Josef. "Don't you know," he almost scolded me, "people are God on this earth, so if the villagers don't attend, then the illness won't be cured? Nothing finished! What, you, alone kill a bull? What makes that true? It is the villagers that make the sacrifice real."[23]

Tavo Robert, who lived in a neighboring town, explained the necessity of witnesses more fully: "You need the other villagers *[fokon'olona]* because people didn't create themselves but were made by Zanahary and borne by the ancestors. If you kill a bull and don't call the *fokon'olona* but only your family and your children, then Zanahary and the ancestors won't accept it, because there are no witnesses. The reason you call people of each town and the villagers is to prove you've really paid, really kept your promise. But if only you and your family sacrifice the bull, it is as if you were a butcher, because the *fokon'olona* didn't attend."

The image of community as one where people join together to construct an official memory and help their neighbors to unlock ancestral blessing is most fully expressed in the speech made in response to the sponsor's speech prior to the sacrifice of the bull. Ideally, the respondent is someone who stands in for the other ancestries that comprise the community, and his speech inevitably emphasizes how normal the actions of the first group are, despite the fact that people often sacrifice in order to rectify potentially embarrassing situations. By the time the respondent is done, any misdeeds or follies that have been revealed seem perfectly normal, as if the actions of the sacrificing ancestry were the epitome of humanity and anyone faced with a similar set of predicaments would have done the same thing. The perfect, self-evident reasonableness of anything revealed by the speech maker is constituted through the "answer" of the respondent. For example, if the organizer's speech reveals that two brothers have fought, and that they wish to rectify the situation, the respondent might invoke the proverb "One seed doesn't rattle" to talk about how normal sibling tension is. Likewise, if one of the reasons that the sacrifice is performed is to wash a child who had accidentally eaten excrement and been defiled, the respondent might go on about how raising children is terribly hard, using stock phrases to make the event part of the larger human predicament. By using proverbs and stock phrases, the respondent generalizes the events and makes them seem a part of a shared human condition.[24]

The effect of the responding speech is to make the witnesses complicit with the sponsors in assuring their successful acquisition of ancestral blessing. When an ancestry negotiates relationships in sacrifice, they say they *mangala* with a bull. The word *mangala* means "to take, grab, or steal," and it is precisely this act of not-quite-theft to which the assembled villagers act as accomplices. Thus, the official memory produced in sacrifice, built out of these numerous different negotiations, is arrived at through the public enactment of consensus. By acting as witnesses and partaking of the sacrificial bull, other members of the community express their acceptance of the memory the sponsor is trying to create.[25] Recall that no one but Pierre would tell me about Bototsara's son Jonasy, who had been expelled. In effect, people's silence on the matter suggested that they were indeed good witnesses: they had sanctified the official memory, and they stood by that official version of events long after the sacrifice had occurred.

Official Memories: An Initial Summary   Let me extract from the morass of various transactions that we've considered here a rough pattern to the process of creating official memory. According to the official memory created in sacrifice:

1. Ambodiharina is a world of mutually nurturing ancestors and descendants;

2. Ambodiharina is a world free of social tension;

3. The different ancestries work as witnesses to help each other unlock ancestral blessing;

4. Ambodiharina is a world where the narrative of colonial power can be "washed" and reconfigured as a narrative of ancestral power; and

5. Ambodiharina is a world where the inequalities that resulted from Betsimisaraka's differential access to the structures of colonial power can be leveled through sacrifice.

Viewed from this "official" perspective, sacrifice plays a crucial role in producing the "ancestral" side of Ambodiharina that dominates everyday life.

We might conceptualize this official memory as a form of what Gilbert Ryle (1949) long ago called "knowing that," the kind of knowledge that people gain from explicit propositions, that tells them how the world works and how it is supposed to be. As Tanya Luhrmann (1989) points out, this is a linguistically acquired form of knowledge, and it is well suited to the elaborate form of the sacrificial speech through which official memory is conveyed. Ryle contrasts "knowing that" to "knowing how," the knowledge of skills—like driving a car—that one can perform but not necessarily explain. In the following pages, I use this term more broadly to show how the practice of commemorating ancestors—not just the techniques of ritual but the messy practices of organizing the ritual and bringing it off—pulls against this idealized, official memory with an alternate kind of procedural understanding. In Ryle's discussion, the distinction between "knowing how" and "knowing that" is simply supposed to highlight two separate but interrelated sides of the process of knowing. In transposing this distinction to the domain of social remembering in sacrifice, I want to highlight the ways the two kinds of memory are in tension with each other, a tension in which the "knowing how" (complexities of practice) undermines and subverts the declarative official memory of "knowing that." Unofficial memories emerge from local practice and social relations, where we see that things are not so neat as the official memory would like people to believe.

UNOFFICIAL MEMORIES

In the following section I bring the official memories just sketched into tension with the unofficial memories with which they coexist. In order to do so, I abstract several aspects of the official memory and contrast them with the unofficial memories implicit in local practice. I should stress that, because the interpretations that follow are not a part of the dominant discourse, I was not aware of them when I attended Zakatiana's ceremony. At the time, my focus was on mastering procedural knowledge and I could not see the unofficial memory it encoded. Rather, I became aware of these alternate memories over the course of my first period of fieldwork and then again in talking to people in 1997. Thus, my discussion is based on my cumulative understanding of many different sacrifices in the area, but I bring the discussion back to Zakatiana's case where appropriate.

Ambodiharina Is a World of Mutually Nurturing Ancestors and Descendants   The first and most obvious way in which local practice belies the official memory produced in sacrifice lies in people's beliefs that ancestors are not always nurturing. Instead, they are often perceived as rapacious ghosts who make their descendants sick. Though people talk about the cruel side of ancestors (see Josef's reflections in chapter 3), this belief is routinely embedded in the sequence of events that leads up to any sacrifice. What happens is that the sick person will visit a diviner and be told that he or she has to throw a sacrifice in order to be cured. Usually, the process begins when the sick person "gives voice" by going to the great house of the ancestor he or she believes is causing the illness, invoking the ancestor over honey and rum, and promising that the ancestor will, eventually, get a sacrifice. In so doing, the sick person must acknowledge, and thus constitute, his or her own weakness and meaninglessness before the ancestors, who are the source of all meaning and strength.

The process forces people to acknowledge that all the good things that happen—the rice, the incredible coffee yield, the birth of so many grandchildren—is not due to their own labor but to ancestral blessing. This emphasis on ancestral blessing is of course part of official ideology. What is not part of the official ideology is that ancestors inflict violence on their descendants if their power is not adequately recognized. The danger of ancestors is also implicit in the medicine that the sick person gets from the diviner. Thus what everybody at Zakatiana's sacrifice knew, but no one said, was that the reason Zakatiana had been sick in the first

place was because of his ancestors' wrath. When I suggested that sometimes descendants might want to give a sacrifice to thank ancestors of
their own accord, I was always told that it was a preposterous idea—
people had to be made sick before they would give anything.

But in the case of Zakatiana's ceremony there was yet another element
at play, because his sacrifice was a *sambatra,* the kind of ceremony that
men perform when they have numerous sons. According to official rhetoric, people perform a *sambatra* in order to thank the ancestors for bestow-
ing sons on them. But the sacrifice also involves a peculiarly male form of
boasting, where the sponsors aggressively display their wealth, implicitly
declaring not only the strength of their ancestors but also their own. This
element of boasting was evident throughout Zakatiana's speech, when he
kept returning to the fact that he was honoring people not with mere rum
but with a bull. But it was particularly evident at the end of the ceremony,
when he told people returning home to announce the fact that he had
sacrificed, carrying news of his wealth and power to the wider surrounds.

Some of the nicknames for a *sambatra,* which include *laza* (renown)
and *deradera* (preening or bragging), capture this element of boasting.
People always emphasized that circumcision ceremonies were one kind
of sacrifice that men brought on themselves, typically by bragging at another person's circumcision that they too had many sons and could pull
off a sacrifice even more sumptuous than the one they were attending.
Indeed, this was the reason for Zakatiana's *sambatra* as well. As he explained in his speech, he had promised to throw a *sambatra* and had not
followed through until he had been forced to do so by illness inflicted by
ancestors. The hint of punishment in every *sambatra* (indeed every
sacrifice) suggests that sacrifices are also occasions on which men taunt
their ancestors, an interpretation implicit in another informal name for
a circumcision celebration, "bringing out" boys, which connotes a man
flaunting his sons in front of the ancestors. Since sons are critical to their
father's future constitution as a powerful ancestor, the *sambatra* is a
double-edged act that builds up ancestral power but also implicitly threatens ancestors with their future obsolescence. A man may use the ritual
to flaunt his power in front of his ancestors, but he does so through the
medium of his most precious asset, his sons, which the ancestors may
take away at any time.

Ambodiharina Is a World Free of Social Tension   The fights that break
out either during the planning of sacrifices or their performance, as well
as participants' heavy use of magic for protection from possible harm,

flagrantly contradict the official memory of harmony produced in sacrifice. Josef once remarked, "Cattle make people fight." When I asked him why, he cryptically responded that it was simple: it came from love. But while Josef makes it sound like people fight *over* cattle, which is partly true, it is also true that they fight *through* them; the bull is an object around which a veritable force field of people's competing intentions and desires coalesce. Though I had read about the historical connection between sacrifice and politics in Grandidier (1958) before arriving in Ambodiharina, I was stunned by the degree to which the equation between the two still held. Possessing one's own *jiro,* which symbolizes the ability to sacrifice, continues to constitute ritual and political autonomy. The metaphoric equation between control over sacrifice and political autonomy is particularly clear in the way people speak about how slaves, people who were considered politically and ritually dependent, gained autonomy. People always said that the slaves had "begged" for permission to "make standing" *jiro* of their own, and they used the same word to describe this process as they did to describe Madagascar's independence from France *(fahaleovan-tena).* People often remarked that there used to be only a few great houses in the town, and men were constantly trying to create new great houses in order to control them. The more I learned about the histories of local political divisions, the more it became clear that they had taken place in the context of sacrifice.

Sacrifices, then, are an important moment of political reckoning. Because they are large intervillage and interfamily events, all sorts of people come from the surrounding area to partake in the festivities. With all those people gathered together in one place, people told me, one can never be sure whose intentions are "clear and true" *(mazava)* and whose intentions are of a more shadowy nature. I was told again and again that you could not see into the hearts of people, which meant that you could not see people's true intentions and motives. No one is more at risk than the person sponsoring the sacrifice, who always goes to a diviner to have his or her *vintana,* or astrological position, "read" in order to predict the possible outcome of the event.[26] If the diviner finds the day inauspicious, the sponsor may ask him to try and "throw" the harm away. Josef explained the practice this way: "There is only a single day and if your work is not clean, then there might be catastrophe: death, the town burns, or the bull kills someone. That danger looks for someone to sit on—the day of begging for blessing is terribly difficult. You rejoice and some terrible thing sneaks in, and so you're forced to protect yourself. Each to his own disease. Yet there is only this day. You forbid [the disease] so it doesn't show itself." To illustrate his point, Josef told me the story of Maman n'i Telo's sacrifice, which had been held on her ancestral court-yard, south of the village. Everything had gone smoothly until the mid-dle of the invocation, when a fire broke out northwest of the town, burn-ing another woman's house to the ground. People assumed that the tragedy of the fire, intended for Maman n'i Telo, had been ritually "thrown" onto someone else.

The diviner may also protect the master of the sacrifice with medi-cines. When I asked Ratsara why one needed protection for a sacrifice, he answered with a proverb: "The leaves of trees were made to shelter the children of living people." Although the proverb might be taken lit-erally, since Betsimisaraka do make their livelihood from the forest, in this case it was used metaphorically to refer to the magical power of leaves and their protective properties. Even if the master of the event chose a day that was auspicious and trusted it, he nevertheless had to protect himself against the malice of other people who might seek to "turn" the day and harm him. Though I have focused on the way the sponsor sought to protect himself, other participants also attempt to protect themselves. As a result, the days before a ceremony are a busy time for the three di-viners in Ambodiharina, as various parties seek their protection. During the days before a massive sacrifice to inaugurate a new tomb, for exam-ple, Tsaravintana was so busy dispensing protective medicine that all of his rice work was temporarily pushed aside.

To hear people talk about what it is like to organize and produce a sacrifice is to realize that sacrifices are intensely competitive events, at which the local order is both made and remade in a continually shifting pattern of alliances and antagonisms requiring continuous negotiation. The fear—and perhaps expectation—that a sacrifice will lead to fights was always evident in the first question that people would ask me when I arrived back from sacrifices in neighboring towns: Were there any fights? Sometimes these fights are about which family had contributed more for the bull, or who had brought the most rice. At other times they were about the way in which the ritual was actually carried out. In all cases, material contributions and ritual actions are read as indicative of a per-son's ability to command resources as well as of their love and devotion for particular people.

Ideally, the enormous investment that a family makes in a sacrifice en-ables all members of the family to receive blessing from their ancestors equally. This ideal of solidarity and shared connection to ancestors is ex-pressed in the aphorisms "Where the ancestors are concerned all must eat" and "With talk of ancestors one doesn't need differentiation." The ideal of equal participation is symbolically achieved through the equal division of the bull, which is a metaphor for the blessing received from ancestors. The attempt to achieve equality among the living means that every last bit of the bull is divided among the witnesses, each of whom is scrupulously given his or her share. The attempt to achieve equality in one's relationship to the dead means that all ancestors are called to "come and eat." Failure to call the name of an ancestor—whether related through blood or marriage—is a grave offense and can even lead to divorce. As Josef put it, sacrifices make people fight because of love, or— to amplify his point—precisely because people are never loved in exactly the same way.

Intentional oversight—favoring one branch of one's family over another seemingly through oversight—is a major source of conflict. It is precisely because of an intentional oversight that Zafilahy's family had split up during a circumcision sacrifice some years earlier. He and his brother had built houses next to one another, but when their sister threw a circumcision celebration, she proceeded to lead the dancers around the elder brother's house and ignored the younger brother's. Her actions so wounded her younger brother that he settled permanently in another village in the country, while his great house stood empty in town. In yet another case, a man had objected when some boys had tried to steal some of his sugarcane during a circumcision celebration, which is an accepted part of the ritual.[27] The next year, when a different family held a circumcision celebration, they refused to include his house in the proceedings, symbolically marking his expulsion from the community. In this context the painstaking care with which the elders at Zakatiana's celebration made the dancers circle each great house and prayer post makes sense. The elders knew that to fail to do so was to disrespect the ancestors associated with those houses, and that it would almost certainly cause a serious fight.

The degree to which sacrifices are sites of power struggles became clear to me when I returned to Ambodiharina after finishing my dissertation and decided to sponsor my own sacrifice to thank the villagers for their support during my earlier fieldwork. During my initial visit there had been some mild tension regarding which families had access to me; initially, some people had been frightened of me. Those people who took me in, however, were later perceived to have gained an advantage once people realized I was in fact not a spy or the granddaughter of a settler coming to reclaim land.

I had intended the sacrifice as a gift for the entire town. However, it was not long before the family who had been most responsible for caring for me claimed that, since they had been responsible for me, the sacrifice had to be done at *their* great house, which gave *them* control over the proceedings, drawing me into the process of empowering *their* ancestors. Other people countered that I had been "brought by the government" (since I had been introduced to the village by a government official, the *delegué*), and that the sacrifice should take place at the "foot of the flag," the symbol of the state. A meeting was held to determine what would be done, and eventually, by sheer force of will, I think, my family won out and duly sacrificed the bull on their courtyard. But at least some of the community members were still angry, and during the proceedings young men broke into the great house and stole some of the meat that had been reserved for honored guests. At first, I was mortified by the level of conflict and assumed that it was only at the anthropologist's sacrifice that people would behave in such a manner. As it turned out, numerous people reassured me by telling me about all the times that fights had broken out at *their* sacrifices, leaving broken loyalties and new groupings in their wake.

Looking back at my field notes, I realized that many of the conflicts in sacrifice that I had heard of were precisely about the expression of everyday tension in the context of ritual: since ritual embodies the articulation of social hierarchy, it was in ritual that the hierarchy was contested. For example, one fight I heard narrated at a sacrifice was the story of two cousins, Iaba n'i Jerome and Iaba n'i Namo, who were related to each other as "child of women" *(zanañy vavy)* and "child of men" *(zanañy lahy)*, respectively. Typically, "children of men" are believed to have closer ties to ancestors and are responsible for caring for ancestors and working as *tangalamena*. In this case, however, the crosscutting hierarchy of younger and elder siblings undermined the hierarchy, placing the child of men below the child of women. Iaba n'i Jerome was a "child of women," but he was also much older than Iaba n'i Namo. The elders in the family had collectively passed control over ancestors to Iaba n'i Jerome with the proviso that eventually he would hand over control of the ancestors to Iaba n'i Namo. But Iaba n'i Jerome was loath to part with his position of power. Tension over who would control the ancestors had been building for some time, and the situation finally exploded at a circumcision ceremony, when Iaba n'i Jerome's son told his uncle, "You are not master of this sacrifice." The comment insulted the uncle by implying that he was not entitled to participate in the event, and he became so angry that he left and refused to participate in the rest of the proceedings. A few months later at the Fête des Morts, tensions were still simmering. The two families had divided "houses," but they still shared an ancestral tomb and thus were forced to come together to deal with caring for their shared ancestors.[28] A fight broke out again, this time between the men's sons, but the fathers got involved when they tried to separate the young men, and one of them was decked by his nephew in the ensuing struggle.[29]

According to the speech I witnessed, however, the conflict described was long over and the division had already occurred. Iaba n'i Namo had successfully seized control of the family's ancestors and was using the sacrifice to erase all prior signs of contest or previous genealogies of ancestral control. The effort to "wash" the fight was in effect an attempt to reconstitute symbolically the relationship between the two brothers and to dispel any ancestral wrath they might have incurred through their struggle. This example illustrates how the direction of social tension— from that of everyday life to the ritual context of sacrifice and back again—is highly porous: people use ritual to express tensions that have developed in everyday life, and they use ritual to mend tensions that have emerged in everyday life. But their efforts are not always successful. Even when sacrifice is used to restore and create ideal relationships, the bitterness and jealousy that caused the sacrifice in the first place sometimes linger on. As Lemontana, the man who had been forced to sacrifice a bull in reparation to his family, commented, "But I see to this day my family continues to hate me—the proof of this is they haven't set foot yet in my house. They continue to be jealous and hate me although the bull is now dead."

The Different Ancestries Work as Witnesses to Help Each Other Unlock Ancestral Blessing   Though the practice of witnessing creates an image of an ideal community produced in sacrifice—where people join together to create official memories and help their neighbors unlock ancestral blessing—social relations, as we have seen, are rarely so simple. The ongoing conflicts that run throughout sacrifice also inflect the official purposes of witnessing. Take, for example, the case of Bototsara and his son Jonasy. Though the community participated as witnesses, it is not clear on what grounds they did so. Rumors about Bototsara suggested that he had powerful magic that enabled him to transgress social norms without suffering any consequences. The community came, but it may have been out of fear of Bototsara rather than desire to support his actions. Though this is a particularly dramatic example, this tension between the sponsor and the wider community is an important subtext running through most response speeches. At one sacrifice the respondent admonished the sponsor's family thus:

> We see those cattle and we think they are many. It is like when you look and see many huge ships scuttling over the sea, and then look again only to find a poor fisherman's pirogue fighting the waves. Don't do that, please, but share well, for there are many. There was once a man who said he did not play with pebbles [tsy milalao vato lalaka]. If we get a share as we do [when that ancestry makes a sacrifice], then truly it will be our lot and our share. We've come to eat, for we've put down our livelihood. Make us full so that when we go home we say, "I've never seen such a good sacrifice." But if we go home gossiping, "Eh, look what they've done over there," don't do that for we have come to feast. Cook those cattle quickly, for we, the assembled, have heard.

The speech highlights the antagonistic relationship that weaves through the complicity linking sponsors and their witnesses, for both groups hope to receive ancestral blessing, and they require each other in order to do so. The blessing, however, is double edged, for, like the notion of *rangitra* discussed earlier, blessing is used to explain why some people are luckier and more successful than others. Behind the ideal of equal blessing for all lurks the fact that some inevitably get more (health, happiness, wealth, whatever) than others. The "man who said he did not play with pebbles" (a proverb chosen to indicate his generosity and avoidance of petty disputes) was a man named Tsaravoky (whose name, appropriately, meant "replete" or "satisfied"), a *tangalamena* well-known for the generosity with which he shared sacrificial meat. It was quite common for older men to use proverbs to describe themselves. In this case, the comparison was in turn used by the respondent to push the sponsors subtly toward generosity with the meat and the ancestral blessing, as well as the subsequent prosperity the blessing might bring.

The following image, which is frequently used to close the respondent's speech, also captures the teasing rivalry between the sponsoring ancestry and the wider community: "May they have money in the hundreds while we get money in the thousands. You carry [the burden—a reference to the ancestors] on your head while we here carry [the burden] across our shoulders."[30] The rivalry is expressed in the reference to money. Everyone wants the sacrifice to provoke a windfall, and each person hopes it will fall in his or her favor. The image of carrying, however, is more complex and has reverberations beyond the sacrificial context. People often used bodily metaphors or images of carrying a burden to describe the relationship between ancestors and their descendants. Human beings carry their ancestors on their heads *(tatovina)*; the ancestors crouch upon the heads and shoulders of their descendants. So, although the respondent roguishly taunts the sponsors, urging them to share the blessing, ultimately the sponsor's speech acknowledges what everyone already knows, despite the talk of sharing: blessing is really intended for the masters of the sacrifice. "You carry on your head, while we carry on our shoulders," the speech says. One might imagine the ancestors of the masters of the ceremony riding on their descendants' heads, spraying water-cum-blessing down onto their descendants, while the assembled community, who carry on their shoulders, are fortunate to catch what blessing slips past.[31]

Ambodiharina Is a World Where the Narrative of Colonial Power Can Be "Washed" and Reconfigured as a Narrative of Ancestral Power   As we saw earlier, people use sacrifice to reverse the effects of colonization. Rather than have their ways of seeing and being, of building houses, and of making a living shaped by cultural forms introduced by French colonialism, they attempt to appropriate the power associated with colonial rule in order to create the power of their ancestors. Critical to the success of these rituals in asserting this reality is the masking of roots. As much as possible, the *fafy kafe* and house-washing rituals rework the meanings associated with coffee and tin-roofed houses, thereby hiding the social relations that make ancestral power in a colonial and postcolonial world possible. Yet the claims to a successful symbolic appropriation implicit in sacrifice are contested in practice in two ways. First, when we consider these practices in light of French officials' explicit desire to make Betsimisaraka enter a cash economy, it becomes apparent that these processes of ritual recoding mask a greater *economic* connection to the world of *vazaha*. Betsimisaraka never lived in isolation, and they were subject to powerful outsiders before the French ever came, as chapter 2 made clear. But the fact that they want to buy commodities like tin for their roofs, or want to grow coffee for cash and thus are reliant on the cost of coffee on the world market, suggests that the French were indeed successful in making Betsimisaraka at least partially dependent on a different set of encompassing forces.

Second, the symbolic absorption and reworking of the meanings associated with the symbols of colonial power achieved in sacrifice are implicitly contested by the fact that, in commemorating ancestral sites of memory, people often implicitly commemorate the ways in which colonial rule reconfigured their relations with one another. The case of a sacrifice made by the Antehengitra ancestry provides a good illustration of how an activity aimed at commemorating ancestors also contains the colonial past. Like Boto's family described in chapter 5, the Antehengitra fled during colonial times because of the corvée requirement and went to live with a Creole planter on his concession "in the forest." Although they moved their house to the planter's concession, their tomb, the other important site of memory, remained in Ambodiharina. Following independence, many of the descendants of the Antehengitra continued to live on the former concession. After a while, someone fell sick and the family realized, through divination, that the ancestors were calling them home. The Antehengitra reluctantly left their refuge with the *colons,* and one faction returned to Ambodiharina, while another group moved to the neighboring village of Benavony. Not yet satisfied, the ancestors inflicted another bout of illness on those who had settled in Benavony, forcing still more people back to Ambodiharina. Meanwhile, some of the group did manage to stay on in Benavony, perhaps because, as descendants of women, they were considered to be less strongly attached to ancestors and thus were less likely to fall sick. However, the stage was set for conflict, as those who remained in Benavony were senior in years to those who returned to Ambodiharina, and thus they were assumed to have power over their more junior relatives.

One day during my stay, distant relatives came from the south to bring a bull to sacrifice. The elders at Benavony did the correct thing and directed the people to the *tangalamena* at Ambodiharina, who agreed to carry out the sacrifice. Later, however, the Benavony children-of-women faction rebelled. They claimed that Ampasimbola, the concession to which the family had fled during colonization to avoid the government's corvée requirement, was the original ancestral locale, not Ambodiharina, and that the sacrifice should take place there. However, the *tangalamena* who lived in Ambodiharina refused to sacrifice the bull at the former concession. He refused for two reasons, one explicit, the other implicit. First, he claimed that the "real root" of the ancestry was in Ambodiharina, and to sacrifice anywhere else was to court ancestral wrath. What he did not publicly mention, but what everybody assumed, was that he knew that to sacrifice at the old concession was implicitly to rekindle a great house *(trano be)* there, which might actually make the ancestors demand that he inhabit it! Since he was quite happy living in Ambodiharina and had no desire to live on the old concession, it was in his interests to have that side of the family's history erased.

When I returned in 1997, it turned out that the fight over which house to honor—the one that represented the ancestors' attempts to adapt to the constraints of colonial times or the one that marked their precolonial allegiances—had caused the group to split in two. By 1999, it was revealed that the man who had encouraged the people to sacrifice at Ampasimbola had had his own reasons for wanting them to do so: he himself wanted to throw a circumcision celebration there that would symbolically mark the concession as his own. By encouraging the visitors to sacrifice there he created a precedent, thereby activating a certain facet of the past, one he hoped would work to his advantage. The case clearly illustrates the tension between the memory of powerful ancestors promulgated in sacrifice and the actual practice underlying the organization of sacrifice. Whereas the former seeks to deny the power of the colonial past, the later demonstrates both its undeniable relevance and the way that people themselves may seek to benefit from it in the present.

Finally, memories of colonization are embodied in some of the contradictory characters, like Giselle and Guy, who occupy the fringes of many sacrifices. As several scholars have argued, colonial contradictions are sometimes embodied in the persona of mad people, those who weave the rags and tatters of the colonial encounter into a powerful commentary on contradictory colonial relations.[32] Giselle and Guy disrupted the text of the ancestral performance, potent reminders to local people of the way in which French practices and the experience of French colonial power had invaded their midst. They put into words what for others remained unspoken. As I later discovered, Guy was the descendant of a Creole, and he had fought with Zakatiana over land taken by his Creole ancestors that Zakatiana had tried to claim. He was an anomaly, a descendant of *vazaha* yet not rich. Giselle was a similarly contradictory character. She had been married to a *vazaha,* who later died and left her destitute. I never figured out whether people perceived her exaggerated performance of Frenchness ("Ahh Chérrrrieeee, viens ici, Chérie") as pathetic or parodic. Perhaps it was a bit of both (see fig. 14).

Ambodiharina Is a World Where the Inequalities That Resulted from Betsimisaraka's Differential Access to the Structures of Colonial Power Can Be Leveled through Sacrifice   Nowhere is the weight of the colonial past more apparent than in people's uneasy perception that sacrifice is never adequate to erasing social inequalities built up out of people's differential success in the colonial past, and may even reinforce them. For example, people who can earn money through their participation

Figure 14. Giselle, formerly married to a *vazaha*, 1993. As a woman who smoked, drank, dressed like a European, and insisted on speaking French, Giselle embodied memory of the colonial past. Photo by Jennifer Cole.

in wider economic and state networks may be forced to throw a sacrifice and share their blessing with the wider community. Nevertheless, the wealth required for sacrifice means that every sacrifice is also a performance of wealth and strength; the fame and glory that accompany sacrifice are one way for the sponsor to build up both his ancestors' reputation and his own. The differential access to the wealth needed to sponsor sacrifices suggests that the sociosymbolic manipulations made possible through cattle sacrifice are never equally available to all. Since cattle sacrifice is supposed to procure ancestral blessing, those who have wealth to begin with can use their wealth to beget ancestral blessing and more wealth. Consequently, every sacrifice contains within it two contradictory impulses, making it a site for the simultaneous erasure and instantiation of inequalities.

The tension between the ideal of equality and the reality of inequality is particularly palpable when sacrifices call together different branches of a family who have been differentially affected by the institutions brought by French colonialism. As country and city inhabitants meet on ancestral terrain, the full significance of where people have made their fortunes, and the tension between a common root and divergent branches, becomes apparent. Take, for example, the case of Sampy, whom I mentioned in chapter 5. Sampy was both lucky and adept at manipulating opportunities brought by colonial rule, and he turned some of the new practices introduced during colonization to his advantage. The result was that his descendants became rich, while those of his younger brother grew increasingly poor. Partially because of her father's wealth, one of Sampy's daughters, Josephine, was able to move her family to Mahanoro to take advantage of schooling opportunities. Now, all of her children—Sampy's grandchildren—have either married people in the government or found government jobs themselves. The oldest daughter married a judge, the second daughter works as a state-record keeper, and her son works in the forestry department. And it was Sampy's great-granddaughter who met and brought me, the visiting anthropologist, to stay, creating yet another kind of potentially useful connection. Although the family enjoys what is considered a much more prestigious lifestyle in Mahanoro, like many Malagasy who live outside their natal villages they regularly return home to take care of their ancestors. When this happens, fights often occur in which the country cousins evoke the inequalities rooted in the colonial past, reminding Sampy's descendants why they have done so much better. As Anselme, one of the grandchildren, who was a physical education teacher, explained, "Everything, everything comes out during sacrifices. They [the country relatives] all start to cry and say how we don't love them, don't share with them. Pindy [a particular cousin] even threatens to do *grigri* [a pejorative French term for divination or magic]. But Grandma isn't scared, she just gets mad!"

Anselme's statement illustrates the fact that jealousy *(fialonana)*, which people always claimed was a particularly Betsimisaraka emotion, is an important part of the structure created in relation to colonial rule and the ways its effects linger on in the present. People rarely talk about this kind of thing—when I tried to ask Anselme's grandmother about it, she just laughed uncomfortably and changed the subject. But the memories of colonization remain in the structure of discomfort evident whenever the town family returned for a visit.

COLONIALISM IN THE BLOOD

This chapter has examined sacrifice as a practice for creating official memory, focusing on how it works as a transforming device, mediating and constantly re-creating an "original" tradition that enables the Betsimisaraka, despite profound change, to remain "the many who will not be sundered." I have shown that people use this ritual to create official memories, and that inevitably these official memories are undermined and brought into tension with unofficial memories that emerge in practice. The coexistence of official and unofficial memories within a single sacrificial performance suggests that sacrifice is deeply heteroglossic, in Mikhail Bakhtin's sense of the word. Bakhtin (1981) argued that as a literary form, the novel contains multiple social languages, multiple voices that compete for dominance and pull at one another at any one time. Likewise, sacrifice always includes multiple, and sometimes contradictory, levels of meaning and even different kinds of memory in tension with each other in the structure of the rite.[33]

The way sacrifice continuously reweaves and incorporates outside interventions and importations, recasting their meanings and causing people to remember them anew, has implications for the metaphors that we use to think about the impact of the colonial past. Although it is obvious that colonial transformations occurred, were they ever capillary? Or were they arterial—affecting some sites and not others? If we use *capillary* in the Foucaultian sense to refer to new subjectivities created through new forms of knowledge, then the answer to the question is that they were clearly not capillary. And if by *capillary* we mean the total transformation of Betsimisaraka in line with French plans, then here too the

answer is that they were clearly not capillary. Perhaps this level of control was never achieved anywhere, and certainly the language of partiality
and incompleteness now dominates accounts of colonial power. But does
that mean there were somehow pure "autonomous zones" untouched
by colonial effects, as implied by Achille Mbembe's discussion of a "domain of the night" (1991), where a rebel could use dreams as a private
spiritual realm through which to fight off the French?

The Betsimisaraka practice of cattle sacrifice suggests that the language
of partiality—of blood vessels or autonomous zones—does not hold up
under scrutiny. Earlier I cited Megan Vaughan (1991), who suggests that
most colonial interventions in Africa took place at the level of the group.
Consequently, she poses the question as to whether colonial power in
Africa was productive of individual subjectivities. Based on the Betsimisaraka material, where we can see how French efforts to impose new
subjectivities intersected with individuals' efforts to adapt themselves to
new circumstances, I would say that it was. But since the meanings associated with these new practices were mediated and transformed by
cattle sacrifice, those subjectivities were not necessarily the ones promoted
by colonial discourse. Rather, we should revise the blood vessel metaphor,
since the Betsimisaraka case suggests that the blood that runs in the social body has itself been transformed. In a process parallel to the literal
intermixing of blood that took place as Creole settlers bore children by
Betsimisaraka women, the blood of the social body has been hybridized
and reconfigured through the blood of sacrificial cattle. The French never
did replace or destroy the techniques of memory through which Betsimisaraka remake themselves, and so Betsimisaraka were active agents
in this process. As a result, Betsimisaraka were not made into French
people, but nor was any domain of life left untouched by the colonial
experience. The partial nature of colonial rule is best imagined not in
terms of coverage but rather through the *style of interweaving* that has
taken place as Betsimisaraka have developed a variety of hybrid forms
that encode competing meanings and reflect the mutually constitutive nature of ancestral and colonial histories.

To be sure, the process of cultural reification that so many anthropologists have suggested is a product of colonial rule, is also evident here,
illustrated in the *vazaha* versus Malagasy ways of doing things that exist in different forms throughout Madagascar. But ultimately, the ancestral and the colonial are shifting signifiers, for Betsimisaraka use sacrifice
as a means of weaving and reweaving themselves together as Betsimisaraka. In the process, they continually reinvent what they think of as Bet-

simisaraka, so that some aspects of the colonial past are absorbed so completely into memory that they simply become the matrix for the next cultural act.

However, although the Betsimisaraka practice of cattle sacrifice is clearly a hybridizing mechanism, I am wary of adopting an overly celebratory tone in discussing "Betsimisaraka hybridity." My experience of talking to many older people who lived through a large part of the French colonial period suggests that new practices and forms were desired because they could empower, but that they were also feared, and the mastery achieved through these sacrifices was never total. Recall that in Ratsara's discussion of the need for a house washing *(fafy trano)* he portrayed the Malagasy and the *vazaha* as two mutually opposed orders. My analysis of the ritual shows that these contrasts are undermined and broken down constantly both in daily practice and in the ritual itself. Nonetheless, the ritual also reinforces the appearance of differences as it incorporates some elements of *vazaha* practice and makes them Betsimisaraka. The contrast between the *vazaha* and the Malagasy may be a kind of optical illusion, produced through what are in fact deeply intermingled social practices, but they nevertheless continue to have tremendous salience in social life. Rather than be too quick to celebrate hybridity, we must remember that these hybridizing practices exist in a dialectical relationship with processes that create categorical distinctions like Malagasy versus *vazaha*.

This chapter, together with the preceding chapters—where I discussed other practices through which Betsimisaraka construct the past, and the way these practices articulate with the social hierarchy—gives us the pieces that will allow us to begin to understand the unstable erasure of the colonial past with which I began. But before doing this, we must look at an example where these various practices failed to work. The kind of breakdown I describe in the next chapter does not occur often. Nevertheless, rupture is an important part of Betsimisaraka historical experience, and analyzing why and how it happens will give us new insights into the fragile nature of the memory-for-everyday-life that I have described thus far.

CHAPTER 7

Reversing Figure and Ground

The Memory of the 1947 Rebellion and the Elections of 1992–93

The traumatized, we might say, carry an impossible history within them.
                    — *Cathy Caruth*

The subalterns make their own memories, but not as they please.
                    — *Shahid Amin*

In the preceding chapters we have seen the ways in which Betsimisaraka memory techniques work to incorporate, mute, and socially exclude— if never totally erase—memories of the colonial past. During the national elections of 1992–93, however, the relationship between these various memory mechanisms changed, and the colonial memories that normally seeped into people's consciousness became a flood, dramatically upsetting the normal sense of village life and causing people considerable worry and distress. Significantly, it was not memories of colonial transformations that preoccupied people but memories of a dramatic episode of colonial violence: the repression of the 1947 rebellion.

Much of the writing on how people remember traumatic events focuses on the impact of trauma on individual memory.[1] People who have witnessed or experienced the deaths of others or have been threatened with death can find themselves suffering from flashbacks, emotional numbing, and an overwhelming sense that they have lost control over their lives. These kinds of responses have been documented in people who have experienced any of many different types of traumatic situations, ranging from those who have suffered natural disasters to veterans of the Vietnam War (see Erikson 1976; Herman 1992; cf. Young 1995). Though there is clearly cultural variation in terms of what people experience as traumatic, the responses are similar enough to one another that they have been classed as "post-traumatic stress disorder" (see Manier n.d. and Young 1995).

The case of how villagers in Ambodiharina remember the rebellion of 1947 is interesting precisely because it does not fit into this framework very well.[2] The rebellion *was* a traumatic event, one that tore Betsimis-araka society apart, pitted neighbors against each other, and caused massive suffering and death. And colonial administrators' descriptions of blank-faced Betsimisaraka walking around in a terrified daze seem to qualify as descriptions of what we might think of as trauma. However, no one I know in Ambodiharina or any of the surrounding villages experience any of the symptoms that are thought of as the typical sequelae of trauma.[3]

But if the events of 1947 did not leave people with the symptoms of post-traumatic stress disorder that have been documented among other survivors of violence, the events did mark them deeply. The Betsimisaraka have at least partially dealt with the horrible things that happened during 1947 by means of a strategy that is surely common to other war survivors but is rarely talked about: silence. There appears to be a social injunction against talking about the events, so that in everyday life the events appear—and perhaps they are—forgotten.[4] The silence that surrounds the events of 1947 does not indicate that those memories are, in Freudian terms, repressed by internal, psychodynamic processes. Nor does it mean that a person would not tell someone about the events if they were asked, or that people did not share their stories immediately after the events. What it does mean is that, in the years following the rebellion, the generation that lived through 1947 has learned, through certain subtle turns of mind, to avoid the topic. Kai Erikson (1976) suggests that traumatic wounds inflicted on individuals can combine to create a mood, an ethos, even a group culture, that is different from the sum of the private wounds that make it up. In Ambodiharina, what formed after 1947 was a tacit agreement *not* to remember the terrible things that happened. In other words the generation of Betsimisaraka who lived through 1947 practice a form of "directed forgetting" or "directed ignoring," in which they intentionally turn their minds away from the events.[5] By this I do not mean to say that today survivors have to *work*, even fifty years later, to create this effect. But as we shall see, they did consciously work on their memories immediately after the events, and this orientation has become a habit of mind. As Laurence Kirmayer (1996, 188) notes, it is easy to forget when there is a tacit agreement not to remember: "Like a magician performing sleight of hand, every gesture of social life then points us away from details which would provoke memory and recollection."

During the elections of 1992–93, however, the conditions that most of the time enabled this kind of directed forgetting broke down, and people vividly remembered the rebellion. A visit to Mahanoro by Zafy Albert, a contender for the presidency, prompted the shift. A tense calm settled over Ambodiharina as people waited to see what would happen. Eventually, Ramaresaka broke the ominous silence that had enveloped the town and began to make explicit what was going on. "Here they come again, those politicians, come to bother the people. There are cars piled on cars in Mahanoro! We're like cattle who don't know which way to turn," she said, cupping her hands to the side of her head to make cow ears and swiveling them about, like a cow desperately pulled in many directions: "Oh, here they come again, bothering the little people." Her husband, Tsaravintana, broke in at this point. "You," he said, directing himself to his adolescent son and daughter sitting nearby, "you haven't ever seen fighting. You don't remember when the French bombers flew over Betsizaraina." But Ramaresaka interrupted him before he could finish his story: "The French soldiers came in 1947 and took everyone who was MDRM. 'Join the MDRM, join the MDRM,' people shouted, but everyone who joined was taken off and put in prison. Old Jean Kaluka was taken and imprisoned in Tamatave, but God was good and he made it back to his ancestral homeland. That money the government promised the martyrs of 1947 never came. And here comes that double-dealing once again. I'm not getting involved in any *politique* . . . We hid from the bombers in the forest, whispering to the children not to cry as the planes whirled overhead. The French, they came and fired along the coast with machine guns. You could hear them all the way to Ifasina [the neighboring town]!" Ramaresaka stopped for a minute to spit tobacco juice expertly between the slats of the hut, giving Tsaravintana a chance to chime in. "During the time of the flight we'd dig holes in the ground and hide roosters in them so that nobody could hear them crow." "People here," Ramaresaka added, "they've become like animals, easily frightened. There's no peace now."

Ramaresaka and Tsaravintana were not alone in seeing a close association between the upcoming elections and the failed rebellion of 1947. Among the generation of people—male and female—who had actually lived through the events of 1947, the upcoming political elections evoked a flood of painful memories. Whether the conversation began with the current political changes or the rebellion, people inevitably evoked one event in order to illuminate the other. For example, I once asked Josef about why he refused to participate in any of the political meetings held in Ambodiharina as various representatives of the different parties came through to woo the villagers. His answer was straightforward:

> We saw politics kill. All of us old people have seen politics kill—everyone who entered the MDRM was thrown in prison and killed. Now it's for the youth to do. Those MDRM, they opened an office. You paid taxes, got a card. It was that list used by the government to call the MDRM. When the political parties came by last week, ten younger men volunteered to set up an office. Kids! Haven't seen anything. They gave their names, and that is all it takes if something goes wrong. All the [male] elders here [raiamandreny], they were almost captured. The only thing that saved them was not having an ID card. And 1947 will come again! Chaos! All these parties tugging at each other so only the people will suffer.

Realizing that people now seemed moved to discuss an event about which I had been curious, I asked Rafaly what happened in 1947. "Well," he began, "in 1947 it started with the Europeans [vazaha], like what's happening now, everyone fighting for seats." He went on to describe a situation that was, in fact, eerily similar to the buzz of political activity going on in the village at the time:

> The colons came with the government, not just the district chiefs but the colons too. They descended on Ambodiharina, writing people down, electing people. When those elections were finished they picked Jean-Paul, mother's brother of Tsiny [Zama n'i Tsiny], Masovato, Jonahandro, Robert Alika, and then they took the list away. Then the Many Spears [Marosalohy] arrived, came from the south. The Malagasy had no weapons, just sticks, spears in their hands. But the Europeans [vazaha] came and captured everyone—took everyone on the list, the elders in the town, and threw them into prison. The MDRM were all in one room. Not just here, but all over the country, they threw them into prison. Maybe eight hundred people were crushed in there together and they all died. Only those graced by Zanahary [God] escaped. Here, it was only Jean Kaluka and Jean-Paul who survived.

The sudden appearance of memories of the 1947 rebellion, and particularly their prominence in public discussions and debates within Ambodiharina, is particularly striking given their absence in daily life. What kinds of structures, practices, and emotions mediate how people remember a war some forty-five years later? Why did memories of 1947 appear *now*, and how might their appearance add to the memory story I have told so far? In this chapter I show how memories of the rebellion were evoked by three critical changes. First, the particular events surrounding the elections of 1992–93 created circumstances uncannily like those that had preceded the rebellion. Second, people experienced a profound surge of fear during the elections. Fear recalled the flight of 1947; their fear also articulated with, and was produced by, a powerful image of moral critique. Third, a critical minority in Ambodiharina expressed political dissent, and elders who had lived through the rebellion used their memories as a rhetorical tool to try and bring them to their senses and make them understand what was at stake in the choices at hand. These changes in the social and emotional terrain explain *why* the rebellion was remembered; the narrative structuring of people's memory narratives suggests some of the ways in which their interpretations of the rebellion were being re-membered. Like the Hutu mythicohistorical narratives documented by Liisa Malkki (1995, 103), memories of the rebellion also "served as a paradigmatic model and interpretive device for giving meaning to and acting upon the sociopolitical present." In so doing, they may have reshaped people's memories, making some future interpretations of the events more likely than others.

INTERPRETING THE REBELLION

In order to understand why Betsimisaraka who lived through the rebellion remembered an episode of state violence when they were simply asked to vote, we must examine what actually occurred in 1947. I do so in two parts. First, I set the rebellion in the context of colonial history and consider historical interpretations of the event.[6] Second, I trace what the archives tell us about what probably happened in the district of Mahanoro.

THE WIDER HISTORICAL CONTEXT

The events of 1947 must be read against the wider background of numerous changes that began to occur in European colonies during the 1940s. The rebellion was both a war of independence and a popular revolt against state structures, and the immediate reasons for it lie in the various changes that took place in Madagascar during and just after

World War II. In 1940, the colonial administration aligned itself with Vichy France, which in turn sparked a successful British invasion of the island. After an initial period of state withdrawal, the British handed control of Madagascar over to the Free French, who proceeded to use Madagascar as a reservoir of men and raw materials for the war effort. The colonial government increased forced labor, sending men deep into the forest to tap rubber but giving them little food and no pay. In addition, the government seized land for its use without providing an explanation. In 1943–44 a terrible famine broke out in the south of the island. In order to prevent starvation, the administration set up a Rice Office to control requisitions. Peasants hated the office because they were forced to donate their entire crop yield, creating a huge black market in rice. Throughout Madagascar, villagers bore the brunt of the requisitions and were left without rice for their own consumption.

Beginning in 1945, however, a number of changes occurred that suggested the French were going to relax their control on political activity and perhaps encourage the replacement of the colonial empire with a new French Union based on mutual consent rather than force.

World War II was thus followed by a liberalization of the colonial regime. The government outlawed forced labor and abolished the *indigénat*, the separate law regulating Malagasy citizens. A number of political changes held the promise of increased autonomy for Madagascar via the political process. Yet the *colons* inhabiting Madagascar opposed the liberalization of the regime. Consequently, the reforms, decreed at the upper level of the colonial government, were never applied. Those involved in the political process were deeply disappointed. At the village level, both the forced-labor system and the Rice Office, though bitterly hated by the peasants, continued to operate.

Economic hardship and political constraints produced by World War II provide important historical context for the rebellion, but other factors must also be taken into account. The Malagasy case is similar to what occurred in Vietnam in 1946, when anticolonial fighting broke out just as the French were trying to reassert control following their absence during World War II (Wolf 1969). The German occupation of France, the British invasion of Vichy-aligned Madagascar, and the anticolonial rebellion that took place in Vietnam combined to give educated Malagasies involved in the independence movement the sense that French influence was on the wane.

The decision to start the rebellion was further strengthened by the profound faith that, should Malagasies fight for their independence, they would be helped by outside forces provided by the British, the Americans, or the United Nations. According to Jacques Tronchon, this belief was due to widening Malagasy awareness of an international context, fostered in part by the men who were elected as deputies to the political party of the MDRM, and who represented Madagascar's interests in the French assembly. In 1945 the deputy called Joseph Ravoahangy declared, "The great nations have resolved to establish a new order, to no longer allow force to dominate the world . . . A new order in which the people will be sovereign and free to govern themselves. A new order that will respect the rights and dignity of human beings without distinction of creed or color" (Tronchon 1986, 134). These ideas were expounded by the United Nations in the San Francisco Charter, which asserted that the UN recognized the fundamental equality of all nations and would guarantee their rights, and further that the UN recognized the necessity of independence for all nations. This faith in outside intervention was critical in the organization, beginning, and maintenance of the rebellion.

Such was the wider political and social context for the events of 1947. The more local causes of the rebellion, however, were rooted in the growth of the Malagasy independence movement following World War II, and particularly the formation of the MDRM.[7] Founded by Joseph Raseta and Joseph Ravoahangy—two men long involved in nationalist politics—and the Betsimisaraka author Jacques Rabemananjara, the party initially had a nationalist platform that advocated autonomy for Madagascar within the context of a French union. In response to the growth of the MDRM, the French created a puppet party—the Parti des Déshérités de Madagascar (Party of the Disinherited of Madagascar, PADESM). Nevertheless, by the time of the provincial elections in June of 1946, the MDRM candidates won three-fourths of the votes cast.

When the rebellion broke out, the colonial government in Madagascar reacted by calling it an MDRM plot and immediately imprisoned the three MDRM deputies. Circumstantial evidence was readily available. The rebels had attacked the military garrison at Moramanga in the name of the MDRM, and the names of the deputies were constantly invoked among the rebels. The French further argued that, because the MDRM was composed largely of people from the high plateau, the Merina had provoked the rebellion. At the time, the French insistence on blaming the deputies, the MDRM, and the Merina allowed the colonial government to destroy indigenous political development in the country, thereby reinforcing the French presence. In 1949, Pierre de Chevigné blamed the rebellion on "several embittered and ambitious men [who] have ex-

ploited, in the name of a supposed nationalism, the credulity of a population, destitute of any notion of politics" (Tronchon 1986, 87). I shall
return to these explanations when we consider villagers' interpretations
of the events. Curiously, Betsimisaraka express exactly the same sentiments today when they talk about the rebellion.

However, the colonial thesis of an MDRM-Merina-led rebellion considerably oversimplifies the case. Tronchon (1986), for example, coun-
ters the idea by noting that during World War II, when French control
over the island was at times relatively loose and seizure of power possible, the Merina remained friendly to the French. Moreover, those Merina who advocated change did so within the limits imposed by the colonial system. Further, most of the fighting took place on the east coast,
outside of Imerina. As for an MDRM-led plot, Tronchon argues that the
leaders had everything to lose and nothing to gain from a rebellion. When
the rebellion took place, the MDRM were in the process of trying to
obtain autonomy for Madagascar using the existing political process.
The leaders were thus committed to the use of legal means, created by the
French, in their struggle for independence. While certain sections of the
MDRM participated in the rebellion, the leaders of the MDRM sought
to distance themselves from the events, condemning the rebels and their
actions. Finally, Tronchon suggests that, had the MDRM organized the
rebellion, the coordination between higher and lower levels would have
been better.

New information about the rebellion is likely to emerge over the next
several years, since enough time has passed that the archives are now accessible. For now, many scholars agree that the proximal causes of the
rebellion lie in the nature of the MDRM and its political affiliations. The
MDRM was not a hierarchical structure but rather a loose coalition of
different organizations and personal networks. Although elite officials
in the party sought Malagasy independence through peaceful, legal
means, other secret societies used the administrative structure put in place
by the MDRM to further their own political goals. In particular, the secret societies known as the Parti National Malgache (National Malagasy
Party, PANAMA), formed in 1941, and the Jina, founded in the south
in 1943 by Monja Jaona, were readier to obtain independence by violent means (cf. Allen 1995). Initially supportive of the deputies' efforts,
the secret societies eventually grew impatient with the slow legal process
and demanded violent, and immediate, action. Propagandists circulated
in the countryside. They declared that "the authority of the deputies has
replaced that of France," and they advised people, under threat of force,

to stop working on colonial concessions. They also announced that the ancestral land belonged to the deputies and that all Europeans would soon die. If the MDRM deputies had immense popularity and prestige in some quarters, they had relatively little power over the secret societies that eventually decided to follow their own, more radical policy and set off the rebellion.

According to this thesis, the members of the secret societies used the cover of the MDRM and the immense popular appeal of the deputies to prepare to obtain Malagasy independence by force. But even this compromise explanation, which posits a dichotomy between a peaceful leadership and a radical base, may be too simple. At least some elite members of the MDRM publicly advocated the use of violence in the struggle for independence, and not all areas swept up in the rebellion were affiliated with the Jina or the PANAMA.[8]

THE REBELLION IN MAHANORO DISTRICT, VIEWED FROM FRENCH MILITARY REPORTS

One aspect of the rebellion that is important to keep in mind is that it was characterized by considerable regional diversity among only loosely coordinated groups. As a result, a thorough understanding of the events requires many microhistories of what happened in different areas of the country; I offer one for Mahanoro District below.[9] In some respects the history of what happened around Mahanoro District conforms to the overall picture described above; in other ways it diverges. The particular pattern of events, in turn, helps to explain the specific ways the rebellion has become embedded in local memory. Despite the infamous malleability of human memory, there is a relatively close correlation between the documentation available in the archives and what people in the Mahanoro area remember.

Colonial administrators in the district of Mahanoro first identified signs of unrest beginning in June of 1946, when they reported that propagandists for the MDRM had "created an ambiance favorable to revolt" by urging the locals to break with the French.[10] Throughout July, August, and September, a group of MDRM propagandists, all of whom were identified as originating from the high plateau, "worked the population," urging them to burn their dry rice land (tavy) as an act of rebellion.[11] By October of that year, colons and administrators alike complained that they were having trouble finding workers. That same month, the district chief sent a telegram to the capital announcing that ten workers had left a construction site, saying that they were no longer willing to work; the telegram also noted that it was impossible to obtain new workers. Likewise, the summary political report for that month observed that it was impossible to complete the coffee harvest because so many workers had deserted. As Monsieur Barbe, a *colon* whose concession was located just outside Mahanoro, wrote, "Today I can't even find a guard to protect my harvest."[12]

Throughout the early part of 1947, support for the MDRM intensified in the Mahanoro region, largely organized by a party secretary and two cantonal delegates. In addition, numerous people—particularly those who worked in government positions, like the schoolteacher from Betsizaraina and the school foreman for Mahanoro—joined the party and were active in recruiting new members. It was the local branch of the MDRM that was responsible for arranging a visit by Rabemananjara, one of the three elected deputies in the MDRM party, to Mahanoro on 6 February 1947, just prior to the provincial elections. The tenor of his speech was strongly anti-French. "It is not for you to enlighten us on the subject of France, nor our love," he said, "for here it is fifty-two years that we have learned how the French colonize: Through fear, forcing us to harvest their coffee, by forcing us to gather their rubber, by forcing us to grow rice for the administration, by having brought us plague, by putting us in prison. So we Malgaches can no longer believe in your words of love, sirs, for we have been terrorized for too long. We no longer believe your words, for we have heard them enough over the last fifty-two years."[13] On 12 February, the list of MDRM candidates won in the provincial assembly. Local administrators later identified the first serious act of rebellion as having taken place just after the elections, in February 1947, when the *chef de canton* for Ambohimilanja, located to the west of Ambodiharina, came to reprimand peasants who burned new rice land. He was held hostage in his house until the Guard Indigène rescued him[14] (see fig. 15).

Much of the east coast was in a state of latent insurrection throughout late 1946 and 1947. However, the date that is commemorated as marking the beginning of the rebellion is midnight, 29 March 1947. Although the rebellion officially broke out on that date, with the attack on the military garrison at Moramanga, the repercussions were not felt in the district of Mahanoro till early May.[15] According to local administrators, the delay was due to their swift action in arresting some sixty-six members of the MDRM, whom they assumed would otherwise have begun

Figure 15. Interrogating the *chef de village,* 1947. During the rebellion, French colonial administrators and military officials tried to draw Malagasy administrators into helping them locate rebel groups. Courtesy of Agence Nationale d'Information Taratra.

the revolt. Within a few days of the arrests, rebel bands from Nosy Varika and Soavina in the south and Moramanga to the north converged on the area surrounding Mahanoro, attacking and burning concessions and stealing cattle. Administrators observed that many of the rebel leaders from the area around Masomeloka were *ancien combattants* recently returned from fighting in France. A good number of leaders, however, were also recruited from the area around Salehy and Betsizaraina, which lay across the river from Ambodiharina and was one of the areas most heavily affected by the appropriation of land that took place under the French.

At least initially, Senegalese, Bara, and local volunteers, many of whom burned the surrounding villages, carried out the repression of the rebellion. Despite losses inflicted by French troops, the rebels kept launching repeated attacks throughout the month of May and into June. By early June, however, French repression had taken on a more systematic quality, including the repeated bombings of the area around Mahanoro. With the arrival of the Seventh Company of the First Regiment of Moroccan Sharpshooters on 31 July, Moroccan soldiers based in Mahanoro, but who had camps set up in the surrounding villages, began the work of

Figure 16. Waving the white flag of surrender, 1948. Toward the end of the rebellion, French officials relied on local people to contact their relatives who had fled into the forest, advising that refugees should wave a white flag of surrender when they emerged. Courtesy of Agence Nationale d'Information Taratra.

pacification. According to one administrator, the military pacification was "quick and bloody," and the rehabilitation of the district began only late in 1948[16] (see fig. 16).

INCITING MEMORY

The democratic elections of 1992–93 reminded older villagers of the rebellion of 1947 because the pattern of state withdrawal and reimposition, in conjunction with the calling of new elections during 1992–93, bore a striking resemblance to what they had experienced just prior to the rebellion of 1947.

THE WITHERED STATE

As I mentioned in chapter 1, in the fifteen years preceding my arrival in Ambodiharina, state agents had taken less and less of an active role in village life. The withdrawal of the state meant that numerous tasks that might have fallen under state jurisdiction were delegated to other domains. In the past the local council *(fokon'olona)* had completed collective tasks. Now, however, the responsibilities delegated to it increased while the resources necessary to execute them decreased. The lack of resources and, more important, the lack of a higher power that could organize people in collective action made the village council tremendously difficult to mobilize. Elders would complain that in their day they had completed such useful work as the building of the schoolhouse, the maternity ward, and the government buildings; nowadays, they said, the youth did nothing.

In fact, it took an enormous effort to get even the tiniest collective tasks completed. For example, when the midwife complained that her kitchen roof needed fixing, a task that in theory the village council was responsible for, it took weeks and repeated requests before the necessary manpower could be mobilized, even though everyone in Ambodiharina loved the midwife. Numerous collective jobs should have been completed, including the clearing of the irrigation canals between the rice fields and the building of a small footbridge along the path out to the embouchure. People even agreed that such tasks were intrinsically good and beneficial to the community, but when it came to the question of actually doing them no one was willing to make the effort. "Each to their own," people would respond to my endless queries about why no community efforts were ever taken to clear up even the most minor problems. In the absence of an outside structure that could mobilize people to form a larger collective unit, people fell back on the smaller units of kin and friendship. The ghosts of the state-imposed system remained, but it was not particularly effective. Despite the lack of services and the decline in the standard of living, most villagers were happy enough to be left alone.

REIMPOSING THE STATE: THE VIEW FROM THE CENTER

But if the peasants around Mahanoro were relatively quiescent about the impoverishment and subsequent withdrawal of the state, this was hardly the case among wealthier and better educated segments of the population. It was these people, in urban centers throughout the island but particularly in the capital city of Antananarivo, who went on strike against the growing poverty and corruption that accompanied President Ratsiraka's policies. Eventually, the Forces Vives (Herivelona)—a coalition of different groups linked by their common opposition to Ratsiraka's party, the Vangaurd of the Malagasy Revolution (AREMA)—organized a strike. One of their major demands, which echoed events happening in other African countries during the early 1990s, was for Madagascar to institute a democratic political process. The strike was successful and forced Ratsiraka to concede to a referendum. In August of 1992 a referendum approved the drafting of a new constitution, which in turn provided for the scheduling of new elections three years earlier than planned. In November of 1992 a preliminary round of presidential elections was held, followed by a final round in February of 1993.

In the capital city of Antananarivo, the geographic base of the Forces Vives movement and the political and symbolic center of the Merina, people responded to the new changes optimistically. For these Malagasy, the new demands for democratization signaled that Madagascar, previously aligned with countries like Libya and North Korea under Ratsiraka's socialist state, was now reorienting itself toward the capitalist countries of the West. These people hoped that the new political and economic policies would stop the country's rapid descent into ever-increasing poverty and provide much-needed economic growth. They believed opening up Madagascar would bring new opportunities; they poised themselves to take them.

REIMPOSING THE STATE: THE VIEW FROM THE EAST COAST

The majority of Betsimisaraka villagers in the area surrounding Mahanoro did not see things this way. Rather than perceiving the changes as a progressive step toward democracy and potential economic growth, they interpreted the new changes through a thicket of fear, rumor, and emotionally charged memories based on their local experience. Didier Ratsiraka, president since 1975, had long identified ethnically, as well as allied himself, with the Betsimisaraka. Ratsiraka's ancestral homeland, Niarovan'ivolo, was located not far from Ambodiharina.[17] Ratsiraka made the most of his ethnic association, parading it publicly whenever possible. When Ratsiraka's family held a tomb opening, villagers proudly told me, he behaved just like a real Betsimisaraka. This was no city slicker who had forgotten his ancestral ways! No, they would say, nodding approvingly, Ratsiraka had followed ancestral custom to the letter, sacrificing numerous cattle, eating happily off the traditional eating mat *(fandambanana)*, even using the traditional palm-leaf spoon *(soroka)*. Further, Ratsiraka knew how to honor local custom by strategically thanking villagers for their support with occasional gifts of fishing nets and sacrificial bulls.

Forced to accede to the new elections, President Ratsiraka was quick to play the ethnic card by evoking the ghost of Merina hegemony in an attempt to turn to his own advantage the political and social divisions created during the Merina conquest in the nineteenth century. Politically motivated rumors, which opposition supporters claimed were started by Ratsiraka's men, were whispered throughout the countryside. These rumors typically started with assertions about the past: Merina had enslaved the Betsimisaraka and subjected them to indignities like having to mourn the death of the Merina queen's dog and having to carry six eggs to Antananarivo to help mix cement for the queen's palace. They inevitably concluded with an ominous reading of the future: if Zafy Albert, the Forces Vives' candidate, won, Betsimisaraka would once again be forced to carry the tax collector on a palanquin on his provincial rounds.

In addition, Ratsiraka called the protests aimed at toppling his regime a "prelude to ethnic conflict" and asked the national assembly to ratify a proposition enabling him to move the national capital from Antananarivo to Tamatave, the provincial capital of Betsimisaraka country. He also invited various rural leaders from the east coast to visit his bunker near Antananarivo. The picture of village elders *(tangalamena)* paying homage to Ratsiraka—an image that reproduced in contemporary terms an act of political allegiance derived from the precolonial past—was televised nationally.[18] Since there is no television in Ambodiharina—let alone electricity—no one saw it. But people nevertheless got the gist of the political message, which was passed on by word of mouth: Ratsiraka was an ethnic Betsimisaraka, and in turn, Betsimisaraka should remain loyal to him in the face of a potential Merina threat.[19]

What further contributed to the association that elder people made between the elections and the rebellion was the visible reassertion of state presence that took place throughout 1992 and 1993, echoing what had occurred prior to the rebellion. Though the interim government put in place by the Forces Vives was still in flux, it soon began to assert its new, no-nonsense policies.[20] In the spring of 1993, tax forms arrived for just about everyone. They were usually inaccurate—more than one villager gleefully displayed a tax slip that grossly underrepresented the actual amount of land farmed—but those taxes they did owe were duly paid.

Moreover, one of the first measures instituted by the Forces Vives government was a census. High school students from Mahanoro—people like my friend Bienaimée who came from "good" families—were hired by the state to work for a period of one month. They were trained in

Ambodiharina, and then sent out to tiny villages scattered throughout the countryside. From the time of Merina dominance to this day, villagers have been expected to provide state-affiliated guests with food. But in this case, fear and painful memories of the colonial period shaped upcountry villagers' reactions, and the high school students were left puzzled and hungry. Villagers throughout the region were terrified that the new census meant that the old colonial regime, complete with impossibly high taxes and forced labor, would be reimposed. Many students returned to say that the upcountry people had abandoned their villages and moved to their camps in the fields. Those who did remain and who consented to fill out the forms pleaded with the students not to write down the names of their children. As one baffled student recounted, "They would beg, 'Please, please, write down my name but leave off the names of my children and grandchildren. I am old and have seen much, but they are still young. Please don't make them suffer.'" In short, people were convinced that the census was merely the first step before the government would seize control of their lives once again.

Finally, the government expressed a renewed concern for, and control over, the clearing of certain kinds of land. While the French had expressly forbidden the clearing of dry rice land and declared certain areas of land off-limits, these laws had been relaxed under Ratsiraka.[21] As salinization grew increasingly severe and the rice yields from wet rice land less abundant, people like Ramaresaka and Liliane and Solo, as I explained in chapter 3, sought new land to farm. Their attempts to expand their meager harvests were foiled, however, as local officials declared that the entire marsh area along the coast was off-limits. After repeated visits by the man from the forestry department, it was determined that everyone who had planted rice in the marsh zones would be forced to abandon their fields and return to the less productive land closer to the village.

And judging from the promises of various campaigners, people assumed that things would only get worse. The various parties all promised a more active state, one that would actually provide important services to the region. While many villagers approved of the idea of a new school or free medical supplies, their feelings about state involvement more generally remained ambivalent.

THE EMOTIONAL EVOCATION OF MEMORY: FEAR

Memories of the rebellion were prompted further by the villagers' growing sense of fear—one of the primary emotions they had experienced during the rebellion.[22] The fear was generated by the reimposition of the state, but it was exacerbated by a set of rumors that started to circulate among the villagers about blood thieves, and a dramatic incident that took place when some political thugs flagrantly disrupted life in town.

I first learned about the blood thieves (*mpaka-ra,* also referred to as heart thieves [*mpaka-fo*] or, in other parts of Madagascar, liver thieves [*mpaka-aty*]) after I had gone away to the capital for a visit and returned to find everyone in Ambodiharina in a panic. When I innocently asked Legros, Tovolahy and Babette's six-year-old boy, who was my most faithful swimming companion, if he would like to go swimming in the embouchure, he replied in a whisper that we could not possibly. Blood thieves were at work. If we even went near the embouchure they would surely kill us, he told me, take our blood and sell it to their employers, who lived "somewhere up north."

Over lunch that afternoon, Ramaresaka explained what had caused the rumors of blood thieves. As it turned out, the rumors were rooted in an actual murder that had occurred on the embouchure. I should emphasize here that the murder had, as far as anyone could tell, nothing to do with the tensions caused by the elections. Yet, the murder and people's attempts to explain it served to heighten their fears about the elections and resonated with older people's worries about the renewed possibility of state violence. What happened was that in the middle of the afternoon a young boy from one of the poorest families in Ambodiharina had gone out to the sandbar that separates the lagoon from the ocean, in order to do some net fishing. He disappeared and was found a few days later, his arm and leg on one side of his body torn off and his insides eaten out by sharks. The signs of a struggle remained in the sand. Violent crimes are extremely rare in Ambodiharina. Although drunken youths at a sacrifice or ball will fight, the event is usually so scandalous that people discuss the occurrence for days. I heard of only two murders in the entire district that had taken place in recent years, and both these involved cases of theft and summary justice. Most murders that occurred happened for a reason—people knew the cause and sequence of events. This murder was different. Not only were there no witnesses to the crime, but it was horrific: people kept returning to the description of the body, its arm and leg chopped off, and murmuring that only a monster could have committed such a deed.

Given the brutal, inexplicable nature of the murder, collective village opinion held that there could be only one possible culprit: the dreaded blood thieves. Rumors of blood thieves have a long history in Madagascar and have been documented by numerous observers.[23] Although versions of the blood-thief story vary, there are a number of common themes. Early versions of the blood-thief rumor held that the thieves were *vazaha* who stole the hearts and blood of Malagasy children during the night and either ate them or fed them to huge beasts, who gave *vazaha* their amazing powers. According to the description provided by Maurice Bloch (1971b), heart thieves have black beards, blue eyes, and large dogs. But heart thieves are not limited to European *vazaha*. Rather, in keeping with the notion that the word *vazaha* refers to anyone who has acquired the habits and material goods associated with a European way of life, heart thieves may also be found among Malagasies, particularly functionaries and government agents. Thus Gerard Althabe (1969) notes that in the central Betsimisaraka region near Brickaville, administrative agents were often identified as heart thieves. Rumors of heart thieves could have very real consequences: in 1963 two Malagasy government officials were identified as heart thieves and killed by a mob (Lumière 1963, cited in Jarosz 1994), and suspicions of heart theft could lead villagers to drive strangers from the community.

Throughout that spring, rumors about blood thieves continued to fly. Women were afraid to let their sons out to fish at night, and no one would venture into the woods alone. Numerous tales were told about how so-and-so was almost caught and killed on the road to Mahanoro. The level of fear was so great that one would have thought murder was a regular occurrence in the district, not something that occurred only once every decade or so. Villagers wondered repeatedly about the blood thieves and recalled an earlier blood thief who had lived in the area, Paul Kamena. This man, so the story went, lived in Betsizaraina, across the river. He was married to a Merina woman with whom he owned a shop. The shop was so full of goods that it was dark inside. One day Paul Kamena went to Antananarivo and returned with a car. Everyone was puzzled as to where he got the money to buy the car. As it turned out, his Merina father-in-law was employing him to kill people and take their blood. Whenever there was a fair in Mahanoro, Paul Kamena would await solitary drunks and kill them as they were walking home. Then, one day Paul Kamena failed to find a victim. It was time to come up with the blood payment, and so eventually he was forced to kill his sister's son. But because the boy's death was due not to God's will but to murder, his ghost kept appearing and telling people who had caused his death. Eventually, the villagers could stand it no longer and lured Paul Kamena into the woods and killed him.

These rumors and stories heightened people's fear, but it was not until a second event occurred in July that people's suspicions of heart thieves were confirmed. One evening during the full moon, Poly went down to unlock his canoe to go out night fishing. He bent down to undo the lock when suddenly someone hit him from behind with a stick. Poly held up his hand to ward off the second blow and turned to see Mborika, someone to whom he was closely related. By early the next morning there was no one in the village who did not know that Mborika was a heart thief and had tried to kill his cousin, Poly. People began to nod their heads as the various pieces of the puzzle fell into place. Soon everyone was convinced that Mborika was employed by *vazaha* from up north who paid him to kill people in order to obtain their blood. "Ahhh," I heard more than one person say, "of course Mborika is a heart thief! He hasn't worked rice for a year and yet he manages to live so well. And he claims he was selling pigs in Tamatave, but really he was going to attend a rendezvous with his employers."[24]

There was, however, one final event that linked the fear produced by the political changes and heart thieves to the particular activities associated with the elections. This event concerned one of the villagers, some AREMA officials, and some baby crocodiles. In the same breath that Ramaresaka recounted the story of the murder on the embouchure, she launched into a related story about how an important taboo had been broken in the town.

Jean, the Merina shopkeeper whom I introduced in chapter 3 as one of the villagers "not of the village," was one of the most ardent supporters of the Forces Vives. He also made no effort to hide his disdain for local customs. For some time, Jean had been raising baby crocodiles in a small cement basin in his backyard, sold to him by Rafaly, descendant of the Zafimalaone and alleged heir to the sacred history and power of the Mangoro River. Bringing crocodiles into town is an ancestral taboo for the entire town of Ambodiharina, a fact that Rafaly, particularly, would have known—but no one bothered Jean about his transgression until the arrival of the AREMA officials.

Then one day, around the time of the primary elections held in November, some ministers and cronies of Ratsiraka's stopped at Ambodiharina to deliver propaganda for the elections. They came into Jean and Maman n'i Talata's tiny shop, intending to harass Jean because he was a member of the Forces Vives. While Jean ran and hid at the midwife's house, Maman n'i Talata and her fifteen-year-old daughter, Talata, sat in the shop and endured the comments of the swaggering officials as they helped themselves to handfuls of cigarettes and swigged down most of the lemonade in the shop. Hours passed, and when Jean would not appear the officials started to threaten that they would throw grenades and blow up the shop if Jean did not show up soon. Meanwhile, Maman n'i Talata sat and watched, her daughter crying quietly at her side. Finally, the men got up to look at the crocodiles kept outside. A few ardent AREMA supporters gathered outside and told the men that it was taboo to keep crocodiles in the town. At this point one of the men drew his pistol and shot the baby crocodiles to pieces, splattering them over the yard. The men grew bored waiting for Jean and left, but not before they announced to all the villagers that they should boycott Jean and Maman n'i Talata's shop.

BLOOD AND MEMORY

I will return to Jean and some of the villagers' attempts to handle the intrusion of the AREMA politicos at the end of this chapter. At this point, I wish to pause for a minute to comment on what the blood-thief rumors might tell us about how people remember the colonial past. Although it would be easy to dismiss the rumors of blood thieves as irrational superstition, many scholars working in Africa have shown that such rumors are highly revealing of political concerns: they embody people's inchoate awareness of larger political processes. Luise White (2000), for example, has documented "vampire stories" that spread throughout east and central Africa. As she observes, "Game rangers were said to capture Africans in colonial Northern Rhodesia; mine managers captured them in the Belgian Congo and kept them in pits. Firemen subdued Africans with injections in Kenya but with masks in Uganda. Africans captured by vampires *(mumiani)* in colonial Tanganyika were hung upside down, their throats were cut, and their blood drained into huge buckets" (4–5). White argues that far from mere gossip, these rumors are important historical sources in their own right; she suggests that stories of vampires were ways in which ideas about relations of race and tools of extraction could be debated, theorized, and explained. And she suggests that vampire stories work as a form of evidence precisely because they insert themselves into daily life and thought in such powerful ways.

White is interested in vampire stories for what they can teach us about evidence and history writing, but anthropologists have also suggested that these kinds of stories might form powerful critiques about certain kinds of extractive relationships (see also Bastian 1993, 1998). For example, in her discussion of a Sierra Leonean politician and a diviner, Rosalind Shaw (1996, 34) shows how debates in the Sierra Leonean press about evil medicine men reveal "powerful metaphoric statements about the abuse of the productive capacities of others." She argues that this postcolonial critique of state elites is informed by an older moral discourse about extractive processes that began with the slave trade. Adeline Masquelier (2000, 87) shows that Nigerian rumors of Igbo headhunters are an important piece of the Nigerian "moral imagination" (Beidelman 1986). The rumors are part of a "more encompassing discourse of otherness through which marginal Nigerians articulate local experiences of power and violence so as to locate themselves in relation to an elusive modernity that is always somewhere else." Writing of rumors of heart thieves in Madagascar, Lucy Jarosz (1994) notes that "these rumors give voice to the individual and collective anxieties of being drained of life and having the core of the body stolen to feed external forces and powers" (433). Jarosz suggests that rumors of heart thieves construct landscapes of fear, an expression that captures the extreme anxiety produced by the combination of the elections and the heart thieves.

Rumors of blood thieves are intricately entwined with memories of 1947 and memories of violent extraction more generally. It is striking that the very same people whose most important ritual rests on equating cattle and people, and who use the blood of sacrificed cattle to incorporate and subdue colonial memories, also used the idiom of blood in a situation where colonial memories were overwhelmingly and frighteningly present. But blood figures in the two contexts in very different ways. Whereas the blood of cattle purifies and transforms, human blood pollutes. People need to ritually cleanse themselves of the blood of birth, and part of the reason Zakatiana used the sacrifice described in chapter 6 to cleanse his wife, who had cared for him while he was sick, was because his blood had polluted her. People control the death of cattle, but with blood or heart thieves people lose control and become the hapless victims of others. Blood in its proper place—inside the body—is proper to good health; when people are weak they often say that "they don't have enough blood" *(tsy ampy ra)*. Hearts are even more closely linked to the local elaboration of the relationship between mind, body, and self. People perceive the heart as the locus of the self and emotion, and often they contrast the deceptive nature of people's words with the real feeling that hides in their hearts. The words that mean "to hold a grudge" *(entim-po,* enthusiasm *(mafana fo),* and even "to be emotionally moved" *(mikasika fo)* are all created using the syllable for heart—*fo.*[25]

People may say that cattle are equivalent to humans, and they take their lives, but the blood-thief scare implies that humans are *not* equivalent to cattle. The blood-thief rumors represent a powerful inversion of what is supposed to happen with blood, and they are linked with the opposite kind of memory processes. Unlike the process by which Betsimisaraka use the blood of cattle to domesticate and incorporate, and thereby forget, their experience of colonial power, the blood-thief rumors suggest a process of being overwhelmed by violent processes of extraction, which in turn led to powerful memories. In contrast to other examples of this type of phenomenon, no supernatural power appeared to be involved. Rather, blood-thief rumors as they were told during the elections were about people within the community selling out: the thief who actually did the evil deed was a normal person who betrayed the community by working for outsiders.

I read these rumors as condensed memories of the colonial past. Blood-thief rumors appear to have emerged during the colonial period, and rumors of community members stealing and selling the blood of others are a powerful way to comment on extractive processes run amok. But the blood-thief rumors are not exactly the same kind of memory as the historically specific memories associated with the rebellion. Psychologists who study memory make a basic distinction between kinds of memory that illuminates the way blood-thief rumors and memories of the rebellion overlapped and informed each other during the elections. On the one hand, semantic memory refers to the structures of knowledge that help us to order our interpretations of the world (for example, knowing winter is cold). On the other hand, episodic memory refers to memory of events like the election. Blood-thief rumors have been documented in times of social unrest throughout twentieth-century Madagascar. We might think of them as a kind of semantic memory: they are rumors that have lost historical specificity and that kaleidoscope—that collapse and recombine—different historical periods, creating a structure of moral knowledge. What perhaps had been memories—or even fantasies—of specific episodes or relationships becomes condensed into a form of moral knowledge about extractive relationships and forms of betrayal more generally. During the elections, this knowledge of blood thieves helped to create the context in which evoking memories of the rebellion made sense.

THE REBELLION AS RHETORICAL DEVICE

A final factor that made people remember the rebellion was dissent within the village and the way memories of 1947 worked as a powerful rhetorical device to further incite memory.

For the most part, people in the capital of Antananarivo assumed that the Betsimisaraka were uniformly loyal to Ratsiraka and his political party, the AREMA. Like the French before them, who believed that the Merina had masterminded the rebellion and tricked the Betsimisaraka into fighting, elite Malagasy also assumed that Betsimisaraka loyalty to Ratsiraka was entirely due to his manipulation. In both cases, urbanites assumed that the Betsimisaraka were simple peasants incapable of making political decisions of their own. In fact, although the argument for Ratsiraka's manipulation may hold in terms of urban areas like Tamatave, in which the state was an active presence, in rural areas state agents had considerably less control. Correspondingly, the question of whom to vote for was more open and there was a good deal of discussion about the relative merits of the different candidates and parties. Villagers remained keenly aware that they were in the minority and that most of the country had decided to choose a new leader. And although those who had lived through the rebellion were, for the most part, staunch in their support of Ratsiraka and the AREMA, they had to contend with a vocal minority of people for whom the platform of the Forces Vives offered welcome changes.

The people who comprised the Forces Vives were people like Piso, Pierre, and Jean, whom I categorized in chapter 3 as "villagers not of the village." The tension between Forces Vives and AREMA supporters, the former being younger, better educated, and less parochial, combined elements of intergenerational tension with differences of class and experience beyond the village.[26] Family links were important as well. At least two villagers known to be members of Forces Vives were the parents of children who had gone off to live in Tamatave or Antananarivo. The children became exposed to the new ideas associated with the Forces Vives while living in the "big town," and then persuaded their parents to change their political views as well.

Whether locally born or merely residing in the village, pro–Forces Vives villagers either did not participate in, or were less committed to, the local memory that many villagers had so carefully constructed through cattle sacrifice. They also saw the role of the state in regulating human relations differently than AREMA supporters, who evoked memories of the rebellion and state-linked violence in their conversations. Though these people knew about the rebellion, of course, they had not lived through it or experienced it in any direct way. Untroubled by painful memories of state intrusion, Forces Vives supporters would defend their political views with talk of the negative side of the local past, which they perceived as a hindrance to social progress. Pierre, for example, justified his support of the Forces Vives by saying that the colonial government had forced people to grow coffee, cloves, and vanilla for cash. Today, he complained, there was no enforcement and people had grown poorer and lazier as they returned to the ancestral practice of growing only rice. He was not the only one to voice this kind of sentiment. All of the people I spoke to who were Forces Vives members, or even better-educated members of the AREMA, expressed shockingly regressive ideas about the necessity of instituting a colonial-style state in order to "take the natives in hand" and foster social change.[27]

In short, Forces Vives supporters took a modernist position on the role of the state. They believed prosperity derived from increased government intervention and the social services the government would provide. Schooling, new roads, increased social service positions—all of these were seen simultaneously as signs and causes of progress. In turn, for such interventions to work, certain aspects of the village past—sedimented in particular practices and orientations—would have to be erased.

Faced with this vocal minority of people who had a vision of the world other than that provided by ancestral custom, village elders tried to use their memories of the rebellion as a rhetorical tool with which to justify their pro-AREMA position and shape the outcome of the elections. If the reimposition of state power and the elections provided the wider social and political context that sparked people's memories of the rebellion, it was the act of trying to shape people's feelings as they decided who to vote for that created the microcontext in which memories of the rebellion were evoked. Consider, for example, the words of Ramaresaka, who told a young woman about the troubles of the times:

> The government is getting worse and worse, ever since the Forces Vives showed up. We don't like the way things are being run—there are too many tiny political parties throughout the country. But in this town we choose Ratsiraka. When I was in my youth, the rebels came and we suffered for nine months hiding in the forest. The only thing that saved us was that during that time it didn't rain. Since the time of Ratsiraka there isn't a job that hasn't been finished! Maybe it is good to have many political parties but I still have my

preference. Democracy! All it means is, "Join this party here, join this party here." That is what they all say. But you can't join if it isn't clear *[mazava]* to you—you just stay with your own. My brother likes Zafy Albert, and we come from one stomach, but I follow Ratsiraka. Each to his own. We were hit hard during the rebellion. Some had parents and lost them; they've learned and no longer dare. Many died. Died. People's work gets worse, and whatever you want to buy the price has gone up—not enough food. It won't do, the way they're running the country; it's not progressing. People are more and more selfish. It's like a country with no one to lead, no one to govern.

Ramaresaka's statement implies that while issues of ethnic loyalty are not irrelevant, neither do they tell the whole story. The force of her narrative, however, derives from references to memories of 1947. Her argument slides between the present and the past, constantly returning to the events of the past—"When I was in my youth, the rebels came and we suffered for nine months hiding in the forest"—to justify her mistrust of the "too many tiny political parties" in the present. As a result, she remains loyal to Ratsiraka.

Ramaresaka was not alone in evoking the events of the rebellion as a justification for her political decision to support Ratsiraka. For example, Josef also referred to the rebellion in order to justify his decision not to become involved in contemporary politics. "There didn't used to be this problem, so many parties pulling at each other. Just one party. But now there are too many and it's hard for anyone to know whom to pick," he explained. And then, continuing on: "A man from Maroankanzo came, and he explained that Malagasy were to ask for independence, and that those who became members of the party would be elected to replace the *chef de bureau* and the *chef de quartier* and the *chef du village*. But it was his caprice, and when the Europeans came they took those people away [and they died]. When that happened the rebel army came from their base in Maroankanzo and struck. So when the RPSD [a political party] came last week and asked me to join, I said, 'No thanks, I'm too old for that. I've seen too much.'"

In evoking the events of 1947, both Ramaresaka and Josef exhibit what David Middleton (1997) terms "conversational remembering," or the use of the past as a discursive resource intended to persuade and engage the interlocutors. Ramaresaka's reference to the rebellion did more than draw an analogy between the two events: her story was also a set of moral claims intended to persuade the young woman standing before her about their collective past and, therefore, implicitly, about their future. So, too, when Josef compared the events immediately before the rebellion to the

contemporary situation of parties constantly courting votes, he effectively
dismissed the opposition party as clever tricksters. Here again, he displayed his vision of the past as a rhetorical tool used to control his future by influencing the election.

Notions of Governance: Attitudes toward the State   In order to clarify why many villagers wanted to discredit the Forces Vives, their understanding of democracy, so proudly touted by the Forces Vives, has to
be explored briefly. Villagers expressed strikingly divergent views on the
meaning of democracy and elections. Choice was the advantage of democracy emphasized by the various political propagandists when they came
through town to court votes. Older villagers, however, tended to associate choice with social chaos. When I asked a wide variety of people
what they thought *democracy* meant, they responded by saying either
that they had no idea or that the word was trotted out by so many different parties that it had ceased to have meaning for them at all. As Josef
observed, "In these times, things have changed so quickly I don't know
what to make of it. It's not like it was before, when there was just one
party. Now there are too many political parties! There are so many that
the people don't know which one to choose. All of them talk about
democracy, so we've no idea what it really means. I'm scared the commotion [rebellion] will come again." People like Josef may have claimed
that they no longer knew whom to choose, yet subtle criteria of custom
and honor converged so that candidates of some parties were better received than the others. For example, as we saw in chapter 5, it is customary for someone who has profited from a particular piece of land to
thank the "creatures of the land" with a sacrifice, just as individuals thank
their ancestors when their desires are realized. As I mentioned earlier,
this practice was extended to the arena of state politics during Merina
and French colonial rule, when officials used sacrifice to assure local co-
operation. Ratsiraka attempted to use this tradition to his own ends: he
paid for a bull to be sacrificed to the town's ancestors as a token of thanks
for their support.

On the day of the event, villagers gathered in the town hall to hear a
long political speech that proclaimed both Ratsiraka's loyalty to the local population and his hopes that they in turn would show their loyalty
to him when they went to vote. Afterward, the crowd poured out of the
house toward the other end of the town, where the bull was tethered. A
wreath of red flowers with five hundred Malagasy francs (twenty-five
cents at the time) was attached to the bull's horns, a gift to anyone brave

enough to tussle with him. By this time, most of the participants were fairly drunk on local rum and a few were brave enough even to run with the bull. Young boys strutted about drunkenly, wearing bits of the wreath, and humming the theme song for Ratsiraka's political platform of "Federated States" (Etats Fédéres). They vaguely declared their intention to fight anyone foolish enough to express loyalty to the opposition candidate Zafy Albert. Eventually, the bull was tethered at the base of the stone monument commemorating independence. Rather than calling out the names of individual ancestors, as one would at a family sacrifice, the ritual leader invoked the names of various towns, and by default all of their inhabitants, past and present.

For Forces Vives supporters, Ratsiraka's gift of a sacrificial bull was evidence of his corruption, a desperate attempt to buy the villagers' votes. But the AREMA supporters read the situation differently: it was one more piece of ever-mounting evidence that Ratsiraka, unlike the Forces Vives, respected local conventions. In fact, many people I spoke with cited "democracy," which was discussed so frequently by the Forces Vives and their supporters, as the justification for what was considered by village standards to be bad, disrespectful behavior. Several people complained that democracy merely meant the right to slander one's opponent. Justin, formally a rural policeman during the first republic and now an employee in a town office, told me that, from his observations of practice, democracy meant one could do as one pleased in order to further the chances of one's own candidate, even if this meant harming someone else. He then recounted how Forces Vives supporters had marched in Tamatave with "Ratsiraka's coffin." They were not put in prison, he said, because this was "democracy" and each person had a right to his opinion. The implicit subtext, however, was that the protesters should, in fact, have been put in prison, because miming Ratsiraka's death clearly expressed the desire for it to occur, an act tantamount to witchcraft. In short, the model of statehood and democracy used by elite groups in Antananarivo was perceived by many in Ambodiharina as chaotic and threatening. Justin concluded by saying that these days there were no limits on what people could do—"Theirs was a country without a ruler, a house without a central post."

The assumptions behind Justin's criticisms of the Forces Vives' behavior, particularly the association of political agreement and proper social behavior, are further illuminated by an incident that took place during the first month of my stay in the village. At the time, I was staying temporarily with Dere, a retired army officer come home to farm, while repairs were completed on the roof of my house. Dere's old, ill-tempered but rich uncle Bototsara was father-in-law to Piso, who, as I mentioned earlier, was an outspoken supporter of the Forces Vives; this was the same Bototsara who sacrificed a cow to end his relationship with his son. Early one morning I was called to Bototsara's great house, where a number of elders had gathered. Furious with Piso, Bototsara successfully demanded that Piso apologize and pay a specified amount of rum as reparation for having borrowed plates purchased with AREMA money to feed the Forces Vives officials. Further, Bototsara knew she was a good friend of Rasage, a nurse-midwife, and herself a Forces Vives supporter, and he accused Piso of speaking ill of him to her.[28] The next time he went for an injection, he feared, she might refuse to give him one, whereupon he might die. The rum was duly purchased and poured out, and Piso apologized publicly to Bototsara and the other male elders of the family. While the incident appeared relatively trivial, even ludicrous, from my perspective, it was taken quite seriously by those involved. Bototsara actually threatened to chase Piso from her house, which he owned, and a number of women who had watched from the sidelines shook their heads as they warned me "that girls shouldn't fight with big men."

Two readings of these events seem particularly compelling. First, one could interpret Bototsara's anger as resulting from Piso's rebellious beliefs. While dissent by strangers may have been tolerated, within the family the difference of opinion was interpreted as treason. Moreover, because of Piso's presumed influence over the nurse-midwife, a person who had the power to give or withhold healing, the political dissent shaded into fears of witchcraft. There is, however, another interpretation. After all, it was common knowledge that Bototsara disliked Piso and disapproved of her marriage to his nephew because she had started out as a maid in his sister's bar. Perhaps he was indifferent to the potential political threat Piso represented and had simply used the political differences to demean Piso symbolically and assert his dominance.

I suspect it was a combination of motives that conspired to produce the humiliation of Piso in the great house that morning. In any case, the incident speaks to a larger notion of correct political behavior, where major political and social decisions are left to important members of the community, who are then assumed to have the power to sway their descendants and followers. When elders do not succeed in convincing their children or subjects of a particular political position, conflict may ensue. This phenomenon is hardly restricted to contemporary Ambodiharina. Françoise Raison-Jourde (1991), for example, writes that nineteenth-century missionaries to Madagascar were perplexed when they found that whole descent groups converted to Christianity en masse. The mass conversions followed the conversions of powerful social superiors and were made, at least initially, for strategic reasons rather than because of a change of faith.[29] When the Merina queen converted in 1869, she sparked off an enormous wave of conversions throughout her kingdom, as villagers hastened to demonstrate their political and religious loyalty. So too with political allegiances in Ambodiharina.

Many villagers argued that, ideally, everybody should agree. For example, Josef told me that they too would vote for whomever Zafilahy, the villagers' chosen representative to the government, voted for. The value placed on conformity to local authority was echoed by Justin, who emphasized that regardless of who people really thought should lead the country, they would always follow the lead of the majority; no one wanted to be singled out as different.[30] After independence, he explained, everyone had been members of the Parti Sociale Democrate (Social Democratic Party, PSD)—the party of President Tsiranana at the time of independence. When Ratsiraka came to power in 1975, everyone had joined the AREMA. Now, he said, people were waiting to see who would win and which party to join. Whoever took power, he said, the people would follow.

Villagers' mistrust of the political changes of 1993 is thus rooted in a particular idea of leadership and how collective decisions ought to be reached. The "democratically minded" Forces Vives sought to create an imagined community premised on impersonal ties of citizenship, one in which debate was an accepted part of the political process. In order to achieve this goal, Forces Vives advocates asked people to engage in the contentious activity of breaking away from old loyalties and conventions in order to build the imagined political community anew. In contrast, pro-Ratsiraka villagers argued for a community based on personalized, hierarchical connections, one in which male village elders were ideally equal to one another but all were equally subject to the state. Paradoxically, however, they assumed that allegiance within this hierarchy would mean that, although a few might benefit from their links to the state, generally autonomy would be granted at the local level. The elder villagers' mistrust of political changes was rooted in a particular local conception of the political process. Thus, while Ratsiraka's sacrifice and other aspects of the AREMA's behavior were highly political, they were not perceived that way by the villagers. As one man observed, ever since 1947 the word *politique* had meant "to lie."[31] In turn, village elders' commitment to supporting state power in the interests of local autonomy had been reinforced through the negative effect of participating in the events of 1947. In invoking the rebellion, many pro-AREMA villagers implied that political activity as they experienced it would automatically lead to chaos, destruction, and death.

SPARKING MEMORY: AN INITIAL SYNTHESIS

In sum, the convergence of three factors accounts for why older villagers remembered the rebellion of 1947 during the elections of 1992–93. First, as I suggested earlier, the provincial elections immediately preceded the attack on the garrison at Moramanga, which constituted the outbreak of the rebellion. As a result, their first experience of state elections came to be associated with the outbreak of violence, and they have come to see elections not as part of the modern political process but as a prelude to catastrophe. In light of this association, it becomes clear why peasants were unwilling to vote in elections sponsored by the colonial government just after the rebellion and even into the 1950s (Raison-Jourde 1997). This association of elections with state violence that came into play during 1992 to 1993 was reinforced by the way the reimposition of the state after a prolonged absence mimicked Ambodiharina's relationship to the state just prior to 1947.

But the association of elections, state presence, and violence alone is not enough to account for why people in Ambodiharina remembered the rebellion, for the association of elections with rebellion does not *necessarily* operate all of the time. The association is a matter of judgment, not an automatic reflex, for other elections occurred both before and after the elections of 1992–93, and in these cases people did not appear to draw such a strong connection between the two events. The critical, additional elements at play during the elections of 1947 and again in 1992–93 were twofold. First, villagers perceived the elections as an invitation to participate in political activities in opposition to the state. Although several villagers' narratives suggest that many villagers believed that the MDRM was a state party, the rebellion and its repression made people keenly aware that it was not. Consequently, in 1992–93 what people seemed to fear most was not the voting per se. Rather, what provided the additional cue to memory was the fact that once again the need to vote was perceived as indicative of a larger political rift that placed villagers in opposition to state power. The idea that people feared oppositional politics and not elections per se was supported when I asked

the one man I knew who had lived through the rebellion but nevertheless supported the Forces Vives why, unlike the other villagers, he was
not afraid to vote for them. He explained that in 1947 the MDRM had
been opposed to the state, while today the Forces Vives had successfully
seized power from the AREMA and demanded the elections. Although
other villagers would have argued the contrary, from his point of view
he was siding with the state by voting for the Forces Vives, who held the
interim government.

The final element, however, was the emotion of fear that brought these
disparate elements together and created a pervasive mood that led people
to expect that things might turn out as they had in 1947. Villagers' narratives of the rebellion attest that the overwhelming sensation they experienced during the rebellion was terror: they feared the colonial government with its bombs, the Moroccan and Senegalese soldiers with their
guns, and the rebel leaders with their impossible demands, summary justice, and homemade weapons. And what was evoked by the new census,
the tax forms, the threats that they would have to carry the tax collector on a palanquin if Zafy Albert won, and above all the rumors of blood
thieves was fear: fear of the state, fear of violence, fear of social retribution. Yet as I have shown, this fear combined with the blood-thief rumors to create a potent moral knowledge and critique. Taken together
with the similarity of historical events and local social tensions, it was
this combination of symbolic, emotional, and moral factors that made
remembering the rebellion a reasonable and necessary act, providing
people with a powerful metaphor with which to interpret the political
changes of 1992–93.

The French bequeathed electoral politics to Madagascar as part of the
legacy of colonization; at least overtly, elections symbolize democracy
and the modern "civilized" political process. But the potential for elections to evoke fear and disaster under certain conditions suggests that,
for Betsimisaraka, the symbolism of elections is more complex and contains within it several possible connotations. As Bartlett once observed,
symbols have double or multiple significance. While one part of a symbol is obvious and constituted by the "face value" of the symbol, the
other part may produce an effect "without being purposively attended
to, this part constituting the 'hidden value' of the symbol." Moreover,
when two groups come into contact, "the old lives still in the new[;] . . .
if some social storm and stress appear, there is reversion. The 'hidden'
value once more becomes the 'face' value. The old group lives again for
all to see, and we say that history repeats itself" (1923, 278, 289).

THE REBELLION REMEMBERED

Villagers' memories of the rebellion reveal much about both their experience of state politics and the work of memory, for there is a reciprocal relationship between their interpretation of the events, their use of the events as political commentary, and their selective representation of what happened. Any villager who lived through the events and experienced them firsthand has a tale to tell. As always, however, some people are better storytellers, having more of an eye for salient detail, than others. In giving an account of how villagers remember the rebellion, I start with one particularly thorough account that was told to me during the elections, and then go on to consider additional versions of the events and the different ways they were explained and interpreted.

TELO'S STORY

It used to be that the government forced taxes from us. Those under the age of twenty didn't have to pay, but still we suffered. They forced the taxes out of us, whether we liked it or not. There was *lavangady* [a work brigade]. They'd say you were only going to work for a month, but instead you'd stay there for three months, serving the *colons*. Later, with Ravoahangy, Raseta, and Rabemananjara, and the MDRM, things changed a little because the Malagasy were saddened by colonization. Ravoahangy, Rabemananjara, and Raseta decided to help us. So the MDRM was formed. Many, many men here joined the MDRM, but later the government cracked down and came to capture all members and locked them in prison. There were nine men from here who were imprisoned in the government jail in Mahanoro. Once the members were imprisoned, things changed—the land was in commotion and the rebel army arrived, entering the town from the south.[32] The rebel army was still marching from the south when the airplanes came and dropped fliers on the town that read, "Hear ye all Malagasy, the Hova [Merina] are coming, a black army is coming, choose your sides well." Many, many of those fliers were sprinkled over the forest and into the town. Everyone asked themselves, "What is this? We'll only suffer in the end." And the rebel army kept marching north, and the rumors flew. "Telonono is coming," and then, "They've arrived in Nosy Varika."[33] It was coming ever closer. Finally they reached Masomeloka, and then they arrived here. All those who had helped the French in Masomeloka fled north to Mahanoro. They would pass through here and say, "The commotion is coming; it has already arrived in Masomeloka." And the army kept moving north, and finally they arrived here.

They arrived late at night. We were already asleep. They came knocking at the doors, "Are you kin? Are you kin?" *[Havana ve?]* They pounded on the walls of the houses, all carrying their sharpened sticks in case there were Europeans. They terrorized us. "The French enslaved us" they said, "Now we are going to chase them out." So everyone joined the rebel army, and we crossed the river and went to burn down Ampetika and Betsizaraina. We almost got all the way to Mahanoro, but the Europeans [vazaha] came from Mahanoro with Senegalese soldiers.[34] When they arrived at Tsangambato, they found the rebels had cut the bridge. The car was stuck there, and so the French army crossed the canal in canoes in order to reach Ampetika. When the French arrived, they caught some of the looters still there and shot them—all those who had stayed behind [to loot] died; some of them were shot in the water, some on land. The rebels, they took all the cattle from Ampetika and herded them across the water and took them off to the south to eat them. We who remained here in town formed an army, part of the Marosalohy. There was a government granary over to the north by the ferry's port and we set up camp there and waited for the French so that we could tell people to flee when they arrived.

The French came at first cock's crow. There were two boats full. At that time the embouchure was over there to the east and the tide was going out. "It's a boat," some people said. "No, it's just water lilies"; and we waited there, on the ferry's moorings. The boats moved to the south and then edged back here—there were two of them. We called out, "Who is there?" but there was no reply. When we saw that, we fled. It was the French and with them someone from here who'd worked for the government and fled to Mahanoro to warn them—a traitor. They came with the Senegalese troops. We arrived at the bridge, when they fired; everyone scattered, fleeing for their lives. Some swam to the west, others to the south. We fled and went to Benavony, then to Ambodisovika. The French retreated and the airplanes came to bomb us. How many people died—even the chickens and geese! The wounded, you couldn't even count. All the women and children fled, and we [those who had joined the Marosalohy] were told to return to town; the others scattered into the countryside. Then the French returned again and dropped bombs. Not a soul was left alive. Finally they burned the town! Burned! No house was left, nowhere for the rebel army to camp, and so we went and stayed in the country at Niarovana, Ambodisovika, and Andranotsara. The women were still in the forest.

Eventually, other people in the rebel army captured us. They accused us of bringing the French! "You brought the enemy into the town and so we are going to punish you." The rebels, they thought we were guilty of bringing in the Europeans. They sent us to Ambodiriana, near Nosy Varika. There were many of us there—people from Ifasina, Salehy, Ambodiharina, Vohilava— we were all sent there. Many died. Later they moved us to Ambahy. "It's because you were on night guard that our enemies, the French, came in. We are going to punish you." We stayed there for a few months. Then they brought us to Nosy Varika, led by the rebel chief. "We're entering Nosy Varika, for it is a small town and we will take it easily." Many bands came to fight in Nosy Varika, from the south and from the west. But there were French soldiers there. They lit a fire in the town. The soldiers looked down on us from the hill where the barracks were. They saw all of us there in the town and they aimed the machine guns at us. All dead! That is what happened. Those who lived spoke to the general, the general of the rebel army. We begged permission to flee but they forced us to stay. "We'll get them back no matter what," he said. But we said, "What happened in Nosy Varika was terrible, and if you want to send

us back there better to send us home to die in Mahanoro. If we die here our
bones will be lost."

They imprisoned us at the priest's house at Ambodiriana. They'd tie
people's hands and feet and make a pulley out of you by throwing the rope
over the house beam to hoist you up, and then they would spear you—because
you didn't follow orders. Then they'd drop you on the ground and feed you
skin of cow for you were a prisoner and so didn't deserve to eat good food.
But we begged again and again and eventually they let us come home.

That is when the Moroccans arrived. They came to bring people up out
of the forest.[35] We'd been in the forest for nine months! No force, just flight!
"Come up," they said, "we won't kill you." Some Malagasy believed them,
for they could no longer stand life in the forest, and then they would come
up and bring the rest of the family. "Come up, come up," they would say,
"we've already moved back to town. Come up but don't stay here in the
forest." That's what happened then. When we came up, there was a Captain
Pau, a Moroccan, and we crawled on all fours coming into the town. They
waited in the road with their machine guns ready. We carried a white flag before us and they gestured to us to come forward. Then they'd ask us why we'd
fled, and we told them, "We've suffered too much! Death! Children and
spouses, all dead. It's better to flee." All the generals asked, "Who are your
leaders?" And I listed them, naming them all. I feared for my life [marary ho
faty] and wanted to save myself even though I too had participated. They gave
me a paper. "This paper is for you," they said. "No matter who you meet,
then, show them this so they won't shoot you. And go back to town. Don't
stay anywhere without a [French] army in case those rebels still in the forest
try to kill you." So we came out, but there was no food. We made salt from
dried *via* [a kind of plant that grows in water] stalks. We'd clean it like coffee, and when it was dry we'd put it on our food to make it salty. But later it
gave us scabies. And you couldn't leave the town and go into the forest alone,
for fear that those rebels who hadn't yet come up would kill you. So we shel-
tered in the church, and each family rebuilt his house on the ancestral courtyard. You asked what happened in 1947—well, that is what happened.

THEMES IN THE REBELLION NARRATIVES: THE MDRM

Other villagers confirmed Telo's memories and added several important
elaborations that suggest two recurrent themes in people's memories of
the rebellion. The first is the role of the MDRM. The second is the violence committed by the rebel army. Velonmaro's story, for example, helps
clarify why everyone I knew believed that the MDRM was at the root
of the rebellion; it also closely jibes with the account of colonial administrators given above:

Rasolofo [who later became the rebel general Mongosolofo] was a Betsileo,
and he kept making speeches, getting people to join the party. Then Rabem-

ananjara came here and gave a speech in Mahanoro. He said that we were
going to get back our ancestral land, that colonization was finished, and that
the *vazaha* would go home. "From now on," he said, "we're going to get our
independence!" He went back to Vatomandry and gave an ultimatum: on this
day, come attend a speech. He even gave the money for us to go there. He
spoke, "We Malagasy have been enslaved for a long time, but from now on
we're going to get our independence. But before we do so we're going to have
to fight." Even the *colons* attended. And Rabemananjara said, "You *vazaha*,
get your bags ready and go wait at the edge of the sea." It wasn't just him but
Raseta and Ravoahangy. He explained they had a party and needed people
to join, and he said that the Americans would come and help, and they started
signing people up for the party. We went home, and only a week [had] passed
when the army came with the *colons*. "Where are all the MDRM?" they asked.
They made us all gather, men and women, and kept asking where the MDRM
were. Some weren't even here but had gone off upcountry, and they sent their
kin to get them. They beat the people, asked them why they'd joined the party.
Some of the people were missing, and they even took their mothers and put
them in prison.

Although most analyses of the rebellion argue that the Jina and
PANAMA used the MDRM as a façade behind which to hide their more
radical activities, no one I knew in Ambodiharina or any of the surrounding villages had ever heard of either of these groups.[36] Read in conjunction with French archival reports, Telo's and Velonmaro's narratives
suggest that, contrary to the widespread historical interpretation that the
MDRM was mainly in favor of the legal negotiation of independence,
the MDRM—not the PANAMA or the Jina—was at least partially responsible for the violence that took place in Mahanoro District. But what
neither Telo's nor Velonmaro's narrative conveys is the sense of horror
and outrage felt by most villagers at joining what they perceived as a
state-sponsored political party without fully understanding the terrible
consequences.

Ramaresaka articulately explained that the MDRM was responsible
for the events, together with the idea that it was all an elaborate ploy in
order to kill Betsimisaraka:

We used to have MDRM here, but then they were all taken by the government during the time of the chaos and killed. All dead. Even my father was
captured . . . Everyone gathered at the town hall, and the guns went like this
[pointing at my chest]. "Pah! Pah! Pah!" went the whips. Our clothes, they
were in tatters, just rags. We were all crying. "Allez! Allez! Allez!" the soldiers were screaming. Our father was captured then—he'd just come back
from fishing and threw down his nets and was off. "To the office! To the office!
To the office!" Then they [the French] came back later and caught everyone
who had joined the MDRM. Yet those people had been forced to join! It wasn't

their heart's will *[sitra-po]*; they were forced! The politicians came and they said, "You must join this party, join this party!" Just like what is going on now. There were seven or eight men captured and sent away. They were all chosen, selected. "Here, you, come join up!" You know, people in the town who were heads of families; and the government came and picked people, those who knew a little more than average. But they tricked us! They came from Tananarive, Raseta, Rabemananjara, Ravoahangy, and they chose people here to be in their party; but the French government came and captured them all, everyone. It was all a lie.

Or as Botoroa said, echoing Ramaresaka, "It all came from the Merina, a trick. They provoked us while we died and they sat by." Moreover, most of the people who experienced the events of 1947 emphasized that they were forced to join the MDRM. As Jesoa, Josef's older brother explained, "No one knew how to do 'politics.' The MDRM, they came and picked those with a bit of learning and made them join. We had no choice." Whether people were actually forced to join remains questionable. Nevertheless, it seems likely that the MDRM leaders, most of whom held what were viewed as prestigious positions, such as schoolteacher or foreman, exerted a good deal of pressure in trying to make peasants join the party. In some areas they achieved this by promising people that if the MDRM obtained power, people would no longer have to pay taxes and could clear as much slash-and-burn rice land as they pleased. In other areas MDRM activists gave small gifts of salt, sugar, and fabric to people as incentives. In short, many feel that they were forced to join the party and then were punished for it despite their minimal understanding of what was at stake.

THE THEME OF INTERNAL VIOLENCE AND THE MAROSALOHY

Returning once again to the thread provided by Telo's narrative, we find that another central motif in villagers' memories of 1947 is the violence committed by the Marosalohy (Many Spears). Emphasis on rebel violence does not appear in villagers' descriptions in all regions of Madagascar affected by the rebellion, and this calls for explanation.[37] In part, the particular rebel band that operated in the area, which French archival sources say "committed atrocities without precedent," helps explain the focus on local violence.[38] It may also have been due to a gap between ideals—for at least some rebel bands left documents suggesting that they were firmly committed to a vision of a more just and humane country—and practice. But it is linked as well to the different ways people experienced violence inflicted by the rebels and violence inflicted by the French.

The violence inflicted by the French army—starting with the arrest and imprisonment of the suspected MDRM members, and continuing with the bombing of the villages and the extensive suppression of the rebellion with greatly superior weapons—was terrifying, but it was a relatively distant form of violence. The French pilots could fly over the villages and bomb them without ever seeing a Malagasy face, just as the French soldiers who shot and killed the rebels attempting to flee after their raid on Ampetika never confronted the bodies. To be sure, some widely circulated memory-narratives focused on the specific acts of brutality committed by the French. For example, several people told me of the innocent man who was shot by a French official because he claimed not to know who destroyed the ferry. Still others spoke of the family of Chinese merchants who were machine-gunned to death by Moroccan soldiers in the French army, who then took all their possessions. But the violence done by the French was more often portrayed in terms of superior weaponry, and only rarely in terms of interpersonal malice.[39]

In contrast, the violence inflicted by the rebel army was of a more intimate kind. It involved the abuse of power between people who perceived themselves as equals, and sometimes people who were related as neighbors and kin. Frequently it also involved stories of betrayal, as people who inhabited the same village used the rebellion to settle old scores. Only twelve years after the rebellion ended, the French left, but the peasants of the east coast who had harmed each other had to continue to live on in one another's company. Internal violence, while perhaps exacting a lesser number of victims, was equally, if not more, traumatizing for the villagers.

As Telo explained, the Marosalohy arrived and imposed a reign of terror. Many of the rebel leaders had served in France, a fact noted by villagers and colonial administrators alike. In turn, the rebel army was modeled on the rebels' experience of the French army.[40] All able-bodied men in the village were recruited; no choice was allowed, and resisters faced death. When they recounted their narratives, many men who had joined the rebel army began their stories with a patriotic slogan—"I joined the rebel army to free my ancestral land." But they inevitably followed it with a telling caveat: "And besides, they killed you if you didn't join; they said you were a friend to the Europeans." Anyone who avoided joining the rebel activities or showed the slightest reluctance was suspected of being a European sympathizer. Despite fear of punishment, many men tried to flee to avoid joining the rebel army, but most were caught. As Zafiroa explained, "I fled into the forest. I didn't want to be in the army. But my friend betrayed me. He told the rebel leaders *[lehiben'ny Maros-alohy]*, "Here is a young man who should be in the army." So the Maros-alohy, came and caught me. The sergeant asked me why I was hiding in the forest. I said I was afraid. "We have knives and sticks, and they have guns," I said. "If they shoot from across the lagoon, then the bullets reach all the way here. That is why I am afraid." So they made me join the army. I wasn't courageous, and when we'd go on attack I would slip into the forest. All the brave ones, they were killed."

While those men judged to be able fighters were made to join the army and go on forays to attack neighboring concessions, villagers with special skills were made to contribute them to the rebel cause. Josef, for example, explained that Maniry, who had been a blacksmith, was made to work for the rebel army forging spears. Likewise, Jesoa, who was one of the few villagers who could read, was made to act as secretary to the rebel army, writing down people's rations and rank and reading roll call *(mamaky l'apel)* to make sure that all were present. The reservists, former soldiers who had fought in France, became the "sergeants," the "corporals," and the "chiefs": all others were supposed to follow their orders, as the group became the mirror image of the violent colonial state. So great was the abuse of power committed by those who became leaders in the Marosalohy that no villager I spoke with referred to them without adding some kind of disparaging remark, emphasizing that they were simply pretending to power to which they had no right.[41]

Aside from feeling betrayed by the MDRM, villagers also bitterly remember the settling of accounts that occurred between those who had benefited in some way from the colonial regime and those who had not. Anybody who had either fled to avoid the government corvée requirement or gone to live with and work for a *colon,* and anyone who had participated in the system by acquiring schooling and then working as a subaltern functionary, was singled out and punished. As Felix, a man who lived in a neighboring village, explained, "Anyone who had worked for the Europeans! Eeeeee! They fled the rebel army. If you had a name like "doctor," "teacher," "*chef de canton,*" then that meant you were associated with the French, and the rebel army took them all down to kill in their camps." The camps Felix referred to were two different military camps to the southwest of Masomeloka, where traitors were tried and sometimes killed, among them the local government official in Ambodiharina who had been responsible for choosing people to perform corvée. Felix explained how his father had almost died, not at the hands of the French but of the rebel army:

> Everyone else hated those people who worked for the Europeans! That man, people would say, he didn't side with us under the French but went and lived with a European. Well, at that time my father was a teacher, and when you were a teacher it meant you were friends with the French. So when the rebel army came through, they tied him with barbed wire and took him off to their camp in Ambahy to be tried, where there was a chief who almost killed him. They arrived there, and they tried him [natao ny tribunal] along with others from Ambodiharina. "Manambelona, what is your work?" "I'm a teacher," my father replied. So the rebels gave him a sack filled with money of many different denominations and left him to count it in a certain amount of time. Well, he was teacher and knew how to count, and so the hour wasn't even over and he'd counted all the money. "Ah," said the chief of the rebel army, "you give learning to our children, you're not our enemy." And so they let him live.

Forced to count money to prove his worth to his ancestral land, Manambelona was saved by his wits and, any Malagasy would add, God's grace. The most vivid memories of 1947 are all about the imponderable question of how some survived while others did not. Telo's story reflected a similar theme when he recounted the story of how he and one of his brothers, Letsara, had survived because of their special skills:

> When the French were here I never served the general corvée. I worked as a blacksmith. All those who carried the palanquin, they really served. But if the palanquin was broken, I would fix it. No pay—just a different kind of corvée. Whatever they asked, you did it. A machine broken, I would fix it. Sometimes I would build new palanquins. I lived here then, and they would come with their orders. One night after the rebellion had started and the rebels were here waiting for the French to attack, my brother Letsara played the accordion and everyone in the village danced. It was then that the Europeans attacked. The rebel leader, he came and wanted to know how the Europeans had managed to enter the town. They accused my brother of helping the Europeans. He was supposed to be on guard that night and had failed his job. So they took him off to their camp at Antananantefasina to try him. The general asked him, "What do you do?" And he replied, "I'm an accordionist. Whenever people rejoice, then I make them dance!" "Ah!" said the chief of the Marosalohy, "then you shan't die." Then it was my turn, and just at that moment I noticed that the general's watch was broken. "Give me your watch," I said, and I fixed it. So the general let me go. That night we gathered together for a ball and everybody rejoiced. Our little bit of learning had saved us.

Letsara died before my arrival in the village, but I heard references to his story from several elders, though because of prohibitions on discussing ancestors only his brother had the authority to legitimately recount the story in detail. Clearly, the image of the joyful accordionist who made music and danced when he should have been on guard—or "doing *la patrie*" *(mañano patrie),* as it was referred to by the rebels—and who almost died because of it, captured people's imaginations. Retold in the context of the election, it became an image through which people meditated on the injustice of the rebellion and the way it had cruelly warped their relations with one another.

Another theme that emerged repeatedly in people's narratives of the rebellion, particularly women's, was the way in which violence committed in 1947 was inflicted indirectly through flight and the subsequent deprivation that people suffered while living in the forest. For example, Ramaresaka recalled the following story: "I was twelve or so when the rebellion started. I'd just started to go to school when the troubles came, so I never finished school. For a year we fled into the forest and hid, fleeing farther and farther. My mother was terrified. She'd been harvesting rice when we heard the shots ring out in the embouchure. She was scared and decided to take us to her ancestral homeland upcountry. We fled. All the things in our house, our cows and chickens—we left it all and fled with the rebel army." Ramaresaka's story of flight was echoed by all, with minor variations. While those who had kin to the southwest, which was considered relatively safe, were able to seek refuge there, those who did not were forced to seek work and shelter among strangers. As one old woman explained, "It was terrible. Hunger everywhere. We fled when the harvest was just ready and then had nothing to eat. We worked for people planting rice in the country and found food." But if women's narratives emphasized flight, they also tended to emphasize the fact that the hardship experienced during flight dehumanized everyone involved. For example, Ratody remarked that if one was fleeing with a child, no one wanted to come along, because the child might cry and reveal one's whereabouts to the army. Reni n'i Jacqueline referred to similar asocial behavior when I asked her what had happened to her during the events: "We fled to the west, digging a huge hole in the ground where we hid all our possessions; but those who came up [out of the forest] first stole them all." Or as one man summed it up, referring to their asocial subsistence during the nine months of flight, "We lived like animals in the forest" (see fig. 17).

Figure 17. A woman emerging from flight in the forest, 1948.
Villagers who spent nine months in the forest suffered severe
malnutrition. Courtesy of Agence Nationale d'Information
Taratra.

TROPES AND CONVENTIONS:
THE NARRATIVE SHAPING OF MEMORY

As Michael Lambek and Paul Antze (1996) remind us, memories are shaped by the narrative conventions of particular places and time. There are two related tropes that I see as especially prominent in structuring people's memories of the rebellion in a particular direction. The first trope is that of the redemptive actions of local people in the midst of violence. The second related structuring device is their denial of their agency in the events and their tendency to see the rebellion as a Merina-MDRM plot.

Stories of Redemption   Though many people's narratives highlighted the theme of internal violence among villagers or violence by the Marosalohy, there was an implicit softening of internal violence when these stories ended with redemption. For example, many of the narratives I mentioned reached a climax in which a rebel chief relented when he realized a would-be victim had indeed contributed something to the struggle (as in the case of the teacher or the accordionist), or when another villager interceded. Rafaly, for example, had lost two brothers in the initial attack on the concession of Ampetika. Recall that Rafaly's father's brother-in-law was a *colon*, and the other villagers envied him both because of his arrogant behavior and because he had long been exempt from fulfilling the corvée requirement. During the rebellion, Rafaly's father was caught and brought to the camp at Ambahy, where he was tried for having colluded with the *vazaha*. It was only when Rafaly arrived on the eve of his father's execution, and explained that the old man had already lost two sons in the attack on Ampetika, that the rebel leaders relented and spared the old man's life. Rafaly concluded his story by emphasizing that the ancestors got rid of Moroccan soldiers charged with overseeing the resettlement of the village by mysteriously dumping sand on their shelter and forcing them to leave.

Similarly, Ramaresaka emphasized that her aunt had come upon Sampy, who as I mentioned in chapter 5 had grown rich under the French, just as they were preparing to take him off to Ambahy to try him. She interceded on his behalf, begging the rebel leader to let him off; since she was the *chef de canton's* mistress, people listened.[42] Josef had also been caught by a rebel patrol when he went to find his family where they were hiding to the west; they had called him a deserter and prepared to bring him to trial. The man they brought him to, however, happened to be his old neighbor, Iaba n'i Rasoa, who recognized him and let him go free.

Overall, these narratives are powerful parables of the villagers' goodness *despite* the circumstances; they are part of a familiar genre of narrative that appears to accompany every twentieth-century atrocity we know of, from those in Nazi Germany to Rwanda to Kosovo.[43] In the Betsimisaraka context, they tend to emphasize villagers' brushes with death and dehumanization, both of which emanate from the outside.

Denying Agency   Related to their emphasis on local redemption, villagers' memory narratives deny both any heroic element to the rebellion and any shred of active agency on their part. This denial of heroism is peculiar, given that the rebellion was part of an independence struggle, which men, at least, clearly knew, since their narratives often began by referencing this fact.[44] It is even more intriguing given that Ratsiraka, whom these same villagers politically supported, tried to foster an interpretation of the rebellion as one of a series of heroic national struggles. Ratsiraka justified many of his policy decisions on the basis of their being "a consecration of what the martyrs of 29 March 1947 had always demanded" (Leymarie 1973, 34, cited in Covell 1989). He attempted to portray his first regime as a vindication of Malagasy struggles for independence, of which the rebellion was the most explicit and the most violent.

Yet as we saw, the villagers' interpretations of the events not only denied any element of heroism but also repeatedly sided with the French colonial interpretation, which stressed that the Merina-MDRM tricked them and led a credulous population astray. Several factors account for their view. First, the villagers' absolute denial of any heroism had much to do with the fact that the French managed to shape people's interpretations of the events during pacification, when people's fear and suffering were still fresh. French military records actually say that the soldiers wanted to provoke a "psychological shock" in both the rebels and the populations who had abandoned their villages.[45] During pacification, French colonial administrators used a number of different methods to punish the Betsimisaraka for the rebellion and to ensure that a negative image of the events remained in their minds. For example, Chantal Valensky (1999) has shown that rituals of humiliation were an important part of the pacification process. These rituals were aimed at emptying the rebellion of any political content and stripping it of any heroic qualities that might have contributed to future political protest. French officials

Figure 18. Deposition of rebel spears, 1948. The French military forced
surrendering rebels to depose their spears in front of a French tribunal
in a symbolic gesture of submission. This photograph and the next were
part of a series used by French officials as propaganda to reassure the French
public that they had stamped out the rebellion. Courtesy of Agence Nationale
d'Information Taratra.

purposefully used their knowledge of Betsimisaraka cultural practice to
stage numerous public ceremonies in which rebel leaders were made to
depose their spears before French generals in a symbolic gesture of obedience and subordination. Often, cattle were sacrificed and rebel leaders were forced to revoke the vows of loyalty they had made to the rebel
cause and to publicly apologize and swear loyalty to the French instead
(see figs. 18 and 19).

    A further element that helps explain why Betsimisaraka memories of
the rebellion remain entirely negative despite Ratsiraka's attempts to give
them a positive, nationalist spin lies in another type of "ritual of humiliation" that administrators organized subsequent to the rebellion. Comparing the problem of postrebellion Betsimisaraka society to France following the liberation, administrators in the Mahanoro area argued that
they needed a way to reassert the authority that the rebellion had so seriously compromised. Their solution was to organize public tribunals in
which respected Betsimisaraka elders and community members were

Figure 19. Ritual of submission, 1948. In a cattle sacrifice staged by the French military, rebels were made to retract their oath to the rebel cause. Courtesy of Agence Nationale d'Information Taratra.

made to judge and mete out punishment to people who had actively participated in the events. The punishment was called a "skin cleansing" *(sasa hoditra)* and involved anywhere from ten to twenty days of public labor spent rebuilding the very schools or maternity wards that these individuals had destroyed in their alleged "frenzy of madness."[46] According to the district chief in Mahanoro, the "skin cleansing" was remarkably successful. "This practice of airing dirty laundry *en famille* has had an astonishing success," he observed. "The judges have judged with a zeal that compromises them definitively in our favor. The guilty have accepted their punishment with relief for the fear of the police which haunted them, as did the absence of punishment for a crime they considered to be sacrilege[,] for they had raised their hand against their elders."[47] Moreover, as the district chief was quick to point out, the "skin cleansing" served a double purpose. On the one hand, it encouraged those who had participated in the rebellion to publicly repudiate their actions and even to help rebuild the symbols of colonial rule they had just torn down. On the other hand, it allowed the district chief to recoup some of the economic loss inflicted by the rebellion. The administrator noted that more than three thousand rebels were condemned to "skin cleansing" of ten to twenty days of work, totaling forty-two thousand days of free labor with which the district of Mahanoro was literally rebuilt, saving the colonial government some two million francs.[48]

As for why the villagers saw the events as a MDRM-Merina plot, there are several possible explanations. First, as I discussed, they heard the MDRM say things that led them to expect a violent confrontation with the French. Second, many of the people most active in recruiting new members to the MDRM were from the high plateau. These initial perceptions were validated during the pacification, when the Moroccan soldiers who settled the area around Mahanoro repeatedly told Betsimisaraka that the Merina were responsible for the event, to the surprise and approval of French civilian administrators, who perceived this interpretation to be to their political advantage.[49] The same report that notes this fact also observes that Betsimisaraka mistrust of Merina substantially increased following the rebellion, and that even Merina subaltern functionaries who worked in the area were surprised by the "racism of this people previously known as tolerant before the rebellion."[50]

Yet when we consider gendarme reports from the area along with comments people sometimes let slip, we find that the experience of the Betsimisaraka belies such simplistic categorizations. To be sure, Merina organizers and the MDRM dominated the initial phase prior to the outbreak of violence. But during the nine months that followed, *some* of the rebel leaders in the Mahanoro area were either Merina or Betsileo, but *many* of the rebel generals they interacted with were Betsimisaraka who had come from the area to the southwest of Ambodiharina. Tangola, Lepako, Tody Velona, Zeka—these are the names of Betsimisaraka rebel leaders in this area, and they were people named in French archival reports as having considerable autonomy in organizing the local struggle.[51]

Given the fact that many people's experience clearly contradicted an easy indictment of the Merina, why did they choose to believe the soldiers' propaganda? Why did they buy the French story more generally? The creation of an authoritative version of the events in rituals tells part of the story, but manipulation by the French alone can not account for why the French version worked. I believe that part of the reason people believed the soldiers' and administrators' propaganda is that it selectively represented some aspects of people's actual experience. It was of course a version of events that helped the French to destroy the independence movement, and it helped to reawaken a kind of regionalist thinking (Merina versus *côtiers* [coastal groups]) that remains in place to this day. But believing in this version was not a total distortion, for it worked by selectively highlighting some aspects of what occurred and downplaying others. The French interpretation was a partial truth, and it gave those Betsimisaraka who were not in fact a core part of the planning of the rebellion a way to mitigate the pain of defeat. Like the trope of internal goodness despite violence, the externalization of blame allowed people to ignore the violence they had done to each other, to act as if it were entirely the fault of external forces. In this regard, a French administrator was correct when in 1948 he remarked that blaming the MDRM and the Merina enabled Betsimisaraka to forget quickly the disastrous consequences of their own actions.[52] It also meant that villagers could avoid blaming their own ancestors, for whom they claimed to have entered the struggle and whom they had supplicated for support, but who essentially had left them to die.

The villagers' attempt to downplay their agency and to distance themselves from the "real" participants, echoing the French colonial narrative with its emphasis on "masterminds" and "innocent populations," is equally apparent in the contradictory narratives I elicited when I asked what people had done when they returned to the village. Earlier I mentioned that local *colons* came and burned the village following the attack on Ampetika. For southern Betsimisaraka, burning is the worst possible kind of annihilation because it destroys the ancestral *hasina* on which the social order is based. When I asked villagers whether they had performed a sacrifice in order to cleanse the town and return it to its prior state, the answers I received were contradictory. Josef, for example, claimed that nothing had been done. When I pointed out that he himself had taught me that cattle sacrifice was necessary after a fire, he answered that in this case it was not, because villagers had not started the fire. It was the *colons,* Josef insisted, not the villagers who had burned the town. But Soavelo, a tiny, white-haired old woman thought differently: "We killed a bull to cleanse the burned town. And we invoked the ancestors and said that if a Malagasy, master of the ancestors here, led Europeans to burn the town then here was the cow that would judge him [before God]. But if the European's force that makes him a European *[mahavazaha anazy]* made him burn the town, well then, there was nothing we could do."

It may be that local family politics played a role in Josef and Soavelo's divergent interpretations. Many people blame Sampson (the man mentioned in Telo's speech as a traitor)—the man who was *chef de quartier* and the sole member of the PADESM, the puppet party created by the French to combat the MDRM—for leading the band of Creole soldiers to burn the town. Because Josef was related to Sampson, he may have chosen to downplay his participation in the events, whereas Soavelo, who came from a different ancestry, had no reason to do so. But while they disagreed on whether the cleansing actually took place, the assumptions behind their positions were the same. For both of them, cleansing the village was only necessary if a Betsimisaraka had been responsible for the act. The logic of externalization was echoed in other tales of post-1947 sacrifice that were told to me. Whenever cattle were sacrificed in cleansing rituals, the harm that had been done was symbolically thrown out of the community, and the blame for people's actions was displaced onto the government. As Reni n'i Jacqueline explained, "We sacrificed two cows to cleanse ourselves. Malagasy killed other Malagasy, but they didn't mean to. We washed that before God, gave it to God to judge. [In the time of the rebellion] there were those who did wrong, but they weren't to blame, as it was all the government's fault."

Uneasy Contradictions   As should be clear by now, villagers' memories were rife with contradictions, both in terms of their accounts of their actions and their interpretation of the events. The tropes of goodness and the lack of agency that they used to organize their stories contributed to a selective erasure of some elements of what happened. Yet the contradictions in their memories only mirrored the contradictions in their subjective experience of colonial and postcolonial politics. Ambodiharina occupied a low-level but not trivial position in the colonial hierarchy, for it was the canton seat, the one large village in the area before one reached Mahanoro; it boasted a school during colonial times but was, nevertheless, in most ways still a rural village. Though many villagers were involved in the colonial system at only the lowest, most exploitative level of serving, by fulfilling the corvée requirement, many others gained some kind of education or experience, either from working for *colons*, learning from missionaries, or working in the army. The people who lived in Ambodiharina were *not* indifferent to national politics—many of them recalled having put down their work to go hear the deputy Rabemananjara speak in Mahanoro and again in Vatomandry, though they emphasized that Rabemananjara and the MDRM paid for their transport. They joined the MDRM, hoping to gain access to political power and material goods offered by the party, and they went with the rebel army to burn the local colonial concessions.

Yet while these people actively participated in the events, they were never the masterminds, and, perhaps not unlike most participants who get swept up in grand historical events, their experience was more than they had bargained for. Ultimately, they experienced the rebellion as a civilian population that *was* partially implicated but found itself nevertheless caught between two armies and the violent logic of military command. Though the terrible events of the rebellion have not recurred, the villagers' subsequent experience of national politics is much the same: a few professional political organizers coming through and singling out a few well-respected people for involvement in state politics. Though only the village traditionalists (AREMA) feared a recurrence of the rebellion, both groups noted the continuities in political experience.

Writing of colonial transformations in Merina notions of political morality, David Graeber (1996) suggests that the outcome of certain key historical contests tends to define the terms of moral discourse. The greater the battle, the more painful the defeat and the more likely people are to reject the very things they once fought for. In Imerina, the key institution no one will defend is slavery, which was abolished at the time the government upholding it was destroyed by the French. This case helps illuminate Betsimisaraka interpretations of their terrible defeat in 1947, for survivors of the rebellion believe that it was a huge mistake for mere peasants to contest the authority of the state. One villager even said that the rebellion was suicidal, and that next time they would do just what the government asked, while another remarked that if it were to happen again she would head straight for town rather than flee into the forest. In this sense, Betsimisaraka survivors of 1947 would agree with the adage that "might makes right"; their defeat proves how foolish their involvement in oppositional politics actually was. At the same time, however, the lesson of their defeat is that one must discredit political participation involving an oppositional stance toward the state. The defeat of 1947 has indeed transformed the parameters of moral discourse, but in a way that elite understandings of politics would have been hard pressed to predict. Today, many rural Betsimisaraka perceive Ratsiraka's gift of a sacrificial cow as proper etiquette, whereas the "democratic" rhetoric of the Forces Vives is read as a prelude to death.

POSTSCRIPT: THE CLEANSING OF THE EMBOUCHURE

Let us return to how some of the people in Ambodiharina—the people who vividly remembered the rebellion and were most caught up in the rumors about blood thieves—handled the disruptions caused by the people organizing the elections. After harassing Jean, the AREMA officials went away—after all, they were outsiders, city slickers from Mahanoro who had little at stake in the village. The consequences of their actions, however, proved more difficult to dispel. The AREMA officials had overtly bullied some in the community because of their political beliefs, thus forcing the community to recognize and deal with tensions that many people would have preferred to remain covert. For weeks after the events at Jean's shop occurred, tensions in Ambodiharina ran high. People talked about the upcoming elections, remembered the trauma of 1947, and spoke ominously of how no good would come of the competitive jostling going on among the different parties. They speculated on the murder at the embouchure and worried about the constant threat of blood thieves. Finally, they worried about the breaking of the crocodile taboo and what should be done to resolve the matter. All of this was exacerbated by a terrible drought that hit the region: the rains were late in coming, and everywhere people complained that if the drought continued there would be no spring harvest and they would all starve.

After weeks of talking about the various events from every possible angle, it was decided that things had gone too far: the community had become too defiled by the different occurrences. Something had to be done. A meeting of the various male elders decided that Jean would be made to pay a fine of rum *(fafy)* for breaking the taboo. Rafaly, the would-be master of the Mangoro who sold Jean the crocodiles, was demoted. Like his arrogant father who had worked for the *vazaha* and who was then almost killed by the rebel chief, he had flouted community norms. Rafaly could remain *tangalamena* for his own family, but in the eyes of the wider community he no longer commanded any respect or power.

Finally, the council of *tangalamena* decided that an additional cleansing would have to be done at the embouchure, a cleansing that people hoped would rid the community of the different ills that had plagued it. A day was chosen and Zafiroa—a Zafimalaone descendant of the last-born brother who had used his position in the colonial administration to seize control of the water (see chapter 5)—was called down from Ankarembelona to officiate. That morning a group of us filed out to the embouchure, picking our way through the woods and across the swamp until we arrived at the sandy shore that edged the lagoon. We gathered at the edge of the sand, facing east, toward the ocean, and although for weeks there had been nothing but sun, clouds gathered as Zafiroa began the speech announcing the reason for the cleansing. Too much had happened in the community he said, and we washed the death of the boy who had been killed on the embouchure and the breaking of the taboo in the town. As Zafiroa poured the rum into the waves and began the invocation of the Zafimalaone ancestors associated with the water, the clouds broke and the rain began to pour down. We returned to the village drenched to the bone. The drought had broken and the social order had been partially restored.

CHAPTER 8

Constructing
a Betsimisaraka
Memoryscape

Youth has the illusion of hope; the adult has
the illusion of recollection.
> —*Soren Kierkegaard*

I began this book by likening Ambodiharina to a reversible illusion, an impossible double-image where the eye flickers back and forth between two mutually imbricated images but has difficulty seizing both simultaneously. What should be clear by now is that Betsimisaraka's practices of remembering create this unstable effect as their techniques of memory weave together different aspects of their past and present. That one aspect of the past becomes figure relies on the fact that—indeed requires that—another facet serves as its ground. It remains, however, to specify some of the precise ways this process works and what it might mean for our understanding of how once-colonized peoples remember the colonial period.

BETSIMISARAKA ARTS OF MEMORY

Several practices account for the foregrounding of ancestors' memories that is evident much of the time. The relative privileging of their memories occurs because ancestral sites of memory provide the framework for daily social action and because these sites are constituted through a combination of space and the practices that make space into place. Since people believe that *hasina* needs to be maintained, these places have the power to draw people to them, so that reproducing ancestral memories becomes not simply an act of personal recollection but a force that structures people's actions on a daily basis. The practices that link power and memory are crucial to how Betsimisaraka produce themselves as subjects, in a way that resembles Michel Foucault's vision of subject formation as a process of self-knowledge tied to power relations.[1] The importance of space and sites of memory in sustaining memory—giving it form and thus making it memorable—also resonates with many other theories of memory that emphasize the importance of a spatial framework for remembering.[2]

However, it is also important to emphasize that we are dealing with a situation of multiple, overlapping histories and cultural encounters, so that it is not simply the spatial organization of ancestral sites that suppresses memories of colonialism much of the time. Since the spatial configuration of sites of memory clearly encodes the colonial past, as well as the local past, space and ritual practices like taboo and caring for tombs are insufficient in and of themselves to account for the dominance of ancestral memories.

As I suggested in chapter 6, sacrifice provides the key to understanding how people's memories articulate with a wider social narrative through which a particular kind of historical consciousness is formed. In some ways, Betsimisaraka sacrifice resembles what Godfrey Lienhardt (1961, 252 ff), referring to Dinka sacrificial practice, calls symbolic action. Lienhardt suggests that sacrifice as a healing ritual worked by first using words to remove symbolically the patient's weakness, and then by symbolically replacing that weakness with something strong, in the form of the bull's urine and chyme. The effect, Lienhardt notes, was to "detach weakening from strengthening elements within the situation of the rite *and the consciousness of the participants*" (294, my emphasis).

Similarly, Betsimisaraka also take symbolic action when they transform the meanings associated with the signs and symbols of colonial and postcolonial rule, like the tin-roofed house and the abundant coffee tree and the defiled prisoner. In all cases, this recoding takes place by partially separating old meanings from their previous frames of reference and assigning them new meanings and a new history. Betsimisaraka not only declare the transformation in speech, but they enact it by applying the blood of the bull—a substance that, as we have seen, they believe cleanses and reformulates all it touches—to either the tin roof of the house or the most abundant coffee tree or the tongue of the defiled person. Where houses or coffee are concerned, the cranium of the sacrificed bull, which is nailed to the northeast gable of the house or to the most abundant coffee tree, marks the transformation. No longer the symbol of alien rule or forced labor, the wealth and power once associated with aspects of colonization now stand for the owners' powerful ancestral connections.

The manner in which Betsimisaraka attempt to achieve symbolic action in cattle sacrifice is also similar to Claude Levi-Strauss's idea of bricolage, the creative cobbling together of symbols drawn from different worlds: "The characteristic feature of mythical thought, as of 'bricolage' on the practical plane, is that it builds up structured sets, not directly with other structured sets but by using the remains and debris of events . . . Mythical thought, that 'bricoleur,' builds up structures by fitting together events, or rather the remains of events" (1966, 21–22). However, where the bricoleur fixes a problem using whatever is at hand, it is not clear that he or she does so with long-term intentions or projects in mind.

By contrast, Betsimisaraka sometimes use sacrifice quite purposefully to recast imperfect relationships, the residue of colonial history, and the signs of the postcolonial present, in terms of their own concerns. The practice of sacrifice contains within it many different kinds of reconfigurations, some of which are short-term and ad hoc. Nevertheless, some of these negotiations *do* involve people's deliberate attempts to act upon meanings and perceptions in order to reformulate them mentally and culturally, in keeping with their long-term projects and goals, some of which have to do with the colonial past or the postcolonial present. To say this, is not to argue for the well-worn binary of global dominance and local response. As I have shown, practices of remembering are one mechanism through which different systems have become tangled up in each other, though the way in which participants are conscious of these processes is a wholly different matter. Nor does my analysis privilege a Western fascination with the power of colonialism more than it should. Not all of people's projects are about the colonial past nor the postcolonial present; it would be hubristic to think that they all are. But colonial power impinged on many facets of daily life. The connection that people make between power and memory, and the fact that colonial power partially constituted Ambodiharina as a particular kind of locale, has meant that, in trying to enact local projects, people often have to take account of the colonial past and postcolonial present in which they live.

Let me emphasize, however, that the degree to which people are conscious of these negotiations varies both by generation and the particular negotiation concerned, making the experience of sacrifice and its effects on people highly variable. Foucault once said, "People know what they do; they frequently know why they do what they do; but what they don't know is what they do does" (cited in Dreyfus and Rabinow 1982, 187), a statement that partially captures the way remembering occurs in Betsimisaraka practices of sacrifice. For example, young people who have grown up with house washing and tin-roofed houses often do not know the origins of the practice, so for them house washing is just a part of "Betsimisaraka tradition," as Zakatiana implied in his speech. These younger people may not perceive house washing as being about the colonial past at all, but their ritual efforts do contribute—whether intentionally or not—to the further transformation of meaning. To return to a distinction I used earlier, young people contribute to the incidental transformation of colonial memories. But older informants' statements imply that negotiations like house washing *are* a part of their conscious efforts to survive in a colonial and postcolonial context. And young people are aware of, and intentionally use, other aspects of the rite, like cleansing themselves after having been in prison. Though symbolic action and bricolage come close to capturing what occurs in sacrifice, we might underscore the (sometimes) deliberate and always highly varied nature of people's efforts and call it a kind of *mnemonic manipulation* or strategic remembering.

In fact, as I mentioned in chapter 1, Betsimisaraka in Ambodiharina refer to cattle sacrifice as a form of remembering. Though they literally mean that they use it to commemorate ancestors, the expression is nevertheless telling because sacrifice works as a technique for shaping individual memories. Comparison with two other famous techniques of memory, the *ars memoria* of classical antiquity and written history, illuminates the specificity of Betsimisaraka practice as a memory technique.

In *The Art of Memory,* Francis Yates traces the different techniques of memory from the early Greeks through Renaissance Europe. She shows how classical students of rhetoric sought artificially to extend their memories for particular arguments. They trained their memories by using vivid images of people engaged in different activities for each of the points they wanted to make, which they then placed in different rooms in a house or palace in order to remember the order of the argument. As Yates observes, analyzing Cicero's discussion of the rules for training memory, "The writer has got hold of the idea of arousing emotional affects through . . . striking and unusual images, beautiful, hideous, comic or obscene" (1966, 10). The idea was to use visually moving images to arouse emotion and thus sharpen and extend normally fallible, short-lived human memory.[3]

Like the *ars memoria* of classical antiquity, written history is also a technique for representing and molding people's memories of the past. It does so, however, in a radically different way, because writing enables people to move beyond the natural limits of human memory and to store information in a way not previously imagined possible. The way writing extends memory is, of course, heavily mediated: many historians now emphasize the necessity of understanding the context in which facts are discursively produced, and the way in which context limits or shapes their ability to represent the past in a particular way. To take an example pertaining to Madagascar, in order to understand how highland Malagasy perceived King Andrianampoinimerina, Pier Larson (2000) had to consider both people's political interests at the time and their discursive construction of history, which emphasized some facets of social life and omitted others.[4] Nevertheless, while many historians agree that "the facts" are discursively constituted, some interpretations are considered more plausible than others, and what is considered plausible is at least partially measured by the fit between a given interpretation and available forms of evidence.

Cattle sacrifice also mediates representations of the past and shapes people's memories, but in a way profoundly different from either the *ars memoria* or written history. Unlike the *ars memoria*, Betsimisaraka practice is not about images or the way images intensify memory. Rather, what Betsimisaraka sacrifice shares with the *ars memoria* of the classical rhetoricians is an attempt to harness the power of emotion in the work of making memories. The Greeks and Romans figured out something fundamental about how individual memory works: it is enhanced by emotional arousal. Numerous psychological studies suggest that emotional engagement—the fact that an event matters and that we are emotionally moved by it—is a central component of what makes an event memorable. In a now-classic study, the psychologists Roger Brown and James Kulik (1977) asked adults to remember where they were when President Kennedy was assassinated. They suggest that people retain especially vivid memories of dramatic events—which they call flashbulb memories—and that there is even a special brain mechanism, which they call "now print," that permanently encodes a shocking event on the brain.

Subsequent studies of flashbulb memories, however, suggest that these memories are not seared into the brain as Brown and Kulik initially thought. In a study of how people remembered the dramatic 1986 explosion of the space shuttle *Challenger,* Ulric Neisser and Nicole Harsch (1992) demonstrate that in fact people could have "phantom flashbulbs," memories of events that people were absolutely convinced had happened but which were inaccurate. The subjective sense of the accuracy of the memory was *not* matched in objective fact. Flashbulb memories have also been shown to fade with time. Yet in general the link between emotional events and memorability appears to hold: people retain more details of dramatic events, or events that are personally meaningful, than ordinary, inconsequential events from around the same time. Reflecting on why this should be so, Daniel Schacter (1996) suggests that it may be a combination of strong emotion and the way an emotional event is more likely to be mentally rehearsed that combine to make the event particularly memorable.

Sacrifice and the classical *ars memoria,* then, share an attempt to use emotion to mold memory. But whereas classical rhetoricians tried artificially to generate emotion through surprising images, thereby enhancing the capacity of human memory to retain information, Betsimisaraka use the power of emotion to shape memory to very different ends. In contrast to both the *ars memoria* and written history, which use different techniques but are each concerned with accumulating information, Betsimisaraka use cattle sacrifice as a form of directed forgetting and remembering in order to create a subjective feeling, which is in turn used to enhance the construction of particular meanings.

The emotion generated in sacrifice fosters a particular process of meaning-transformation that is partially captured by Frederic Bartlett's conception of constructive remembering. Bartlett argues that schemas— "active organized settings of past reactions" ([1932] 1995, 201)—form the reconstructive basis through which remembering (as well as perceiving and imagining) takes place. Further, he suggests that when a new practice or item comes from outside the group, its meanings are reshaped. For example, he shows that newly introduced art forms undergo several changes before they finally settle down to a particular local form. He calls this process *conventionalization,* and he suggests that it occurs through processes of assimilation, elaboration, and even exaggeration of an element's existing meanings, but always "positively in the direction along which the group happens to be developing at the time at which these features are introduced" (274).

When villagers ritually "wash" tin-roofed houses, abundant coffee trees, or soldiers returned from the national army, they are erasing memories of the colonial and postcolonial government and recasting them as part of the "direction along which the group happens to be developing"—their narrative about ancestral power. In Bartlett's terms they are changing the meaning of the schema: the schema for tin-roofed houses, coffee, or soldiers remains, but its meaning is transformed, so that it no longer signals vazaha ways but the success of local ancestors. The emotion generated in sacrifice facilitates this process because it means that people are emotionally committed to reading the possible meanings of certain objects and practices in a particular way. As Bartlett observes, "Subjective confidence and the emotional halo [are] liable to lead to inventions, and to a constructive type of remembering" ([1932] 1995, 264, my emphasis).

Consistent with Bartlett's ideas, new processes or experiences that were comparable to already existing local practices—growing coffee, building houses, going to work beyond the village—dominate the reformulation of meanings that takes place in sacrifice. Growing coffee for a colonial economy is arguably a very different process from growing rice on one's ancestral land for one's own subsistence, just as going off to join the army of a modern nation-state is part of a structure that is different from being forced to fulfill the Merina queen's corvée requirement. Nevertheless, the remembered experience of growing rice and being forced to fulfill the queen's corvée requirement provides a template through which the experience of growing coffee or being a member of a national army can be compared, interpreted, and understood. Since Betsimisaraka have local templates for these processes, people recast the meanings of houses and returning soldiers as they pursue their primary goal of reconfiguring their relationships among themselves and between themselves and their dead kin.

Yet if one follows Bartlett too closely, one might mistakenly believe that the process of reconfiguring the meanings of certain practices comes about almost by accident, an organic practice that is simply a "tendency of the group." It is here that my analysis diverges sharply from Bartlett's. As I have mentioned, "washing," the crucial mechanism through which the process of reconfiguration takes place, is a result of people's struggles with one another and their deliberate attempts to transform the signs and symbols associated with colonialism. The struggles that lead to sacrifice are fundamentally about people's always uneven and highly fraught attempts to regenerate themselves and the ways in which these struggles intersect with opportunities for growth and transformation—or alternatively, suffering and death—brought by colonial, and now postcolonial, rule. People in Ambodiharina used ancestral demands for sacrifice in their attempts to control how new opportunities brought by colonial power changed their relationships to one another as some people grew richer or escaped corvée while others did not.

The ultimate articulation of individual and social memory that takes place in sacrifice results in what we might call a "feeling memory," which occupies the fuzzy space between thinking and feeling, similar to what Michelle Rosaldo calls "embodied thoughts": "The crucial point . . . is recognition of the fact that feeling is forever given shape through thought and thought is laden with emotional meanings. I can then argue . . . that what distinguishes thought and affect, differentiating a "cold" cognition from a "hot" [emotion,] is fundamentally a sense of the engagement of the actor's self. Emotions are thoughts somehow felt in flushes, pulses, "movements" of our livers, minds, hearts, stomachs, skin. They are embodied thoughts" (1984, 143). Unlike the *ars memoria* or written history, the emotional memories created in sacrifice are not about knowing the past or retaining information. Rather, through an emotive form of reconstruction, Betsimisaraka's arts of memory enable some Betsimisaraka to retain a particular vision of how the world works and how many, though not all, Betsimisaraka think it *ought* to be.

COLONIAL MEMORIES AS UNOFFICIAL CONSCIOUS

The remembering effected in sacrifice as well as the other practices I have described together produce a quasi suppression of colonial memories, even while Betsimisaraka take as given certain changes wrought by colonial rule that, absorbed into memory and forgotten as history, silently structure the present. In daily life, memories of the colonial past become a bit like a subterranean brook that runs its course without anybody paying much attention, until a person stumbles upon a place where the brook wells up through the earth. But unlike an underground stream that is the product of natural forces, colonial memories are entirely a social phenomenon. They are the residue of historically constructed relationships, with tensions and contradictions that lie just beneath the more obvious order of things. In this respect, colonial memories are similar to what Valentin Vološinov calls the "unofficial conscious." Vološinov argues that the psyche, "like all human structures, is a social entity filled with ideological signs, a product of continual interaction between it and the outer world."[5] As a result, the unconscious is not fundamentally different from consciousness (1976, 85). Rather, the difference between the conscious and the unconscious mind lies in the degree of ideological elaboration. The unconscious is guided by inner speech, a reduced form of social speech that privileges the idiosyncratic, ego-centered aspects of the remembered past. It is a relatively unelaborated ideological realm because it is not yet completely expressed in words and, thus, leaves thought unfinished and incomplete. By contrast, official consciousness is expressed in words that are part of developed ideologies shared openly with others. Vološinov renames this social unconscious of inner speech the unofficial conscious.

Vološinov adds a social dimension to Freud, but he does not deal explicitly with memory and, in particular, never addresses Freud's theory of traumatic memory. Recall that Freud argues that painful memories remain in the psyche but that the ego works to keep them at bay. While I do not agree with Freud's psychodynamic interpretation, Vološinov's revision allows us to think about how social practices might sometimes suppress individual consciousness of painful memories by making them part of the diffuse realm of inner speech. It also suggests that sometimes the social suppression of memories may have a healing effect, allowing people to move beyond elements of a painful past even though in so doing it necessarily limits what it is possible to say. The story I have told for Ambodiharina suggests that in some cases it may be the fact that implicit knowledge remains implicit that liberates; in other contexts, however, it is release—the forcing into consciousness—that heals. Not all remembering is liberatory, but under the right conditions it can be.

Vološinov's concept of the unofficial conscious bears similarities to what Michael Taussig (1987, 366 ff) calls "implicit social knowledge." Taussig defines implicit social knowledge as what "moves people without their knowing quite why or quite how" and "slips in and out of consciousness."[6] The concept also resonates with John and Jean Comaroff's distinction between ideology and hegemony in their account of the colonizing efforts of Christian missionaries in southern Africa (1991), and with Janice Boddy's idea of counterhegemony in Zar spirit possession (1989). All of these discussions share an emphasis on the importance of implicit versus articulated forms of knowledge, highlighting the ways in which implicit forms of knowledge may be expressed in embodied practices and rituals. They also highlight the potentially subversive nature of this knowledge. However, in analyzing the place of colonial memories in Betsimisaraka daily life I have found Vološinov's reanalysis of Freud, and Vološinov's discussion of the "unofficial conscious," particularly useful because his focus on the ideological elaboration that makes speech possible seems to me to best capture the *movement* that is central to the production of memory: from silent, implicit forms of "knowing how" to the more discursive forms of "knowing that." As Maurice Bloch (1998) reminds us, memory and narrative are not the same. Thinking through the dynamics of memory in Ambodiharina reveals what kinds of social and individual processes force implicit forms of memory into consciously constructed narratives.

The distinction between official and unofficial conscious, or explicit and implicit social knowledge, helps us to grasp the location of memories of colonialism in daily life. Clearly, individual memories of colonialism have not been erased. Nor have they been repressed in the psychodynamic sense of the word. Rather, through the articulation of individual and social memory produced through practices related to ≥ *Peace* houses, tombs, taboos, and sacrifice, memories of colonization have been *socially* suppressed. They have been pushed into the background against which the work of commemorating ancestors plays out.

Insofar as sacrifice articulates individual memory with an emotionally anchored master narrative, relegating colonial memories to the unofficial conscious, it initially appears profoundly Durkheimian in spirit. Watching a Betsimisaraka sacrifice, where the members of a great house gather together to cheer in affirmation of their most cherished social values, it is hard *not* to think of Durkheimian collective effervescence, for sacrifice does attempt to mold people's memories in line with a socially constituted master narrative.

But if sacrifice partially shapes people's memories in line with a master narrative, it is a master narrative embraced by some people more heartily than others, and it is here that the analogy with a Durkheimian interpretation of ritual quickly breaks down. Earlier, I suggested that the official memories constituted in sacrifice were like Gilbert Ryle's conception of "knowing that" (1949), but this is true only if we acknowledge that the memories created in sacrifice are different from knowing that the sky is blue. After all, the memories created in sacrifice are the foundational truths that underpin much of Betsimisaraka social life. In this sense, I think that the comparison of official memory with "knowing that" works only if we acknowledge that the particular form of knowledge produced in sacrifice is intensely ideological. Sacrifice is tied to people's efforts to sustain particular social relations and the distribution of power on which they rest. In turn, acknowledging the power relations involved in sacrifice raises the question of which groups benefit from it, and which ones might want to see the world represented and experienced in this particular way.

In Betsimisaraka daily life, the elder men who mediate between ancestors and their descendants are the most obvious group of people who benefit from the official memories produced in sacrifice, because they are the powerful political actors in Ambodiharina. As such, they have the most invested in maintaining the status quo. Yet to say that official memories do not benefit women or youth would be wrong, for insofar as women and younger people also hope to build lives premised on local control, they too benefit from perceiving the world as it is constructed in sacrifice. By contrast the category of people who do not have much to gain by creating the illusion of local autonomy are those people I earlier referred to as "village progressives." Unlike those who embraced official memories that rested fundamentally on creating an imaginary separation that enabled local sovereignty, these people desperately wanted Ambodiharina to be visibly integrated into a wider world in order to reap the material and social benefits that they hoped would follow.

The success of sacrifice as an art of memory, however, is always incomplete. Sacrifice ensures that some memories, and some forms of perception, are easier—more readily accessible and more practiced than others—because they are tied into some people's long-term interests and what some people find a comfortable emotional tone. But sacrifice does not—indeed cannot—guarantee control of people's memories all of the time. There is always tension between the reality promulgated in "knowing that," and what people do in "knowing how," tension that remains submerged much of the time, but only provisionally so. This tension is embedded not only in rituals of sacrifice but in daily life as well.

And so colonial memories remain, although as Vološinov's conception of the unofficial conscious implies, they are more idiosyncratic than the highly elaborated ancestral memories and are made up of many different kinds of memory woven together only unevenly.

I see roughly three ways that memories of colonialism slip into the "knowing how" of ancestral sacrifices and daily life. First, in much the same way that colonial history incidentally slips into ancestral *tantara,* so in organizing ancestral rituals people incidentally commemorate the way their interactions with settlers and the colonial state transformed ancestral sites of memory. Insofar as people rearranged their ancestral sites of memory because of their experience of colonial power, it provides the deep structure for ancestral commemoration, as when Prosper's illegitimate son returned to his father's colonial concession to sacrifice. Second, colonial memory is often evoked in moments of conflict or discoordination, as when the Antehengitra family fought over where their family's sacrifice should be carried out. In these cases, colonial memories are the spanner in the works that illuminate the ideological nature of sacrifice, countermemories that destabilize the dominant ancestral narrative that most people work so hard to produce most of the time.

But colonial memories also enter into "knowing how" in a more deliberate way. They are alternative scripts of the past, and so sometimes people evoke colonial memories quite intentionally as a way of recasting present social relationships or asserting a set of moral claims, though their efforts do not always work. When Pindy accused Bienaimée's grandmother of "not really loving him" because her branch of the family took advantage of colonial opportunities while his did not, he made a set of moral claims both about the past and the present in relation to his family. The claims he made were particularly weighted because they were voiced in the ideologically charged context of sacrifice, where the master narrative of equal ancestral love is enacted. Colonial memory is also expressed by people like Giselle or Guy, whose inappropriate performance of Frenchness leaves everyone laughing and uncomfortable at the same time. And it was also colonial memory that erupted forth in the ravings of old Baomaro when she asked me to punish the villagers who were letting their cattle destroy the vanilla she had planted for tax money, an event that probably happened fifty years ago if it happened at all. Fools and mad people, after all, are those who say what can not be said by others. Most of the time, however, colonial memories are memories that people have not yet put into words because they have not yet encountered the occasions on which to say them. The elections of 1992–93 provided an occasion. Before we can address what happened during the elections, however, I want to step back and theorize the articulation of individual and social memory more generally.

METAPHORS FOR MEMORY

It is an underacknowledged aspect of the history of anthropology that many anthropological or social science theories bear a similarity to, or are elaborations of, the local theories of the people studied, what Alessandro Duranti (1985) calls "famous theories" and "local" theories. For example, Duranti shows that the Samoans and Ludwig Wittgenstein worked out strikingly similar theories of language. Bloch's theory of the ideological nature of ritual bears a striking resemblance to one facet of Merina ideas about ritual (1989). Catherine Lutz (1988) attributes her ideas about emotions to the people on Ifaluk with whom she worked. This same principle applies to the Betsimisaraka, whose practices of reburial provide an especially appropriate metaphor through which to think about the memory puzzle I have described in the previous chapters.

REBURIAL: DIACHRONIC PROCESSES OF REMEMBERING

As I have already mentioned, in the Betsimisaraka version of reburial *(famokarana)*, a practice that exists in many guises throughout Madagascar, the ritual sequence is initiated after an individual gets sick and goes to a diviner, who tells him or her that an ancestor's wooden tomb has rotted and needs replacing.[7] The person then gathers the family together, and, once a diviner has chosen the day, they collectively organize a ceremony.

Prior to the ceremony, the new tomb must be built. The mats that the bones will be spread upon must be woven, and new fabric for shrouds must be purchased. The night before the event, the *tangalamena* and a selected elder or two walk out to the tombs to call the ancestors to let them know not to wander too far because they should be ready in the morning to have their houses changed. The next day the family, along with other people from the community who come to help, walk out to the tombs, and the ceremony begins after the proper invocation.

First, young men complete the heavy work by lifting the lids off the tombs and taking the bodies out.[8] Since people are buried in adjacent tombs according to sex, they take all the men's and women's bodies out, gently laying each on a mat next to his or her tomb. When the tomb is opened and the first bodies taken out, people can identify the bones because they know who died most recently and thus who lies on top. They also know the clothes that the recently deceased were wearing and which blankets they were wrapped in when they died.[9]

Over the course of the ceremony, however, these individual distinctions become unrecognizable as older and older sets of bones are removed. Two groups form, a group of women working on the female ancestors' bones and a group of men, working on the male ancestors' bones. People unwrap the bodies and place them on the mats.[10] Then, men and women gingerly pick the bones out of the bits of cloth and dirt. As people work, methodically sifting through the bones, selecting the bones and contributing them to either the male or female pile, it becomes impossible to know which bone belongs to whom.

These arrangements never take place without negotiation, invention, play, and occasionally, conflict—all the same potential for dissension seen in the examples of sacrifice discussed earlier. Elders often show younger people what to do, encouraging them to join in the work. At the Zafindrabe's family ceremony, where the contents of ten different wooden tombs were emptied in order to move them to a new cement tomb, the entire village was there to help. At a smaller ceremony for Bienaimée's grandmother's family that involved only the substitution of two new wooden tombs for two old ones, Bienaimée's family came from Mahanoro. Though Bienaimée's aunt and grandmother lived in Mahanoro, they remained familiar with the country milieu and got straight to work sorting bones with the rest of their family. Bienaimée and her younger sister, however, who were much better dressed than anyone else, stood and watched the proceedings until someone forced them to sit down on the ground to help. At one point in the ceremony, after most of the work was done, Tsaravintana took the mat that the bones had lain on and, using it as a cape, grabbed Bienaimée's aunt, the well-heeled record keeper from Mahanoro, to dance a mock waltz.

Sometimes unprecedented situations occur and people must decide how to handle them. For example, at the Zafindrabe reburial one of the seven ties used to bind the blanket around the body of a woman after death would not come loose. People kept tugging at the tie uneasily, and the man who was helping the women working on the body was about to get a knife and start hacking at it when Ramaresaka interceded. She took a bit of rum and poured it on the tie, to honor the woman; when she went to pull the tie off, it yielded easily. As Ramaresaka commented, even a dead woman does not want her *sembo* (the traditional wrap worn by women) ripped off of her; but once she had been honored with rum the dead woman did not mind, which explained why the tie came right off.

These different moments of play, participation (forced or willing), and negotiation are crucial to how the literal re-membering of the ancestors is ultimately achieved. By the time people are done, the head bones are all placed together, followed by the neck bones, and so forth, so that by the end of the ceremony people have created two master-ancestors, one for each sex[11] (see fig. 20). What people work to produce, as they literally collapse the generations and create their master-male and -female ancestors, is a cultural archetype—the brother-sister pair that lies at the root of every ancestry. This brother-sister pair is a master symbol that continues through time and is, in this sense, timeless, even as it is continuously negotiated and renegotiated through collective human action.[12]

The same is true of social memory more generally. Individuals carry memories created in social interactions. Through their struggles to enact their particular projects, which are always socially shaped, their memo-

Figure 20. Ritual of reburial *(famokarana)*, 1993. During this ritual, the relatives of the deceased pick through the ancestors' bones and carefully construct two master-ancestors, one male and one female. Photo by Jennifer Cole.

ries are in turn modified. Individual and social memory are coconstituted. Consequently, the metaphor of reburial—the many individual bodies that are broken apart and reconfigured through collective human action into two large, collected ancestors—gives us a way to think of the process through which individual memories might be collected together, and of the transformations that occur as people work to secure their ties to the past, thereby making themselves, quite literally, the many who will not be sundered.

LANDSCAPES OF MEMORY:
SYNCHRONIC HETEROGENEITY IN REMEMBERING

The sequence involved in reburial privileges the temporal, sequential nature of remembering and suggests that certain underlying schemas determine what people are more likely to remember. What this temporal
metaphor of bone turning does not give us is the sense that people are
differently positioned vis-à-vis each other and various memories, though
their positions are always changing. As a result, we must combine the
temporal metaphor that produces an ideal, diachronic prototype with a
spatial metaphor that affords us a view of synchronic variation—the fact
that different people survey the landscape from different positions at any
given moment.

The spatial metaphor I use is the *landscape of memory*, which I borrow from Laurence Kirmayer (1996). Kirmayer compares the narratives
of Jewish Holocaust victims with people who suffered abuse as children.
He notes a striking difference in prototypical trauma narratives between
the two groups. Whereas Holocaust victims are more likely to be bothered by intrusive memories, victims of child abuse may dissociate and
suffer an absence of memory. Kirmayer does not look to psychological
explanations. Instead, he suggests that one may explain this difference
by the particular landscapes of memory that the two occupy. He defines
landscapes of memory as the metaphoric terrain that determines how
difficult or easy it is to remember socially defined events that initially may
be vague or impressionistic. Thus, while child-abuse victims inhabit a
landscape of memory suffused with the private shame of abuse, Holocaust victims experience their memories in a context that publicly rec-
ognizes, and abhors, the suffering they experienced. For Kirmayer, it is
social practices, the larger social context of meaning, and the way that
these converge to create a virtual space of recounting that constitute this
metaphoric terrain.

THE MEMORYSCAPE: UNITING
THE DIACHRONIC AND SYNCHRONIC SIDES OF MEMORY

In thinking through the question of how to account for the relative absence of colonial memories in Ambodiharina in daily life, and their dramatic appearance during the elections, I draw the temporal aspects of
memory embodied in reburial together with the synchronic heterogeneity embodied in landscape. I think of this combined spatiotemporal terrain as a memoryscape. Like Kirmayer, I see the social practices that en-

able individual memory as being crucial to how the articulation of individual and social memory is produced. Unlike Kirmayer, I use the landscape metaphor to refer specifically to the existence of synchronic heterogeneity, and I draw this together with the idea of diachronic transformation that is such an important part of Betsimisaraka practices of reburial.[13] Every group is constantly evolving, and the memoryscape indicates the articulation of individual and social memory that dominates at a particular time; it is constituted by the diachronic tendencies that enable continuity of historical consciousness over time, as well as the way these diachronic tendencies intersect with synchronic heterogeneity that enable any group's transformation.

The memoryscape is not just *of* memory, but *for* memory (Geertz 1973). It indicates the configuration of people's memories at a given moment, as well as how easily people currently access particular memories; and it conditions the possibilities for retaining them in the future. The *memoryscape* includes the array of schemas through which people remember and the social-historical forces that draw these schemas into action and sometimes enable them to be formulated in narrative. It also encompasses the broad spectrum of commemorative practices through which people rehearse certain memories critical to their personal dreams of who they think they are, what they want the world to be like, and their attempts to make life come out that way. In other words, social and individual memory articulate through the practices that facilitate individual memory and the way that these practices intersect with larger patterns of social transformation. As the memoryscape both elaborates some memories and diffuses others, it marks the crystallization of historical consciousness that occurs where social and individual memories provisionally meet.

THE ELECTIONS OF 1992–93:
POSITIONS IN THE MEMORYSCAPE

In chapter 7, I examined the kinds of interpretations, emotions, and social tensions that made older people evoke the rebellion during the elections of 1992–93. Here, I suggest that the idea of a memoryscape provides us with a broader view of the full set of historical memories that were circulating within Ambodiharina during 1992–93. It gives us a way to think about how this pattern articulated individuals' memories with competing social narratives associated with the different groups involved. More specifically, I want to suggest that the historical memo-

ries that emerged during the elections were a product of the interrela-
tionships among three groups in Ambodiharina, and of their different
positioning along the temporal and spatial axes, that I have suggested
constitute a memoryscape.

A unique configuration of individual and social memory characterized each group. Primary memories of the events of 1947 dominated the
memories of the first group. Those who did not directly experience the
rebellion split into two groups, one oriented internally, the other externally. Secondary memories of Merina enslavement, as I mentioned in
chapter 7, dominated the memories of the internally oriented group. The
externally oriented group, the Forces Vives supporters, evoked neither
memories of Merina enslavement nor the 1947 rebellion; instead, a modernist, nationalist perspective that was focused on the present shaped their
memoryscape. Concentrating on each group enables us to revisit in a different register the question of how the traces of colonialism linger on,
not in the larger sense of macrostructural changes but in the more intimate sense of the memories through which people imagine who they are.

THE GENERATION OF 1947

The memories of the older generation that lived through the rebellion
have an emotional intensity that distinguishes them from the memories
of the generations that followed.[14] Expressions of fear tinge their recollection. The rebellion also figures importantly in the ways that many of
these people reckon time, "before the flight" and "after having come up
from the flight" being prime examples. And though rarely publicly discussed, people have integrated the events into their autobiographical
memory, so that someone like Ramaresaka blames the rebellion for her
lack of schooling. Moreover, there is a remarkable homogeneity in the
way that people who survived 1947 interpret the events; while I found
variation in how younger people thought about 1947, survivors' views
were surprisingly similar. But these primary memories were by no means
free of cultural shaping.

When the French introduced practices like growing coffee and building houses with tin roofs, they appear to have assumed that their adoption by the Betsimisaraka allowed only a single kind of interpretation.
As a result, French administrators did not try to shape more thoroughly
what the activities meant because they assumed that meaning was created by participation in the activity: the medium was the message. By

contrast, in the case of the rebellion, French administrators and military alike perceived people's interpretations as being up for grabs, and they worked hard to shape how people read the events. As I showed in chapter 7, the French use of rituals of pacification and cattle sacrifice, local tribunals, and "skin cleansing" enabled the colonial administration to crystallize people's memories in a manner that erased all heroic elements from the events so thoroughly that they have proven irretrievable by subsequent regimes. The elder people in Ambodiharina, like the French colonial administrators who suppressed the rebellion, agree that it was all a MDRM-Merina plot.

It is tempting to conclude that, by reshaping people's memories of 1947 and thereby rooting their version of the past deep within Betsimisaraka hearts and minds, French administrators finally demonstrated the kind of capillary control often attributed to rulers in their position. This conclusion, however, fails to take two factors into account. First, while the French provided the dominant memory-narrative of the rebellion, they had little influence over how these events were interpreted; they could not create or control the conceptual link that Betsimisaraka forged between elections and oppositional politics, and fear. As a result, the French administrators could not control when and how the memories of the rebellion were elicited. Second, it fails to take into account the complex ways in which French administrators and rural Betsimisaraka were— perhaps unintentionally—complicit with each other in managing the aftermath of the events.

The way the older generation remembered the rebellion during the elections was loosely based on the French narrative, but they reinterpreted it to their own ends in a way that deliberately emphasized the dangerous side of state-local relations. When people remembered the rebellion during the elections, they also talked about the violent settling of accounts that took place during the rebellion, as we saw in the narratives examined in chapter 7. The harm they had done to one another, however, was *never* the first thing that people talked about. Rather, it was the secondary discourse, the unsettling aspect of past events that tagged along with the overt story of state violence whenever a curious interlocutor, including the anthropologist, probed too long.

As I have suggested, the crucial advantage of interpreting the rebellion as a Merina-MDRM plot was that it enabled people to persistently displace responsibility and agency for what happened *outside the community.* This externalization of agency and people's tendency to represent themselves as tossed about by more powerful forces are partially factual, but these narrative devices also enabled them to narrate their memories in such a way as to downplay the violence and highlight the kindness that came from within the community. I see this structuring of memories of 1947 as yet another form of directed forgetting, which is similar to what people practice in sacrifice when they try to erase their differences by "washing" disputes and reinstating them with proper, harmonious social relations. Though the French certainly did not intend this outcome, the ironic convergence between the Betsimisaraka and the French perspective on the events has partially enabled the foregrounding of state violence and the downplaying of local violence. *Amnesty* and *amnesia* come from the same root, and this strategy enabled people in Ambodiharina to live with each other. French administrators complained about the Betsimisaraka's tendency to blame the Merina, which they claimed enabled the Betsimisaraka to forget quickly the consequences of their own actions. But the French surely helped along the process of memory-transformation by means of their interested attempts to shape how the rebellion was interpreted and remembered. A good deal of the secret history of the rebellion is precisely about local participation. This is the aspect of 1947 that no one really wants to talk about, and it is in the process of being erased as people focus on the tyranny of the state. The transformation is further fostered by the disappearance of memories over generations, as the story is slowly simplified in line with people's contemporary concerns.

MEMORIES OF MERINA ENSLAVEMENT

If the great majority of younger villagers happened to agree with their elders on whom to vote for, they justified their choices with reference to different aspects of the past. Whereas older villagers chose the rebellion memories, younger villagers talked more about a possible reenslavement by the Merina. The evocation of memories of enslavement by the Merina also exhibited directionality, for the *only* aspect of the Merina-Betsimisaraka relations that was evoked was a history of enslavement. I do not want to downplay the fact that Merina exploited Betsimisaraka in the past. Nevertheless, it seems important to acknowledge that the focus on enslavement considerably simplifies the complex relations that formed between Merina and southern Betsimisaraka over the years. For example, there had also been periods in the past when the relationship was reversed, when Betsimisaraka worked as intermediaries carrying Merina to sell as slaves at the coast (Pier Larson, personal communication).

Betsimisaraka may have suffered during Merina domination of the area, but they also intermarried with Merina; in many ways they learned to live with their dominators, just as they lived with the Creole settlers who came after them. Many older people who had not lived through Merina domination but whose parents had, had a rather moderate view of Merina presence. Several of them said that the Merina had kept cattle nearby, and that they had always had fairly friendly relations.[15] But this complex history of interaction was absent from the evocation of these memories during the elections.

This difference between the memories that the two groups chose to evoke, despite a shared ideological perspective, may be explained by the fact that—in comparison to memories of enslavement by the Merina, which circulated in the public sphere—in everyday life the elders tended to suppress their narratives of the rebellion. Perhaps it was the relative familiarity of Merina enslavement narratives and their integration into official consciousness that made them seem more relevant to younger people than the more hidden memories of the rebellion. Younger people could also express their political position via these narratives without evoking the history of local inequalities, which they may not have known about or could strategically forget. In any case, because these memories of enslavement by the Merina were secondary memories— memories of events that no one had directly experienced—the people who evoked them were people who could integrate memories of Merina enslavement into their autobiographical narratives in a meaningful way. This process is clearly illustrated by Monsieur George.[16]

Though he was born during the colonial period, long after Merina rule had ended, Monsieur George often referred to memories of Merina domination. Son of a Betsimisaraka mother and Merina father, Monsieur George detested the Merina and had forbidden his children from marrying them. His decree caused considerable tension within the family when his daughter fell in love and had a child with a local man of Merina descent (when she protested that he was really Betsimisaraka, Monsieur George responded, "I *know* where their tomb is") and then proceeded to sneak around and lie to her father. Monsieur George disliked the Merina because his mother had been courted and impregnated by a Merina prince, who then rejected her because of her coastal—and thus, implicitly, slave—origins. The story he told me went like this:

> My mother's older sister worked for a *vazaha*, and the *vazaha* decided to move to Fianarantsoa.[17] They took my mother too. At that time my father went down there from Antananarivo seeking wealth. He was carried in the red

palanquin, the mark of princes, seeking cattle to buy and sell. He saw my mother and courted her *[mañano l'amora]* hither and yon. And my mother got pregnant *[nahazo kibo]*. My father went home to tell his father about her: "Papa, there is a girl I love, she's already pregnant." My grandfather asked, "The child of whom? Where is she from?" And my father told him where she was from. "Then she's a slave," he said; "we don't need any of that." My mother was furious, and she returned home, where my mother's brother raised me.[18]

Monsieur George's reasons for distrusting Merina differ significantly from the clichéd memory-images allegedly circulated by Ratsiraka's men. They differed in that they were entirely personal, rooted not in a mythologized and dramatized past of enslavement (which is not to say that Merina-Betsimisaraka relations were not tainted by the very real history of slavery) but in a personal history of suffering and perceived injustice. Though he had never lived through Merina oppression, its effects had tangibly affected his life (growing up without his father, which was something he often mentioned) and had become a central part of how he thought about himself and his place in the world. For Monsieur George, these memories were part of the memoryscape of everyday life.

I never talked politics with Monsieur George, and I am not sure where he stood on the matter of the elections. However, the importance of personal positioning in determining whether secondary memories resonated was equally apparent when people in Ambodiharina responded to rumors of a return of enslavement by the Merina. Among young people, those individuals whose situations were directly threatened by Ratsiraka's potential loss of power found these memories most convincing. For example, Babette and Tovolahy, who were both in their twenties, were among the people I knew who talked about the Merina-enslavement rumors the most. Recall that Babette's father *and* uncle both worked in Ratsiraka's army. Though neither Babette nor Tovolahy had experienced the same kind of personal tragedy as Monsieur George as a result of Merina-Betsimisaraka interactions, the fact that the male relatives most important to Babette's well-being made their living working for Ratsiraka gave them powerful reasons to find the memories of enslavement by the Merina compelling.

THE FORCES VIVES

Memory processes for the younger generation that supported the Forces Vives contrasted with the memories evoked by the inward-looking younger villagers. These people had surely learned of both the 1947 rebellion and enslavement by the Merina secondhand, but they chose to evoke neither set of memories.

Earlier, I remarked that the advantage of the way the older generation manage their primary memories of 1947 is that it has allowed them to downplay the violence they did to each other and to live with their own concerns most of the time. The potential cost, however, is high. The events of 1947 are not discussed in daily life, they are not integrated into socially structured rituals of remembering, and they seem very distant from the experience of contemporary young people.[19] As a result, young people often know about the events—how their parents or grandparents escaped, where they fled, and so on—but they have not always internalized the (largely unspoken) moral lessons and emotional stance that accompany them. As we saw in the example of memories of the Merina, one way secondary memories gain power is through their integration into autobiographical life narratives. By keeping their primary memories outside the public sphere, the older generation made this convergence of personal history and the rebellion less likely to happen among younger people in Ambodiharina.[20]

This muting of local memories of the rebellion makes it possible for the state's narrative of the rebellion eventually to take pride of place. By 1999, this was already beginning to happen in the capital, as the Malagasy newspapers announced the state's version of events, which focused on transmitting the story of the struggle for independence, and national unity, to future generations. Whether this version will take hold in rural areas is open to question, since most rural people I knew never read newspapers and, at least as late as 1999, schooling was minimal for all but a few children whose parents could afford to send them to Mahanoro. But it is worth noting that, like the narratives evoked during the elections, the state version completely ignored the internal violence among peasants that had taken place. Unlike people's primary memories, however, it also glossed over the fact that mainly coastal people had died, as well as similarities between the violent colonial state and its postcolonial counterpart.

Whether the Forces Vives' attitude in 1993 was particularly pronounced because of the general erasure of the rebellion from daily life, or whether it was due to intrinsic differences between primary and secondary memories, is difficult to say on the basis of my observations. But what is sure is that the adherents of the Forces Vives were able to distance themselves from the moral-political commitments of older villagers as well as those adopted by inward-looking younger villagers. This distancing also meant that they could change their orientation to the history of the village's relation with the state, as well as to the moral stance it implied.

CONTENDING POSTCOLONIAL MEMORIES

The three major positions that people occupied in the Betsimisaraka memoryscape that emerged during the elections have implications for how we think about the effects of colonialism, which anthropologists sometimes refer to as "the postcolonial condition." In the introduction, I raised the question of what Betsimisaraka memory practice might tell us about the consciousness of rural postcolonial peoples. Akhil Gupta (1998, 11) suggests that "what constitutes the experience of modernity as 'postcolonial' in a country such as India is the acute self-awareness of [a] temporal lag and spatial marginality" vis-à-vis the metropolitan center, an observation that resonates with those of others writing on the postcolonial condition.[21] Drawing from information included in the preceding discussion of Ambodiharina, I believe that how the postcolonial condition is experienced, even in small rural villages, is more varied than Gupta implies. It is profoundly crosscut by lines of generation and social status. Equally important, as I have emphasized here, is the presence or absence of certain kinds of memories, which, as they are absorbed into people's autobiographical narratives, have profound implications for how people think about their circumstances. If the experience of living in the aftermath of colonialism did *not* engender a sense of marginality for older people in Ambodiharina, as it has done in so much of the formerly colonized world, this is surely related to the older generation's experience of state violence, and their efforts to avoid contact where possible.

Though younger localists and the Forces Vives disagreed on which group should control the state, neither of them experienced the same kind of fear as their elders. As postcolonial theorists would expect, and as Gupta argues, these groups *did* experience a profound sense of spatial marginality and a deep desire to "catch up," though this sentiment was more sharply expressed by the adherents of the Forces Vives. As I showed in chapter 7, it was the relative absence of memory in the Forces Vives group that made "reminding" those who had "forgotten" the events of 1947 such an important part of the pro-Ratsiraka villagers' political strategy and forced these memories into the public sphere.

It is ironic, then, that the real violence of the rebellion saved those people who survived it from a symbolic violence of a different sort, the symbolic violence of a second-class modernity, where one perpetually imagines oneself vis-à-vis a center that lies elsewhere and that one can never attain. During routine colonialism, the colonial state was at pains to make the Betsimisaraka imagine themselves in terms of larger forms of collectivity, and by the end of the colonial period it had partially succeeded. But the violence it inflicted during 1947 had the opposite effect. The generation that experienced 1947 firsthand were deeply influenced by colonial policies and had pursued many new opportunities, but their response to the violence of the repression was to drop any form of state politics and turn in on themselves.[22] One administrator described the local scene in 1949 this way: "The old customs have regained favor, people are attending more and more to their elders, there is a return to paganism that is almost disconcerting. This includes a wave of circumcisions around the month of September, the meticulous cleansing around the tombs[,] which appears to be spreading in imitation of Europeans, and the numerous cattle sacrifices that appear to have exceeded 800 in this year alone.[23] Perhaps this return to traditional values is normal after a period of crisis like the rebellion, for we have ourselves experienced it in France after the armistice."[24] The survivors of 1947 were working to reconstruct Ambodiharina as the center of the world. They were also working hard to do the impossible: to keep everybody else out.

These observations about what happened after the rebellion, as well as the way in which the memoryscape shifted during the elections, makes visible some key aspects of the memoryscape that I first perceived as part of the dominant tenor of daily life during my fieldwork in Ambodiharina. What was at stake in the elections, and in the older generation's deliberate evocation of the violent colonial past, was an attempt to protect a memoryscape heavily influenced by colonial interventions. The generation of people that had shaped the dominant tenor of daily life in Ambodiharina were the people who had experienced the most intense period of French colonial rule. These people were responsible for elaborating on many of the symbolic boundary-maintaining practices manifest in contemporary sacrifice. Historical records suggest that Betsimisaraka practiced sacrifice from at least the sixteenth century on, when precolonial traders crossed the east coast. They also tell us that sacrifice was used in war and was an important part of the constitution of hierarchical communities from at least that time. In the sacrifices I witnessed, the structuring of hierarchy was certainly important, but what was particularly striking were the processes of reversal or incorporation—the "washing" of people, houses, and coffee. As I have shown, this reversal or purification involves taking practices or people that were "outside" and making them "inside," incorporating their power or reversing the appropriation of people and wealth by pulling them in and making them ritually and materially commit to the ancestral order. Although there is evidence of some of these processes in earlier historical accounts, the heightened concern with creating symbolic boundaries is surely a result of this generation's attempt to assert mastery over their increased interactions with the outside world in circumstances that were less and less of their own choosing. The observation supports many accounts of colonial contexts, which emphasize the way "age-old tradition" springs in part from people's experience of colonial rule.[25] It also suggests that this process included the psychological and cultural constitution of particular kinds of individuals, and that individuals actively participated in this process. Betsimisaraka drew some elements of the colonial experience into the deepest part of themselves as, in their efforts to control their memories, they restructured some of the ways that memories are made.

The structure of the memoryscape created through sacrifice and sustained in sites of memory belongs to this generation more than it does to the kind of people who joined the Forces Vives, who have had more experience of the outside world. Not surprisingly, it is these older people who work to maintain it. It benefits them because sacrifice as memory work ensures the protection of locality over and against all threats that come from the outside. This older generation, as well as the other people in Ambodiharina who attempt to live their lives in very local terms, need to believe in this narrative in order to maintain a sense of control over their world. Thus, it is not the village progressives—Pierre, Piso, or Jean, among others—who inhabit the daily memoryscape that I first described. Rather it is Josef—whose father died in prison as a member of the MDRM, and whose status derived primarily from his deep knowledge of ancestral custom—who works to sustain this particular formation of the memoryscape. And it is Ramaresaka—someone who never learned to read because her parents hid her away so that she would not be raped by soldiers during the repression, and who now invests so much effort in creating a group of loving children around her—who works to keep this memoryscape in place.[26]

The status quo, as I have suggested, was a structure of feeling and set of sociocultural arrangements that had been shaped and inflected by the colonial encounter. For the older villagers of Ambodiharina, the status quo was a condition they had learned to live with and more or less control following the departure of the French in 1972. It was this sense of local control that the pro-AREMA villagers, who envision their lives in very local terms, sought to protect. They drew on their memories of the rebellion because, for them, their first-person experience as elders made these memories a powerful tool. For people like Piso, however, the stakes were different. The elections held out the hope of change and the possibility of attaining some of the benefits of modern life for which she worked hard. The crisis of the elections suggested that a new configuration of the memoryscape was emerging.

The dynamic interaction between individual and social memory visible throughout this analysis suggests that the old dichotomy between individual and social memory needs to be rethought. Rather than seeing individual and social memory as fundamentally opposed, we might follow the Betsimisaraka and look at the practices through which individual and social memory are articulated and sustained. As we have seen, Betsimisaraka have developed multiple arts of memory to selectively shape consciousness and create continuity with the past. These mechanisms range widely in their material embodiment and social organization. But as I have sought to demonstrate here, the memoryscape in which they coalesce is always but a fragile truce among contending social forces.

EPILOGUE

Looking Back

Memoryscapes in Time

Oh young Malagasy, natives of Madagascar,
your island is calling you!
   —*Le lieutenant chef de Bureau Politique*
    de la Rénovation Malgache, 1947

After the cleansing on the embouchure, life in Ambodiharina settled
down. But the wheels that had been set in motion at the national and international levels ground ahead. On 7 February 1993, the presidential
election was finally held throughout the country. For all the panic that
had occurred during the preceding weeks as people worried about blood
thieves and older people talked about the rebellion, the day of the elections was astoundingly calm. People lined up at the schoolhouse and cast
their votes, their thumbs marked with red ink. A few weeks later we
learned that Zafy Albert, leader of the Forces Vives had won. Locally,
however, most people had voted for Ratsiraka. Older villagers were upset,
but they seemed resigned: "Whomever the people elect," pro-AREMA
villagers told me, "we will follow." The panic about the elections, and
the massive surge of memory, had passed.

But in many ways the panic that older people felt about the 1992–93
elections and their fears about a recolonization (recall the old people begging the census takers, "Please, please, write down my name but leave
off the names of my children and grandchildren") were a remarkably
prescient interpretation of the changes taking place.

When I first began to think through the flood of memories that I had
witnessed during the elections of 1992–93, I thought that the villagers,
because of their relative lack of access to information about national political processes, had gotten it wrong. After all, they were interpreting

the move toward democracy that was sweeping Africa in the wake of the cold war as a prelude to recolonization and a harbinger of state violence. At the time, I thought of the rebellion as what Jerome Bruner (1966) called a "pre-emptive metaphor," an experience that is so powerful that people use it to (mis)interpret later experiences. Now, six years later, after observing, on periodic visits to Madagascar, the changes that have taken place, I think differently.

One of the fears that people expressed during my earlier stay—fears that would occasionally punctuate the local round of rice work I described earlier—was of recolonization. Specifically, those people who had experienced French colonization firsthand feared that the people who had earlier settled the area around Ambodiharina would come back to claim their land, which many Betsimisaraka had started to farm and use since the departure of the remaining French nationals in 1972. In late 1993, when I left Ambodiharina, these fears seemed unfounded. Soon after, however, a series of changes took place that suggested the villagers were right: a new colonization *was* taking place.

When Zafy Albert took power, he declared that his republic supported open market capitalism and embraced contacts with France and the United States. As with many other African countries, Madagascar's economy came increasingly under the control of the World Bank and the International Monetary Fund (IMF). Between the time I left in December of 1993 and my return in 1997, the currency was devalued three times. And the peasants grew poorer. During this short period, Zafy's government was repeatedly accused of corruption, like Ratsiraka's government had been before him. Eventually, he was unable to secure the loans from the IMF needed to keep Madagascar's economy going.

In 1997, Ratsiraka was voted back into power, and he remains in power as I write. When villagers voted for Ratsiraka in 1992–93, they supported him on the assumption that his policies would be favorable to them, a combination of selective investment and benign neglect. When Ratsiraka was reelected, however, he began to enact many of the policies that villagers had initially held against Zafy Albert, who had been operating under pressure from the IMF. These changes included increased state control of the practice of burning land, as well as a policy forcing people to inhabit villages and not move out to their small camps in the fields—exact replicas of the policies of the earlier colonial governments.

The result of Ratsiraka's new policies is that outsiders have been returning to Madagascar for business. In the area around Ambodiharina, this has meant the literal return of people who had formerly colonized the area, which may signal the creation of new kinds of neocolonial relations.

Akhil Gupta (1998) persuasively argues that the apparatuses of development and environmentalism have created new global regimes of governmentality that continue, in new guise, the structures and relationships created under colonialism. In Madagascar, new patterns of translocal connections have emerged with the recent change of government on the island. In some cases, these connections are new, forged between agencies like the World Bank who have allowed Madagascar to trade national parks for debt. It is still too early to talk of a pattern, but in the older settler regions of the east coast, which have little forest left to protect, some French and Creole settlers who created ties to Madagascar under the umbrella of the French empire, and sometimes even before, have returned. Many of these former *colons* are motivated in part by tremendous colonial nostalgia, and they long for the places they inhabited when they were young and enjoyed relative freedom and wealth.

Following the mass exodus of foreigners that took place in 1972, the area that had been Ampetika (what Joseph Gallieni had called at the turn of the century "our most beautiful concession"), and the site of villagers' experience of forced labor, was purchased by the Société Codal. The Codal was a trading company that collected local produce—pepper, coffee, and vanilla—for export. During the late 1980s and the early 1990s, at the height of state bankruptcy and the withdrawal of state presence, people from around the area who had lost their land to settlers during the colonial period, but who still coveted it, began to return little by little. They planted their crops on the edges of the old concession. And then the former settlers started showing up, kicking people off the land and not even allowing them to claim their harvests.

In 1997, I had the odd experience of meeting, while in California, a French couple who had once been settlers in Mahanoro. This man's name had cropped up repeatedly when I asked Betsimisaraka about the colonial period, and I had come across it in the archives because he was one of the primary owners of Ampetika. He and his wife spoke nostalgically of Mahanoro and said they wanted to return to Madagascar to reclaim the land they had abandoned when they fled the country in 1972. They told me that their daughter had gone back to Mahanoro, staying in the only *vazaha* hotel in town, and that their former workers came throughout the night, in twos and threes, begging their old mistress to return. Colonial nostalgia again, but of a more ambivalent sort.[1]

When I returned to Madagascar, local people told me that the husband had come back to visit the area around Ampetika. He had never gone to see the people managing the Codal, but visited instead the peasants inhabiting the edges of their old concession, cozying up to them with gifts and money. I can only guess at his plans. Descendants of another old Creole family—people related to the old foreman from Ampetika, whom I quoted in chapter 2—also came back and started a hotel. They had wives in Réunion, people said, but they had started second families in the Mahanoro area, marrying local women as a way of forming new patterns of local connection, much as their great-grandfathers had done before them. In 1999, I received a letter announcing that another man, also the child of settlers who had left in 1972, had also come to Ambodiharina and had started claiming land in order to plant vanilla. Unlike in colonial times, these people can not use the government apparatus to force Betsimisaraka to work for them, but they can try to take their land. When they are the descendants of former *colons* who legally registered that land, their claims usually win in a court of law. And because many peasants remain afraid to enter government buildings, where, as one Betsimisaraka proverb has it, "You only go to die," people in the area have done little so far to contest this state of affairs. Whether these new kinds of relationships can be accurately called colonial is questionable; as I have shown, exploitative relationships such as these predated colonial rule, and we now think of colonialism proper as a phase associated with the creation of nation-states. But from the local point of view, these relationships are often experienced in much the same way.

　　These events show that the older villagers had good reason to fear the changes foreshadowed by the 1992–93 elections. These people drew on their memories in their efforts to protect their children. As it turns out, the older villagers got what they wanted and Ratsiraka was returned to power. In the meantime, however, global forces had shifted the conditions for national policy. Consequently, although older villagers may have gotten what they wanted, they did not get what they had hoped for.

Notes

CHAPTER 1. INTRODUCTION

Epigraph: Raymond Williams, *Marxism and Literature* (Oxford University Press, 1977), 130. © by Oxford University Press. Reproduced by permission of Oxford University Press.

1. The individual who is chosen to represent the community's interests to the state is called the "government *tangalamena*," or *tangalamena fanjakana*.

2. Throughout this book I use the word *locality* in the sense described by Arjun Appadurai (1996) and Akhil Gupta and James Ferguson (1997), as a phenomenological quality and structure of feeling that "is produced by particular forms of intentional activity and that yields particular sorts of material effects" (Appadurai 1996, 182).

3. Throughout the nineteenth century, France and England competed for control over Madagascar. Virginia Thompson and Richard Adloff (1965) persuasively argue that, with the opening of the Suez Canal in 1869, England wanted to eliminate French influence in Egypt and so agreed to grant France a free hand in Madagascar. In 1890, Britain and France agreed that France would maintain control over Madagascar, while England would get the island of Zanzibar. Theoretically, the slave trade between Madagascar and the Mascarene Islands stopped in 1817, when the Merina king Radama I signed a treaty with General Robert Farquhar declaring that in exchange for abolishing the slave trade, King Radama would receive technical support from the British. In practice, however, Réunion Island continued to rely on Madagascar for illicit shipments of slaves.

4. French policy was hardly unified: while some French colonial theorists argued in favor of "assimilation," others argued for "association," in which the colonies would be administratively associated with the metropole but would retain more cultural autonomy. For a discussion of assimilation theory in French colonial policy, see Lewis 1962.

5. It took so long to get to Antananarivo, which was only 150 kilometers away, partly because of the condition of the roads and partly because the driver of the *taxi-brousse* refused to enter Antananarivo at night for fear of being attacked by bandits and robbed.

6. Two other prominent examples of this approach, which have different theoretical orientations but share a common focus on the way people creatively respond to the penetrations of the world system, are Aihwa Ong's *Spirits of Resistance and Capitalist Discipline* (1987) and Jean Comaroff's *Body of Power, Spirit of Resistance* (1985). In each case, we learn how local cultural beliefs and practices provide a medium through which people resist and transform disciplines and values imposed on them from the outside, making continuity of historical consciousness possible.

7. For an illuminating discussion of Sahlins's approach and its implications for understanding the history of colonized peoples, see N. Thomas 1989.

8. See Dirks 1992a and 1992b, and Cohn 1987.

9. See the volume edited by Cooper and Stoler (1997), as well as Stoler 1989.

10. The issue of what to call Ambodiharina—a town or a village—is tricky. Most Euro-Americans looking at Ambodiharina would perceive it as a village; however, when Betsimisaraka use the word *town (tanàna)* they mean simply what is opposed to the bush: it can be as little as two houses grouped together (see chapter 2). Throughout this book I refer to people living in Ambodiharina as villagers but often refer to Ambodiharina as "the town," in keeping with local usage. As should be clear from the argument developed in this book, referring to people as villagers is by no means intended to somehow dehistoricize or romanticize their situation.

11. There is a large body of literature in anthropology that focuses on schemas and their role in "internalizing" culture (see D'Andrade and Strauss 1992 for a good introduction). I have chosen to highlight Bartlett's work because he focuses squarely on the problem of remembering.

12· In response to attacks saying that his model did not take into account the social and political context in which writing occurs (Street 1984; see also Halverson 1992), Goody has modified his position. See Goody 1986, 1987.

13. I should point out that while Piso and the storekeepers were not from Ambodiharina, both the midwife and Pierre were. Despite their education, Pierre and the midwife both felt constrained by the form of ancestral memory I describe in chapter 4.

CHAPTER 2. COLONIAL INTERVENTIONS INTO BETSIMISARAKA LIFE

1. Larson (1996) persuasively argues that in Imerina the phenomenon of ethnogenesis in fact predates the French colonial period.

2. The term I have translated as "king" is *mpanjaka*. In many parts of Madagascar, the term is gender neutral and is best translated as "sovereign" or "monarch"; in the past both Sakalava and Merina have been ruled by "queens" as well as "kings." I have glossed the term *mpanjaka* as "king" because Betsi-

misaraka imagine rulers as being male, since only men are able to invoke the ancestors (see Cole and Middleton 2001).

3. The way in which Betsimisaraka create community in sacrifice differs from the practices of other, more hierarchically ordered groups on the east coast (such as the polities around Manambondro [see P. Thomas 1996]). Each group is able to sacrifice their own cattle; the privilege is not reserved for a particular ancestry. The group relies on others in the community to attend the sacrifice in order to make it efficacious.

4. I was denied access to the Merina archives for the Mahanoro area because of their poor condition. As a result, I have relied on Manassé Esoavelomandroso's account of Merina rule in this area (1979), which is based on this same set of archives.

5. For a discussion of the administration of the east coast province of Imerina, see M. Esoavelomandroso 1979.

6. The word *hova* was mistakenly used by the French to refer to the Merina as an ethnic group. The word actually refers to Merina commoners as opposed to nobles *(andriana)* or slaves *(andevo)*.

7. Archives de la République Démocratique de Madagascar (Archives of the Democratic Republic of Madagascar), Antananarivo (hereafter ARDM), Serie 363–75, "Monographie du District de Mahanoro, 1950."

8. Ibid.

9. Archives de l'Evêché de Tamatave, Madagascar, Lettres d'Uclès, 10 December 1882, Letter from R. P. Lacomme to R. P. Cazet, Prefet Apostolique de Madagascar.

10. As I mentioned in chapter 1, Creole planters of the east coast were pivotal in lobbying for French colonization of Madagascar. Later, they formed a reactionary and politically powerful group, whose interests were often at odds with those of the metropole. See Boiteau 1958.

11. According to Fremigacci (1976), the term *marécageux,* taken up by Deschamps in his *Histoire de Madagascar,* was coined in the 1930s.

12. The Creole and French *colons* have been gone for many years. I suspect, however, that at least superficially the feel of commerce in the countryside around Mahanoro is much the same today as it was then. The Réunionais have been replaced by *métisse* Chinese traders, who continue to inhabit small wooden shacks with verandas and corrugated tin roofs, selling small quantities of cheap foreign goods (inevitably imported from China) and chewing tobacco, or buying rice and coffee in season and selling them for a profit, or collecting cloves and raffia for sale to national companies like Somacodis or Codal for export.

13. Centre des Archives d'Outre Mer, Aix-en-Provence (hereafter CAOM), Serie IID, Rapports Politiques et Economiques des Circonscriptions (hereafter Serie IID), 221, "Rapport Politique, Vatomandry, 1951."

14. CAOM, Serie IID, 128, "Rapport d'Ensemble sur la Situation Politique et Administrative du District de Mahanoro du 1 Octobre 1896 au 31 Decembre 1898."

15. ARDM, Cabinet Civil, Supplément, Serie D178, "Concession Deville de Sardelys à Mahanoro."

16. Under colonial rule, administrative divisions changed continually, making it difficult to specify precisely the responsibilities of different administrators. Suffice it to say that the administrative divisions were nested one within the other, with each level responsible to the next highest level. For example, the *chef de village*, who was responsible for making sure that government laws were enforced, reported to the *chef de canton*, who in turn reported to the *chef de district*.

17. Ibid. It is also cited in Fremigacci 1976.

18. The art of formal oratory is highly developed in Madagascar. Though people refer to large political meetings as *kabary*, technically *kabary* can be both official speeches made to convey the will of the government and the formal oratory made at ancestral events. For a discussion of the formal properties of *kabary*, see Keenan 1974.

19. CAOM, Serie IID, 128, "Rapport d'Ensemble sur la Situation Administrative de la Circonscription de l'Année 1899."

20. Ibid.

21. See Jaquier 1904 for a discussion of French policy on labor in Madagascar.

22. ARDM, Cabinet Civil, Supplément, Serie D178, Letter from de Sardelys to Governor General Gallieni, 1900.

23. ARDM, Cabinet Civil, Supplément, Serie D361, "Rapports et Communications des Chefs de Provinces sur l'Application de l'Arrète de 1900 Supprimant les Prestations."

24. CAOM, Serie IID, 220, "Rapport Politique et Administratif, Vatomandry, 1915."

25. CAOM, Serie IID, 220, "Rapport Politique, Vatomandry, 1914."

26. ARDM, Cabinet Civil, Supplément, Serie D176, Letter from Gallieni to Monsieur L'Administrateurs des Colonies, Chef de la Province de Vatomandry-Mahanoro, April 1904.

27. Ibid.

28. Ibid.

29. See also Feeley-Harnik 1991 (129) for Madagascar, and Rabinow 1989 and Wright 1991 for French colonies more generally.

30. CAOM, Serie IID, 128, "Administrative Report from Chef de District Chesse to Governor General Gallieni, 1899."

31. CAOM, Serie IID, 221, "Rapport Politique, Vatomandry, 1928."

32. CAOM, Serie IID, 129, "Rapport Politique, Mahanoro, 1933."

33. Ibid., "Rapport Politique, Mahanoro, 1934."

34. CAOM, Serie IID, 128, "Rapport d'Ensemble sur la Situation Administrative de la Circonscription pendant l'Année 1899."

35. CAOM, Serie IID, 221, "Rapport Politique, Vatomandry, 1951."

36. CAOM, Serie IID, 129, "Rapport Politique, Mahanoro, 1934."

37. CAOM, Serie IID, 219–20, "Rapport Politique et Administratif, Vatomandry, 1903."

38. The key verb here is *manaiky*, which means simply "to agree": the concept of the *fokon'olona* is based on the notion that any decision that affects all the people inhabiting one locality should be arrived at by consensus, and that the consensus should endure beyond the particular moment that people assemble.

39. CAOM, Serie IID, 219–20, "Rapport Politique et Administratif, Vatomandry, 1903."

40. CAOM, Serie IID, 221, "Rapport Economique, Vatomandry, 1932."

41. Archives de l'Evêché de Tamatave, Madagascar, Lettres d'Uclès, Letter from R. P. Lacomme to R. P. Cazet, 10 December 1882.

42. Ravoahangy was a member of the Vy Vato Sakelika (Iron, Stone, Branches, VVS), a nationalist secret society formed during World War I and disbanded by the French in 1916.

43. More recently, Fremigacci (1999) argues that French military power has been grossly overestimated. Instead, he suggests that most deaths were due to exposure, and that the number of people actually killed in the military campaign was relatively small. Regardless of the number of people who died or how, the rebellion is remembered to this day as a terrible atrocity, which has played an important role in shaping Betsimisaraka political subjectivity.

44. Throwing dogs in water is the way that Betsimisaraka dispose of dogs' corpses (it is taboo to bury them). Thus, attaching a human body to a dog symbolically as well as physically degrades the victim by equating him or her with dogs, the lowest form of animal life.

45. ARDM, Affaire Politique, MDRM "1947," Serie D870, "Notes et Rapports Province Tamatave."

46. ARDM, Affaire Politique, MDRM "1947" Series D872, D873.

47. Ibid.

48. Services Historiques de l'Armée de Terre (hereafter SHAT), Serie 8H176, "Note de Service, Juillet 1947."

49. ARDM, Affaire Politique, MDRM "1947," Series D872, D873, D879.

50. CAOM, Serie IID, 221, "Rapport Politique, Vatomandry, Rapport Annuel, 1949."

51. Ibid.

52. Ibid.

53. Ibid., "Rapport Annuel, 1948."

54. CAOM, Serie IID, 129, "Rapports Politiques, Mahanoro, 1933."

55. CAOM, Serie IID, 221, "Rapport Politique, Vatomandry, Rapport Annuel, 1948."

CHAPTER 3. LOCAL WORLDS

Epigraph: Arundhati Roy, *The God of Small Things* (Random House, 1997), 31. © by Random House.

1. During my fieldwork in 1992–93, Mahanoro was called the *fivondronam-pokon-tany*, an administrative unit corresponding to "district," and Ambodiharina was the next largest administrative unit, *firaisam pokon tany;* smaller satellite villages were called simply *fokon-tany.*

2. If the *tangalamena* does not want to live in the great house because it is inconvenient—for example, if it is too far from his fields—he may ask another member of the family to live there in his stead. However, he would have to be present for all ritual occasions.

3. I should note here that Pierre's father was unusually well-informed about

events in the outside world. Most of the villagers did not know that the United States existed, let alone that there had been a war between the United States and Iraq.

4. For example, Graeber (1996) suggests that on the high plateau the word *miaramila* is often used as a euphemism for slaves.

5. See Graeber 1996 and Evers 1999 for discussions about the contemporary relevance of slavery on the high plateau.

6. When I was in Madagascar in 1992–93, people had begun to live in their fields, as the requirement to inhabit the town was not enforced. I returned in 1997, however, to find that the government had once again started to enforce the rule about inhabiting the town.

7. According to local histories, the Zafindrenian had intermarried with the Zafimalaone, becoming related as children of sisters.

8. Betsimisaraka sacrifice both bulls and cows, though they prefer to sacrifice bulls, and for circumcision celebrations only a bull may be used. Throughout this book I mainly refer to bulls when talking about cattle sacrifice, though I also mention cows. The confusion stems from the fact that in Malagasy the word for cattle—*aomby*—is gender neutral, and people often specify *aomby lahy* if they mean a bull.

9. As it turned out, the *tangalamena* did know quite well who it was he had seen with the cow. He told his wife, who immediately pointed out that they were related through a tie of blood brotherhood, and that if he divulged the name of the person he risked being in violation of the blood bond and thus might bring suffering and death on his family. He therefore decided to keep quiet and endure considerable social opprobrium.

10. Typically, the name of the Christian God is translated as *Andriamanitra*, while *Zanahary* is used to refer to a supreme God or creator, but one less tied to Christianity. Occasionally people used the terms interchangeably, but *Zanahary* was used much more frequently than *Andriamanitra*.

11. Izy tompony tsara sady tompony ratsy.

12. Sasany manasaha, manome heloka mijaka "vanona ianareo" dia ho tonga ny tany dia mamparary, mangataka. Avy vava ny olombelona mijaka—eeee zareo nahavita trano dia tsy natao fomba. Voa maika Zanahary manome aretina, malady mahareñy raha Zanahary.

13. Nirina was a twin, born to an Antembahoaka family who was tabooed from raising a second twin. Though apparently in the past, one twin from a pair would have been killed, today state and missionary organizations have intervened, and one twin is usually placed for adoption. People in the Mahanoro area who are childless know that children can sometimes be adopted from this area, and go there expressly to do so.

14. For example, people always wanted to ask Tsaravintana to be their blood brother because he was such a well-respected healer. One instance in which Tsaravintana agreed to the ceremony was with Lemontana, a man who lived near Andrambomaro and sold *betsa* to the entire region. Lemontana became a blood brother to Tsaravintana, and then asked him to manage his *betsa* depot in Ambodiharina because the previous person who had done so had stolen too much money. I discuss Lemontana's story further in chapter 6. While Ramaresaka and

Tsaravintana both had several blood siblings, some people were too afraid of the curse involved in the ritual and did not participate in the practice. Josef said a taboo *(fady)* prevented him from blood brotherhood, because he found the mutual curse required for the ceremony distasteful. My landlady also refused to do the ceremony though she did not say why; Ramaresaka always claimed it was because the woman was stingy and hated having guests in the house.

15. For discussion of the way in which the ritual formerly associated with the royal bath was displaced onto the celebration of July 14 during French colonization, and then onto the celebration of June 26 after independence, see F. Esoavelomandroso 1989 and Sharp 2001, respectively.

16. Raising pigs always caused tension, because many Betsimisaraka do not eat pigs and, moreover, believe that if a pig touches the prayer post they will have to cleanse the infraction by means of a sacrifice.

17. Betsimisaraka believe that if someone dies during a celebration, one should ignore the death and follow the celebration. To do the contrary is considered bad luck, as if one is asking for more deaths rather than seeking happiness.

18. They had shops in Masomeloka and various other towns, though not in Nosy Varika, where the local shop is run by a *métisse* Chinese merchant. The grandfather had emigrated at the turn of the century from what is now Pakistan to Mauritius, moving to Madagascar around 1920.

CHAPTER 4. BETWEEN MEMORY AND HISTORY

Epigraph: Milan Kundera, *The Book of Laughter and Forgetting*, trans. Michael Henry Heim (Knopf, 1977), 130. © by Alfred A Knopf, A Division of Random House.

1. Within Malagasy studies, conceptions of history have been most thoroughly explored for those people who formed precolonial kingdoms, particularly the Merina (Delivré 1974; Berg 1980; Larson 2000) and the Sakalava (Feeley-Harnik 1978, 1991; Lambek 1998; Sharp 1995). This discussion of Betsimisaraka conceptions of historical practice offers an interpretation of Malagasy conceptions of history among a people who never belonged to a monarchy. What is striking is that—in contrast to Sakalava, where historical consciousness expressed through possession reveals "an intense awareness of effects of outside forces on the local political economy" (Sharp 1995, 76)—Betsimisaraka continue to construct historical narratives in almost entirely local terms.

2. Some pioneering works in this field are Price 1980, Rosaldo 1980, and Rappaport 1990.

3. Another way we might think about this idealized version of memory is to compare it to Bourdieu's notion of habitus (see chapter 1); Nora's conception of memory also has certain similarities to what psychologists call habit memory.

4. In fact, it seems quite likely that what people learn from history books in school does seep into and color their memories, and that people often forget the source of certain memories and come to think of them as their own, a process that psychologists call "source amnesia."

5. In several studies—for example, Feeley-Harnik 1978 and Bloch 1998— *tantara* is explicitly contrasted to *angano* (folktales), which are "lies told by the

ancestors." Among Betsimisaraka I knew, it was remembering—*mahatsiaro*—
that was typically used in order to emphasize connection to the past.

6. Following the rebellion of 1947, several people erected stones *(tsangambato)* for their fathers, who had died in prison as part of the French roundup of
members of the MDRM.

7. The idea that living Betsimisaraka are the standing stones of the ancestors has interesting parallels with beliefs of other Malagasy groups. In her analysis of the Vezo, Rita Astuti (1995) notes that each village is supposed to have a
prayer post, or *hazomanga*, at which ancestral supplications are made. Astuti
then describes how she gradually realized that the term *hazomanga* was used to
refer not to an actual post, but rather to the old man in charge of making ancestral supplications. The original *hazomanga* had been left in the south when
the Vezo had moved northward, and was metaphorically projected onto the body
of the elder.

Astuti further contrasts Vezo practice with a Zafimaniry practice described
by Bloch (1995a). Zafimaniry liken elders to the hard, straight sticks that old
men often carry with them through the forest. Hardness and straightness are qualities associated with ancestorhood, qualities that an old man obviously lacks.
When Zafimaniry talk about an elder, they are in fact likening the elder to his
stick; the elder becomes the stick. The Zafimaniry, through their association of
the man with his stick, attempt to introduce the fixity of death into what is perceived as an ephemeral and vulnerable life. In contrast, Astuti argues that, for
the Vezo, who have left the actual *hazomanga* far to the south, the focus is on
reconciling the ever-moving bodies of people with the fixity of ancestors (embodied in the object of the *hazomanga*). "Whereas the Zafimaniry seem to be
trying to insinuate the ancestors' permanence into life," she writes, "the Vezo
aim to introduce the fluidity of life into the fixity of ancestorhood" (1995, 102).
Like both the Vezo and the Zafimaniry, elements of Betsimisaraka practice reveal a preoccupation with the tension between life and death, movement and stasis. Yet where Zafimaniry seek to achieve permanence through an association
with ancestors, and Vezo force their ancestors to move with them in the person
of the *hazomanga*, the statement that people are the ancestors' standing stones
in fact reveals what people believe the ancestors *wish* their descendants were:
from the point of view of ancestors, descendants should obediently and endlessly
repeat and honor their desires; they should become like living stones, never moving beyond an area already delimited through prior ancestral action.

8. Taboos have been extensively documented in the literature on Madagascar. For other examples, see Rudd 1960, Van Gennep 1904, Lambek 1992, and
Graeber 1995. For an intriguing example of ancestral practice itself becoming
taboo, thereby marking distance from the past, see K. Middleton 1997.

9. In this region there are two different words used to refer to prohibitions:
fady, which usually refers to taboos imposed by healers, and *sandrana*, which
refers to the taboos imposed by one's ancestors. The latter are considered more
powerful and hence more important to obey.

10. Babette became convinced that she had eaten a fish that had accidentally
come into contact with a fish in her husband's net and which was taboo for her.
Eventually Babette's toothaches became so severe—I would find her with a scarf

wrapped around her head and her cheek so swollen that she was unrecognizable—
that I took her to get her tooth pulled. The toothaches cleared up after that, but
since Babette also became infinitely more careful about what she ate, it became
impossible to say which cure was more effective. In fact, most villagers would
not try to privilege one over the other—the two cures would be perceived as
complementary.

11. Fandrambeazana an-aty ala fa mihinana dia an-tanana my.

12. The relationship between houses, the commemoration of ancestors, and
the promotion of one's self appears widespread in Madagascar (for another example from the east coast, see P. Thomas 1998). What appears to distinguish
Betsimisaraka practice is that they expect people to actually live in the houses in
order to keep ancestral memory alive. Simply building large houses—which, judging from the number of huge empty houses in the countryside surrounding Antananarivo, appears to be standard on the high plateau—would never be enough.

13. The people of Madagascar have long been known for their huge expen-
ditures of time and money on building tombs for the dead (see Astuti 1995; Bloch
1971b; Graeber 1995; Feeley-Harnik 1991, 1997; Kottak 1980; and K. Middleton 1988). Two related themes dominate the literature on Malagasy mortuary practice. On the one hand, there is a concern with permanence, and many
groups such as the Merina and the Antandroy build huge cement tombs meant
to last forever. Numerous observers, colonial and modern, have noted how paltry and temporary the houses of the living are in comparison to those constructed
for the dead (K. Middleton 1988). On the other hand, there is a simultaneous
concern with change, particularly the opportunity to renew and renegotiate one's
links to the dead (Bloch 1971a; Graeber 1995; Feeley-Harnik 1991).

14. It is difficult to know whether to phrase this in the singular or the plural.
Typically one person was named as the "founding" ancestor, but individuals might
also associate the tomb with their father or mother, thus downplaying the propensity of tombs to stand for named, eponymous ancestors (see Graeber 1995 for a
discussion of the association between tombs and particular founders in Imerina).

15. Complaints about the cost of building tombs were a regular feature of
conversation in Ambodiharina in 1992–93 and again in 1997 and 1999.

16. Although Betsimisaraka tombs seem to have long been made out of wood
and shaped roughly like canoes, there is substantial variation among those tombs
built by different villages. In the neighboring village, for example, the tombs lay
on top of the ground, rather than half buried, while at still another cemetery a
small house had been built over the tombs to protect them from the rain.

17. The fact that the fragility of the materials results in frequent interaction
between ancestors and descendants raises the question as to how the current fashion for cement tombs—which Betsimisaraka prefer because they last longer and
thus save them the work and money of having to change wooden tombs every
few years—will alter their relationship to their ancestors.

18. People claimed that at various times the tombs looked like *lakana,* the
dugout canoes that Betsimisaraka use as boats, but I never actually saw one and
today this seems to be no longer the case.

19. The burial party rips the reed mat that the body lies on in order to prevent witches from using it to work evil.

20. The lid of the tomb is called the *rangolahy.*

21. Unlike in Imerina, where couples can request to be buried together, even wrapped in the same cloth, Betsimisaraka do not bury people of the opposite sex together. The closest the couple could come to being buried together was for the man to be buried in his ancestral tomb and for the woman to have a separate grave located in the same cemetery.

22. It also seems plausible that, as villagers struggled to eke out a living with decreased buying power—enforced by the austerity measures of the IMF—they expressed an inchoate awareness of wider, global forces in local, moral terms, ones that had emotional power and salience within the village world.

23. While stories of interpersonal tension caused by caring for houses were ubiquitous, stories of tension focusing on tombs, the other important concrete structure of memory, were less frequent, perhaps because, by the time people actually needed to build a whole new tomb or move a tomb, it typically meant that they had already broken most of their ancestral attachments and were well on their way to putting roots down in a new place.

24. The Betsimisaraka use a classificatory system of kinship, and so every male in the ascending generation might be referred to and treated as a "father."

25. Soron-tany arahin'ny ovy.

26. I think that people were particularly uneasy because Koto had left his teenage sons in Ambodiharina on their own. They both subsequently caught tuberculosis, and one of them died.

27. Although I have investigated the topic in the archives in both Madagascar and France, the exact sequence of events that led to the adoption of the Fête des Morts by the Betsimisaraka remains murky. Archival sources in the national archives at Antananarivo suggest that the practice may have started as early as 1895, when the French attempted to start a national day of commemoration for those who had died fighting for Madagascar and for France. However, given the sharp division between the Catholic Church and the colonial state, it is not clear how or why the day chosen was the first of November, associated with the Catholic holy day of Toussaint, rather than the eleventh of November, associated with the French state. The practice is even more puzzling given that those people who did convert during the colonial period primarily chose Anglicanism; it is only recently that Catholicism has gained a great number of converts (see also Cole and Middleton 2001).

28. The use of ancestral names among the Betsimisaraka contrasts with the practice of the Sakalava, among whom royal praise names, given at the time of a monarch's death, index precise historical periods (see Feeley-Harnik 1978 and Lambek 1998).

29. Lambek (1998) similarly reports that historical knowledge among the Sakalava belongs to certain people.

CHAPTER 5. THE POWER IN THE PAST
AND THE COLONIAL IN THE ANCESTRAL

Epigraph: Michael S. Roth, "Remembering Forgetting: *Maladies de la Mémoire* in Nineteenth-Century France," Representations 26 (Spring 1989):

49. © by The Regents of the University of California Press. Reprinted by permission.

1. As throughout this book, the question of which tense to use remains a tricky one. I use the present tense to describe the general processes and the past tense to describe the way colonial structures shaped the projects of an earlier generation of Betsimisaraka, who are now ancestors; but these processes continue to play out today, though in different patterns.

2. The paradigmatic form of spirit possession in Madagascar is *tromba,* as practiced by the Sakalava of the northwest coast, where spirits are named historical personalities that were once associated with the Sakalava monarchy (see Feeley-Harnik 1978, 1989, 1991; Lambek 1998; Sharp 1993, 1995). However, Hilde Nielssen's 1999 study of *tromba* in the region of Marolambo (only 130 kilometers to the west of Ambodiharina) reports that spirits were wood and water sprites or people who came from far away. She argues that *tromba* practiced in Marolambo was decidedly ahistorical and, in fact, provided an alternative source of power to that of ancestors. By contrast, Betsimisaraka in Ambodiharina did conceive of *tromba* in terms of ancestors, though these ancestors did not represent historical personages in any clearly demarcated way. Had the phenomenon been more important to local practice, I suspect that I might have found the same kind of "incidental history" that I found concerning tombs, houses, and taboos, which I discuss in chapter 4. For other discussions of Betsimisaraka practices of spirit possession, see Althabe 1969, Lahady 1979, and Emoff 1996. For a discussion of spirit possession and colonial memory in Niger, see Stoller 1995.

3. In his study of spirit possession and music, Ronald Emoff (1996) describes spirit possession practices in urban Tamatave as deeply implicated in how they remember colonial power in ways that appear somewhat similar to the kinds of remembering and reconfiguring that I describe regarding cattle sacrifice in chapter 6.

4. In many historical sources the name *Betanimena* is used to refer to the various ancestries found to the south of Andevoranto.

5. The concern with responding to speech, which is evident in so many facets of Betsimisaraka practice, is tied to the importance of witnesses, which I discuss in the context of sacrifice in the next chapter.

6. Actually, singling out one ancestor is a risky business, because if one gives to one ancestor one has to give to all. Although one may choose to "honor" one's mother by making and fulfilling a vow to her great house, one must also, of course, call one's father and his ancestors as well.

7. Note that Telolahy was in fact Zafisoa's cousin—the two men were children of two brothers. Telolahy was child to the older brother, while Zafisoa was child to the younger brother. There was considerable tension between the two, which was standard between cousins. This was further exacerbated by the fact that Zafisoa had prestige and monetary income from his job in the army, which further complicated the ambiguous relationship between "older" and "younger" siblings.

8. That Betsimisaraka carry historical knowledge with them as a sign of their political power and legitimacy has parallels with the Sakalava practice in which

warring factions run away with ancestral relics to found new kingdoms farther up the west coast (see Feeley-Harnik 1991).

9. Izaho zanaka niteraka harivahariva. Ka tafahiratra ny maso, dia efa alina ny andro.

10. This proverb is often placed at the beginning of a speech *(kabary)*. The proverb is used as a "remover of blame," the traditional part of a *kabary* in which the speaker begs his audience not to blame him for presuming to stand before others and speak (Keenan 1974).

11. The young woman explicitly compared her quest for history to mine, in turn suggesting that people thought the real reason I was interested in history was so that I might claim land.

12. Omeo vohitra izahay, omeo tanana.

13. In this case the word *mazoto* connotes "keen" with reference to knowing about ancestral traditions, a usage also documented among the Merina by Bloch (1971b).

14. Izaho olona vaohiasa—note the use of the word *work* in the ancestral context: all activities one undertakes for ancestors are referred to as work. See also the discussion in chapter 3.

15. As Ann Stoler (1989) observes about Sumatra, class created important divisions among colonial settlers. Though this observation may easily be derived from any perusal of archival reports for the area, the class divisions were made particularly clear when I met a couple in California who had been French *colons* in the area, and whose family had in fact owned Ampetika (see the epilogue). The wife said that she had never associated with the local Creole families, who were considered a "different sort."

16. *Lavangady* means "long spades" (from *lava*, or long, and *angady*, or spade) and is the term for the male work teams sent to labor for *colons*. Men were forced to weed and clear around coffee trees, while women were made to collect the coffee. Betsimisaraka called the women's brigades *mavoloha*, or "yellow heads," a reference to the way workers' heads became yellow from the pollen on the coffee plants.

17. These observations dovetail with Africanist work done on the construction of tribalism in Africa (see Vail 1989).

CHAPTER 6. MEMORY

Epigraph: Friedrich Nietzsche, *On the Advantage and Disadvantage of History for Life,* trans. Peter Preuss (Hackett Publishing, 1980), 8. © by Hackett Publishing Co. Reproduced by permission of Hackett Publishing Co. All rights reserved.

1. A *jiro* may not be dug up and removed, nor may a house be removed—once a house is built on ancestral land it must stay there. To remove it is a grave offense called *mamadika tany mena*—"turning over red earth"—which results in a fine that must be paid publicly in order to cleanse the wrong.

2. British Library, Manuscripts Division, N. Mayeur, "Histoire de Ratsim-ila-hoe, Roi des Bé-tsi-miçaracs," Additional Manuscript 18129, Folios 82–144.

3. For a discussion of the intersection between ancestors and colonial discourse, see Cole and Middleton 2001.

4. In her analysis of Bastille Day during the French colonization of Madagascar, Faranirina Esoavelomandroso (1989) demonstrates the way in which French and Merina alike appropriated the rites to their own ends.

5. As a classic topic in the anthropology of religion, blood sacrifice has been theorized from diverse perspectives. Early theorists saw sacrifice as a gift to the gods (Tylor [1889] 1958), a communion with gods created through a shared meal (Robertson Smith 1889), and a form of mediation that enabled contact between the sacred and the profane (Hubert and Mauss [1899] 1964). In the context of early structural-functional anthropology, the sacrificial schema proposed by Hubert and Mauss—which focuses on how sacrifice, by putting people in contact with the divine, enables the transformation of social status—provides the implicit model on which most studies of sacrifice have been based. Scholars have focused on how sacrifice mediates the individual's relation to God and absolves humans of their sins (Evans-Pritchard 1956), and how sacrifice works as a kind of symbolic action that shapes people's moral and mental dispositions (Lienhardt 1961). They have also examined how sacrifice enables the negotiation of lineage authority (J. Middleton 1960), and how, by killing animals, people subjugate the wildness of life to the social order (Bloch 1985). For the reader familiar with debates on sacrifice, all of these classic theories are apparent in the pages to come. For example, Betsimisaraka would agree with E. Evans-Pritchard's 1956 contention that "cattle substitute for the lives of men." And like William Robertson Smith (1889), they see sacrifice as a communal meal, an occasion when the dead and the living come together to feast. Finally, as John Middleton (1960) might predict, lineage politics are also negotiated at these events.

6. Betsileo country is located just to the west of Betsimisaraka country, in the southern portion of the high plateau.

7. Many people claimed that to *mandahy lahy,* or "dance men," was what made a *sambatra* a *sambatra,* as opposed to another kind of sacrificial celebration. The songs sung during the dancing were either about water and blessing or about how boys who were "danced" didn't bleed from the circumcision operation. One popular song went as follows: "Dance that child, dance, children who are danced don't bleed" (Rango zaza rango, zaza rangoina tsy mandeha ra).

8. The money is called either *fafy rano* or *soron'afo* or *elan-kelan-tanana*—"blessing."

9. The tree is called either a *ramiavona,* which means "haughty tree," or a *hazoambo,* "high tree"; either way the association is with cleanliness and spiritual efficacy.

10. Na lahy na vavy, na madinika na maventy, Iaba n'i Baomena mangataka tsodrano amaraina, ario ny asa sy ny tondra-tena, nahavelona ny antso antso dia tongava.

11. Giselle's other famous antic took place when President Ratsiraka flew in for a spot of campaigning, and she got up on the dais while he was speaking and tried to dance with him.

12. Godfrey Lienhardt (1961) reports a similar belief among the Dinka.

13. It is inevitably men who gather around the *tangalamena* to call the ancestors' names, although villagers claimed that it was perfectly acceptable for women to "present names" *(manatoro anarana)* — which means that they tell the names to their *tangalamena*, who then actually calls them out.

14. Given the logic behind taboos described in chapter 3, it seems likely that these taboos were originally prescribed to accompany medicine used to protect the children about to be circumcised. Today, however, the children have been circumcised previously and the taboos have simply become part of what makes the ceremony an efficacious way to obtain blessing.

15. I was told that previously all of the rice that is specially pounded for the *sambatra* would be used to sprinkle the populace, a sign of abundance and blessing.

16. There are two other ways people may try to manipulate their relationships with ancestors, which did not take place at Zakatiana's sacrifice but which are quite common: people may choose to abandon their mother's taboos, and they may attempt to remove the curse of a parent who has died. The first case usually occurs when the children have gone to live with their father, and it requires that the father's kin come and beg the mother's kin to release the children from their obligations. However, people can request this absolution only if they have no intention of either working, living, or being buried in their mother's ancestral land. Despite a patrilineal bias and the official line that children are buried with their father, a good many people do end up living and dying with their mother's kin. Shared prohibitions are one definition of a tomb group, and one must respect the taboos in order to make it into the tomb; removing maternal taboos is a calculated risk, a decision to affiliate with one group rather than another.

The other case occurs when people attempt to "return the words of an angry parent" who subsequently died. For example, at one sacrifice the speech maker recounted the following story: "Telolahy left his ancestral homeland. He never saw or knew anything that happened in his ancestral land. His father died and he never came. But his father, before he died, said, 'That child really went out to seek his fortune! We never caught a glimpse of him.' Telolahy has arrived home. And so now we cleanse that blame!" Clearly, this case involved a parent's anger and disappointment over his child's departure. Although the son could not be sure that his father would absolve him and remove the curse, he could nevertheless try to transform his relationship to his father's ghost.

17. See also Bloch 1995b, Feeley-Harnik 1980, Huntington 1988, and P. Thomas 1998.

18. I thank Karen Middleton and Michael Lambek for discussions on this topic.

19. The word literally means "to spray, to scatter," as done with seeds or, in the case of a blessing, water.

20. Unfortunately, at the time I recorded these stories people did not mention which sect of Christianity people had converted to (whether Catholic or Anglican, the two most active missions in the area).

21. My assumption is that, because he couldn't walk, they helped him to relieve himself. Cleansing is usually required after coming into contact with blood or excrement (see chapter 7).

22. Zavatra tsara mila namana, fa ny zavatra ratsy tsy mila olona mbara tsisy mahita izay sitra-po hataonao. Amin'ny zavatra tsara koza dia tsy vita ianao ireka tsy maintsy misy namana amarina zavatra karan'izany—zavatra tsara mila namana.

23. Zanahary ambony tany ny olombelona, ka raha tsy hiatrika ny fokon'olona dia tsy afaka ny aretina. Tsisy raha vita. Ianao ireka mamono aomby? Inona raha mahamarina izany? Ny fokon'olona mahamarina an-azy.

24. This desire to normalize the events revealed in sacrifice explains why one tends to find more proverbs in the response to the speech than in the speech itself, which is often presented in straightforward narrative form.

25. In some cases, the *fokon'olona* may be pitted against the person throwing the sacrifice. Thus, in the case of a rich man who is arrogant and makes himself hated by the other villagers, the *fokon'olona* may be only too happy to have the ancestors force him to sacrifice a bull. In this case, the community of the dead combines with the *fokon'olona* against a particular individual who has probably transgressed social norms of reciprocity.

26. *Vintana* is particularly important for understanding the politics of sacrifice, because it mediates contact between the living and the dead. When people see a diviner for almost any kind of illness, the likelihood of cure depends on whether the *vintana* of the diviner is stronger than that of the patient. It is considered crucial that a diviner have a strong *vintana*, for a *vintana* weaker than that of the patient may lead to misdiagnosis. One reason that people frequently go to several different diviners is to ensure that they find one with a stronger *vintana*, someone who can really cure them. Cure results when the diviner is able to "crush" the patient's destiny. In the context of sacrifice, each person is positioned relative to others via their *vintana*. Moreover, the people's *vintana* are always perceived as fighting it out with one another, allowing some people to triumph, while others fall sick and die, some to carry out a sacrifice successfully, while the sacrifices of others end in disaster.

27. See Bloch 1986 (55 ff) for a discussion of "stealing" ritually required plants in Merina circumcision celebrations.

28. If a split in tombs were to occur, which was quite likely, then they would literally divide up the bones so that each group would get some.

29. Iaba n'i Namo and Iaba n'i Jerome's conflict is also interesting because it demonstrates the way in which the conflict between brothers is expressed through their children: the two brothers never fight, even though they are battling for ancestral power. Rather, all tensions are mediated through the children. For an example of how, among the Zafimaniry, tensions and desires that elders can not express may be expressed by their children, see Bloch 1999.

30. Zareo ahazo vola an-aliny izaho koza ahazo an-etsiny. Anareo mitatao, izahay manao anjañiro.

31. Images of carrying are used in a variety of different contexts to refer to caring and responsibility, and different ways of carrying an object have different connotations. The image of carrying something on a stick over one's shoulder *(mitarozo)*, which is typically how men carry objects, could also signify that either one's mother or father has already died. Conversely, to refer to someone as "carrying over one's shoulders a stick with a bundle tied to each end" *(lan-*

320					Notes to Pages 217–224

jañivo) means that one is "of a living mother and father" *(velon-dray velon-dreny)*, an important symbol of intergenerational continuity that recurs throughout Malagasy ritual practice (Bloch 1986). Finally, the image of carrying something on one's head frequently refers to carrying one's ancestors, but it also refers to the way one might carry an offering or gift. The progression of the generations is said to follow the body from head to toe. The ancestors sit on one's head, while one's great-great-great-grandchildren are referred to as "offspring of the knees," and one's great-great-great-great-grandchildren as "offspring of the soles of the feet."

32. See Comaroff and Comaroff 1987 and Price 1998.

33. Bakhtin's conception of language is a useful tool for conceptualizing ancestral practice in Madagascar more generally. See Cole and Middleton 2001.

CHAPTER 7. REVERSING FIGURE AND GROUND

Epigraphs: Cathy Caruth, ed., *Trauma: Explorations in Memory* (Johns Hopkins University Press, 1995), 5. © by Johns Hopkins University Press. Reproduced by permission.

Shahid Amin, *A Subaltern Studies Reader, 1986–1995,* ed. Ranajit Guha (University of Minnesota Press, 1997), 187.© by The Regents of the University of Minnesota Press. Reproduced by permission.

1. A number of different scholars have followed a Halbwachsian route by focusing on the political needs that mediate and structure how a nation remembers a war. Jeffrey Herf (1997, 1), for example, has examined how the "mixture of belief, interest, ideology and drive for power," which shaped very different forms of public memory of the Jewish Holocaust, was constructed in East and West Germany. Similarly, Peter Novick (1999) has investigated why the memory of the Jewish Holocaust has become such a powerful one in contemporary American life, charting the ways that it moved from the margins to the center of American Jewish discourse with the changing circumstances of American Jews. Marita Sturken (1997) has shown the complex cultural forms that help structure how Americans remember Vietnam.

2. The Betsimisaraka case in fact supports Allan Young's 1995 critique of post-traumatic stress disorder as the "harmony of illusions."

3. In my subsequent work in Tamatave I came across one woman who claimed that her heart condition started the day she learned her husband had been arrested for allegedly participating in the MDRM. Significantly, however, this woman was among the lucky few who received a pension from Ratsiraka, and although I do not want to dismiss her suffering, I also think it important to place her narrative in terms of a discourse of rights to state compensation.

4. Françoise Raison-Jourde (1989) reports that, when she taught at the University of Antananarivo in the 1960s, she would ask the students what they wanted to know about Malagasy history. They would inevitably reply, "Why don't our parents ever talk about 1947?"

5. I am borrowing the terms "directed forgetting" and "directed ignoring" from the psychological literature, which has demonstrated that people can eas-

ily block out certain factors not considered essential information, and that they can train their minds away from certain topics. See Zacks and Hasher 1994; and Bjork, Bjork, and Anderson 1998.

6. The official history that I give here is based on the work of Jacques Tronchon, whose book *L'Insurrection Malgache de 1947* (1986) was researched in the early 1970s, before the archives involving the rebellion were open to the public. My subsequent archival research for the area of Mahanoro suggests that Tronchon's vision of what happened is correct overall, though subsequent regional studies may add nuance to the larger picture.

7. For a discussion of the early nationalist movement in Madagascar, which certainly predates the formation of the MDRM, see Boiteau 1958, Randrianja 1989, and F. Esoavelomandroso 1981.

8. During a notable part of one conference organized to commemorate the rebellion, members of the MDRM apologized to the audience for what had happened.

9. The sketch of the events in Mahanoro District is based on my construction of French archival documents housed the Malagasy National Archives (ARDM), the French colonial archives, and the French military archives (SHAT).

10. CAOM, Serie IID, 221, "Rapport Politique, Vatomandry, 1948."

11. ARDM, Affaire Politique, MDRM "1947," Serie D870, "Rapport Annuel."

12. Ibid.

13. ARDM, Affaire Politique, MDRM "1947," Serie D870, extracts from a letter from Monsieur l'Administrateur Pont au Sous Gouverneur Simon, February 1947.

14. In fact, many acts of brigandage and small-scale rioting occurred throughout 1946, suggesting that it is perhaps more useful to think of the rebellion of 1947 as forming part of a continuum of resistance to colonial rule, rather than as an isolated and unique event.

15. CAOM, Serie IID, 129, "Rapport Politique Année, 1948."

16. Ibid.

17. At least this is what people in Ambodiharina claimed—I have heard other people claim other locales as Ratsiraka's *tanin-drazana*.

18. I should specify that to televise something nationally in Madagascar in fact means to televise it to the limited number of places that have televisions and satellite dishes, which means the capital city of Antananarivo as well as provincial capitals like Tamatave and Diégo-Suarez. Although the image of the *tangalamena* was most likely intended to convince Betsimisaraka to remain loyal to Ratsiraka, the great majority of people that were meant to receive the message were unlikely to see the broadcast.

19. This opposition of Betsimisaraka versus Merina in turn glosses over important regional, cultural, historic, and class divisions among the peoples of the central east coast.

20. Zafy Albert won only 45 percent of the votes in a November election, and Ratsiraka 29 percent, making it necessary to hold another election in February 1993.

21. Jean Fremigacci (1976) notes that the French *colons* took all the land that was good for irrigated rice farming, leaving dry rice cultivation—by means of

slash-and-burn agriculture *(tavy)*—as the only option for most villagers if they were to avoid starvation. The cultivation of large amounts of land using slash-and-burn techniques, and the subsequent problem of deforestation, is a historical result of French policy and had little to do with age-old native custom.

22. The fact that fear appeared to heighten people's memories of the rebellion dovetails with a considerable body of research on memory that demonstrates the way moods and emotions may shape how and what we remember. See Schacter 1996, Christianson and Safer 1996, and Bower 1981.

23. For examples, see Althabe 1969, Bloch 1971b, Blot 1964, Gintzburger 1983, Jarosz 1994, and Molet 1979.

24. The reader may want to know what actually happened to Mborika. By the time I left the village there was lots of talk, but no action: Mborika continued to live in the village and to farm, but people wanted relatively little to do with him.

25. The syllable *fo* is elaborated in cultural practice in other parts of Madagascar as well. For example, see K. Middleton 1995 and P. Thomas 1997.

26. For discussions of intergenerational politics and new forms of power, see Bayart 1981 and Geschiere 1988.

27. Their expression of desire for change coming from outside is similar to that documented by James Ferguson (1992) for Zambia, except that the Forces Vives supporters did not express out and out colonial nostalgia. And of course, this group did not have direct experience of the colonial state.

28. The nurse-midwife was a woman in her early forties, born and raised in a neighboring village but with strong roots in Ambodiharina. She had gone to school in Tamatave, and thus she had extended experience outside the village.

29. The practice seems to have occurred in parts of southeast Asia as well. In Vietnam, for example, after the arrival of the French, entire villages converted to Catholicism.

30. An enormous literature has grown up around the topic of peasants' so-called traditional bias and their alleged resistance to change, particularly in the realm of economics. For example, in Africa, writings on witchcraft have focused on how witchcraft beliefs act to limit accumulation (Ardener 1970). Cyprian Fisiy and Peter Geschiere (1991) argue the inverse. In Asia, debates surrounding the moral economy of the peasant have focused on the subsistence ethic in relation to peasant rebellions (Scott 1976), while in reference to Latin America the topic has been addressed in George Foster's theory of limited good (1965). I want to emphasize that I am focusing on political dissension and not the question of economic difference.

31. The use of the word *politique* to denote lying and trickery is widespread throughout Francophone Africa.

32. The rebel army is referred to locally as the Marosalohy, or the Many Spears. I have chosen to refer to them simply as the rebel army to make the text more accessible.

33. *Telonono* literally means "three breasts." She was allegedly a woman who had powerful medicines that would protect soldiers in fighting. Though she is cited as a real person in the archives (Jean Fremigacci, personal communication),

people I knew in Ambodiharina thought the name referred to a kind of medicine, not an actual human being.

34. The French used troops from their other colonies, mainly Morocco and Senegal, in order to repress the rebellion, hence the frequent references to these groups in survivors' narratives.

35. Note that linguistically in Malagasy the town is always referred to as being "up." Hence one says, "Let's go up from the fields." Further, ascendance is associated with light and superiority, thus the town is high and light in contrast to the dark "forest" *(ala)* surrounding it, even though that forest may be merely cassava fields and rice paddies and, only much farther out, actual forest.

36. Tronchon (1986), for example, argues in favor of the PANAMA-Jina thesis, an argument that I found in French archival documents regarding the rebellion as well. See SHAT, Serie 8H114.

37. Zafimaniry memory narratives, for example, primarily concern the brutality of the French army (Bloch 1998).

38. SHAT, Serie 8H177, Dossier 4, "Activité des Bandes Rebelles."

39. The villagers' emphasis on the superior weaponry of the French is particularly significant given Fremigacci's recent revisionist account of the rebellion (1999), which stresses that the French were hampered by outdated weapons that had minimal capacity to kill. From the villagers' perspective, we can see that no matter how inefficient the gun or old the bomber plane, it is still accurately perceived as more efficient at killing people than handcrafted spears or garden stakes sharpened to serve as spears.

40. SHAT, Serie 8H177, "Rapport d'Ensemble sur les Evénements de Madagascar," Piece No. 16, 27 February 1947: "In the region of Nosy Varika and Mahanoro a group of ex-military repatriated from France exists which has taken the form of the old VVS. The members of this group are each supposed to kill two Europeans when the revolt breaks out."

41. The fact that the abusive behavior of the rebels was modeled on their experience of the French army implies that their behavior was perhaps learned during their time in France, a fact that speaks ill of how Malagasy soldiers were treated in the French army (see Valensky 1995).

42. That the rebels allegedly listened to the *chef de canton's* mistress when they were in the midst of trying to destroy the French state and set up an alternative chain of command is intriguing, not least because it suggests that they remained keenly aware of the fact that their rule had not yet been legitimated.

43. While I was writing this, the atrocities in Kosovo were a constant topic of discussion on public radio. The stories broadcast from Kosovo, which all focused on the loyalty or betrayal of friends, family, and neighbors, were strikingly similar to people's narratives of 1947.

44. Curiously, this was not true of women's narratives, which is perhaps linked to gendered division of historical agency.

45. SHAT, Serie 8H199.

46. CAOM, Serie IID, 129, "Rapport Politique, 1949."

47. Ibid.

48. Ibid.

49. Ibid.

50. Ibid. Though the *côtier* (coastal) versus Merina tension is represented as a colonial product, I suspect it waxed and waned throughout the colonial period, and that the experience of 1947 served as a pretext to reawaken these tensions. As one colonial administrator in Mahanoro observed, "The *côtier's* old hatred has rekindled from its ashes and burns with a violence which we must try and control, especially since it can be used to produce regionalism, which appears to be the direction of our current policy."

51. ARDM, Affaire Politique, MDRM "1947," Series D872, D873.

52. CAOM, Serie IID, 221, "Rapports Politique, Vatomandry, Rapport Annuel, 1948."

CHAPTER 8. CONSTRUCTING
A BETSIMISARAKA MEMORYSCAPE

Epigraph: Soren Kierkegaard, *The Sickness unto Death,* trans. Howard V. Hong (Princeton University Press, 1941), 58. © by Princeton University Press. Reproduced by permission of Princeton University Press.

1. See Foucault 1982.

2. For example, see Casey 1987 and Halbwachs [1950] 1980.

3. Fabian's discussion of the paintings of Tshibumba Kanda Matulu provides an African example of an art of memory that shares the focus on visual imagery first described by Yates (1966).

4. I would like to thank Pier Larson for an e-mail discussion on this topic (October 7, 1999).

5. See Emerson 1983 (9).

6. There is a curious convergence between Taussig's concept of "implicit social knowledge" and what psychologists call implicit memory, which Schacter describes as a "subterranean world of non-conscious memory and perception normally concealed from the conscious mind" (1996, 165).

7. There are several variations of this practice; for example, a family might change only the women's tomb one year and the men's the next, depending on what was needed. People who can afford it have begun to move their ancestors to cement tombs. Though this is a practice that probably originated with the Merina, it is remarkable that, although Merina have lived in the area since the nineteenth century, people have only now begun to take up the custom in great numbers. While one might expect this move to cement tombs to give rise to the Merina practice of *famadihana,* in which people remove the bodies and rewrap them in silk shrouds, most people I knew said they did the practice so as not to have the trouble of changing the tomb so frequently. They claimed that moving their ancestors to cement tombs would decrease their interactions with the dead because of the expense.

8. More than once people asked me to take photos of them with a particular relative's bones.

9. People avoid changing the tomb if there is a body that is still "wet," but bodies that have already dried are often still recognizable to kin.

10. People then try to keep parts of the mat that the bones have lain on—

which they take home to sleep on—since these are believed to bestow blessing and fertility on the possessor.

11. In some cases a sacrifice is held right away to announce to the ancestors that they have a new house. At other times, the sacrifice is postponed until people can come up with the money to pay for the cow. When the sacrifice is held, it marks the only joyful occasion at which no extra negotiation (cleansing, removing curses, etc.) is attempted: the focus is on remembering ancestors and that alone.

12. The archetype of the male and female master-ancestors underlies many of the cultural practices I have described, including the aphorism "We are the ancestors' standing stones," as well as the continual pull that people both submit to and struggle against as they inhabit their ancestral sites of memory. Yet there is a fundamental tension in the way in which this archetype—which is equally male and female—plays out in everyday life. As I demonstrated in chapters 4 and 5, it is primarily their fathers' sites that both daughters and sons work to maintain. At the same time, it is sons who are most likely to break away from ancestral control. In daily life, as I have argued, women are more closely linked with the ideal of memory, which is more closely associated with reproduction, while men are symbolically tied to the dangers and necessity of history, which in its idealized form stands for change. The symbol of the male and female master-ancestors appears to suggest that both are necessary to survive. Though it oversimplifies the complexities of what occurs either in bone turning or in sacrifice, we might see the two forms of ritual as standing in dialectical relationship to each other. Bone turning holds out an iconic ideal image of the social order, while sacrifice gives people a way to achieve it despite the fact that history propels them forward in space and time.

13. For a similar use of the landscape metaphor in order to capture the idea of multipositionality, see Appadurai 1991.

14. In referring to "the generation of 1947," I follow Katherine Newman (1996), who sees generational identity as forming when people who are coming of age have lived through a particularly dramatic experience that then gives a certain shape to what she calls "moral architecture."

15. The fairly mild view that some Betsimisaraka in the Mahanoro region had of Merina contrasts quite sharply with what Ronald Emoff (1996) reports for the Tamatave region, where anti-Merina sentiment was quite strong. In my subsequent research at the University of Tamatave, I also found that an epithet that northern Betsimisaraka students frequently hurl at southern Betsimisaraka is that they are "friends of the Merina."

16. Secondary memories can also become powerful through their integration into group narratives—as in Vamik Volkan's concept of a "chosen trauma," where a particular event becomes definitive of group identity and is transmitted from one generation to the next (1991).

17. Fianarantsoa is a town located on the southern end of the high plateau and is inhabited by Betsileo.

18. Monsieur George's rejection by his Merina grandfather and subsequent identification with his maternal, Betsimisaraka, kin caused him great bitterness and plagued him throughout his life. He used to tell me teasingly that when he

died he would ask *le bon dieu* just why he had inflicted a mixed identity on him—straight hair (the alleged mark of a Merina) and the dark skin of a Betsimisaraka. Monsieur George died in June of 1994, and I like to think that his questions were answered.

19. Incomplete transmission—which is one kind of forgetting—is of course fundamental to all historical development, but in this case I think it has also been exacerbated as a result of the contradictory ways in which older villagers experienced the rebellion. In other areas of Madagascar, where the rebellion played out in a different manner, I would expect the pattern of remembering to look different.

20. In fact, I don't have a single example of a young person evoking the rebellion as a justification for their political beliefs.

21. See Prakash 1995 and Chakrabarty 1992. For an example taken from rural Madagascar that shows that some rural areas of the country do suffer from a sense of profound marginality, see P. Thomas n.d. For a critique of recent postcolonial writing, see Ong 1999.

22. For example, one administrator remarked in 1949 that the Betsimisaraka were trying to mend their relationship with the government and forget their painful past by voting for the person they knew the French wanted, so that they would be left in peace. See CAOM, Serie IID, 129, "Rapport Annuel, Mahanoro, 1951."

23. Based on my experience of the region around Mahanoro, this is an extraordinary number of sacrifices. I attended over 25 sacrifices while I was there, but even assuming that I never heard about a portion of the sacrifices that took place, there could not have been more than 75, if that.

24. CAOM, Serie IID, 129, "Rapport Politique, Mahanoro, 1949."

25. See Dirks 1992a and 1992b, Feeley-Harnik 1984, Shaw 1997, and Wilmsen 1989.

26. When we take into account the importance of generation in positioning people in the memoryscape, a variable that Halbwachs ([1950] 1980) emphasizes as well, it becomes clear that the particular formation of memory visible in daily life circa the 1990s is similar to what Raymond Williams calls a "structure of feeling." He defines this as "characteristic elements of impulse, restraint and tone; specifically affective elements of consciousness and relationships: not feeling against thought, but thought as felt and feeling as thought: practical consciousness of a present kind, in a living and interrelating community" (1977, 132). For Williams, "structures of feeling" are a mode of experience that have not quite settled into a formal ideology, and they are frequently tied to particular generations. He emphasizes that structures of feeling are often visible after the fact, when they have been formalized and a new structure of feeling is about to emerge. I argue that the processes of remembering and forgetting that I have delineated here play a role in this process.

EPILOGUE. LOOKING BACK

1. For a discussion of colonial nostalgia in Zambia, see Ferguson (1992).

Glossary

akanjobe Traditional shirt worn by men and made from raffia fiber.

ala Forest.

ambanivolo Literally, "under the bamboo": the countryside.

An'ala mizina Literally, "the dark forest": the name of the forest where several ancestries' tombs are located.

andevo Slave.

andriana Person of high status; nobility.

andry iankinana Literally, a "house post to lean on": a powerful person in social life.

angady Spade.

angano Folktales.

anjara Destiny; share (can be used to mean both "one's lot in life" and "a share of meat").

antòka Stake used to tether a grazing bull.

Aomby misolo ny aina olombelona. "Cattle substitute for the lives of men."

aomby Cattle (gender neutral).

aomby lahy Bull.

asa Private, domestic work related to making a living; the ritual activity that enables communication with ancestors.

asoasony Part of a circumcision ceremony, in which participants present the fattiest cooked meat to Zanahary and the ancestors.

avy niakatra tamin'ny filofana Literally, "since we came up from the flight": the time from the end of the 1947 rebellion to the present.

betsa Locally made sugarcane beer.

biby Literally, "animal" or "creature"; a spirit who possesses people.

bokin-drazana Ancestral book.

colon Settler.

côtiers Coastal groups.
delegué Tax collector.
deradera Preening or bragging.
dokitra Large domestic bird.
entim-po To hold a grudge.
fady Taboo imposed by ancestors or a healer.
fafy Ritual of reparation in which either rum or a cattle sacrifice is used to restore proper social relations.
fafy kafe Coffee-cleansing ritual.
fafy rano Blessing; permission.
fahaleovan-tena Independence.
fahavalo Bandit.
fahavanonana Ritual of cattle sacrifice celebrating the birth of many children to
  an individual or couple.
fahavazaha Colonial period.
famokarana From the words meaning "to bring up": refers to the ritual in which
  ancestors' bones are moved from an old tomb to a new one.
fanafody Medicine.
fandambanana Traditional eating mat.
fanjakana The government.
fanompoana Corvée.
farabolana Last words uttered before death, which bind one's descendants.
fatidrà Blood siblingship.
fialonana Jealousy.
filoha be Big chief.
filohany Village head.
finaritra Literally, "pleasing"; in the past this word was part of the Betsimisaraka
  greeting.
firaisam pokon tany Administrative unit.
fivondronam-pokon-tany Administrative unit corresponding to "district" under
  the French.
fo Heart.
fody Species of weaver finch.
fokon'olona Village council—an institution used for popular participation that
  has been appropriated by successive state regimes since the nineteenth century.
fokon-tany Smallest administrative unit.
gasy Adjectival form of *Malagasy;* usually used by rural Betsimisaraka to refer
  to themselves.
grigri Pejorative French term referring to African practices of divination.
hasina Power; a plant used for ritual purposes and for building fences around
  courtyards.
Havana ve? Literally, "Are you kin?" Greeting used by the rebel army when they
  entered villages along the central east coast during 1947.
hazoambo or *ramiavona* Literally, "high tree" or "haughty tree": a special kind
  of tree that helps add generative power to the circumcision celebration.
hazomanga Term used in southern and western Madagascar for the prayer post
  at which invocations are made to the ancestors.

hetra Tax defined in relation to surface area.

Ho ariana raha tsy manome aomby. "We will expel you from the community if you do not sacrifice a cow."

hova Merina commoners; also used by colonial sources to refer to all Merina.

ilo Coconut oil.

indigénat Collection of French colonial laws regulating indigenous Malagasy.

isampangady Tax levied on "each spade," meaning each worker.

jaka pandroana Honor bestowed during rituals held at Christmas and again on June 26, Malagasy Independence Day.

jiny Word occasionally used in place of *rangitra*.

jiro Prayer post shaped like the horns of a bull and erected specifically during a circumcision ceremony; all subsequent cattle sacrifices take place here.

kabala Traditional raffia shroud.

kabary Large political meeting; official speech made to convey the will of the government; formal oratory made at ancestral events.

kadaka Dish made of cooked cassava.

karazana Kinds or ancestries.

la politique des races Modified form of indirect rule that divided the peoples of Madagascar into different groups according to their customs.

lañañana Long bamboo tubes for carrying water.

lakana Dugout canoe.

lambaoany Mass-produced wrap worn mainly by women, but also worn by men in spirit possession ceremonies.

lango Savory dish prepared by grilling still-green rice.

lanjañivo Literally, "carrying over one's shoulders a stick with a bundle tied to each end": used metaphorically to signify that one's mother and father are still living.

lava Long.

lava tsynatohy Accordion ball held following a cattle sacrifice.

lavangady Literally, "long spades": male work teams sent to labor for *colons*.

laza Fame.

lehiben'ny Marosalohy Rebel chief.

lofo Funerary sacrifice.

loi-cadre Law passed by the French government in 1956 that gave greater administrative freedom to the colonies.

mañano l'amora Literally, "to love"; to court.

mañano patrie Literally, "doing *la patrie*": the circulation of bands of rebels in a particular area.

mafana fo Enthusiastic.

maha toetra olona maventy The character of a grown person.

mahatsiaro Literally, "make not set apart": to remember.

mahavazaha anazy That which makes one a European.

maitresse de couture Seamstress.

mamadika tany mena Literally, "turning over red earth": refers to the fact that one is forbidden from removing a house once it has been built in a specific place.

mamadika Literally, "to turn"; also used to mean "to betray."

mamafy rano To spray water; synonymous with giving blessing.

mamafy Literally, to "spray"; used frequently in the sense of cleansing through payment of a ritual fine, especially cattle sacrifice.

mamaky l'apel Roll call performed by rebel soldiers during the 1947 rebellion.

manaiky To agree.

manatoro anarana Literally, "to present names": the act of revealing ancestral names that can be used in ritual.

mandahy lahy Literally, "to dance men": the celebration of male offspring in a circumcision ceremony.

manefa voady To "pay" a vow.

mangala To take, grab, or steal.

mangalatra anjara To steal another's fate.

mangataka tantara To beg for history.

manofa Belief that cultivating certain kinds of plants, like ginger or coffee, may kill one.

manome bon To give credit.

manome voninahitra To give honor.

marary ho faty To fear death.

marécageux Creole settlers who came to Madagascar prior to colonization and claimed small pieces of property.

masiaka Cruel.

masina Powerful; efficacious.

maty tampoka Sudden death.

mavoloha Literally, "yellow heads": female work brigades forced to harvest coffee on the colonial concessions; workers' heads became yellow from the pollen on the coffee plants.

mazava To be clear and true.

mazoto Keen, eager.

métisse Of mixed blood.

miadilahy To compete.

miaramila Army, soldiers.

mifanta To swear.

mifindra Literally, "to move"; the "movement" of a spirit to another person.

mikasika fo To be emotionally moved.

mikoka Piercing yell that a *tangalamena* uses when he wants the ancestors' attention.

mirombo Spirit possession party.

mitarozo Literally, "to carry something on a stick over one's shoulder": used metaphorically to refer to someone who has only one parent still living.

mody mandry To die.

mpaka-aty Liver thief.

mpaka-fo Heart thief.

mpaka-ra Blood thief.

mpanjaka Ruler, monarch, or king.

mpifady Tabooed men and women who guard the children being celebrated at a circumcision ceremony.

mumiani East African term meaning "vampire."

nahafoy tena To give of oneself; the state of having given of oneself.

nahazo kibo To become pregnant.

namana Friend; spouse.

natao ny tribunal To hold a court trial.

nitsangana Literally, "made standing": adopted.

Ny anarana tsy mba maty. Literally, "Names never die"—the idea that ancestral names live on in ritual

ody tsiny Medicine against blame.

Olombelona tsy miofo. Literally, "Living people don't shed"—a proverb meaning people only live once.

olon-kafa Non-kin.

petits colons Small settlers.

potagères Vegetable gardens.

raha indô Literally, "things you have to carry"—used metaphorically to refer to the way men take care of women's relationships to their ancestors.

raha misy asa atao Literally, "if there is work to do": ritual work associated with ancestors.

raha sarotra Literally, "difficult things": death.

raharaha Spirit who possesses people.

raiamandreny Mothers and fathers; elders.

rangitra Spirit that accompanies each living being, tree, or rock and makes them powerful.

rangolahy Tomb lid.

razana Corpse; ancestor.

renin-jaza Mothers of the children celebrated at a circumcision sacrifice.

ro Anything eaten as an accompaniment to rice.

sambatra Literally "joyous"; circumcision celebration.

sandrana Taboos imposed by one's ancestors.

sasa hoditra Literally, "skin cleansing": penance or type of punishment.

sembo Traditional wrap worn by women.

service des domaines Bureaucratic office in charge of titling land.

sikidy Divination.

sitra-po Literally, "heart's will": volition.

sokoza Tiny bird.

soroka Traditional palm-leaf spoon.

soron'afo or *elan-kelan-tanana* Money contributed by witnesses to a sacrifice.

tache d'huile Literally, "oil spot": policy used by General Joseph Gallieni in his conquest of Madagascar.

tamin'ny tonta Period during the eighteenth and nineteenth centuries when the slave trade produced continuous raids and fighting between ancestries.

tanàna Town, as opposed to the bush.

tangalamena fanjakana Individual who is chosen to represent the community's interests to the state.

tangalamena Person in charge of invoking the ancestors; the stick he uses to strike a bull that is about to be sacrificed.

tanin-drazana Ancestral homeland.

tantara Story; historical narrative.

tany masiaka Literally, "cruel land": used metaphorically to refer to land with a spirit who prevents people from being able to live there.

tany ravo White clay used in rituals of ancestral blessing.

tatovina To carry the ancestors on one's head.

tavy Dry rice land cleared by slash-and-burn methods.

taxi-brousse Bush taxi.

tena izy Literally, "really it": the most significant part of a ritual.

toaka Locally brewed sugarcane rum.

toby Provisional house built near fields in the forest.

tompon ny zaza Master of the child.

Tongo-dray mahery. Literally, "The father's foot is stronger": proverb expressing the idea that adult children are more likely to live in the ancestral land of their father than that of their mother.

trano be Great house.

tranon-drazana Literally, "ancestors' house": tomb.

tromba Spirits who possesses people.

tsaky Salty, fatty food that accompanies alcohol consumption.

tsangam bato Literally, "standing stone": a commemorative stone or megalith sometimes erected to commemorate an event; usually, a substitute for a body that has been lost and can not be brought back to the ancestral tomb.

tsikafara Cattle sacrifice intended to fulfill a vow.

tsiny Illness-inducing, murderous blame.

tsitsika Invocation of the ancestors.

tso-drano or *mangataka tso-drano* To beg for ancestral blessing, also refers to a request for historical knowledge.

tsy ampy ra Literally, "not enough blood": refers to feeling weak or ill.

tsy fanin'olona That which "is not done by people."

tsy mety afaka That which can not be removed.

tsy milalao vato lalaka Literally, "to not play with pebbles": proverb referring to a *tangalamena's* generosity in dividing sacrificial meat.

tsy roa kianja Literally, "not-two-courtyards": bad magic.

vahiny Strangers.

valo-ila Literally, "eight parts": metaphorically refers to the eight branches of a family through which people reckon descent (see also *valo-razana*).

valo-razana Eight ancestors.

varika A kind of lemur.

vary oraka First rice-growing season of the year.

vary vato Second rice-growing season of the year.

vazaha Europeans; sometimes used to mean Merina, Europeans, or any government bureaucrat or representative of the state.

velon-dray, velon-dreny Literally, "children of a living mother and father"; often used in rituals to symbolize intergenerational continuity.

via Edible marsh plant consumed in times of scarcity.

vily A kind of smelt found only in river mouths and considered a great delicacy.

vintana Astrological position; bad luck or bad fate.

voady A vow.

voakabaro To be disciplined.

voanjo Literally, "seeds": the term used to refer to Creole settlers.

zafimanorotrano Literally, "offspring who burn houses": great-great-great grandchildren.

zama Mother's brother.

zanañy lahy Literally, "child of men."

zanañy vavy Literally, "child of women."

zana-malata Mixed-blood descendants of European pirates who inhabited the east coast of Madagascar during the eighteenth and nineteenth centuries.

zo Rights; the honor that comes from participating in social life.

References

ARCHIVAL DOCUMENTS

ARCHIVES DE LA RÉPUBLIQUE DÉMOCRATIQUE
DE MADAGASCAR (ARCHIVES OF THE DEMOCRATIC
REPUBLIC OF MADAGASCAR, ARDM), ANTANANARIVO

Affaire Politique, MDRM "1947"
Serie D870, Lutte Engagé
Serie D872, Affaires "Rebellion Malgache"
Serie D873, Poursuites contre le MDRM et Ses Membres "Attentat à la Sûrété
    de l'Etat"
Serie D879, Déposition des Temoins, 1947

Cabinet Civil
Serie D84, Province de Vatomandry

Cabinet Civil, Supplément
Serie D130, Rapports Economiques
Serie D176, Textes et Documents de Principe (Tamatave, 1881–1912, 1918–31)
Serie D178, Concessions
Serie D361, Travail et Main d'Oeuvre (Organisation du Travail)

Monographie du District
Archives Nationales Serie 363–75

ARCHIVES DE L'EVÊCHÉ DE TAMATAVE, MADAGASCAR

Lettres d'Uclès

BRITISH LIBRARY, MANUSCRIPTS DIVISION

N. Mayeur, "Histoire de Ratsimila-hoe, Roi des Bé-tsi-miçaracs," Additional Manuscript 18129, Folios 82–144.

CENTRE DES ARCHIVES D'OUTRE MER (CAOM), AIX-EN-PROVENCE

Serie IID, Rapports Politiques et Economiques des Circonscriptions

128, Mahanoro
129, Mahanoro
219, Vatomandry
220, Vatomandry
221, Vatomandry

SERVICES HISTORIQUES DE L'ARMÉE DE TERRE (SHAT)

Serie 8H114, Cabinet Militaire
Serie 8H176–177, Deuxième Bureau
Serie 8H199, Documentation

OFFICIAL PERIODICALS

Guide-Annuaire de Madagascar et Dépendances à l'Usage des Colons Planteurs, Commerçants, Industriels, Fonctionnaires, et Voyageurs. République Française. Imprimerie Officielle, Tananarive.
Journal Officiel de Madagascar et Dépendances. République Française. Imprimerie Officielle, Tananarive.

WORKS CITED

Adas, Michael.
1992.   "From Avoidance to Confrontation: Peasant Protest in Precolonial and Colonial Southeast Asia." In *Colonialism and Culture,* ed. Nicholas Dirks, 89–126. Ann Arbor: University of Michigan Press.
Allen, Philip M.
1995.   *Madagascar: Conflicts of Authority in the Great Island.* Boulder, Colo.: Westview Press.
Althabe, Gerard.
1969.   *Oppression et Liberation dans l'Imaginaire.* Paris: Francois-Maspero.
Amin, Shahid.
1997.   "Remembering Chauri Chaura: Notes from Historical Fieldwork." In *A Subaltern Studies Reader, 1986–1995,* ed. Ranajit Guha, 179–239. Minneapolis: University of Minnesota Press.

Appadurai, Arjun.
   1996.   *Modernity at Large*. Minneapolis: University of Minnesota Press.
   1991.   "Global Ethnoscapes: Notes and Queries for a Transnational An-
            thropology." In *Recapturing Anthropology: Working in the
            Present*, ed. Richard G. Fox, 191–210. Santa Fe, N.M.: School
            of American Research Press.
   1981.   "The Past as a Scarce Resource." *Man* 16, no. 2:210–19.
Ardener, Edwin.
   1970.   "Witchcraft, Economics, and the Continuity of Belief." In *Witch-
            craft Confessions and Accusations*, ed. Mary Douglas, 141–60.
            London: Tavistock.
Astuti, Rita.
   1995.   *People of the Sea*. Cambridge: Cambridge University Press.
Aujas, L.
   1927.   *Les Rites du Sacrifice à Madagascar*. Tananarive: Imprimerie Mo-
            derne de l'Emyrne, G. Pitot et cie.
   1905–06. "Essai sur l'Histoire et les Coutumes des Betsimisaraka." *Revue
            de Madagascar* 11:187–96.
Bakhtin, Mikhail M.
   1981.   *The Dialogic Imagination*. Austin: University of Texas Press.
Bakhurst, David.
   1997.   "Memory, Identity, and Cultural Psychology." In *Collective
            Memory: Theoretical, Methodological, and Practical Issues: Pro-
            ceedings of the Small-Group Meeting: European Association of
            Experimental Social Psychology*, ed. David Bakhurst, 13–22. Bari,
            Polignana a Mare: Dipartimento di Psicologia, Universita de Bari,
            May 14–17.
Bartlett, Sir Frederic Charles.
   1995.   *Remembering: A Study in Experimental and Social Psychology*.
            1932. Reprint, Cambridge: Cambridge University Press.
   1924.   "Symbolism in Folklore." In *Proceedings of the Seventh Inter-
            national Congress of Psychology*, 278–89. Cambridge: Cam-
            bridge University Press.
Bastian, Misty.
   1998.   "Fires, Tricksters, and Poisoned Medicines: Popular Cultures of
            Rumor in Onitsha, Nigeria, and Its Markets." *Etnofoor* 11, no.
            2:11–32.
   1993.   "'Bloodhounds Who Have No Friends': Witchcraft and Locality
            in the Nigerian Popular Press." In *Modernity and Its Malcontents:
            Ritual and Power in Post-Colonial Africa*, ed. Jean Comaroff and
            John Comaroff, 129–66. Chicago: University of Chicago Press.
Bayart, Jean François.
   1981.   "Le Politique par le Bas en Afrique Noire." *Politique Africaine*
            1:53–81.
Beaujard, Philippe.
   1991.   *Mythe et Société a Madagascar*. Paris: Editions de l'Harmattan.

Beidelman, Thomas O.
   1986.   *Moral Imagination in Kaguru Modes of Thought.* Bloomington:
            Indiana University Press.
Bellelli, Guglielmo, Antoinetta Curci, Giovanna Leone, and Fabrizio Stasolla.
   1997.   "Flashbulbs as Collective Memories." In *Collective Memory:*
            Theoretical, Methodological, and Practical Issues: Proceedings
            of the Small-Group Meeting: European Association of Experi-
            mental Social Psychology, ed. David Bakhurst, 65–76. Bari,
            Polignana a Mare: Dipartimento di Psicologia, Universita de
            Bari, May 14–17.
Berg, Gerald M.
   1980.   "Some Words about Merina Historical Texts." In *The African*
            Past Speaks: Essays on Oral Tradition and History, ed. J. C. Miller,
            221–39. London: Dawson.
Bjork, Elizabeth Ligon, Robert A. Bjork, and Michael C. Anderson.
   1998.   "Varieties of Goal-Directed Forgetting." In *Intentional Forget-*
            ting: Interdisciplinary Approaches, ed. Jonathan M. Golding
            and Colin MacLeod, 103–37. Mahwah, N.J.: Lawrence Erl-
            baum Associates.
Bloch, Maurice.
   1999.   "Eating Young Men among the Zafimaniry." In *Ancestors, Power,*
            and History in Madagascar, ed. Karen Middleton, 175–90. Lei-
            den, Netherlands: Brill Publishing.
   1998.   *How We Think They Think.* Boulder, Colo.: Westview Press.
   1995a.   "People into Places: Zafimaniry Concepts of Clarity." In *The An-*
            thropology of Landscape, ed. E. Hirsch and M. O'Hanlon,
            63–77. Oxford: Oxford University Press.
   1995b.   "The Resurrection of the House amongst the Zafimaniry of
            Madagascar." In *About the House: Levi Strauss and Beyond,* ed.
            J. Carsten and S. Hugh-Jones, 69–83. Cambridge: Cambridge
            University Press.
   1989.   "The Disconnection between Power and Rank as Process." In *Rit-*
            ual, History, and Power, 46–88. London: Athlone Press.
   1986.   *From Blessing to Violence.* Cambridge: Cambridge University
            Press.
   1985.   "Almost Eating the Ancestors." *Man* 20, no. 4:631–46.
   1971a.   "Decision-Making in Councils among the Merina of Madagas-
            car." In *Councils in Action,* ed. A. Richards and A. Kuper, 29–62.
            Cambridge: Cambridge University Press.
   1971b.   *Placing the Dead: Tombs, Ancestral Villages, and Kinship Orga-*
            nization in Madagascar. New York: Seminar Press.
Blot, B.
   1964.   "D'ou Vient la Croyance aux 'Mpaka Fo.'" *Lumière* (Antana-
            narivo, Madagascar) (9 February).
Boddy, Janice.
   1989.   *Wombs and Alien Spirits: Women, Men, and the Zar Cult in*
            Northern Sudan. Madison: University of Wisconsin Press.

Boiteau, Pierre.
1958.   *Contributions à la Histoire de la Nation Malgache.* Paris: Editions Sociales.
Bourdieu, Pierre.
1977.   *Outline of a Theory of Practice.* 1972. Reprint, Cambridge: Cambridge University Press.
Bowen, Elenore Smith [Laura Bohannan].
1964.   *Return to Laughter.* New York: Anchor Books.
Bower, G. H.
1981.   "Mood and Memory." *American Psychologist* 36, no. 2:129–48.
Breuer, Josef, and Sigmund Freud.
1957.   *Studies on Hysteria.* New York: Basic Books.
Brown, Roger, and James Kulik.
1977.   "Flashbulb Memories." *Cognition* 5:73–99.
Bruner, Jerome S.
1966.   *Toward a Theory of Instruction.* Cambridge: Harvard University Press, Belknap Press.
Caruth, Cathy.
1995.   *Trauma: Explorations in Memory.* Baltimore: Johns Hopkins University Press.
Casey, Edward S.
1987.   *Remembering.* Bloomington: Indiana University Press.
Catat, Louis.
1895.   *Voyage à Madagascar, 1889–1890.* Paris: l'Univers Illustré.
Christianson, S. A., and M. A. Safer.
1996.   "Emotional Events and Emotions in Autobiographical Memories." In *Remembering Our Past: Studies in Autobiographical Memory,* ed. D. C. Rubin, 218–43. New York: C.U.P.
Clifford, James, and George Marcus, eds.
1986.   *Writing Culture: The Poetics and Politics of Ethnography.* Berkeley and Los Angeles: University of California Press.
Cohn, Bernard.
1987.   *An Anthropologist among the Historians and Other Essays.* New Deli: Oxford University Press.
Cole, Jennifer.
1998.   "The Uses of Defeat: Memory and Political Morality in East Madagascar." In *Memory and the Postcolony,* ed. Richard Werbner, 105–25. New York: Zed Books.
Cole, Jennifer, and Michael Cole.
1999.   "Re-fusing Anthropology and Psychology." In *Bartlett, Cognition, and Culture,* ed. Akiko Saito, 135–54. New York: Routledge.
Cole, Jennifer, and Karen Middleton.
2001.   "Ancestors and Colonial Power in Madagascar." *Africa* 71, no. 1 (March-April).
Cole, Michael.
1996.   *Cultural Psychology: A Once and Future Discipline.* Cambridge: Harvard University Press.

Comaroff, Jean.
1985.   *Body of Power, Spirit of Resistance*. Chicago: University of
           Chicago Press.
Comaroff, Jean, and John L. Comaroff.
1991.   *Of Revelation and Revolution*. Vol. 1. Chicago: University of Chi-
           cago Press.
Comaroff, John L.
1997.   "Images of Empire, Contests of Conscience: Models of Colonial
           Domination in South Africa." In *Tensions of Empire*, ed. Fred-
           erick Cooper and Ann Laura Stoler, 163–97. Berkeley and Los
           Angeles: University of California Press.
Comaroff, John L., and Jean Comaroff.
1997.   *Of Revelation and Revolution*. Vol. 2. Chicago: University of Chi-
           cago Press.
1992.   *Ethnography and the Historical Imagination*. Boulder, Colo.:
           Westview Press.
1987.   "The Madman and the Migrant: Work and Labor in the Histor-
           ical Consciousness of a South African People." *American Eth-
           nologist* 14:191–209.
Connerton, Paul.
1989.   *How Societies Remember*. Cambridge: Cambridge University
           Press.
Cooper, Frederick.
1996.   *Decolonization and African Society: The Labor Question in
           French and British Africa*. Cambridge: Cambridge University
           Press.
1994.   "Conflict and Connection: Rethinking Colonial African History."
           American Historical Review 99, no. 5:1516–45.
1992.   "The Dialectics of Decolonization: Nationalism and Labor Move-
           ments in Post-War Africa." Paper presented at "Power: Thinking
           through the Disciplines," Comparative Studies in Social Theory,
           January 24–26. University of Michigan, Ann Arbor.
Cooper, Frederick, and Ann Laura Stoler, eds.
1997.   *Tensions of Empire*. Berkeley and Los Angeles: University of Cali-
           fornia Press.
Covell, Maureen.
1989.   *Madagascar: Politics, Economics, Society*. New York: Francis
           Pinter.
Crowder, Michael.
1964.   "Indirect Rule—French and British Style." *Africa* 34, no. 3:197–
           205.
D'Andrade, Roy, and Claudia Strauss.
1992.   *Human Motives and Cultural Models*. Cambridge: Cambridge
           University Press.
Das, Veena.
1995.   *Critical Events: An Anthropological Perspective on Contempo-
           rary India*. Delhi: Oxford University Press.

Davis, Natalie, and Randolph Starn.
1989.   "Introduction." *Representations* 26 (spring): 1–6.
de Certeau, Michel.
1984.   *The Practice of Everyday Life*. 1974. Reprint, Berkeley and Los Angeles: University of California Press.
Delivré, Alain.
1974.   *L'Histoire des Rois d'Imerina: Interprétation d'une Tradition Orale*. Paris: Klincksieck.
Deschamps, Hubert.
1960.   *L'Histoire de Madagascar*. Paris: Editions Berger-Levrault.
1949.   *Les Pirates à Madagascar*. Paris: Editions Berger-Levrault.
Dirks, Nicholas B.
1992a.   "Castes of Mind." *Representations* 37:56–78.
1992b.   Introduction to *Colonialism and Culture*, 1–25. Ann Arbor: University of Michigan Press.
Douglas, Mary.
1966.   *Purity and Danger: An Analysis of Concepts of Pollution and Taboo*. New York: Praeger.
Dreyfus, Hubert L., and Paul Rabinow, eds.
1982.   *Michel Foucault: Beyond Structuralism and Hermeneutics*. 2d ed. Chicago: University of Chicago Press.
Duranti, Alessandro.
1985.   "Famous Theories and Local Theories: The Samoans and Wittgenstein." *Quarterly Newsletter of the Laboratory of Comparative Human Cognition* 7, no. 2:46–51.
Edwards, Derek, and David Middleton.
1986.   "Joint Remembering: Constructing an Account of Shared Experience through Conversational Discourse." *Discourse Processes* 9, no. 4:423–59.
Ellis, Stephen.
1985.   *The Rising of the Red Shawls*. Cambridge: Cambridge University Press.
Emerson, Caryl.
1983.   "Bakhtin and Vygotsky on Internalization of Language." *Quarterly Newsletter of the Laboratory of Comparative Human Cognition* 5, no. 1:9–13.
Emoff, Ronald Gene.
1996.   "Musical Transformation and Constructions of History in the Tamatave Region of Madagascar." Ph.D. diss., Department of Anthropology, University of Texas at Austin.
Erikson, Kai T.
1976.   *Everything in Its Path*. New York: Simon and Schuster.
Esoavelomandroso, Faranirina V.
1989.   "Les 14 Juillet à Antananarivo au Temps de la Colonisation." In *Ravao ny Bastille: Regards sur Madagascar et la Revolution Française*, ed. Guy Jacob, 145–58. Antananarivo: Editions CNAPMAD.

1981.   "Differentes Lectures de l'Histoire: Quelques Reflexions sur le
            VVF." *Recherche, Pâedogogie, et Culture,* no. 50:101–11.
Esoavelomandroso, Manassé.
    1985.   "Les Revoltés de l'Est, Novembre 1895-Février 1896: Essai d'-
                Explication." *Omaly sy Anio* nos. 21–22:33–47.
    1979.   *La Province Maritime Orientale de la Royaume de Madagascar
                à la Fin du XIX Siècle.* Antananarivo: FTM Antananarivo,
                Madagascar.
Evans-Pritchard, E. E.
    1956.   *Nuer Religion.* Oxford: Clarendon Press.
    1940.   *The Nuer: A Description of the Modes of Livelihood and Polit-
                ical Institutions of a Nilotic People.* New York: Oxford Univer-
                sity Press.
Evers, Sandra.
    1999.   "The Construction of History and Culture in the Southern High-
                lands: Tombs, Slaves, and Ancestors." In *Ancestors, Power, and
                History in Madagascar,* ed. Karen Middleton, 257–82. Leiden,
                Netherlands: Brill.
Fabian, Johannes.
    1996.   *Remembering the Present: Painting and Popular History in Zaire.*
                Berkeley and Los Angeles: University of California Press.
Fanon, Frantz.
    1963.   *The Wretched of the Earth.* 1961. Reprint, New York: Grove Wei-
                denfield, Universitaires de France.
Feeley-Harnik, Gillian.
    1997.   "Madagascar: Religious Systems." In *The Encyclopedia of Sub-
                Saharan Africa,* ed. John Middleton, 86–89. New York: Charles
                Scribner's Sons, Macmillan Library Reference.
    1991.   *A Green Estate: Restoring Independence in Madagascar.* Wash-
                ington, D.C.: Smithsonian Institution Press.
    1989.   "Cloth and the Creation of Ancestors in Madagascar." In
                Cloth and Human Experience, ed. Annette B. Weiner and Jane
                Schnieder, 73–116. Washington, D.C.: Smithsonian Institution
                Press.
    1984.   "The Political Economy of Death: Communication and Change
                in Malagasy Colonial History." *American Ethnologist* 11, no.
                1:1–19.
    1980.   "The Sakalava House." *Anthropos* 75:559–85.
    1978.   "Divine Kingship and the Meaning of History among the Saka-
                lava of Madagascar." *Man* 13:402–17.
Feld, Stephen, and Keith Basso.
    1996.   *Senses of Place.* Santa Fe, N.M.: School of American Research.
Ferguson, James.
    1999.   *Expectations of Modernity: Myths and Meanings of Urban Life
                on the Zambian Copperbelt.* Berkeley and Los Angeles: Univer-
                sity of California Press.

1992.   "The Country and the City on the Copperbelt." *Cultural Anthropology* 7, no. 1:80–92.

Fisiy, Cyprian F., and Peter Geschiere.

1991.   "Sorcery, Witchcraft, and Accumulation." *Critique of Anthropology* 11, no. 3:251–78.

Fortes, Meyer.

1957.   *The Web of Kinship among the Tallensi.* London: Oxford University Press.

1945.   *The Dynamics of Clanship among the Tallensi: Being the First Part of an Analysis of the Social Structure of a Trans-Volta Tribe.* London: Oxford University Press, in association with International African Institute.

Fortes, Meyer, and E. Evans-Pritchard, eds.

1987.   *African Political Systems.* 1940. Reprint, New York: KPI, in association with International African Institute.

Foster, George.

1965.   "Peasant Society and the Image of Limited Good." *American Anthropologist* 67:293–315.

Foucault, Michel.

1988.   "Technologies of the Self." In *Technologies of the Self: A Seminar with Michel Foucault,* ed. Luther H. Martin, Huck Gutman, and Patrick H. Hutton, 16–49. Amherst: University of Massachusetts Press.

1982.   "The Subject and Power." In *Michel Foucault: Beyond Structuralism and Hermeneutics,* ed. Hubert Dreyfus and Paul Rabinow, 208–26. Chicago: University of Chicago Press.

Fremigacci, Jean.

1999.   "1947 sur le Terrain: Forces Coloniales contre Insurgés dans le Secteur Sud." *Madagascar 1947: La Tragédie Oubliée,* ed. Francis Arzalier and Jean Suret-Canale, 177–89. Pantin, France: Le Temps de CeRISES.

1993.   "l'Etat Colonial Français, du Discours Mythique aux Realités (1880–1940)." *Materiaux pour l'Histoire de Notre Temps,* nos. 32–33 (July-December): 27–35.

1985.   "Les Difficultés d'une Politique Colonial: Le Càfe de Madagascar à la Conquête du Marché Français (1930–1938)." *Omaly sy Anio,* nos. 21–22: 277–305.

1976.   "La Colonisation à Vatomandry-Mahanoro, Esperances et Desillusions (1895–1910)." *Omaly sy Anio,* nos. 3–4:167–247.

Freud, Sigmund.

1965.   *The Psychopathology of Everyday Life.* New York: W. W. Norton.

1963.   *Therapy and Technique.* New York: Collier.

Friedlander, Saul.

1979.   *When Memory Comes,* trans. Helen R. Lane. New York: Farrar, Straus, Giroux.

Gallieni, Joseph S.
1908.   *Neuf Ans à Madagascar.* Paris: Librarie Hachette.
1905.   "Instructions a MM. les Chefs des Provinces Cotières sur la
           Réorganisation Territoriale et Administrative du Pays Betsi-
           misaraka." *Journal Officiel de Madagascar et Dépendances*
           974:1234.
1901.   *Voyage du General Gallieni: Cinq Mois Autour de Madagascar.*
           Paris: Hachette.
Geertz, Clifford.
1973.   "The Growth of Culture and the Evolution of Mind." In *The In-
           terpretation of Cultures,* 55–83. 1962. Reprint, New York: Basic
           Books.
Geschiere, Peter.
1988.   "Sorcery and the State." *Critique of Anthropology* 8:35–63.
Gillis, John.
1994.   Introduction to *Commemorations: The Politics of National Iden-
           tity,* ed. John Gillis, 2–24. Princeton: Princeton University Press.
Gintzburger, G.
1983.   "Accommodation to Poverty: The Case of Malagasy Peasant
           Communities." *Cahiers d'Etudes Africaines* 92, nos. 23–24:
           419–42.
Goody, Jack.
1987.   *The Interface between the Written and the Oral.* Cambridge:
           Cambridge University Press.
1986.   *The Logic of Writing and the Organization of Society.* Cam-
           bridge: Cambridge University Press.
1977.   *The Domestication of the Savage Mind.* Cambridge: Cambridge
           University Press.
Goody, Jack, and Ian Watt.
1963.   *The Consequences of Literacy: Comparative Studies in Society
           and History* 5:304–45.
Graeber, David.
1996.   "The Disastrous Ordeal of 1987: Memory and Violence in Rural
           Madagascar." Ph.D. diss., Department of Anthropology, Univer-
           sity of Chicago.
1995.   "Dancing with Corpses: An Interpretation of Famadihana, Arivo-
           nimamo, Madagascar." *American Ethnologist* 22:258–78.
Grandidier, Alfred, and Guillaume Grandidier.
1958.   "Histoire des Betsimisaraka." In *Histoire des Populations Autres
           que les Merina,* by G. Grandidier and R. Decary, 21–70. Vol. 3
           of *Histoire Physique, Naturelle, et Politique de Madagascar. Se-
           rie: Histoire Politique et Coloniale de Madagascar.* Antananarivo:
           Imprimerie Officielle.
Gupta, Akhil.
1998.   *Postcolonial Developments.* Durham, N.C.: Duke University Press.
Gupta, Akhil, and James Ferguson.
1997.   "Beyond "Culture": Space, Identity, and the Politics of Differ-

ence." In *Culture, Power, Place: Explorations in Critical Anthropology,* 33–51. Durham, N.C.: Duke University Press.

Hacking, Ian.
1996.   "Memory Sciences, Memory Politics." In *Tense Past: Cultural Essays in Trauma and Memory,* ed. Paul Antze and Michael Lambek, 67–88. London: Routledge Press.

Halbwachs, Maurice.
1980.   *The Collective Memory.* 1950. Reprint, New York: Harper and Row.

Halverson, John.
1992.   "Goody and the Implosion of the Literacy Thesis." *Man* 27, no. 2:301–17.

Hamilton, Carolyn.
1998.   *Terrific Majesty: The Powers of Shaka Zulu and the Limits of Historical Invention.* Cambridge: Harvard University Press.

Hannerz, Ulf.
1986.   *Transnational Connections: Culture, People, Places.* London: Routledge.

Head, Sir Henry.
1920.   *Studies in Neurology, in Conjunction with W. H. R. Rivers.* London: H. Frowde, Hodder, and Stoughton.

Herf, Jeffrey.
1997.   *Divided Memory: The Nazi Past in the Two Germanys.* Cambridge: Harvard University Press.

Herman, Judith.
1992.   *Trauma and Recovery.* New York: Basic Books.

Hubert, Henri, and Marcel Mauss.
1964.   *Sacrifice: Its Nature and Function.* 1899. Reprint, London: University of Chicago Press.

Huntington, Richard.
1988.   *Gender and Social Structure in Madagascar.* Bloomington: Indiana University Press.

Hurvitz, David.
1980.   "A Record of Anjoaty History in Vohemar, Madagascar." Ph.D. diss., Department of Anthropology, Princeton University.

Hutchins, Edwin.
1995.   *Cognition in the Wild.* Cambridge: MIT Press.

Jacquier, L.
1904.   *La Main-d'Oeuvre Locale à Madagascar.* Paris: Henri-Jouve.

Janet, Pierre.
1973.   *L'Automatisme Psychologique.* 1889. Reprint, Paris: Société Pierre Janet.

Jarosz, Lucy.
1994.   "Agents of Power, Landscapes of Fear: The Vampires and Heart Thieves of Madagascar." *Environment and Planning D: Society and Space* 12:421–36.

Keenan, Elinor Ochs.
1974.   "Conversation and Oratory in Vakinakaratra, Madagascar."

Ph.D. diss., Department of Anthropology, University of Penn-
sylvania.
Kierkegaard, Soren.
1983.   *The Sickness unto Death.* Princeton: Princeton University Press.
Kirmayer, Laurence J.
1996.   "Landscapes of Memory: Trauma, Narrative, and Dissociation."
         In *Tense Past: Cultural Essays in Trauma and Memory,* ed. Paul
         Antze and Michael Lambek, 173–98. London: Routledge.
Koonz, Claudia.
1994.   "Between Memory and Oblivion: Concentration Camps in Ger-
         man Memory." In *Commemorations: The Politics of National
         Identity,* ed. John Gillis, 258–80. Princeton: Princeton University
         Press.
Kottak, Conrad P.
1980.   *The Past in the Present: History, Ecology, and Cultural Variation
         in Highland Madagascar.* Ann Arbor: University of Michigan
         Press.
Kundera, Milan.
1980.   *The Book of Laughter and Forgetting.* New York: Alfred A.
         Knopf.
Lahady, Pascale.
1979.   *Le Culte Betsimisaraka.* Finanarantsoa, Madagascar: Librarie
         Ambozontany.
Lambek, Michael.
1998.   "The Sakalava Poesis of History: Realizing the Past through
         Sakalava Spirit Possession." *American Ethnologist* 25, no. 2:
         106–27.
1996.   "The Past Imperfect: Remembering as Moral Practice." In *Tense
         Past: Cultural Essays in Trauma and Memory,* 235–54. New York:
         Routledge.
1992.   "Taboo as Cultural Practice among Malagasy Speakers." *Man*
         27:254–66.
Lambek, Michael, and Paul Antze.
1996.   "Introduction: Forecasting Memory." In *Tense Past: Cultural Es-
         says in Trauma and Memory,* xi–xxxviii. New York: Routledge.
Lambek, Michael, and Andrew Walsh.
1997.   "The Imagined Community of the Antankaraña: Identity, His-
         tory, and Ritual in Northern Madagascar." *Journal of Religion
         of Africa* 27, no. 3:308–30.
Larson, Pier M.
2000.   *Becoming Merina in Highland Madagascar: History and Mem-
         ory in the Age of Enslavement, 1770–1822.* Portsmouth, N.H.:
         Heinemann.
1996.   "Desperately Seeking 'The Merina' (Central Madagascar): Read-
         ing Ethnonyms and Their Semantic Fields in African Identity His-
         tories." *Journal of South African Studies* 22:541–60.

Lave, Jean.
1988.   Cognition in Practice: Mind, Mathematics, and Culture in Every-
             day Life. New York: Cambridge University Press.
Leguéval de Lacombe, B. F.
1840.   Voyages à Madagascar et aux Iles Comores, 1823–1830. Paris:
             L. Desessart.
Levi-Strauss, Claude.
1966.   The Savage Mind. 1962. Reprint, Chicago: University of Chicago
             Press.
Lewis, Martin.
1962.   "One Hundred Million Frenchmen: The 'Assimilation' Theory
             in French Colonial Policy." Comparative Studies in Society and
             History 4, no. 12:129–53.
Leys, Ruth.
2000.   Trauma: A Genealogy. Chicago: University of Chicago Press.
1996.   "Traumatic Cures: Shell Shock, Janet, and the Question of Mem-
             ory." In Tense Past: Cultural Essays in Trauma and Memory, ed.
             Paul Antze and Michael Lambek, 103–45. London: Routledge.
Lienhardt, Godfrey.
1961.   Divinity and Experience. Oxford: Clarendon Press.
Loftus, Elizabeth F.
1993.   "The Reality of Repressed Memories." American Psychologist
             48, no. 5:518–34.
Luhrmann, T. M.
1989.   Persuasions of the Witch's Craft. Cambridge: Harvard Univer-
             sity Press.
Lutz, Catherine.
1988.   Unnatural Emotions. Chicago: University of Chicago Press.
Malkki, Liisa.
1995.   Purity and Exile: Violence, Memory, and National Cosmology
             among Hutu Refugees in Tanzania. Chicago: University of Chi-
             cago Press.
Manier, David.
Forthcoming. "Remembering Past Harm: A Sociocultural Approach to
             PTSD and Traumatic Memory." In Remembering in Socio-
             Cultural Context, ed. William Hurst and David Manier. New
             York: Russell Sage Foundation.
Mantaux, Christian G., and Harold Adolphe.
1972.   "Documents Officiels Inédits sur Elizabeth Marie, Sobobie Be-
             tia, Reine de Sainte Marie et du Royaume de Foulpoint." Bul-
             letin de l'Académie Malgache 50, no. 1:63–113.
Masquelier, Adeline.
2000.   "Of Headhunters and Cannibals: Migrancy, Labor, and Con-
             sumption in the Mawri Imagination." Cultural Anthropology 15,
             no. 1:84–126.

Mbembe, Achille.
    1991.   "Domaines de la Nuit et Autorité Onerique dans les Maquis du Sud-
              Cameroun (1955–1958)." *Journal of African History* 31:89–121.
Memmi, Albert.
    1961.   *The Colonizer and the Colonized.* 1957. Reprint, Boston: Bea-
              con Press.
Middleton, David.
    1997.   "The Social Organization of Conversational Remembering: Ex-
              perience as Individual and Collective Concerns." *Mind, Culture,
              and Activity* 4, no. 2:71–85.
Middleton, David, and Charles Crook.
    1996.   "Bartlett and Socially Ordered Consciousness: A Discursive Per-
              spective, Comments on Rosa." *Culture and Psychology* 2:379–96.
Middleton, David, and Derek Edwards.
    1990.   "Conversational Remembering: A Social Psychological Approach."
              In *Collective Remembering,* ed. David Middleton and Derek
              Edwards, 23–45. London: Sage.
Middleton, John.
    1960.   *Lugbara Religion: Ritual and Authority among an East African
              People.* London: Oxford University Press.
Middleton, Karen.
    1997.   "Circumcision, Death, and Strangers." *Journal of Religion in
              Africa* 27, no. 4:341–73.
    1995.   "Tombs, Umbilical Cords, and the Syllable Fo." In *Cultures of
              Madagascar: Ebb and Flow of Influences,* ed. S. Evers and M.
              Spindler, 223–35. Leiden, Netherlands: International Institute for
              Asian Studies.
    1988.   "Marriages and Funerals: Some Aspects of Karembola Political
              Symbolism (South Madagascar)." Ph.D. diss., Department of An-
              thropology, Oxford University.
              Forthcoming. "Memory, Alliance, and Landscapes of Power in
              the Karembola (Madagascar)." *Journal of the Royal Anthropo-
              logical Institute.*
Mitchell, Timothy.
    1988.   *Colonizing Egypt.* Berkeley and Los Angeles: University of Cali-
              fornia Press.
Molet, Louis.
    1979.   *La Conception Malgache du Monde, du Surnaturel, et de l'Homme
              en Imerina.* Paris: Editions de l'Harmattan.
Neisser, Ulric, ed.
    1982.   *Memory Observed: Remembering in Natural Contexts.* San Fran-
              cisco: W. H. Freeman.
Neisser, Ulric, and Nicole Harsch.
    1992.   "Phantom Flashbulbs: False Recollections of Hearing News
              about *Challenger.*" In *Affect and Accuracy in Recall,* ed. Eugene
              Winograd and Ulric Neisser, 9–31. Cambridge: Cambridge Uni-
              versity Press.

Newman, Katharine.
1996.   "Ethnography, Biography, and Cultural History: Generational
          Paradigms in Human Development." In *Ethnography and Hu-
          man Development: Context and Meaning in Social Inquiry,* ed.
          Richard Jessor, Anne Colby, and Richard A. Shweder, 371–93.
          Chicago: University of Chicago Press.
Nielssen, Hilde.
1999.   "Manao Tromba: En Studie av Aandekulten Tromba Blant Bet-
          simisaraka paa Ost Madagaskar (Hovedfagsoppgave)." *Norsk
          Antropologisk Tidsskrift* 10, no. 2:97–110.
Nietzsche, Friedrich.
1980.   *On the Advantages and Disadvantages of History for Life.* 1874.
          Reprint, Indianapolis: Hackett Publishing Company.
Nora, Pierre.
1989.   "Between Memory and History: Les Lieux de Memoire." *Rep-
          resentations* 26 (spring): 7–25.
Novick, Peter.
1999.   *The Holocaust in American Life.* New York: Houghton Mifflin.
Ong, Aihwa.
1999.   *Flexible Citizenship.* Durham, N.C.: Duke University Press.
1987.   *Spirits of Resistance and Capitalist Discipline: Factory Women
          in Malaysia.* New York: State University of New York Press.
Ortner, Sherry B.
1989.   *High Religion: A Cultural and Political History of Sherpa Bud-
          dhism.* Princeton: Princeton University Press.
Osborne, Peter.
1995.   *The Politics of Time: Modernity and Avant-Garde.* London:
          Verso.
Piehlar, G. Kurt.
1994.   "The War Dead and the Gold Star: American Commemoration
          of the First World War." In *Commemorations,* ed. John Gills,
          168–85. Princeton: Princeton University Press.
Piot, Charles.
1999.   *Remotely Global: Village Modernity in West Africa.* Chicago: Uni-
          versity of Chicago Press.
Prakash, Gyan.
1995.   *After Colonialism: Imperial Histories and Postcolonial Dis-
          placements.* Princeton: Princeton University Press.
Price, Richard.
1998.   *The Colonel and the Convict.* Beacon Press: Boston.
1980.   *First Time: The Historical Vision of an Afro-American People.*
          Baltimore: Johns Hopkins University Press.
Rabearimanana, Lucille.
1997.   "Evénement de 1947 et Construction Nationale." Paper pre-
          sented at "Colloque Internationale sur le Cinquantenaire de l'In-
          surrection de 1947," Département de l'Histoire, Université d'An-
          tananarivo, Madagascar.

Rabinow, Paul.
  1989.   *French Modern: Norms and Form of the Social Environment.*
             Cambridge: MIT Press.
Raison-Jourde, Françoise.
  1997.   "Les Prolongements du Soulèvement dans la Mémoire et dans
             le Contact avec des Administrés." Paper presented at "Colloque
             Internationale sur le Cinquantenaire de l'Insurrection de
             1947," Département de l'Histoire, Université d'Antananarivo,
             Madagascar.
  1993.   "Une Transition Achevè ou Amorcèe." *Politique Africaine* 52:6–19.
  1991.   *Bible et Pouvoir à Madagascar au XIX Siècle: Invention d'une
             Identité Chretienne et Construction de l'Etat, 1780–1880.* Paris:
             Editions Karthala.
  1989.   "Une Rébellion en Quête de Statut: 1947 à Madagascar." *Revue
             de la Bibliothèque Nationale* (Paris) 34:24–32.
Randrianja, Solofo.
  1989.   *Le Parti Communiste de la Region de Madagascar, 1930–39: Aux
             Origines du Socialisme Malgache.* Antananarivo, Madagascar:
             Foi et Justice.
Ranger, Terence.
  1993.   "The Invention of Tradition Revisited: The Case of Colonial
             Africa." In *Legitimacy and the State in Twentieth-Century Africa,*
             ed. Terence Ranger and Olufemi Vaughan, 62–111. Oxford:
             Macmillan.
  1983.   "The Invention of Tradition in Colonial Africa." In *The Inven-
             tion of Tradition,* ed. Eric Hobsbawm and Terence Ranger, 211–
             62. Cambridge: Cambridge University Press.
Rappaport, Joanne.
  1990.   *The Politics of Memory: Native Historical Interpretation in the
             Andes.* New York: Cambridge University Press.
Robertson Smith, William.
  1889.   *Lectures on the Religion of the Semites.* Edinburgh: A. and C.
             Black.
Rosa, Alberto.
  1996.   "Bartlett's Psycho-Anthropological Project." *Culture and Psy-
             chology* 2:355–78.
Rosaldo, Michelle Z.
  1984.   "Toward an Anthropology of Self and Feeling." In *Culture
             Theory: Essays on Mind, Self, and Emotion,* ed. Richard A.
             Shweder and Robert A. LeVine, 137–57. Cambridge: Cambridge
             University Press.
Rosaldo, Renato.
  1989.   "Imperialist Nostalgia." *Representations* 26 (spring): 107–22.
  1980.   *Ilongot Headhunting.* Palo Alto: Stanford University Press.
Roseman, Sharon.
  1996.   "'How We Built the Road': The Politics of Memory in Rural Gali-
             cia." *American Ethnologist* 23, no. 4:836–60.

Roth, Michael S.
  1989.   "Remembering Forgetting: Maladies de la Mémoire in Nineteenth-
             Century France." *Representations* 26:49–68.
Roy, Arundhati.
  1997.   *The God of Small Things*. New York: Random House.
Rudd, Jorgen.
  1960.   *Taboo*. Oslo: Oslo University Press.
Ryle, Gilbert.
  1949.   *The Concept of Mind*. London: Hutchinson's University Library.
Sahlins, Marshall.
  1985.   *Islands of History*. Chicago: University of Chicago Press.
  1981.   *Historical Metaphors and Mythical Realities: Structure in the
             Early History of the Sandwich Islands Kingdom*. Ann Arbor: Uni-
             versity of Michigan Press.
Saloman, Gavriel, ed.
  1993a.   *Distributed Cognitions: Psychological and Educational Consid-
             erations*. Cambridge: Cambridge University Press.
  1993b.   Introduction to *Distributed Cognitions: Psychological and Edu-
             cational Considerations*, ed. Gavriel Saloman, xi–xxi. Cambridge:
             Cambridge University Press.
Schacter, Daniel.
  1996.   *Searching for Memory: The Brain, the Mind, and the Past*. New
             York: Basic Books.
Schudson, Michael.
  1996.   "Lives, Laws, and Languages: Commemorative Versus Non-
             Commemorative Forms of Effective Public Memory." *Commu-
             nication Review* 2, no. 1:3–17.
  1995.   "The Dynamics of Distortion in Collective Memory." In *Mem-
             ory Distortion: How Minds, Brains, and Societies Reconstruct the
             Past*, ed. Daniel Schacter, 346–64. Cambridge: Harvard Univer-
             sity Press.
  1992.   *Watergate in American Memory: How We Remember, Forget, and
             Reconstruct the Past*. New York: Basic Books.
Scott, James C.
  1990.   *Domination and the Arts of Resistance: Hidden Transcripts*. New
             Haven: Yale University Press.
  1976.   *The Moral Economy of the Peasant: Rebellion and Resistance in
             Southeast Asia*. New Haven: Yale University Press.
Sharp, Lesley A.
  2001.   "Youth, Land, and Liberty in Coastal Madagascar: A Children's
             Independence." *Ethnohistory* 48, nos. 1–2:207–38.
  1995.   "Playboy Princely Spirits of Madagascar: Possession as Youthful
             Commentary and Social Critique." *Anthropological Quarterly*
             68, no. 2:75–88.
  1993.   *The Possessed and the Dispossessed: Spirits, Identity, and Power
             in a Madagascar Migrant Town*. Berkeley and Los Angeles: Uni-
             versity of California Press.

Shaw, Rosalind.
2001.   *Memories of the Slave Trade: Divination and Atlantic Modernity in Sierra Leone.* Chicago: University of Chicago Press.
1997.   "The Production of Witchcraft/ Witchcraft as Production: Memory, Modernity, and the Slave Trade in Sierra Leone." *American Ethnologist* 24, no. 4:856–76.
1996.   "The Politician and the Diviner: Divination and the Consumption of Power in Sierra Leone." *Journal of Religion in Africa* 26, no. 1:30–55.
Shobe, Katharine Krause, and John F. Khilstrom.
1997.   "Is Traumatic Memory Special?" *Current Directions in Psychological Science* 6, no. 3:70–74.
Shotter, John.
1990.   "The Social Construction of Remembering and Forgetting." In *Collective Remembering,* ed. David Middleton and Derek Edwards, 120–38. London: Sage.
Stoler, Ann Laura.
1989.   "Rethinking Colonial Categories: European Communities and the Boundaries of Rule." *Comparative Studies in Society and History* 13:134–61.
Stoler, Ann Laura, and Frederick Cooper.
1997.   "Between Metropole and Colony: Rethinking a Research Agenda." In *Tensions of Empire,* ed. Frederick Cooper and Ann Laura Stoler, 1–56. Berkeley and Los Angeles: University of California Press.
Stoller, Paul.
1995.   *Embodying Colonial Memories: Spirit Possession, Power, and the Hauka in West Africa.* New York: Routledge.
Street, Brian V.
1984.   *Literacy and Theory in Practice.* Cambridge: Cambridge University Press.
Sturken, Marita.
1997.   *Tangled Memories: The Vietnam War, the AIDS Epidemic, and the Politics of Remembering.* Berkeley and Los Angeles: University of California Press.
Sylla, Yvette.
1985.   "Les Malata: Cohésion et Disparité d'une 'Groupe.'" *Omaly sy Anio* (Antananarivo), nos. 21–22:10–32.
Tambiah, Stanley.
1985.   *Culture, Thought, and Social Action: An Anthropological Perspective.* Cambridge: Harvard University Press.
Taussig, Michael.
1993.   *Mimesis and Alterity.* London: Routledge.
1987.   *Shamanism, Colonialism, and the Wild Man: A Study in Terror and Healing.* Chicago: University of Chicago Press.
Taylor, Charles.
1979.   "Interpretation and the Sciences of Man." In *Interpretive Social*

Sciences: A Reader, ed. Paul Rabinow and William M. Sullivan, 25–71. Berkeley and Los Angeles: University of California Press.

Thomas, Nicholas.
1989.   "Taking People Seriously: Cultural Autonomy and the Global System." *Critique of Anthropology* 9, no. 3:59–69.

Thomas, Philip.
1998.   "Conspicuous Construction: Houses, Consumption, and 'Relocalization' in Manambondro, Southeast Madagascar." *Journal of the Royal Anthropological Institute* 4, no. 3:425–44.
1997.   "The Water That Blesses, the River That Flows: Place and the Ritual Imagination among the Temanambondro of Southeast Madagascar." In *The Poetic Power of Place: Comparative Perspectives on Austronesian Ideas of Locality,* 22–41. Comparative Austronesian Project Publication Series. Canberra: Research School of Pacific Studies, Australian National University.
1996.   "Place, Person, and Ancestry among the Tenambondro of Southeast Madagascar." Ph.D. diss., Department of Anthropology, London School of Economics and Political Science.
Forthcoming.   "The River, the Road, and the Rural-Urban Divide: A Postcolonial Moral Geography from Southeast Madagascar." *American Ethnologist.*

Thompson, Virginia, and Richard Adloff.
1965.   *The Malagasy Republic: Madagascar Today.* Palo Alto: Stanford University Press.

Tronchon, Jacques.
1986.   *L'Insurrection Malgache de 1947.* Paris: Editions Karthala.

Tsing, Anna L.
1993.   *In the Realm of the Diamond Queen.* Princeton: Princeton University Press.

Tylor, Sir Edward Burnett.
1958.   *Primitive Culture.* Vol. 2. 1889. Reprint, New York: Harper.

Vail, Leroy.
1989.   Introduction to *The Creation of Tribalism in Southern Africa,* 1–19. Berkeley and Los Angeles: University of California Press.

Valensi, Lucette.
1992.   *Fables de la Memoire: La Glorieuse Bataille des Trois Rois.* Paris: Seuil.

Valensky, Chantal.
1999.   "La Pacification en 1947–1949." In *Madagascar 1947: La Tragédie Oubliée,* ed. Francis Arzalier and Jean Suret-Canale, 151–59. Pantin, France: Le Temps de CeRISES.
1995.   *Le Soldat Occulté: Les Malgaches de l'Armée Françaises.* Paris: Editions de l'Harmattan.

Van der Kolk, Bessel A., and Onno Van der Hart.
1995.   "The Intrusive Past: The Flexibility of Memory and the Engraving of Trauma." In *Trauma: Explorations in Memory,* ed. Cathy Caruth, 158–82. Baltimore: Johns Hopkins University Press.

van Gennep, Arnold.
1904.   *Tabou et Totemism à Madagascar: Etude Descriptive et Theo-rique.* Paris: Leroux.
Vansina, Jan.
1985.   *Oral Tradition as History.* Madison: University of Wisconsin Press.
Vaughan, Megan.
1991.   *Curing Their Ills: Colonial Power and African Illness.* Palo Alto: Stanford University Press.
Volkan, Vamik.
1991.   "On Chosen Trauma." *Mind and Human Interaction* 3, no. 1:13.
Vološinov, Valentin N.
1976.   *Freudianism: A Marxist Critique.* Trans. I. R. Titunik. New York: Academic Press.
Warnock, Mary.
1987.   *Memory.* London: Faber Press.
Watson, Rubie S., ed.
1994.   *Memory, History, and Opposition under State Socialism.* Santa Fe, N.M.: School of American Research Press.
Weiner, Annette B.
1992.   *Inalienable Possessions: The Paradox of Keeping-While-Giving.* Berkeley and Los Angeles: University of California Press.
Werbner, Richard.
1995.   "Human Rights and Moral Knowledge: Arguments of Account-ability in Zimbabwe." In *Shifting Contexts,* ed. Marilyn Strath-ern, 99–116. London: Routledge.
ed. 1998.   "Beyond Oblivion: Confronting Memory Crisis." In *Memory and the Postcolony: African Anthropology and the Critique of Power,* ed. Richard Werbner, 1–17. New York: Zed Books.
White, Hayden.
1987.   *The Content of the Form: Narrative Discourse and Historical Representation.* Baltimore: Johns Hopkins University Press.
1973.   *Metahistory: The Historical Imagination of 19ᵗʰ Century Europe.* Baltimore: Johns Hopkins University Press.
White, Luise.
2000.   *Speaking with Vampires: Rumor and History in Colonial Africa.* Berkeley and Los Angeles: University of California Press.
Williams, Raymond.
1977.   *Marxism and Literature.* Oxford: Oxford University Press.
Wilmsen, Edward.
1989.   *Land Filled with Flies: A Political Economy of the Kalahari.* Chicago: University of Chicago Press.
Wittgenstein, Ludwig.
1953.   *Philosophical Investigations.* Trans. G. E. M. Anscombe. Oxford: B. Blackwell.
Wolf, Eric.
1969.   *Peasant Wars of the 20ᵗʰ Century.* New York: Harper and Rowe.

Wright, Gwendolyn.
  1991.   *The Politics of Design in French Colonial Urbanism.* Chicago:
             University of Chicago Press.
Yates, Francis.
  1966.   *The Art of Memory.* Chicago: University of Chicago Press.
Young, Allan.
  1995.   *The Harmony of Illusions: Inventing Post-Traumatic Stress Dis-
             order.* Princeton: Princeton University Press.
Zacks, Rose T., and Lynn Hasher.
  1994.   "Directed Ignoring: Inhibitory Regulation of Working Memory."
             In *Inhibitory Processes in Attention, Memory, and Language,* ed.
             Dale Dagenbach and Thomas H. Carr, 241–64. San Diego: Aca-
             demic Press.

Index

MDRM *(continued)*
225, 226, 254; origin of rebellion and,
229, 230–32, 256–58
MDRM-Merina plot. 229–30, 258, 268,
269, 292
medicines, 111–12
Memmi, Albert, 18
memorializing practices, 9, 12
memories, flashbulb, 278–79
memory: as an art, 171, 277–79, 281,
284; Betsimisaraka, 106–9; collective,
22–24; colonial suppression of, 281;
definition of, 2, 22; deliberate, 133;
emotion and, 278; feeling, 281; history
vs., 104–6; incidental, 133; individual
vs. social, 1–2, 22–23, 26, 27, 287–88,
290, 300; landscape of, 289; official,
205–6, 283–84; reciprocal, 137–40;
social constructionist view of, 26;
social technologies of, 27(29; unofficial, 206–20. *See also* colonial memories; election of 1992–93; sites of
memory
memoryscape, 290, 298, 299
Merina: control of Betsimisaraka, 12,
40–43; memories of enslavement by,
293–95; rituals, 94, 152, 175, 191.
See also MDMR-Merina plot
Middleton, Karen, 11
mind, extending beyond individual, 1.
See also memory, social technology of
missionaries, 59–60
Mitchell, Timothy, 19, 55
mnemonic manipulation, 277
modernity, 101, 297–98
murder, 239

Nietzsche, Friedrich, 101, 170
Nora, Pierre, 105, 108, 139
nostalgia, 3, 134, 303

PADESM (Parti des Déshérités de
Madagascar), 129, 229, 270
palanquin, 165, 261
PANAMA (Parti National Malgache),
230, 231
parent-child relationship, 92–96
passive resistance, 64–65
Patrick, Michael, 173–75
Piot, Charles, 8
politique des races, 57–58
possession. *See* spirit possession
postcolonial condition, 297–300
power. *See* ancestors; colonial power;
hasina
practices theory, 27–28
prayer posts (*jiro*), 5, 68, 153, 312n7;

construction of new, 178–79, 180,
182, 186, 312n7; control over, 172
prison, 202–3

Rabemananjara, Jacques, 61, 62, 229,
232
Radama I, 35, 40
Radama II, 11
Raison-Jourde, Françoise, 63, 250–51,
320n4
Ramano, 38
Ranavalona I, 11, 40, 43, 129
Ranger, Terence, 21
rangitra, 143–45
Raseta, Joseph, 61, 229
Ratsimilaho, 38, 172
Ratsiraka, Didier, 150; administration of,
13; identified ethnically with Betsimisaraka, 236–37; on 1947 rebellion,
265; opposition to, 235–36; reelection
of, 302; sacrifice of bulls by, 173, 248–
49, 251
Ravoahangy, Joseph, 61, 22, 309n42
rebellion of 1947, 2–3, 7, 163; cause of,
228–31, 256–58; contradictory memories of, 270–71; denial of heroism in,
265; effects of, 62–64; in Mahanoro
District, 231–34; Merina involvement
in, 268; pacification after, 265–68;
remembrance of, 224–27, 234, 245,
246–47, 254–63, 291–93, 296; stories
of redemption from, 264–65; summary
of, 60–62. *See also* MDRM; MDRM-
Merina plot
reburial, 159, 286–89, 324n7
recolonization, 301–2
remembering, 21, 24; constructive, 279,
280; conversational, 247; diachronic
processes of, 286–88; spatial framework for, 275; strategic, 277. *See also*
mahatsiaro
Réunion, 12, 304
rice, 66, 68, 69, 76, 77–78, 321n21
Rice Office, 228
rituals, of humiliation, 265–68. *See also*
cattle sacrifice; rum; sacrifice
Rosaldo, Michelle, 281
Roth, Michael S., 135
Roy, Arundhati, 66
rum, 6; ritual use of, 82, 85, 128, 149,
159, 175, 186, 207
Ryle, Gilbert, 206, 283

sacrifice: as art of memory, 171, 284;
flourishing, 88–89; to new sources of
hasina, 151–52; as symbolic action,
275. *See also* cattle sacrifice

Compositor: Integrated Composition Systems, Inc.
        Text: 10/13 Sabon
     Display: Sabon